AF711843

Banking & Financial Systems

by

Biz Kid$

Publisher
The Goodheart-Willcox Company, Inc.
Tinley Park, Illinois
www.g-w.com

Copyright © 2013
by
The Goodheart-Willcox Company, Inc.

All rights reserved. No part of this work may be reproduced, stored, or transmitted in any form or by any electronic or mechanical means, including information storage and retrieval systems, without the prior written permission of The Goodheart-Willcox Company, Inc.

Manufactured in the United States of America.

Library of Congress Catalog Card Number 2012002793

ISBN 978-1-60525-778-5

1 2 3 4 5 6 7 8 9 – 13 – 17 16 15 14 13 12

The Goodheart-Willcox Company, Inc. Brand Disclaimer: Brand names, company names, and illustrations for products and services included in this text are provided for educational purposes only and do not represent or imply endorsement or recommendation by the author or the publisher.

The Goodheart-Willcox Company, Inc., Safety Notice: The reader is expressly advised to carefully read, understand, and apply all safety precautions and warnings described in this book or that might also be indicated in undertaking the activities and exercises described herein to minimize risk of personal injury or injury to others. Common sense and good judgment should also be exercised and applied to help avoid all potential hazards. The reader should always refer to the appropriate manufacturer's technical information, directions, and recommendations; then proceed with care to follow specific equipment operating instructions. The reader should understand these notices and cautions are not exhaustive.

The publisher makes no warranty or representation whatsoever, either expressed or implied, including, but not limited to, equipment, procedures, and applications described or referred to herein, their quality, performance, merchantability, or fitness for a particular purpose. The publisher assumes no responsibility for any changes, errors, or omissions in this book. The publisher specifically disclaims any liability whatsoever, including any direct, indirect, incidental, consequential, special, or exemplary damages resulting, in whole or in part, from the reader's use or reliance upon the information, instructions, procedures, warnings, cautions, applications or other matter contained in this book. The publisher assumes no responsibility for the activities of the reader.

Library of Congress Cataloging-in-Publication Data

Banking & financial systems / by Biz Kid$.
p. cm.
Includes index.
ISBN 978-1-60525-778-5
1. Banks and banking—Juvenile literature. 2. Financial institutions—Juvenile literature. 3. Financial services industry—Juvenile literature. I. Biz Kid$ (Television program) II. Title: Banking and financial systems.
HG1609.B36 2013
332.1--dc23
2012002793

Attributions for unreferenced images:

Cover background: newart/Shutterstock
Cover dollar vault: YAKOBCHUK/Shutterstock
Career ladder: David Carillet/Shutterstock
Ethics: Image Wizard/Shutterstock

Introduction

Banking & Financial Systems is written especially to introduce teens to the business of banking. Concepts about banking operations, the Federal Reserve, customer services, and other relevant topics are presented to provide an understanding of how banks function within society. *Banking & Financial Systems* prepares students to be competent consumers and employees.

This text is divided into five units. Unit 1 introduces the business of banking. Unit 2 discusses money and banking regulations, including the role of the Federal Reserve. Unit 3 covers services customers need, such as savings, lending, and making payments. Unit 4 discusses the management aspects of the banking business. Finally, Unit 5 provides an overview of the history of banking, including the financial crises of the early 21st century, and discusses the future of banking. Progressing through this text, many opportunities are offered to learn about the banking industry and how it has evolved, new offerings to its clients, and avenues for a future potential career.

A new learning tool has been provided to help students study. QR codes are provided to use with a smartphone to go directly to selected text activities. In addition, the G-W Learning mobile site makes it easy for students to study on the go!

About the Authors

Biz Kid$ is a national financial education–based initiative whose foundation is the Emmy Award-winning public television series that teaches kids and young adults about money and business. The series has also been given the Environmental Media Award for Outstanding Children's Television, the Silver Telly Award for Outstanding Financial Education Series and it has been recognized for Excellence in Contributions for Financial Literacy Education by the Council on Economic Education.

Contributing Authors

Maria Townsley is an educator and a professional writer in business and education. She has written or edited many published books that teach business concepts and tools to students and business professionals.

Cheryl McGaughey is currently an instructor of Finance at Angelo State University in Texas and serves as chairman of the board of a Texas credit union. She has over 30 years experience teaching finance.

Matt Fontaine has been writing for a variety of organizations, businesses, and publications in the Pacific Northwest since 2001. He wrote his first economics text in 2006 and has worked closely with Biz Kid$ since 2009.

Reviewers

The author and publisher would like to thank the following industry and teaching professionals, who provided valuable input into the development of this text.

Ted Brauch
Vice President
Wells Fargo
Jacksonville, Florida

Sandra Cullen
Business/Marketing Teacher
Jemison High School
Jemison, Alabama

Stephen Day
Programs Director
North Carolina Council on Economic Education
Raleigh, North Carolina

Holly B. Laird
Business and Finance Teacher
Leesville Road High School
Raleigh, North Carolina

LouAnn Massey
Business Teacher
Las Cruces Public Schools
Las Cruces, New Mexico

Kim Miller
Marketing Teacher
Holtville High School
Deatsville, Alabama

Debra Moore
Business Education Teacher
Raymond S. Kellis High School
Glendale, Arizona

Julie Moore
Business Teacher
East Porter County School Corporation
Valparaiso, Indiana

Sharmyn Munoz
GRADS Teacher
Gallup Central High School
Gallup, New Mexico

Kimberly Pruiett
Marketing Education Teacher
Winston Churchill High
San Antonio, Texas

Luke W. Reynolds
Insurance Professional

Rhonda Schmaltz
Business Department Chair and Instructor
Ames High School
Ames, Iowa

Jason Weiss
Business Teacher and DECA Advisor
Howard High School
Macon, Georgia

Brief Contents

Table of Contents

Special Features

Chapter Review and Assessment

Special Features

Chapter Review and Assessment

Unit 2 Money and Regulation. . . 84

Special Features

Chapter Review and Assessment

Special Features

Chapter Review and Assessment

Unit 3 Customer Services 146

Excellent Organization

Student Focused

Each chapter and section opener begins with a consistent plan of learning for success.

The **Check Your Banking IQ** pretest opens each chapter with an opportunity to evaluate what the student knows about the banking topic to be presented in the chapter.

A **QR code** makes it convenient to use a smartphone to launch the pretest. Access the pretest without a smartphone on the G-W Learning companion website.

Objectives define the goals for learning the section content and are related to the main headings in the section.

Unit 2 Money and Regulation

6

Check Your Banking IQ

Before you begin this chapter, see what you already know about banking by taking the chapter pretest.

www.m.g-wlearning.com
www.g-wlearning.com

Bank Regulations

Section 6.1 Banking Regulations
Section 6.2 Consumer Regulations
Section 6.3 Recent Banking

amount of risk they can take on. Compared to most industries, banking is heavily regulated. In banking, as in other industries, regulations often follow a crisis. Laws are passed to try to avoid the same mistakes that caused the crisis. Bank regulations are meant to prevent bank failures and protect bank customers, while allowing banks to be competitive.

College and Career Readiness — **Reading Prep.** As you read the chapter, think about the advantages and disadvantages of banking regulations. Do you think regulations help or hurt the banking industry? Use examples from the text to support your opinion.

Scan the code to view a Biz Kid$ video. If you do not have a smartphone, visit the G-W Learning companion website.

www.m.g-wlearning.com
www.g-wlearning.com

122

Chapter 6 Bank Regulations 123

Section 6.1
Banking Regulations

Objectives

After completing this section, you will be able to:

- Explain the conditions that existed in the banking industry during the 1920s and 1930s.
- Describe the provisions of the Glass-Steagall Act.
- Explain why the legislation that created FIRREA and FDICIA was needed.
- Describe how the Sarbanes-Oxley Act increases transparency and accountability in banking.

Terms

bank run
Emergency Banking Act of 1933
Glass-Steagall Act
interest rate ceiling
Federal Home Loan Bank Board
Financial Institutions Reform, Recovery, and Enforcement Act (FIRREA)
Federal Depository Insurance Corporation Improvement Act (FDICIA)
Sarbanes-Oxley Act (SOX)

Setting the Stage for Failure

During the Great Depression, there were huge numbers of bank failures. Over 9,000 banks closed their doors during this time. In 1933 alone, some 4,000 banks failed. Figure 6-1 shows the number of bank failures throughout the 19th and 20th century. Why did so many banks fail? There were several contributing factors, including crop failures in the

Source: The Federal Reserve

Figure 6-1.
Number of Bank Failures

Chapters are divided into smaller **sections** for better comprehension of content that is being presented.

Through the presentation of important business and academic **terms**, a framework is created to build a personal banking glossary.

Reading Prep sets the stage for reading by applying Common Core State Standards for reading.

A **QR code** makes it convenient to use a smartphone to launch the Biz Kid$ video.

Engaging Features

Workplace Spotlighted

Special features in this text bring content to life in a way that allows the reader to understand and apply what is learned. In each chapter, emphasis is given to selected banking topics that are important to building knowledge of financial systems.

Green Banking

Green Banking features share banking tips on best practices for the environment.

Ethical Banking

Ethical Banking presents real-life information and insight on issues that arise in the banking business.

Finance

Careers in Finance
Banking and Related Services

Careers in Finance highlights careers in the Banking Services Pathway of the Finance Cluster to provide awareness of potential banking opportunities.

Biz Kid$ in Action provides real-life examples of banking in practice.

BIZ TIPS

Biz Tips highlight banking facts to add relevance to content.

G-W Mobile

G-W Learning Mobile Site

The G-W Learning mobile site is a study reference to use when you are on the go. The mobile site is easy to read, easy to use, and fine-tuned for quick access.

For *Banking & Financial Systems,* the G-W Learning mobile site contains chapter pretests and post tests, Biz Kid$ videos, and e-flash card vocabulary practices. If you do not have a smartphone, these same features can be accessed using an Internet browser to visit the G-W Learning companion website.

G-W Learning mobile site: www.m.g-wlearning.com
G-W Learning companion website: www.g-wlearning.com

Scan now!

Goodheart-Willcox QR Codes

This Goodheart-Willcox product contains QR codes, or quick response codes. These codes can be scanned with a smartphone bar code reader to access information or online features. For more information on using QR codes and a recommended QR reader, visit the G-W Learning companion website.
An Internet connection is required to access the QR code destination. Data-transfer rates may apply. Check with your Internet service provider for information on your data-transfer rates.

G-W Learning companion website: www.g-wlearning.com

Scan now!

Ongoing Assessments

Outcome-Oriented Learning

Multiple opportunities are provided for self-assessment within the chapter, as well as at the end of each chapter and unit, to check learning as the content is explored.

Checkpoint 3.2

1. Why do people purchase insurance?
2. How do banks make money from selling insurance?
3. What are the biggest costs associated with liability cases?
4. List the major services offered by bank trust departments.
5. What is the major source of income from brokerage services?

Build Your Vocabulary

As you progress through this course, develop a personal glossary of banking terms and add it to your portfolio. This will help you build your banking vocabulary. Write out a definition for each of the following terms, and add it to your personal glossary.

risk
insurance
beneficiary
trustee
trust
estate
estate planning
probate law
treasury and cash management services
pension fund
trading
underwriting
underwriting spread
merger
acquisition

Checkpoint questions provide point-of-coverage assessments at the end of each section. Solutions to the checkpoint questions are located on the G-W Learning companion website.

Review Your Knowledge questions review basic concepts and provide an opportunity to evaluate what has been learned.

Each **Chapter Summary** provides a quick overview and reinforcement of content.

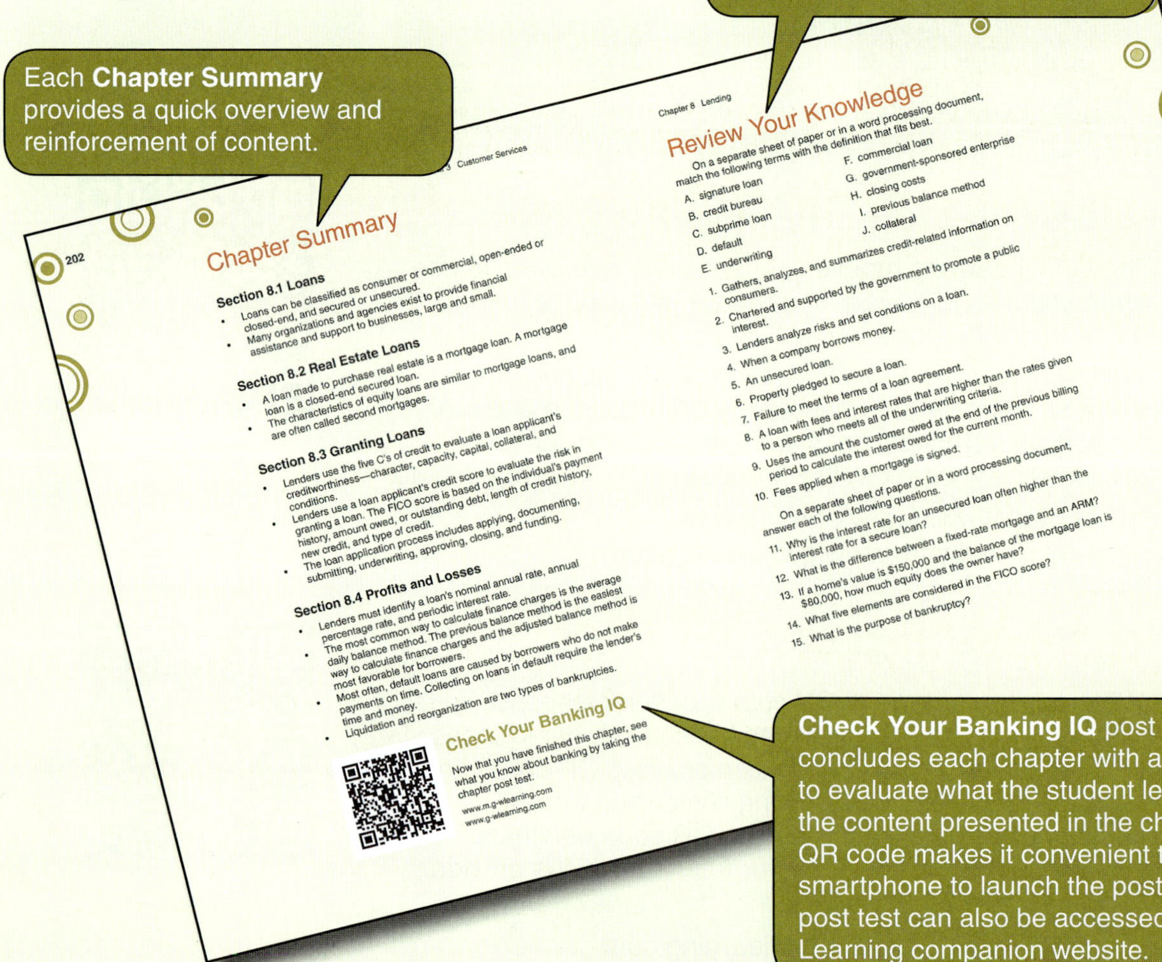

202 Chapter 8 Customer Services

Chapter Summary

Section 8.1 Loans

- Loans can be classified as consumer or commercial, open-ended or closed-end, and secured or unsecured.
- Many organizations and agencies exist to provide financial assistance and support to businesses, large and small.

Section 8.2 Real Estate Loans

- A loan made to purchase real estate is a mortgage loan. A mortgage loan is a closed-end secured loan.
- The characteristics of equity loans are similar to mortgage loans, and are often called second mortgages.

Section 8.3 Granting Loans

- Lenders use the five C's of credit to evaluate a loan applicant's creditworthiness—character, capacity, capital, collateral, and conditions.
- Lenders use a loan applicant's credit score to evaluate the risk in granting a loan. The FICO score is based on the individual's payment history, amount owed, or outstanding debt, length of credit history, new credit, and type of credit.
- The loan application process includes applying, documenting, submitting, underwriting, approving, closing, and funding.

Section 8.4 Profits and Losses

- Lenders must identify a loan's nominal annual rate, annual percentage rate, and periodic interest rate.
- The most common way to calculate finance charges is the average daily balance method. The previous balance method is the easiest way to calculate finance charges and the adjusted balance method is most favorable for borrowers.
- Most often, default loans are caused by borrowers who do not make payments on time. Collecting on loans in default require the lender's time and money.
- Liquidation and reorganization are two types of bankruptcies.

Check Your Banking IQ

Now that you have finished this chapter, see what you know about banking by taking the chapter post test.

www.m.g-wlearning.com
www.g-wlearning.com

Chapter 8 Lending

Review Your Knowledge

On a separate sheet of paper or in a word processing document, match the following terms with the definition that fits best.

A. signature loan
B. credit bureau
C. subprime loan
D. default
E. underwriting
F. commercial loan
G. government-sponsored enterprise
H. closing costs
I. previous balance method
J. collateral

1. Gathers, analyzes, and summarizes credit-related information on consumers.
2. Chartered and supported by the government to promote a public interest.
3. Lenders analyze risks and set conditions on a loan.
4. When a company borrows money.
5. An unsecured loan.
6. Property pledged to secure a loan.
7. Failure to meet the terms of a loan agreement.
8. A loan with fees and interest rates that are higher than the rates given to a person who meets all of the underwriting criteria.
9. Uses the amount the customer owed at the end of the previous billing period to calculate the interest owed for the current month.
10. Fees applied when a mortgage is signed.

On a separate sheet of paper or in a word processing document, answer each of the following questions.

11. Why is the interest rate for an unsecured loan often higher than the interest rate for a secure loan?
12. What is the difference between a fixed-rate mortgage and an ARM?
13. If a home's value is $150,000 and the balance of the mortgage loan is $80,000, how much equity does the owner have?
14. What five elements are considered in the FICO score?
15. What is the purpose of bankruptcy?

Check Your Banking IQ post test concludes each chapter with an opportunity to evaluate what the student learned about the content presented in the chapter. A QR code makes it convenient to use a smartphone to launch the post test. The post test can also be accessed on the G-W Learning companion website.

Outcome-Oriented Learning

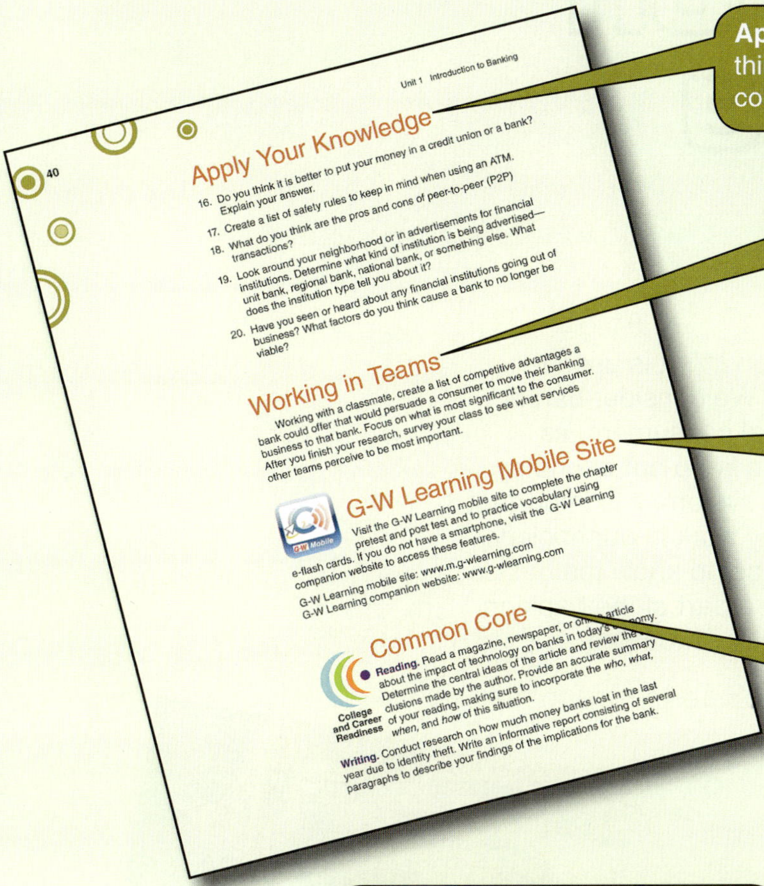
Unit 1 Introduction to Banking

40

Apply Your Knowledge

16. Do you think it is better to put your money in a credit union or a bank? Explain your answer.
17. Create a list of safety rules to keep in mind when using an ATM.
18. What do you think are the pros and cons of peer-to-peer (P2P) transactions?
19. Look around your neighborhood or in advertisements for financial institutions. Determine what kind of institution is being advertised—unit bank, regional bank, national bank, or something else. What does the institution type tell you about it?
20. Have you seen or heard about any financial institutions going out of business? What factors do you think cause a bank to no longer be viable?

Working in Teams

Working with a classmate, create a list of competitive advantages a bank could offer that would persuade a consumer to move their banking business to that bank. Focus on what is most significant to the consumer. After you finish your research, survey your class to see what services other teams perceive to be most important.

G-W Learning Mobile Site

Visit the G-W Learning mobile site to complete the chapter pretest and post test and to practice vocabulary using e-flash cards. If you do not have a smartphone, visit the G-W Learning companion website to access these features.

G-W Learning mobile site: www.m.g-wlearning.com
G-W Learning companion website: www.g-wlearning.com

Common Core

College and Career Readiness

Reading. Read a magazine, newspaper, or online article about the impact of technology on banks in today's economy. Determine the central ideas of the article and review the conclusions made by the author. Provide an accurate summary of your reading, making sure to incorporate the *who, what, when,* and *how* of this situation.

Writing. Conduct research on how much money banks lost in the last year due to identity theft. Write an informative report consisting of several paragraphs to describe your findings of the implications for the bank.

Apply Your Knowledge questions present critical thinking activities that allow individual interpretation of content learned in the chapter.

Working in Teams provides collaborative work experiences to encourage leadership and cooperation.

The **G-W Learning mobile site** contains e-flash cards to practice vocabulary, as well as the chapter pretest and post test and Biz Kid$ videos. If students do not have access to a smartphone, these activities can be completed on the G-W Learning companion website.

College and Career Readiness activities give students an opportunity to apply the Common Core State Standards to improve reading, writing, listening, and speaking skills.

Event Prep creates an opportunity to prepare for competitive activities for career and technical student organization (CTSO) competitions.

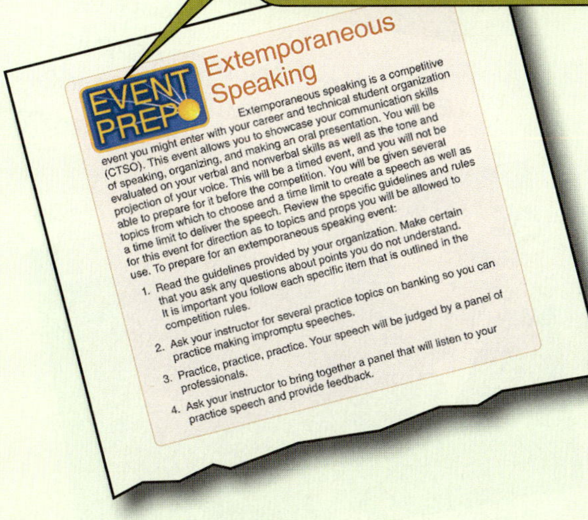
EVENT PREP

Extemporaneous Speaking

Extemporaneous speaking is a competitive event you might enter with your career and technical student organization (CTSO). This event allows you to showcase your communication skills of speaking, organizing, and making an oral presentation. You will be evaluated on your verbal and nonverbal skills as well as the tone and projection of your voice. This will be a timed event, and you will not be able to prepare for it before the competition. You will be given several topics from which to choose and a time limit to create a speech as well as a time limit to deliver the speech. Review the specific guidelines and rules for this event for direction as to topics and props you will be allowed to use. To prepare for an extemporaneous speaking event:

1. Read the guidelines provided by your organization. Make certain that you ask any questions about points you do not understand. It is important you follow each specific item that is outlined in the competition rules.
2. Ask your instructor for several practice topics on banking so you can practice making impromptu speeches.
3. Practice, practice, practice. Your speech will be judged by a panel of professionals.
4. Ask your instructor to bring together a panel that will listen to your practice speech and provide feedback.

The **Unit Assessment** provides an opportunity to measure student knowledge of the materials presented in the chapters in the unit.

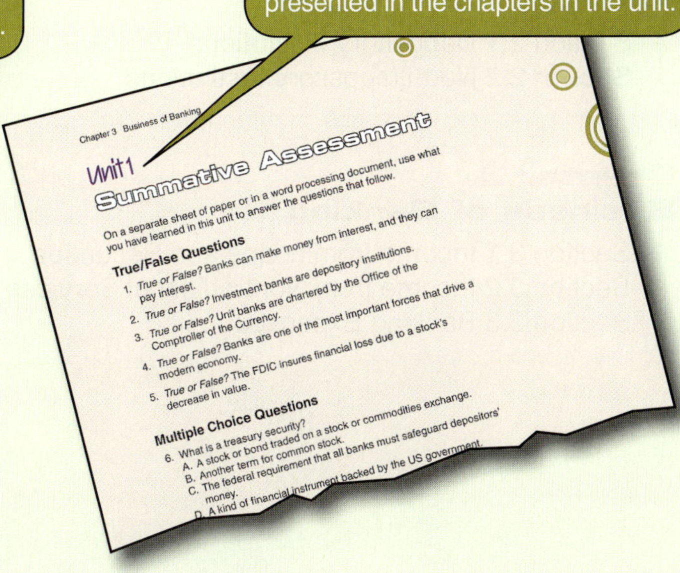
Chapter 3 Business of Banking

Unit 1 Summative Assessment

On a separate sheet of paper or in a word processing document, use what you have learned in this unit to answer the questions that follow.

True/False Questions

1. *True or False?* Banks can make money from interest, and they can pay interest.
2. *True or False?* Investment banks are depository institutions.
3. *True or False?* Unit banks are chartered by the Office of the Comptroller of the Currency.
4. *True or False?* Banks are one of the most important forces that drive a modern economy.
5. *True or False?* The FDIC insures financial loss due to a stock's decrease in value.

Multiple Choice Questions

6. What is a treasury security?
   A. A stock or bond traded on a stock or commodities exchange.
   B. Another term for common stock.
   C. The federal requirement that all banks must safeguard depositors' money.
   D. A kind of financial instrument backed by the US government.

This product also aligns with the National Standards in K–12 Personal Finance Education published by the Jump$tart Coalition for Personal Financial Literacy®.

LISTED ON jumpstartclearinghouse.org

Unit 1

Introduction to Banking

What You Will Learn

Have you ever heard the expression "you can bank on it"? It is used to describe something you can count on with certainty. We consider banks to be reliable, safe places to put our money. Individual consumers, as well as businesses, depend on the banking system to keep our economy running. Banks are the cornerstone of our economic system. It is important to understand the significance of banks and how they work in our society. In the three chapters that make up this unit, you will get to know the basics of banking, the different financial institutions that are a part of the banking industry, and the role banking plays in how business is conducted.

Source: Biz Kid$

Learn about the many services financial institutions provide.

Source: Biz Kid$

Discover how banks make money while keeping the economy moving.

Biz Kid$ in Action

Banking sure has changed over the last few hundred years, especially with the rise of ATMs, online banking, and mobile apps. A century ago, a bank may have been just a single room with one or two tellers, but now many banks have locations all over the world. Today, banks deal more with electronic 1s and 0s than with physical cash. Banks also have had to change to meet the changing banking needs of customers. Now, banks offer a lot more than just savings and loans. They help customers with retirement planning, insurance, investments, and more. Some banks have become specialized. They serve individuals and businesses in specific areas of interest. For example, there are banks that work exclusively with the construction industry. Others assist the aerospace, software, and film industries. Some banks cater to the wealthy. Others help the disadvantaged. There are even banks in high schools run by students!

Banks are not the only thing that changed. The competition has changed, too. Many well-established depository institutions have collapsed or been sold. Some weren't able to keep up with all the regulations. Others took on too many risky loans. Taking the place of the traditional bank are all kinds of similar businesses, like credit unions, community banks, and savings and loans. Customers can even do their banking in grocery stores! Banking sure isn't like the good ol' days anymore.

Banking Bits

What is interest? Interest is a fee that is paid from a borrower to a lender. When you put your money in a savings account, the bank is borrowing it from you. The bank pays you interest. When someone else borrows that money, he or she pays interest to the bank. The amount banks pay to savers is always less than what they charge to borrowers. That's how banks make money.

Quick Tip! Open a savings account as early as possible. The longer you wait, the more likely you are to spend rather than save.

Scan the code to view a Biz Kid$ video. If you do not have a smartphone, visit the G-W Learning companion website.

www.m.g-wlearning.com
www.g-wlearning.com

Let's get started! ⟶

1

Check Your Banking IQ

Before you begin this chapter, see what you already know about banking by taking the chapter pretest.

www.m.g-wlearning.com
www.g-wlearning.com

Banking Basics

Section 1.1
Banking Today

Section 1.2
Banks and the Economy

Banks are one of the most important engines of a modern economy because they hold, protect, and lend money. Banking is a dynamic industry. It has been shaped by advances in technology and an increase in competition. Regulations have also had a big influence. The health of the economy relies on the good will of the financial institutions that work within it. In this chapter, you'll learn the basic definition of a bank, discover different types of banks, and learn about some of the services that today's banks provide.

College and Career Readiness

Reading Prep. Review the table of contents for this text. Trace the development of the content that is being presented from simple to complex ideas.

Scan the code to view a Biz Kid$ video. If you do not have a smartphone, visit the G-W Learning companion website.

www.m.g-wlearning.com
www.g-wlearning.com

Section 1.1
Banking Today

Objectives

After completing this section, you will be able to:

- Describe the purpose of a bank.
- Compare and contrast different types of banks.
- Explain the effect technology has had on modern banking.

Terms

bank
charter
depository institution
reserves
retail bank
Internet bank
commercial bank
money center bank
investment bank
central bank
unit bank
regional bank
interstate bank
national bank
automated teller machine (ATM)
online banking
peer-to-peer payment (P2P)
app

What Is a Bank?

Banks are a type of financial institution. A financial institution is any organization that provides services related to money. Figure 1-1 lists the financial services provided by banks. This includes deposits, loans, and other services. Insurance companies, credit card companies, and stock brokerages are also financial institutions. Many banks provide a range of services such as insurance and investment advice. Not all services are provided by every bank.

Most people and organizations have one or more bank accounts. You probably have one yourself. A bank account lets you deposit and withdraw money, write checks, and earn interest on your savings. You may even have a credit card or a loan from a bank.

The everyday things you do at the bank are only part of what banks do. Basically, banks are organizations that handle money. That can mean a lot of different things:

- protecting money
- lending money
- issuing money (like the Federal Reserve Bank does)
- sending money from one place to another

Deposits	Loans	Other Services
• Savings accounts • Checking accounts • Money market accounts • Certificates of deposit • Retirement accounts	• Car loans • Home loans • Student loans • Business loans • Credit cards	• Insurance • Investments • Trust services • Safe deposit boxes • Money transfers

Figure 1-1.
Common Financial Services Provided by Banks

- keeping track of money
- helping customers get more money
- helping businesses find money

Banks handle money. Most of them also make money. For-profit banks are expected to create profit for their owners. The owners could be individuals, groups, or stockholders. Banks make money by:

- lending money at a higher interest rate than they pay depositors;
- providing services such as safe-deposit boxes;
- charging fees of various kinds.

Because they are so important in our economy, banks are highly regulated. That means they operate under strict rules. Local, state, federal, and international agencies each have a regulatory role. To open a bank, you need a special document called a charter. A bank's **charter** details how the bank is to be operated and how it will be regulated. Charters are issued by federal and state governments.

So what makes a bank a bank? In addition to being financial institutions, banks are depository institutions. In a **depository institution,** customers can give their money to it (make a deposit) and then come back for their money later (make a withdrawal). Banks lend money that customers deposit, charge interest to the borrower, and pay interest to the depositor. No bank keeps 100% of its deposits available, but it must keep reserves on hand for when customers want to take money out. **Reserves** are a percentage of a bank's funds that must be held separately to ensure that the money will be available when customers want to get money from their accounts.

Credit union cooperatives and savings associations are examples of not-for-profit depository institutions. They offer similar services to banks, but instead of making a profit for owners, they return profits to members in the form of lower rates and fees.

Green Banking

Banks are proving that being green can also be good business. Online banking helps reduce fuel consumption by eliminating car trips and minimizing the need to mail printed statements. While meeting customers' demands for green solutions, these services help banks reduce personnel and printing costs. In fact, many banks offer incentives such as higher interest rates to customers who use online banking. That's smart business.

Types of Banks

Consumers and businesses have many options when choosing a bank. There are national banks with thousands of branches as well as ATMs. There are unit banks with only one location. There are even Internet banks with no physical location at all. One way of classifying a bank is by what kind of business it does.

What Does a Bank Do?

Typically **retail banks** provide services for consumers, such as deposit accounts, mortgage, auto, and personal loans as well as credit cards. Those banks that service the needs of businesses are generally referred to as commercial banks.

A newer type of retail bank is the Internet bank. Also known as *online banks,* **Internet banks** have no physical location or building. Customers can do their business with the bank from anywhere they have an Internet connection. These banks sometimes pay higher rates on deposits than other banks because they do not have the expense of maintaining physical locations. However, online banks also do not offer the convenience of in-person service. Even banks with physical locations are offering more online-banking services.

A **commercial bank** focuses on business customers, providing bank accounts along with specialized services such as foreign exchange, investment services, and capital loans. Commercial banks, however, may also provide limited consumer-oriented services, such as personal checking and saving accounts.

Money center banks are very large, often international banks whose primary customers are businesses, other banks, and governments. Large companies often use money center banks to acquire financing for their businesses. Because money center banks play such a large role on the world financial stage, they are susceptible to market conditions worldwide. These banks were hard hit by the global financial crisis that began in 2007.

Regulations instituted after the stock market crash of 1929 stated that banks were prohibited from providing investment services *and* banking services. They had to choose one or the other. As a result, a commercial bank was a bank that took deposits and made loans. A separate entity, known as an **investment bank,** helped companies prepare to become publicly traded companies and otherwise made profit from the stock market. After 1999, banks were once again allowed to provide both kinds of services. Some believe that consequences of this sparked the Great Recession at the beginning of the 21st century.

Governments establish central banks to help stabilize a country's money system. The US established the Federal Reserve System in 1919 to do just that. A central bank, which is part of the Federal Reserve System, is an important mechanism for overseeing a country's banking system. **Central banks** lend money when commercial banks are not able to, regulate banks, and control the money supply.

BIZ TIPS

Retail banks are sometimes called commercial banks even though they serve consumers more often than they do businesses.

Who Owns the Bank?

In some countries, banks are owned by the government. When this is the case, it is called *nationalization.* In the US, banks are not owned by the government. Instead, they are owned by corporations or individuals. Federal and state regulators do, however, have an effect on a bank's operations.

Where Do Banks Operate?

Banks may be classified by how large of an area in which they operate. A bank with one location is called a unit bank. **Unit banks** are usually found in small towns or rural areas. They serve the local customer, tend to invest locally, and know the challenges of the local community.

Banks that branch across a state or a few states in the same region, say the Midwest, are known as **regional banks** or **interstate banks.**

Source: Shutterstock (Supri Suharjoto)

Online banking is just one way that technology has transformed banking.

Regional banks usually specialize in retail banking and do not operate internationally. Depending on the laws governing banking in the state in which it operates, a regional bank may be a member of the Federal Reserve System. The Federal Deposit Insurance Corporation (FDIC) would characterize most regional banks as midsized. National banks may be midsized or characterized as a Top 25. The FDIC classification relates to the bank's size rather than the geographic location it serves.

National banks have offices across the country. Bank of America and Wells Fargo are examples of national banks. National banks are chartered by the federal Office of the Comptroller of the Currency (OCC). National banks do not have to follow state interest-rate caps. Money center banks are national banks. National banks are all members of the Federal Reserve System.

Technology's Transformation of Banking

Once upon a time, you had to visit an actual building to get your banking done. Today, you can bank at a machine, from your computer, or even on your mobile phone.

Automated Teller Machines

Most of us take ATMs for granted and assume they will be on every corner. **Automated teller machines,** or ATMs as they are better known, provide a means of self-service banking. The use of ATMs has become so prevalent that we rarely have to walk into a bank or even go past a drive-through window.

BIZ TIPS

In some foreign countries, such as Japan, ATMs can be used as a way to exchange foreign currency for local money.

ATMs service several banking functions, including getting cash, viewing account balances, initiating cash advances from a credit card, and making deposits. Figure 1-2 provides an overview of the banking services an ATM can provide.

Most banks do not charge a fee to their customers when they use an ATM belonging to the bank. Instead, they impose a fee for ATM transactions to customers of other banks, known as foreign transactions. ATM fees are a source of income for banks.

ATMs can be owned by a bank or other private company. The only part of the ATM experience that is not automated is filling the machine. Employees of the bank or of the ATM's owner must fill the machine with bills periodically and retrieve deposits. However, the records of the transactions completed on the ATM are electronic.

Making Cash Withdrawals	• Original purpose of the ATM • Amount of withdrawals per day is limited • Most popular ATM service
Checking Account Balances	• View a balance even when the bank is not open
Getting Cash Advances	• Get money out of an ATM with certain credit cards • A fee is usually charged • The amount that can be advanced is limited
Making Deposits	• Checks or cash can be deposited • Checks and currency are scanned by the ATM • Funds deposited through ATMs may not be immediately available

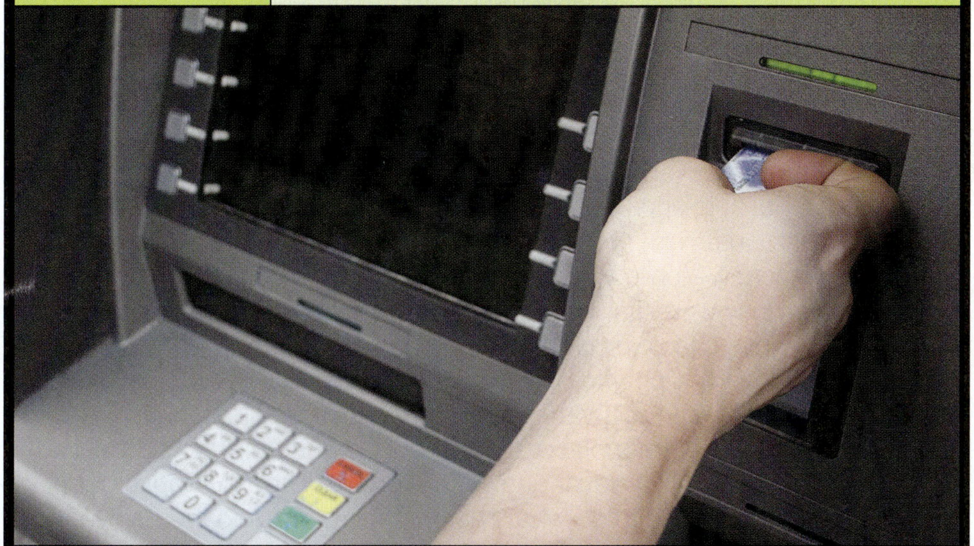

Source of photo: Shutterstock (TimmyQ)

Figure 1-2.
Banking Function Available through Automated Teller Machines

Online Banking

From ordering pizza to video chats with grandma, you can do practically anything online these days. Banking is no exception. **Online banking,** also known as *home banking,* allows customers to conduct financial transactions on a secure website operated by their bank. Today, most banks offer some form of online banking. There are two types of online-banking programs—transactional and non-transactional.

Transactional Online Banking

Transactional online banking allows customers to perform common functions. The functions include transferring funds between checking and savings accounts, paying bills, applying for loans, and purchasing or selling securities (through an affiliate).

Ethical Banking

Did you know that it is unethical and illegal for banks to reveal your personal information to any individual or business? Banks will never reveal a customer's private information for any reason. A customer's information will never be sold or given to anyone who is not approved by the customer. While some banks sell their customer lists to marketing companies, personal banking information, such as account balances, is never sold.

A relatively new transactional online function is person-to-person or peer-to-peer payments. **Peer-to-peer payments (P2P)** allow for an immediate money transfer from one person to another. Suppose you want to send your friend $20 for his or her birthday. Instead of mailing a check or cash, just log on and send a virtual check. All you need to know is your friend's e-mail address or cell phone number. Your friend will receive notification by e-mail or text along with a transaction code from the P2P system and can transfer the $20 into his or her bank account. PayPal™ is a type of P2P payment system.

Non-Transactional Online Banking

Non-transactional online banking is the ability to review information rather than make a transaction. Viewing checking account balances, viewing recent transactions, downloading bank statements, and seeing and printing images of paid checks are all examples of non-transactional activities. Many banks encourage paperless banking to save the environment and money, as well as save the customer time.

Mobile Banking

Applications, or apps, are making their way into banking. **Apps** are computer software programs loaded onto smartphones that let the user perform specific tasks. Banking apps allow mobile devices to be used to handle certain financial transactions. This gives bank customers faster and easier ways of handling their money. Mobile apps are changing the face of banking much as ATMs did when they were first installed in 1972. Figure 1-3 describes the many things banking apps can do, such as mobile phone deposits, text banking, bill payment, locating ATMs, peer-to-peer payments, as well as in-store payments.

As both phones and software programs evolve, mobile banking will become even more commonplace. Customers like the ability to conduct their banking business whenever and wherever they choose. Banks gain by needing fewer employees to do what customers can now do themselves.

BIZ TIPS

While P2P refers to peer-to-peer transactions, B2B refers to business-to-business transactions.

Mobile Banking Services	Allow Customers To...
Mobile Phone Deposit Apps	• Use the camera on a smartphone to take a picture of the front and back (endorsement side) of a check • Receive deposit confirmation
Text Banking	• Use text messaging to find out the balance in an account • Set up automatic text alerts from the bank on balances and other activities
Bill Payments	• Pay bills
ATM Locators	• Find the nearest ATM or banking center
Peer-to-Peer (P2P)Payments	• Make an instant payment to someone
In-Store Payments	• Make a purchase by waving a smartphone at a specially equipped device; the payment is taken directly from the bank account, operating much like a debit card

Figure 1-3.
Mobile Banking Services

Checkpoint 1.1

1. What is a financial institution?
2. What type of bank would a business owner likely use to deposit daily receipts as well as pay invoices and payroll?
3. How are money center banks chartered?
4. What type of bank typically has only one or two locations?
5. PayPal™ is what type of payment system?

Build Your Vocabulary

As you progress through this course, develop a personal glossary of banking terms and add it to your portfolio. This will help you build your banking vocabulary. Write out a definition for each of the following terms, and add it to your personal glossary.

bank
charter
depository institution
reserves
retail bank
Internet bank
commercial bank
money center bank
investment bank
central bank
unit bank
regional bank
interstate bank
national bank
automated teller machine (ATM)
online banking
peer-to-peer payment (P2P)
app

Section 1.2
Banks and the Economy

Terms

- debit card
- banker's blanket bond
- Federal Deposit Insurance Corporation (FDIC)
- financial intermediary
- electronic funds transfer (EFT)
- automated clearinghouse (ACH)

Objectives

After completing this section, you will be able to:

- Describe the economic functions of banks.
- Explain a bank's safekeeping function.
- Explain how credit is essential to a country's economy.
- Define the bank's role as a financial intermediary.
- Discuss why fast and certain access to funds are keys to a banking system.

Economic Functions of Banks

With the help of technology, banks are able to offer a variety of services to customers. There are three basic categories of services offered:

- safekeeping services that protect our money
- deposit services that let our money grow
- loan services that allow us to borrow money

By offering these services, borrowers, savers, buyers, and sellers are able to successfully transact their business. Financial transactions are essential to economic growth. Banking expands the economy and provides jobs, income, investment returns, and tax revenues that benefit all. Individuals, businesses, and governments rely on banks to make our financial world work as shown in Figure 1-4.

Source: Shutterstock (Christina Richards)

The Federal Deposit Insurance Corporation, with its main office in Washington, DC, insures depositors against the loss of any qualifying deposits due to bank failure.

Keeping Money Safe

Our economy functions efficiently because our banking system gives us the confidence that our money, in whatever form within the bank, is safe. Where do you keep your money? Maybe you keep it in your wallet, backpack, or bedroom. Most people keep the bulk of their money in a bank account. A major reason we use bank accounts is that we know our money is safe there. Our wallet or backpack could be lost or stolen. Our bedroom could be burglarized or catch fire.

People want to know their money is secure, and banking is all about security. Banks provide physical security as well as electronic security of our money. In addition, federal deposit insurance protects our money in the event of a bank failure.

Figure 1-4.
Economic Functions of Banks

Protecting money sitting in the bank is only a small part of the safekeeping that banks provide. We rely on banks to keep accurate records of our accounts. Consumers and businesses depend on the records from the bank to help provide a trail of business activities. Much of our banking business occurs not with actual currency, but through access to our bank accounts using checks, ATMs, and debit cards. A **debit card,** also known as a *check card,* allows bank customers to withdraw cash or pay for goods and services in stores or online. Individuals and businesses trust banks to maintain accurate records of their accounts and all account transactions. If we trust the bank enough to put our money in an account, we assume that good records will be kept.

BIZ TIPS

The FDIC insures checking, savings, and other bank deposit accounts. However, the FDIC does not insure securities sold by banks such as mutual funds nor does it cover the contents of safe deposit boxes.

Careers in Finance
Banking and Related Services

What Does a Bank Teller Do?

A **bank teller** is a very important employee in the banking business. When you walk into a bank, the teller is the first person you probably encounter. A **bank teller** must:

- communicate with the customer and provide customer service;
- handle all cash transactions that the customer may need, such as cashing a check, depositing money, or opening various accounts;
- balance the cash drawer at the end of the day; and
- be educated about bank policies, procedures, and emergency operations, such as what to do if a situation of theft presents itself.

What Is It Like to Work as a Bank Teller?

A **bank teller** has a comfortable work environment where the temperature is controlled and the surroundings are pleasant. Professional dress is expected as well as a professional attitude when communicating with customers and fellow employees. Some banks allow tellers to sit, rather than stand, when working at the teller window.

If you are interested in a career in banking, working as a teller is a good way to start learning the business and create a career path.

What Education and Skills Are Needed to Be a Bank Teller?

- high school diploma; college degree preferred
- good math skills
- honest and ethical personality
- customer service oriented

Career Ladder

Regional Vice President

Branch Manager

Bank Teller

Banks are physically protected by state-of-the-art surveillance equipment and security systems. Nearly indestructible vaults are equipped with alarm systems and antitheft devices. Teller windows have bulletproof glass and other safety features.

Banks also guard against internal theft. Tellers and others with access to money must pass strict background checks. In addition, banks perform daily checks on cash drawers and vaults along with audits and internal controls designed to catch employee theft.

Bank-security actions deter many would-be robbers or thieves. However, bank robberies and employee theft still occur. If a robbery does take place, banks are protected by insurance they purchase. Known as a **banker's blanket bond,** this type of insurance covers the bank from losses due to robberies or employee theft.

Customer's insured deposits are protected from loss by the FDIC. The **Federal Deposit Insurance Corporation (FDIC)** insures each depositor up to $250,000 in the case of bank failure. In recent years, a number of banks have been closed. However, because of the FDIC, no customer has lost insured funds.

Extending Credit

Banks are the major lenders in our economy. When we need a loan to buy a car or house, we often get a bank loan. Businesses also borrow from banks to purchase materials or equipment or expand their markets. Bank loans are the primary source of credit for both businesses and individuals. Interest from loans is the main source of revenue for most banks.

Without banks extending credit, borrowers suffer, as does the economy. If consumers need money to buy products, but cannot get loans, then businesses cannot sell their inventory. If businesses do not sell their inventory, the exchange of money slows down.

Consider a common type of bank loan, a car loan. Many people do not have the funds available to pay cash for a new car. If new car loans were not readily available at banks, fewer new cars would be sold. The car dealership would make less money and might lay off some workers. Those workers would have less money to spend since they are not working. Other businesses that rely on sales to the car dealer and its former workers would also be affected.

As you can see, our economy has many pieces. Even if we do not need to borrow, our savings can be used by banks to make loans to those who need them. Both revenue and jobs are created by the extension of credit. The economy relies on banks to provide loans to keep it growing. The loan cycle is depicted in Figure 1-5. This shows how a bank loan cycles through the economy, affecting many in addition to the bank and borrower.

BIZ TIPS

We rely on banks to protect our identity. However, it is the individual's responsibility to be aware of identity theft and take safeguards to protect his or her information. Identity theft is when someone pretends to be you and illegally conducts business in your name.

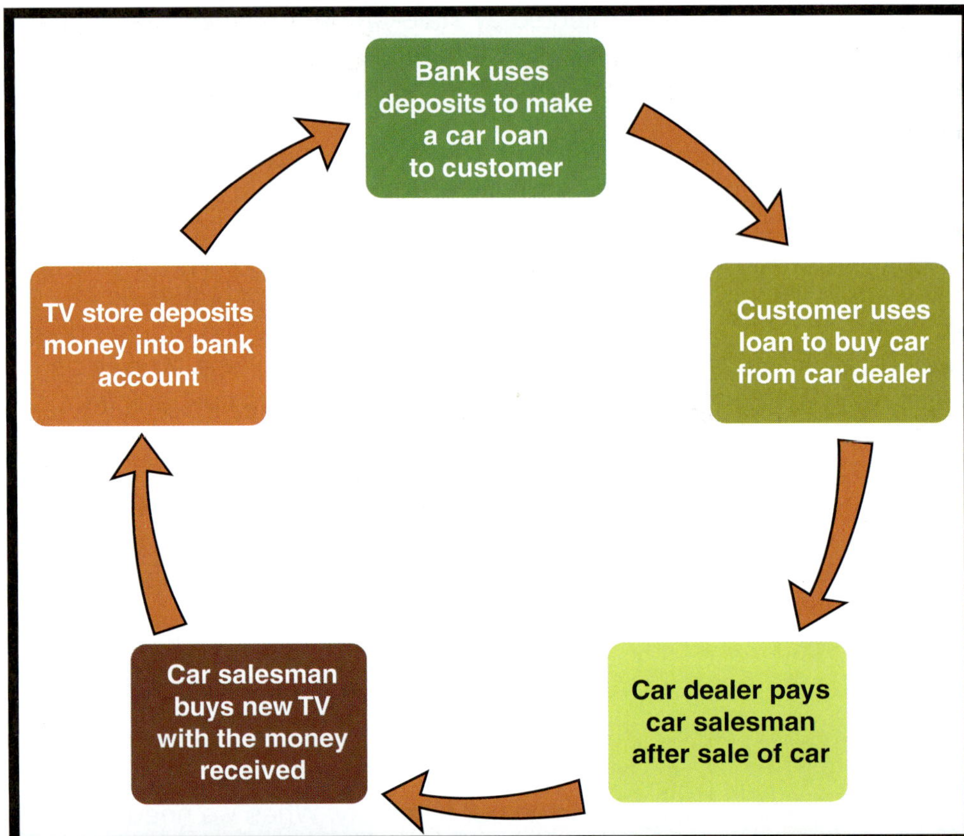

Figure 1-5.
Loan Cycle

Financial Intermediary

A major economic function of a bank is to act as a financial intermediary. A **financial intermediary** is an institution that acts as a go-between in financial transactions. As an intermediary, the financial institution facilitates transactions between the savers and borrowers. Financial intermediaries satisfy the needs of both parties in the transaction and play a critical role in our economy.

For example, savers need a safe place to put their savings. Banks can meet that need by providing accounts that are safe and pay interest. Borrowers, on the other hand, need someone to lend them money and who is willing to accept some risk. Banks use money from savers to make loans to borrowers. In doing so, banks accept the risk that the loan may not be repaid. Both the saver and borrower receive the services that they need.

Transferring Funds

Our economy is fast-paced. Without the transfer and payment systems provided by banks, our economy would slow down to a crawl.

Think of money as a river. Money flows just as a river flows. It takes a long time to travel a mile on a still river, but very little time on a rapidly flowing river. It is the same for money. A money river that flows slowly will take a long time to transfer money between individuals, businesses, and governments. If money moves slowly, the economy also slows down.

Banks make possible a fast-money world where our money moves quickly and securely. **Electronic funds transfer (EFT)** is the electronic exchange of money from one account to another through computer-based systems. Any time you use a debit card or an ATM, you are conducting an electronic funds transfer.

Most funds transfers today involve automated clearinghouses. **Automated clearinghouses (ACHs)** are electronic networks for financial transactions. ACHs process credit and debit transactions and transfer funds from bank to bank. There are several ACHs in the United States, with the Federal Reserve Bank being the largest. About 60% of ACH transactions are handled by the Federal Reserve.

We live in a global economy. Banks can transfer money anywhere in the world at almost any time of the day. Bank customers expect quick access to their money, whether it is from the bank down the street or from the one halfway around the world.

We also live in a world of large-dollar transactions. Banks can just as easily cash a $1 check as they can electronically transfer $1 billion. Although there are some other institutions that can transfer funds, banks handle more transfers than all other institutions combined.

BIZ TIPS

In 1978, the United States Congress passed the Electronic Funds Transfer Act to establish the rights and liabilities of consumers as well as the responsibilities of all participants in EFT activities in the United States.

Checkpoint 1.2

1. What are the three major functions of a bank?
2. What precautions do banks take to safeguard our money?
3. What is the primary source of income for most banks?
4. What is the largest automated clearinghouse in the US?
5. Which type of financial institution handles the most electronic funds transfers?

Build Your Vocabulary

As you progress through this course, develop a personal glossary of banking terms and add it to your portfolio. This will help you build your banking vocabulary. Write out a definition for each of the following terms, and add it to your personal glossary.

debit card
banker's blanket bond
Federal Deposit Insurance Corporation (FDIC)
financial intermediary
electronic funds transfer
automated clearinghouse (ACH)

Chapter Summary

Section 1.1 Banking Today

- Banks are where we deposit our money and the service we use to pay our bills. Most are for-profit businesses and may be owned by individuals or corporations.
- Retail banks typically offer services for the individual consumer—checking, savings, and other services. Commercial banks provide basic banking services along with more specialized services, such as foreign exchange, as well as investment services and capital loans.
- Technology has had a tremendous impact on the banking industry.

Section 1.2 Banks and the Economy

- Banks facilitate the financial transactions that are essential to the health and growth of our economy.
- Banks do a great deal to keep deposits and information safe.
- Banks are the main source of credit for individuals and businesses.
- In its role as financial intermediary, banks make connections between savers and borrowers.
- Fast, reliable access to funds is very important to a banking system.

Check Your Banking IQ

Now that you have finished this chapter, see what you know about banking by taking the chapter post test.

www.m.g-wlearning.com
www.g-wlearning.com

Review Your Knowledge

On a separate sheet of paper or in a word processing document, match the following terms with the definition that fits best.

A. central bank
B. commercial bank
C. Internet bank
D. interstate bank
E. investment bank
F. money center bank
G. national bank
H. regional bank
I. retail bank
J. unit bank

1. Serves the banking needs of consumers.
2. Has no physical bank branch.
3. Serves the banking needs of businesses.
4. Operates globally.
5. Solely provided investment and banking services until 1999.
6. Bank run by a country's government.
7. Usually has only one branch.
8. Operations are limited to one geographic area.
9. Same as national bank.
10. Chartered by the Federal Reserve.

On a separate sheet of paper or in a word processing document, answer each of the following questions.

11. How do banks make money?
12. What is the largest automated clearinghouse (ACH) in the US?
13. What is the special document that details how the bank is to be operated and regulated called?
14. Give two examples of not-for-profit depository institutions.
15. Typically, what three groups do money center banks serve?

Apply Your Knowledge

16. Do you think it is better to put your money in a credit union or a bank? Explain your answer.
17. Create a list of safety rules to keep in mind when using an ATM.
18. What do you think are the pros and cons of peer-to-peer (P2P) transactions?
19. Look around your neighborhood or in advertisements for financial institutions. Determine what kind of institution is being advertised—unit bank, regional bank, national bank, or something else. What does the institution type tell you about it?
20. Have you seen or heard about any financial institutions going out of business? What factors do you think cause a bank to no longer be viable?

Working in Teams

Working with a classmate, create a list of competitive advantages a bank could offer that would persuade a consumer to move their banking business to that bank. Focus on what is most significant to the consumer. After you finish your research, survey your class to see what services other teams perceive to be most important.

G-W Learning Mobile Site

Visit the G-W Learning mobile site to complete the chapter pretest and post test and to practice vocabulary using e-flash cards. If you do not have a smartphone, visit the G-W Learning companion website to access these features.

G-W Learning mobile site: www.m.g-wlearning.com
G-W Learning companion website: www.g-wlearning.com

Common Core

College and Career Readiness

Reading. Read a magazine, newspaper, or online article about the impact of technology on banks in today's economy. Determine the central ideas of the article and review the conclusions made by the author. Provide an accurate summary of your reading, making sure to incorporate the *who, what, when,* and *how* of this situation.

Writing. Conduct research on how much money banks lost in the last year due to identity theft. Write an informative report consisting of several paragraphs to describe your findings of the implications for the bank.

EVENT PREP

Introduction

Career and Technical Student Organizations (CTSOs) are a valuable asset to any educational program. These organizations support student learning and the application of skills to real-world situations. There are a variety of organizations from which to select, depending on the goals of your educational programs. To prepare for any competitive event:

1. Contact the association a year before the next competition to give yourself time to review and decide which competitive events are correct for you or your team.
2. Closely read all of the guidelines. These rules and regulations must be strictly adhered to or disqualification can occur.
3. Follow all of the directions on entry for the events.
4. Review the dress code and code of behavior, and ask any questions before the event.
5. Competitive events may be written, oral, or a combination of both.
6. Communication plays a role in all the competitive events. Read which communication skills are covered for the event you select. Research and preparation are important keys to successful competition.
7. Go to the website of your organization for specific information for the events. Visit the site often as information changes quickly.
8. Pick one or two events that are of interest to you. Print the information for the events and discuss your interest with your instructor.
9. To practice, visit your CTSO's website. Review the competitive events and select those that you will consider entering. Print the description, guidelines, and important dates.

2

Check Your Banking IQ

Before you begin this chapter, see what you already know about banking by taking the chapter pretest.

www.m.g-wlearning.com
www.g-wlearning.com

Financial Institutions

Section 2.1
Depository Institutions

Section 2.2
Non-Depository Institutions

Almost everyone deals with a financial institution at one time or another. Everything from depositing money, to getting a loan, to paying bills is usually done through a type of bank or credit union. Individuals, businesses, and governments all rely on the expertise of financial institutions to help them conduct their money-related matters. There are a variety of financial institutions from which to choose, each with its own unique characteristics.

College and Career Readiness

Reading Prep. Before reading, observe the objectives for each section in this chapter. Keep these in mind as you read, and focus on the structure of the author's writing—was the information presented in a way that was clear and engaging?

Scan the code to view a Biz Kid$ video. If you do not have a smartphone, visit the G-W Learning companion website.

www.m.g-wlearning.com
www.g-wlearning.com

Section 2.1
Depository Institutions

Objectives

After completing this section, you will be able to:

- Describe the various types of depository institutions.
- Discuss types of deposit insurance.

Terms

financial institution
deposit
depositor
stockholder
transaction account
savings account
money market account
savings association
savings and loan association (S & L)
credit union
cooperative
not-for-profit
share account
share draft account
deposit insurance
deposit insurance fund (DIF)
Federal Deposit Insurance Corporation (FDIC)
National Credit Union Share Insurance Fund (NCUSIF)

Financial Institutions

Financial institutions are businesses that offer financial services. Banks, along with credit unions and savings associations, are known as depository institutions. As was introduced in Chapter 1, depository institutions receive money from customers and put the money into a bank account. A **deposit** is money placed in an account. **Depositors** are customers who make the deposits.

Banks are businesses. They are supposed to make money, not just hold onto it. Banks use your deposits to make loans to other customers. By loaning money to customers and charging interest on the loans, the bank is able to generate revenue. The primary business of depository institutions is taking in deposits and turning those deposits into loans. Banks also make money from fees. These fees include ATM-usage fees, overdraft fees, monthly account-maintenance fees, and other fees.

Depository institutions are one of the most important parts of the US economy. They are responsible for most of the money circulating in the country. Most financial transactions, such as paying bills or buying items with a debit or credit card, are done through depository institutions. In addition, when individuals and businesses borrow money, they do so from a depository institution. Our entire financial system is built around the proper functioning of these institutions. Without them, our economy would not function well.

Some familiar examples of depository institutions are commercial banks, savings associations, and credit unions. The characteristics of these depository institutions are shown in Figure 2-1.

Source: Biz Kid$

Banks and credit unions are just two of the many types of financial institutions that play important roles in our economy.

Characteristics	Commercial Banks	Savings Associations	Credit Unions
For Profit	$	$	
Not-for-Profit			$
Owned by Stockholders or Privately	$	$	
Owned by Members			$
Transfers Funds	$	$	$
Accepts Deposits	$	$	$
Makes Loans	$	$	$

Figure 2-1.
Characteristics of Depository Institutions

BIZ TIPS

Depository institutions are also known as intermediaries. Intermediaries facilitate transactions between the savers and borrowers. The bank connects people who are willing to *pay* interest to borrow money with those who want to *earn* interest on their savings.

Commercial Banks

A commercial bank is owned by investors, called **stockholders,** who expect to make a return from their investment. The primary functions of a commercial bank are to transfer funds, accept deposits, and make loans to individuals, businesses, and governments. There are approximately 6,500 commercial banks in the US.

Transfer Funds

Every time you pay for something, you are transferring money from yourself to another party. A **transaction account** is one that allows the owner to use it to pay a third party. Checking accounts are the most common type of transaction account. These accounts may provide us with an online bill payment service, a debit card, or access to an ATM. Checking accounts are used to handle our day-to-day financial needs.

Accept Deposits

Individuals also save money at a bank. **Savings accounts** are deposit accounts that provide a safe place to store your money. Savings accounts do not have check-writing privileges. Banks pay interest on savings accounts. This gives depositors an added reason to save money. **Money market accounts** are a type of savings account that pays more interest than an average savings account. These accounts require a larger initial deposit as well and a minimum balance, often $500.

Make Loans

In addition to offering checking and savings accounts, a commercial bank also makes loans to its customers. Commercial banks make more loans than other depository institutions. Consumers get bank loans to finance the purchase of cars, houses, and sometimes even higher education.

Other Services

Commercial banks also offer a wide assortment of other services. These services vary from bank to bank. You can rent a safe deposit box for your valuables. Many banks sell securities and insurance. Trust departments at banks manage money and other assets for customers. If you have a financial need, chances are there is a bank that can take care of it. Banks today are truly one-stop financial supermarkets.

Many different types of customers use banks. This was not always the case. Years ago, banks were just open to businesses. The name *commercial bank* refers to the services banks performed for commercial enterprises or businesses. Modern banks are open to individuals, businesses, and nonprofit organizations. Banks provide different services for a variety of different customers.

Green Banking

Green banks are changing the way bank loans are made. For example, a traditional banker approves a home loan based on the current value of the home and the borrower's ability to pay. A green banker will also consider the cost savings from new technology, such as solar and geothermal installations. The savings found will give the borrower more money to repay the loan. Sometimes green technology used in building a new home has a higher upfront cost, but actually saves money over the long term. Loan officers at green banks also advise customers on the latest green building innovations that will reduce energy consumption.

Savings and Loan Associations

Savings associations, also known as **savings and loan associations (S & L's),** were originally organized to help people save money. Small deposits once were not accepted by many banks. This meant that many customers had nowhere to save money in small amounts. Savings associations allowed savers with small deposits to open savings accounts just like the investors who had large deposits. Savings associations are also called *thrift institutions.* They were given that name because they encourage people to be thrifty and save.

Originally, savings associations only provided savings accounts and home loans. Because many banks did not make home loans then, savings associations became the leading source of these loans. Today, savings associations offer other types of loans as well.

Savings associations, like commercial banks, operate for profit. They are typically owned by stockholders. However, they may be owned by a single person, a group of people, or a corporation.

Source: Shutterstock (Blend Images)

The Memphis Area Teachers Credit Union was once an occupational membership credit union. It now has a geographic membership requirement.

Credit Unions

Credit unions provide many of the same services as banks and S & L's, but they are owned by their members. This arrangement is known as a cooperative, or co-op for short. A **cooperative** is a business or organization that is owned by its members—members cooperate to run the organization. Credit unions are operated on a not-for-profit basis. **Not-for-profit** means instead of paying profits to shareholders, money made by the credit union is returned to the members. The returned money takes the form of higher interest rates on savings and lower interest rates on loans compared to other types of institutions. **Share accounts** are savings accounts at credit unions. **Share draft accounts** are checking accounts at credit unions.

Another difference between banks and credit unions is the membership requirement for credit unions. To open a credit union account, you must meet membership criteria. The most common criteria relate to employer, occupation, and geography. Figure 2-2 shows the characteristics of each type.

Credit unions tend to be small since they are focused on serving a particular group or community. Because of their size, credit unions may offer fewer services than large banks. Credit unions may:

- have a limited number of deposit accounts available to members;
- only offer savings accounts;
- offer only car loans and not mortgage loans;
- not sell securities or insurance to customers; and
- serve a smaller geographic area than banks, such as having only one office in one city.

BIZ TIPS

Legislation that allowed savings associations more freedom, together with unwise investments and some criminal practices, led to what would become known as the S & L crisis during the 1980s and early 1990s. The number of savings associations fell from over 3,000 in 1986 to around 1,600 in 1995.

Credit Union Membership Type	Characteristics
Employer-based	Open to people working in a particular company. Example: The Deere Employees Credit Union in Illinois is open only to employees of the John Deere Company.
Occupation-based	Open to people who share a common occupation. Example: The Newton Teachers Credit Union in Massachusetts is open to people working in or retired from the Newton public schools.
Geography-based	Open to anyone living, working, or even volunteering or worshiping in specific geographic location. These credit unions are often larger than other types since membership is obtained just by living in a community. Example: The Park Community Federal Credit Union is open to anyone living or working in the nine-county Louisville, Kentucky metropolitan area.

Figure 2-2.
Credit Union Membership Categories

There are more credit unions than banks in the United States. There are currently close to 8,000 credit unions in the US. Banks, though smaller in number, tend to be much larger in size. Banks usually have more deposits, assets, and profits compared to credit unions. Some small credit unions have assets of less than $1 million. It would be very rare to find a bank that small.

Once enrolled, you can stay a member of a credit union even if you no longer meet the membership requirement. Of course, you can close your account at any time just as in other financial institutions. During the Great Recession, many people became fearful of keeping their money in banks. As a result, deposits in credit unions increased greatly. The services credit unions offered also expanded. These institutions began lending not just to individuals, but to certain businesses as well.

BIZ TIPS

Walmart, the *world's retailer,* offers some financial services to its customers. While they do not take in deposits as such, the retailer allows customers to load money onto prepaid debit cards. It also cashes government and payroll checks and conducts wire transfers.

Federal Deposit Insurance

Customers can rest assured their money deposited in a bank is safe. **Deposit insurance** covers the deposits of customers. If an institution fails, the depositors are protected. The depository institutions share their risks and pool their money by paying premiums into the **deposit insurance fund (DIF).** If an institution fails, the DIF arranges for depositors to maintain the insured funds they have in their accounts. Many times a healthy bank takes over the deposit accounts of the closed bank. This allows depositors to keep doing their banking without any interruption. In most years, there are few bank failures and the fund balance grows. However, a number of banks failed as a result of the financial crises and resulting economic downturn in the early 21st century. This affected the fund's growth.

Two federal agencies insure deposits. Banks are insured by the Federal Deposit Insurance Corporation (FDIC). Most credit unions are insured by the National Credit Union Administration (NCUA).

Federal Deposit Insurance Corporation

The **Federal Deposit Insurance Corporation (FDIC)** provides deposit insurance for depositors in insured banks and thrifts. The FDIC is an independent federal agency established in 1933. Thousands of banks failed during the Great Depression. The FDIC was created to promote public confidence in the banks. Since it was started, no depositor has lost a cent of insured funds due to the failure of an FDIC-insured institution.

Prior to the global financial crisis of the early 21st century, the FDIC insured each customer's deposits up to $100,000. To improve confidence in US banks during the crisis, coverage of interest-bearing accounts was raised to $250,000 in 2008. This increase was initially meant to be temporary, but it was made permanent in 2010. Non-interest-bearing transaction accounts, such as checking accounts, are covered regardless of the amount.

Deposits are insured per ownership category per depository institution. Ownership categories include:

- single accounts;
- joint accounts;

BIZ TIPS

Make sure the financial institutions you do business with are federally insured. To do so, simply visit the website for these agencies to verify that the bank is legitimate and federally insured.

- certain retirement accounts, including individual retirement accounts, known as *IRAs;*
- certain trust accounts;
- employee-benefit plan accounts; and
- government accounts.

It is possible for a person to be insured for more than $250,000, depending on the type of accounts opened. For example, Joe Cruz has a savings account (classified as a single account) and an IRA (classified as a retirement account) at the same bank.

$180,000 (savings account) < $250,000 = fully insured

$210,000 (IRA) < $250,000 = fully insured

$180,000 + $210,000 = $390,000 of fully insured funds

However:

$180,000 (joint savings account) + $75,000 (joint interest-bearing checking account) = $255,000 total of the same account type

$255,000 – $250,000 = $5,000 of uninsured funds

The FDIC insures deposit accounts, but not investment instruments, even if they are sold through the bank. Figure 2-3 shows which types of accounts are and are not covered. Banks are required by law to clearly disclose the risks of purchasing non-deposit investment products that they sell. This is to ensure consumers do not think they are protected by deposit insurance for these products.

In addition to its role as an insurer, the FDIC does other important things. It monitors member banks to help ensure that they do things by the book. It also manages banks that are in receivership, meaning banks that have failed.

BIZ TIPS

The Glass-Steagall Act of 1933 established the FDIC and introduced banking reforms. Parts of this act were repealed in 1999 by the Gramm-Leach-Bliley Act. As a result, commercial banks were once again allowed to offer investment services.

National Credit Union Share Insurance Fund

The **National Credit Union Share Insurance Fund (NCUSIF)** was established in 1970 to insure credit union deposits. The NCUSIF is administered by the National Credit Union Administration (NCUA).

Eligible for FDIC Insurance Protection	Not Eligible for FDIC Insurance Protection
Checking accounts	Mutual funds
Savings accounts	Stocks
Money market accounts	Bonds
Certificates of deposit	Annuities
IRAs	Life insurance
401(k)s	Contents of safe deposit boxes

Figure 2-3.
FDIC Insurance Eligibility

The FDIC and NCUA are virtually identical. Both insure accounts up to $250,000 per depositor per ownership category per institution. Credit unions pay insurance premiums to the NCUA just as banks and savings associations pay premiums to the FDIC. They are both backed by the US government. Both agencies have examiners who determine financial soundness of insured institutions. Both insure state- as well as federally chartered depository institutions.

BIZ TIPS

At one time, the Federal Savings and Loan Insurance Corporation (FSLIC) insured savings associations. This federal agency was closed in 1989 as a result of the S & L crisis. The FDIC then began insuring savings associations.

Checkpoint 2.1

1. What do financial institutions do?
2. What are the three types of depository institutions?
3. Who owns commercial banks?
4. What was the original purpose of savings associations?
5. Why was the FDIC established?

Build Your Vocabulary

As you progress through this course, develop a personal glossary of banking terms and add it to your portfolio. This will help you build your banking vocabulary. Write out a definition for each of the following terms, and add it to your personal glossary.

financial institution
deposit
depositor
stockholder
transaction account
savings account
money market account
savings association
savings and loan association (S & L)
credit union
cooperative
not-for-profit
share account
share draft account
deposit insurance
deposit insurance fund (DIF)
Federal Deposit Insurance Corporation (FDIC)
National Credit Union Share Insurance Fund (NCUSIF)

Section 2.2
Non-Depository Institutions

Terms

non-depository institution
investment bank
securities
bond
stock
dividend
securities firm
commission
full-service brokerage firm
discount broker
finance company
consumer finance company
payday lender
business finance company
captive finance company
insurance company
premium
insured

Objectives

After completing this section, you will be able to:

- Define non-depository institutions.
- Describe the role of investment banks in raising capital.
- Explain the purpose of securities.
- Describe the function of finance companies.
- Explain how insurance companies provide risk-management and investment options to their clients.

Other Financial Institutions

The financial marketplace also includes non-depository institutions. **Non-depository institutions** do not accept deposits, although many make loans. Non-depository institutions accept money from their customers to invest in business deals. This spreads the risk and provides a way for customers to invest.

There are a number of non-depository institutions. Investment banks, securities firms, finance companies, and insurance companies are all non-depository institutions.

Investment Banks

When is a bank not a bank? When it is an investment bank. Investment banks are very different from commercial banks and credit unions. They do not take deposits or make loans. Instead, they are specialists in the securities markets.

Investment banks provide services for businesses. They help businesses raise capital to expand. Money is also known as *capital.* A common way for businesses to raise money is to issue securities. **Securities** are financial instruments. They pay interest or give the investor part ownership of the company. Issuing securities is one of the main activities of investment banks.

Source: Shutterstock (Stephen Coburn)

Stocks and bonds are two securities frequently handled by investment bankers.

Investment banks help organizations issue bonds and find investors to buy them. **Bonds** are debt issued by a government or company. If you buy a bond, you are loaning money to that organization. The organization must repay the bondholder for the loan. For example, a city may issue bonds to raise money for a football stadium. First, the bonds are sold. The bonds are held for a specified period of time. Then, the amount borrowed plus interest is paid back to the investor. In certain cases, bondholders receive periodic interest payments while they hold the bond.

Investment banks also assist companies that want to raise capital by acting as an agent to sell stock. **Stock** is a security that gives the purchaser part ownership in the company. This part ownership is called *equity.* Stockholders may receive dividends from the issuing company. **Dividends** are payments. However, not all companies pay dividends to stockholders.

The process of issuing securities is complex and highly regulated. So, companies pay investment banks to manage it. Investment banks act as intermediaries between issuers of securities and investors. This is similar to the role commercial banks play between depositors and borrowers.

Financial instruments themselves have become more complicated. Take for instance, derivatives. In finance, a *derivative* is a contract designed to manage risk and make money. Derivatives are controversial because they are challenging to understand and can have a major impact on the economy.

BIZ TIPS

Until the 1999 Gramm-Leach-Bliley Act, banks were not permitted to engage in investment banking. Now, many large commercial banks have investment banking divisions.

Securities Firms

Securities firms are financial institutions involved in the trading of securities in financial markets. Securities firms are also called *brokerage firms, stockbrokers,* or *bondbrokers.* Securities firms may create and manage funds, such as mutual funds. Mutual funds are made up of a selection of securities and other financial instruments.

Securities firms execute transactions for customers. If you wanted to buy Google stock, you could use the services of a stockbroker. The broker would place the order and charge a fee. A **commission** is the fee for placing the order.

In addition to placing orders, full-service brokers also provide other services. **Full-service brokerage firms** advise customers on which securities to buy. They also help customers manage their investments. Many firms also offer services online.

Discount brokers place orders for customers, too. Commissions are generally less than full-service brokers. Fees may be less, and services offered by a discount broker may be limited. Many discount brokers *only* operate through a website. Today, companies such as E-Trade and Sharebuilder allow customers to trade securities online. Commissions are lower than those charged by full-service brokerages.

Ethical Banking

The Financial Industry Regulatory Authority, better known as FINRA, is a self-regulatory organization that ensures stockbrokers follow established rules of conduct when dealing with customers. Ethical lapses can be punishable by fines and license suspension or revocation.

Source: Shutterstock (Monkey Business Images)

Stockbrokers provide investment advice based on research and suitability to clients' needs.

Finance Companies

Finance companies make profits by issuing loans to both individuals and businesses. They are also known as *loan companies.* Offering loans is the only service provided to customers. Most finance companies are privately owned. There are two major types of finance companies—consumer finance companies and business finance companies.

Consumer finance companies provide personal loans to individuals. They generally make loans to customers who have poor credit. Consumer finance loans commonly carry much higher interest rates than bank or credit union loans.

A relatively new type of consumer finance company is a payday lender. **Payday lenders** make short-term loans designed to cover expenses until the borrower's next payday. Many payday loan customers find they are unable to pay the loan when it is due. Sometimes they get another payday loan, paying more fees in the process. This can lead to a cycle of debt that is very difficult to escape. Payday loans can be very expensive. Interest rates can be 300% or higher.

Business finance companies provide loans for businesses, such as retail stores. The finance company arranges with the business to provide loans on site to customers. For example, a customer wants to buy a computer, but does not have the cash. The computer store can offer that customer a loan. The computer store is not really issuing the loan. The business finance company that works with the computer store is issuing the loan.

Some large manufacturers form their own finance companies. These are known as captive finance companies. A **captive finance company** is formed by a manufacturer to provide loans so the manufacturer can easily sell its goods.

Insurance Companies

Insurance companies are for-profit businesses that primarily sell insurance. They may also sell other products and services. Insurance is an extremely important part of our economy. Individuals, governments, and businesses all buy insurance. Insurance is available to protect just about anything. Some types of insurance, such as automobile insurance, may be required by law. There are two primary ways that insurance companies generate revenue: selling insurance policies and selling investment products.

Insurance is a way to protect against financial loss. By purchasing insurance, the consumer transfers their risk onto the insurance carrier. Insurance can protect us from financial risks we encounter in our everyday lives, such as a car accident or a prolonged illness. Life insurance, property insurance, and health insurance are examples of risk-management products sold to consumers.

The consumer buys an insurance policy by making periodic payments, known as **premiums.** In turn, the insurance carrier agrees to cover losses according to the terms of the insurance contract. An insurance contract is also known as a *policy.* The person or thing covered by the policy is called the **insured.**

Insurance companies also sell investment products such as annuities, whole life insurance, and mutual funds. These investment products are similar to products bought from banks or other financial institutions. Insurance companies earn income from fees they charge to create and manage these products.

BIZ TIPS

Even insurance companies buy insurance. It's called *reinsurance.* The insurance company pays a premium to the reinsurance company, who agrees to pay the insurer in the event of certain kinds of losses.

Checkpoint 2.2

1. What are four types of non-depository financial institutions?
2. How do investment banks help companies raise capital?
3. How do stockbrokers make their money?
4. What is the primary business of finance companies?
5. What are the two ways insurance companies earn income?

Build Your Vocabulary

As you progress through this course, develop a personal glossary of banking terms and add it to your portfolio. This will help you build your banking vocabulary. Write out a definition for each of the following terms, and add it to your personal glossary.

non-depository institution
investment bank
securities
bond
stock
dividend
securities firm
commission
full-service brokerage firm
discount broker
finance company
consumer finance company
payday lender
business finance company
captive finance company
insurance company
premium
insured

Careers in Finance
Banking and Related Services

What Does a Customer Service Representative Do?

Customer service representative (CSRs) provide a valuable link between customers and the bank. They are knowledgeable about all bank services and must be able to sell those services to customers. The services provided by **customer service representatives** include:

- answering customer questions;
- researching and solving customer problems;
- selling bank products to customers; and
- maintaining bank files.

What Is It Like to Work as a Customer Service Representative?

A **customer service representative** may work in a variety of settings. Some work in a call or customer contact center. Others work on the bank floor Since they are often in public view, CSRs are expected to dress professionally.

Customer service representatives are the contact people for customers who need help with their accounts. CSRs are trained on all products that the bank offers and can offer solutions to customer problems.

Working as a **customer service representative** is a good way to start a career in any business. If solving problems and working with the public are things that interest you, this may be a good career opportunity for you.

What Education and Skills Are Needed to Be a Customer Service Representative?

- high school diploma; college degree preferred
- good communication skills
- detail oriented
- desire to solve problems and help the customer

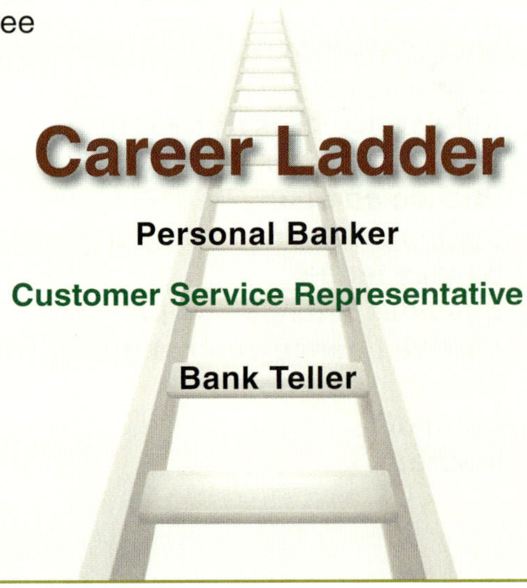

Chapter Summary

Section 2.1 Depository Institutions

- Financial institutions collect and invest funds. Depository institutions include banks, savings associations, and credit unions.
- The FDIC is the largest deposit insurance fund, insuring both banks and savings associations. The NCUSIF insures deposits in credit unions.

Section 2.2 Non-Depository Institutions

- Investment banks help businesses issue securities to raise capital.
- Securities firms place orders from customers to buy or sell securities.
- Finance companies are essentially lenders, making loans to individuals and businesses.
- Insurance companies assume risk from policyholders in exchange for premium payments.

Check Your Banking IQ

Now that you have finished this chapter, see what you know about banking by taking the chapter post test.

www.m.g-wlearning.com
www.g-wlearning.com

Review Your Knowledge

On a separate sheet of paper or in a word processing document, match the following terms with the definition that fits best.

A. checking account
B. deposit
C. dividend
D. equity
E. money market account
F. premium
G. savings account
H. securities
I. share account
J. share draft account

1. Money placed in an account.
2. Checking account with a credit union.
3. Savings account with a credit union.
4. Stock and bonds.
5. Periodic payment made in exchange for insurance coverage.
6. Most common kind of transaction account.
7. Deposit account that does not allow for check writing.
8. Type of savings account that pays higher interest.
9. Payment to stockholders.
10. Part ownership.

On a separate sheet of paper or in a word processing document, answer each of the following questions.

11. Which type of depository institution is owned by its members?
12. Which type of transaction account is used to pay bills or make purchases?
13. What are the most common qualifications for membership in a credit union?
14. What types of institutions do the FDIC and NCUSIF insure?
15. What is the difference between a depository and a non-depository institution?

Apply Your Knowledge

16. Conduct some online research exploring the differences between banks, savings and loan associations, and credit unions. Of the three, which do you think is the best place to put your money? Explain your answer.
17. What are the pros and cons of taking out a payday loan? Why do you think that people are willing to take out a loan with such a huge interest rate?
18. Visit the Securities and Exchange Commission's website to review the terms of the Dodd-Frank Wall Street Reform and Consumer Protection Act. What impact does this law have on how banks and other financial institutions operate?
19. The FDIC offers an online calculator tool called EDIE, the Electronic Deposit Insurance Estimator. EDIE allows depositors to see the extent to which their deposits are insured by the FDIC. Go to the FDIC website and determine if the deposits of you or someone close to you are insured and to what extent. Describe your findings.
20. Do you think that investments should be insured the same way funds in banks are? Why or why not?

Working in Teams

Working with a classmate, create a list of services or products that are offered at both depository and non-depository institutions. Then, create a list of reasons why customers might choose a non-depository institution over a depository institution for a service that is offered at both types of institutions.

G-W Learning Mobile Site

Visit the G-W Learning mobile site to complete the chapter pretest and post test and to practice vocabulary using e-flash cards. If you do not have a smartphone, visit the G-W Learning companion website to access these features.

G-W Learning mobile site: www.m.g-wlearning.com
G-W Learning companion website: www.g-wlearning.com

Common Core

College and Career Readiness

Listening. Practice active listening skills while listening to a broadcast business report on the radio, television, or podcast. Pick a single story and create a report in which you analyze the following aspects of the business story: the speaker's audience, point of view, reasoning, stance, word choice, tone, points of emphasis, and organization.

Speaking. Find a recent story about online banking in a newspaper, magazine, or blog. Prepare a one- to two-minute summary of the material to present orally. Make an audio recording of your presentation. Listen to it. Note ways your presentation was effective and ways that you could improve. If time permits, rerecord your presentation. Listen to how much you improved from your first try.

EVENT PREP

Written Events

A written event is a competitive event you might enter with your career and technical student organization (CTSO). Students who participate are required to write a paper and submit it either before the competition or when he or she arrives at the event. The entrant must also present the paper in front of a panel of judges. Written events can be lengthy and take a lot of time to prepare, so it is important to start early. To prepare for a written event:

1. Read the guidelines provided by your organization. The topic to be researched will be specified in detail. In addition, all final format guidelines will be given including how to organize and submit your work. Make certain that you ask any questions about points that you do not understand.
2. Do your research early. Research may take days or weeks, and you do not want to rush the process.
3. Set a deadline for yourself so that you can write at a comfortable pace.
4. After you write your first draft, ask a teacher to review it and give you feedback.
5. Once you have the final version, go through the checklist for the event to make sure you have covered all of the details. You will be penalized on your score if you omit a direction.
6. To practice, visit your CTSO's website and select a written event in which you might be interested. Research the topic and then complete an outline. Create a list of guidelines that you must follow for this event. After you have completed these steps, decide if this is the event or topic that interests you. If you are still interested, move forward and start the writing process.

Check Your Banking IQ

Before you begin this chapter, see what you already know about banking by taking the chapter pretest.

www.m.g-wlearning.com
www.g-wlearning.com

3

Business of Banking

What do banks, barbershops, and babysitters all have in common? If you said they all begin with the letter B, you would only be partly correct. They are all service businesses. Unlike manufacturers, service businesses do not produce goods for sale in a store. Instead, they provide a variety of services for which customers pay money.

Whether it is a not-for-profit credit union or a multinational bank, all banks have to cover the cost of providing services. If it is a for-profit bank, it also has to provide a return on investment for the owners. This chapter looks at the many ways that banks generate revenue.

College and Career Readiness

Reading Prep. Before reading the chapter, skim the photos and their captions. As you are reading, determine how these concepts contribute to the ideas presented in the text.

Scan the code to view a Biz Kid$ video. If you do not have a smartphone, visit the G-W Learning companion website.

www.m.g-wlearning.com
www.g-wlearning.com

Section 3.1
Income from Loans and Securities

Terms
asset
interest
maturity
liquidity
gain
insufficient funds fee
overdraft program
overdraft
surcharge
account inquiry fee
safe deposit box
money order
inactivity fee

Objectives
After completing this section, you will be able to:
- Describe four common ways banks generate revenue.
- Explain the connection between customer fees and bank profitability.

Income from Traditional Bank Services

When looking at how banks earn income, you must first examine their assets. An **asset** is something owned by an individual or other entity. The two largest assets of banks are loans and securities. Banks extend loans to customers and own the loan until it is repaid. Securities purchased by a bank are owned until the bank sells them.

These loans and securities tend to be the way banks generate most of their income. Increasingly, banks generate a sizable amount of income through the fees they charge.

Interest on Loans

Banks make most of their income by extending loans to customers. Loans are the largest bank asset and produce the largest amount of income. When banks make loans to customers, they charge interest. **Interest** is the fee charged for borrowing money. This is known as *interest income* for the bank. Banks also charge interest on credit card balances.

The main factors that determine how much interest a bank charges include:
- competition;
- market rates; and
- the borrower's creditworthiness.

Banks work hard to balance all of these factors to stay profitable. It is quite a balancing act. Every loan carries a certain amount of risk. Taking this risk into account, the bank must set its rates at levels that are competitive, yet profitable.

Source: Shutterstock (isak55)

Banks are businesses, and businesses are established to make money.

Some customers with poor credit ratings are considered a high risk for not repaying a loan. Poor credit ratings mean that the customer may not be able to repay a loan. Banks charge higher interest rates for customers who have low credit ratings. These risky loans pay a higher interest rate because there is a greater chance of the bank losing money on the loan. However, some loans are considered too risky to be approved at all. Customers who have good credit ratings are considered a good risk for repaying the loan. Therefore, banks are willing to give them lower interest rates. The more risk a borrower represents to the bank, the greater the interest the borrower will have to pay. The lower the risk, the less a borrower has to pay.

Interest on Securities

Loans are not the only ways banks make money. They also invest their money in securities, typically bonds and treasury bills. The interest rate on most loans is higher than the interest rate on most securities. However, banks cannot always make a loan, or at least not a good loan. In that case, banks must put their money into other assets. This is where securities come in.

Securities are investments that represent ownership or debt. One kind of security is a bond. There are many types of bonds. Each type has its own distinct features. Bonds pay interest, but the way the interest is paid differs by type of bond. For the most part, an investor receives the purchase price plus interest back when the bond matures. A bond's **maturity** is the date on which the investor can receive the initial investment.

Banks invest in a combination of long- and short-term securities. Long-term securities have maturities of over one year. Short-term securities have maturities up to one year. In general, short-term securities have lower interest rates than long-term securities. Bonds are a type of long-term security. Many banks invest in treasury bonds issued by the US Treasury Department.

Treasury Securities

There are several types of treasury securities, as shown in Figure 3-1. Treasury bonds pay interest to investors and are issued with maturities of up to 30 years. Bondholders receive interest every six months until the bond matures. Treasury bonds are considered risk-free since they are backed by the US government. Treasury securities are not as sensitive to market risk as are other types of securities.

Short-term securities include treasury bills. Like treasury bonds, treasury bills are issued by the US Treasury Department and are considered risk-free. Treasury bills are issued in terms of 4, 13, 26, and 52 weeks. Banks often invest in treasury securities if they only need to invest for a short period of time.

Green Banking

Like many businesses, banks are heavily dependent on computers for much of their workload. Each bank employee, from tellers to accountants and loan officers, generally has a computer workstation. Many banks have begun to modernize their computer technologies and, at the same time, engage in green banking. Newer computers and printers are more efficient, using less energy to power them. Some banks are replacing desktop computers with laptop or notebook computers to save energy. Laptops are 30% more energy efficient than desktop computers. By upgrading to new computers, banks not only save the environment, but also save money on their operating expenses.

Short-Term Security	Treasury Bills	Also called *T-bills*	• May be purchased from the Treasury or banks • Yield is what the market will pay on maturity • May be resold
Short- to Medium-Term Security	Treasury Notes	Also called *T-notes*	• Fixed interest rate • Sold at auction • May be resold
Long-Term Security	Savings Bonds	Series EE	• Fixed interest rate • Available in paper or electronically • Earn interest for up to 30 years • Nontransferrable
		Series I	• Two methods for paying interest—one is fixed, the other is tied to inflation rate • Earn interest for up to 30 years • Nontransferrable
	Treasury Bonds	Also called *T-bonds*	• Fixed interest rate • Pays interest every six months (up to 30 years) • May be resold

Figure 3-1.
Treasury Securities

BIZ TIPS

Have you ever heard of a *liquid asset?* It means something (the asset) can be quickly sold or traded.

Banks balance interest income with liquidity by purchasing a mix of short- and long-term securities. **Liquidity** refers to the ability to quickly turn an asset into cash. Short-term securities are more liquid than long-term securities. Some short-term securities have maturities of less than a week. A bank can hold a security for a few days, after which point the initial investment plus interest is returned to the bank and ready for another investment.

Bank regulators restrict the types of securities banks can buy. For instance, banks cannot invest in common stock. Stock returns change based on stock market activity. Stocks carry no guaranty for investors. So, regulators consider common stock too risky for banks.

Gains on Securities

Securities can provide banks with income in addition to what would be earned in interest. This happens when a bank sells a security for more than its purchase price. This is known as a **gain,** or increase in income.

While loans are a bank's primary asset, securities are the next most profitable. If loan demand is high and a bank needs money to make loans, they may sell securities even if it means taking a loss. On the other hand, if fewer loans are being made, banks do not want to have money just sitting in a nonearning account. They will buy some securities even if the price is higher than they would like.

Income from Fees

Fees have become a larger source of income for banks in recent years. Many banks have raised fees or put new fees in place to generate more income. Customers face fees for just about every bank service they use. Figure 3-2 shows some of the common fees charged by banks on services they provide.

Many bank fees relate to checking accounts. Banks often charge a monthly service fee just for having a checking account. However, some banks may waive the fee if a customer keeps a certain balance in his or her account or use other bank services. Banks also charge an **insufficient funds fee** if there is not enough money in an account to cover a transaction.

To avoid being charged for insufficient funds, customers can make arrangements with the bank to cover a check. A service called an **overdraft program** provides funds to cover a check written on an account with insufficient funds. Of course, banks charge an *overdraft fee* for this service. Even though your account might have less than (under) the amount needed to cover transactions made, it is still called an *over*draft. An **overdraft** is a negative balance.

The Credit Card Act of 2009 requires that cardholders must declare that they want over-limit transactions covered. If they opt out of having overdraft service, a transaction that goes over their credit limit will be denied. Another major area that produces fee income for banks is credit cards. Banks that offer credit cards may charge an annual fee just to have the card. Credit cards also have other fees, such as *late payment fees* if you do not make payments on time. In addition, those who go over their credit limit will face an *over limit fee.*

BIZ TIPS

Larger banks often have their own trading departments that buy and sell securities.

Checking Accounts	ATM
Insufficient funds fees Overdraft fees Service fees Stop payment fees	Account balance fees Transaction fees—using another bank Transaction fees—using ATM internationally
Credit Cards	**Safe Deposit Boxes**
Annual fees Over-the-limit fees Late payment fees	Rental fees Late rental payment fees Lost key replacement fees
Miscellaneous	
Money order fees Inactivity fees Electronic funds transfer fees	

Figure 3-2.
Common Bank Service Fees

ATM users may see a variety of different fees. Withdrawing cash from an ATM may trigger a fee, known as a **surcharge** or *convenience fee.* Banks often allow their own customers to use their ATMs at no charge, but charge a usage fee to customers of other banks. Many banks now charge a fee just to check your account balance using an ATM, known as an **account inquiry fee.**

Another common bank fee is the *safe deposit box rental fee,* usually an annual fee, paid to the bank to rent a safe deposit box. **Safe deposit boxes** are individually secured containers, usually within a bank vault, used to store valuables.

Money order fees are charged to customers who buy a money order from the bank. A **money order** is purchased in an exact amount payable to a specific party. Banks collect the amount of the money order plus a fee to issue it to the customer.

BIZ TIPS

nce companies ome other financial institutions do not accept money orders as payment because these instruments can be used to conceal money obtained by illegal means.

Banks charge for just about every service they offer. Sometimes you can even be charged a fee for doing nothing. An **inactivity fee** may be charged if a customer does not make a transaction within some specified period. Even a small transaction, such as depositing or withdrawing $1, counts as activity and avoids the fee.

Credit cards often have fees associated with them. These fees include:

- annual fees just to have the card;
- late payment fees if you miss the payment deadline; and
- over-limit fees if you exceed your credit limit.

For example, if your card has a $5,000 credit limit and you currently have a $4,950 balance, buying something costing $100 will put you over your credit limit. The bank will penalize you for going over your limit and impose a fee for this action.

$4,950 (current balance) + $100 (new purchase) > $5,000 (credit limit)

$5,000 – $5,050 = $50.00 over the credit limit

Balance = –$50.00

When you use a credit or debit card at a business, the merchant is charged a fee by the banks for making the service available. The Dodd-Frank Wall Street Reform and Consumer Protection Act limits the amount banks can charge merchants per card transaction.

Checkpoint 3.1

1. What is interest?
2. How do loans earn income for banks?
3. What are the two ways banks earn income on securities?
4. List four types of treasury securities.
5. List three of the fees a bank may charge for checking accounts.

Build Your Vocabulary

As you progress through this course, develop a personal glossary of banking terms and add it to your portfolio. This will help you build your banking vocabulary. Write out a definition for each of the following terms, and add it to your personal glossary.

asset
interest
maturity
liquidity
gain
insufficient funds fee
overdraft program
overdraft
surcharge
account inquiry fee
safe deposit box
money order
inactivity fee

Section 3.2
Income from Nontraditional Services

Terms
risk
insurance
beneficiary
trustee
trust
estate
estate planing
probate law
treasury and cash management services
pension fund
trading
underwriting
underwriting spread
merger
acquisition

Objectives
After completing this section, you will be able to:

- Explain how banks earn income from insurance products.
- Describe types of trust operations and how they provide income.
- Explain how brokerage services operate and provide bank revenue.
- Describe how banks manage the financial assets of certain customers.
- Identify the major investment banking activities.

Insurance Products

If you were asked to name a company that sells insurance, you probably would not name a bank. But, over half of the banks in the United States sell some type of insurance. For many years, banks were prohibited from most insurance activities by the Glass-Steagall Act of 1933. Now, under the Gramm-Leach-Bliley Act of 1999, banks are allowed to offer insurance as well as brokerage and investment banking services. Many banks have even purchased insurance companies to expand the bank's insurance offerings. Insurance can be very profitable, but, just like loans, it poses a risk for the bank.

Insurance provides protection from risk. **Risk** is the chance that something unfavorable could happen to a person or property. Life is full of risks. **Insurance** provides protection from certain risks that can cause a financial loss. The loss may occur from a death, illness, or accident.

Insurance is designed to protect businesses and individuals. If a business or individual has a loss, the insurance policy will pay to cover the loss. Since there are many kinds of possible losses, there are many kinds of insurance products available. The major types of insurance are life, health, and property insurance.

Source: Shutterstock (Kellis)

Insurance is used to manage exposure to financial risk.

Life Insurance

Life insurance protects people from a financial loss in the event of a death. Most individuals want to provide some financial support for their family after their death. This is especially true for people with young children. A life insurance policy will pay a specified amount to a named beneficiary. A **beneficiary** receives the financial protection from the insurance policy. In the case of life insurance, the death benefit is paid to the beneficiary after the insured dies.

Banks often offer life insurance related to loans, such as credit life and mortgage life insurance. Many other types of life insurance are available from banks today. However, traditional life insurance may be a less expensive option for most people than insurance tied to a specific loan. In recent years, there have been several mergers between life insurance companies and bank holding companies. This allows banks to acquire a presence in the life insurance field.

Credit Life Insurance

Life insurance that will pay off a loan if the insured dies is called *credit life.* Borrowers are offered credit life insurance at the time they apply for a loan. Some borrowers assume they must take out credit life insurance as a condition for getting the loan. However, credit life insurance is not tied to loan approval. You are granted or denied a loan based on financial factors.

Mortgage Life Insurance

Mortgage life insurance is very similar to credit life insurance. Mortgage life insurance pays off the loan balance on your home on your death. By purchasing mortgage life insurance, the borrower is assured that the mortgage will be paid should he or she die.

Property and Casualty Insurance and Liability Insurance

Property and casualty insurance and liability insurance cover things, rather than people. Property and casualty insurance covers property we own, such as houses and cars, from losses. If an item covered by the policy is lost or damaged, the insurance company will pay for its replacement or repair.

Liability insurance protects against the financial losses that may occur if the insured is found responsible for property loss or injuries to others. For example, if someone falls on your front steps and breaks his or her leg, you may be responsible for that person's injuries. Liability insurance will pay for the medical expenses of the injured person. The major cost associated with many liability cases are the legal costs. Liability insurance pays your legal costs in liability lawsuits.

The two most common types of property and casualty insurance are automobile insurance and homeowner's insurance. Since vehicles and houses are usually the most valuable things people own, it makes sense to insure them against loss.

BIZ TIPS

Commercial banks, especially large banks, often had investment bank departments prior to the Glass-Steagall Act. With the collapse of the stock market in 1929, many banks failed due to their investment banking activities. The separation of commercial and investment banking was designed to prevent such widespread bank failures in the future.

Ethical Banking

Many banks have a written code of ethics, often available on their websites. A code of ethics states the mission of the bank and the values it strives to uphold. Such a code is essentially a blueprint for how the bank will attempt to uphold its obligation to every party associated with the bank.

Auto liability insurance covers the medical and property expenses of somebody else if you cause an accident. All states require auto liability insurance. Collision insurance pays for damage to your vehicle as the result of a vehicle-on-vehicle accident, regardless of who is at fault. Comprehensive auto insurance covers other types of damage to your vehicle. For example, if a tree falls on your car while parked on the street, comprehensive auto insurance covers the damage.

Homeowner's property insurance provides protection to your home and its contents. Homeowners face a number of dangers to their property, such as fire, theft, hail, and flood. Homeowner's insurance pays for damage to the property as well as the covered loss of personal property inside the home, such as furniture and clothing.

Businesses also need insurance to protect from losses. The two most common types of business insurance, also known as commercial insurance, are property and liability insurance. Business property insurance protects the physical assets of the business, such as buildings, equipment, and furniture.

Health Insurance

Health and disability insurance is now considered very essential. Medical costs today can quickly devastate the finances of an individual or family. Health insurance pays some or all of the medical costs associated with an illness or accident. Disability insurance provides monthly payments to replace income lost when a worker is unable to work due to illness, injury, or disease.

Banks are now offering consumers the option to purchase health-care insurance. Their services are various health plans that can usually be purchased through a bank. Some plans include indemnity health insurance, health maintenance organizations, and preferred provider organizations. Figure 3-3 describes the features of each.

	What It Is	How It Works
Indemnity Health Insurance	Known as a *fee-for-service plan*. Lets the insured go to any doctor he or she chooses.	The insurance pays a portion of covered health-care costs.
Health Maintenance Organization (HMO)	An association of doctors, hospitals, and other health-care providers that provides comprehensive medical services.	The insurance pays part or all of the health-care costs only if the insured uses a doctor that is part of the HMO.
Preferred Provider Organization (PPO)	An association of providers that offers services at a lower cost to subscribers. Gives the insured more choice than an HMO.	The insurance pays part or all of the health-care costs only if the insured uses a doctor that is part of the PPO.

Figure 3-3.
Types of Health Insurance

Trust Services

Banks have been offering trust services since the early 1900s. Trust services involve handling financial assets for a customer. The bank becomes the **trustee,** the person or institution that controls the financial assets for the customer. A legal document is drawn up, known as the trust. **Trusts** define the customer's assets and how those assets should be handled. The trustee manages these assets, but does not own them. The bank generates revenue by receiving a fee for trust services it provides. Trust departments can be quite profitable for a bank.

Trust services are generally only provided by large banks. This is because those services require very specialized skills, such as a legal background, tax planning ability, or security trading knowledge. Smaller banks generally do not have employees with those specialized skills. Trust departments offer services to individual clients as well as business customers. Figure 3-4 provides an overview of trust services offered.

Individual Clients

A major trust activity provided by banks is estate administration. An **estate** is the property and possessions of an individual. The estate may include property, cars, money, and other assets that the person owns. There are two major components of estate administration—estate planning and estate settlement.

Estate Planning

Many people set up a trust and name a trustee in their wills. In many instances, a bank is named as the trustee of an estate. Parents may set up a trust for a child. These trusts usually remain in force until the child reaches a designated age. Once the child reaches the age stated in the trust, the trust is dissolved. The estate's assets are then turned over to the child.

Estate planning is preparing for the transfer of assets after a client's death. A trustee is named in a will to manage the assets of the estate. Family members may not be the best choice to handle an estate as they may not have the financial knowledge and skills needed. Banks are often named as trustees as they are experienced in managing assets, especially financial assets. Trust officers work with a client to set up an individualized estate plan.

Retirement Planning	• Open IRA, 401(k), variable annuity
Estate Planning	• Prepare a will or trust document that arranges for transfer of assets
Estate Settlement	• Determines estate value • Prepares and files all necessary documents • Pays taxes • Distributes assets as called for in the will

Figure 3-4.
Overview of Trust Services

A major objective of estate planning is to minimize taxes. A good estate planner can reduce taxes paid by the estate. Without good estate planning, much of the estate's value may be lost to taxes.

Estate Settlement

The job of the trustee is very important and involves multiple job duties. One of the important duties of the trustee is to settle the estate when the person dies. This may involve:

- paying any debts of the estate;
- managing the assets until the estate is completely settled; and
- preparing and filing tax returns.

Estates must be settled according to state law. Laws that pertain to wills and the distribution of assets after a person's death are known as **probate laws.**

Business Clients

Banks also have business customers. The services that are offered to these customers relate to cash management. **Treasury and cash management services** include accounting services, capital services, collections services, credit card services, and information services. These are outlined in Figure 3-5. Banks are in a good position to offer cash management services because they are already involved in some way with most of the transactions.

Because trust departments are experts in both securities markets and regulatory requirements, they are often hired to manage pension plans for other businesses. **Pension funds** are plans that provide retirement income for the employees of a business.

Contributions from either employees, employers, or both go into the pension fund, and those contributions are then invested. Pension funds often invest in securities. The earnings from these assets generate revenue that can be used to pay employee retirement benefits.

Another example of a service is handling the payment of dividends. If a company pays a dividend to its stockholders, a bank trust department often takes care of it. Managing the payment of dividends is another task that requires expertise companies may not have in their business. Banks are paid for each service they provide.

BIZ TIPS

Did you know that you may be able buy or sell securities at your bank? In fact, some of the biggest banks have either bought brokerage companies or merged with them.

Brokerage Services

Brokerage departments offer a number of services to customers. The major service provided is securities trading. A broker may buy and sell securities for a customer, which is known as **trading.** Although securities brokers are commonly called stockbrokers, they are licensed to trade all types of securities, including:

- common stock;
- bonds; and
- treasury securities.

If a bank has a brokerage department, brokerage commissions produce income for the bank. In addition, brokerage departments may provide other services, such as safekeeping of securities and advice on suitable investments.

Accounting Services	• Payroll • Accounts payable—debts requiring payment in less than 60 days • Accounts receivable—money owed to the business • Cash concentration—improved cash management • Positive or reverse positive pay—guards against cashing fraudulent checks • Controlled disbursement—checks are presented once a day
Capital Services	• Capital expenditures—the purchase of a new building or machinery • Financing • Factoring—the sale of a company's accounts receivable to a third party at a percentage of actual value
Collections Services	• Deposit services—ease of making depositing • Lockbox services—accounts receivable are deposited directly into the bank • Account reconciliation—account updating and balance reporting • Zero balance accounting—one account with only enough funds to cover outstanding checks, while remaining funds are placed in an account where they can make money • Automated clearinghouse services—system through which electronic banking can take place • Armored car services
Credit Card Services	• Processing credit card transactions • Issuing credit and prepaid cards • Credit analysis
Information Services	• Electronic data interchange (EDI)—the transfer of financial information over a closed computer system • Advanced Internet access • Detailed reports and data related to business operations • Wire transfers

Figure 3-5.
Treasury and Cash Management Services

The brokerage business is a natural fit for banks. Banks are heavily involved in securities markets since they buy and sell securities for themselves. Brokerage services are another way to generate income by offering services that are already familiar to most banks.

BIZ TIPS

Hedge funds are private investment funds for very wealthy and very sophisticated investors. These funds employ a variety of strategies to manage a client's investment risk.

Asset Management

Bank trust departments also provide asset management for clients. These clients have large sums invested. Clients who do not have the time or expert knowledge needed to handle their own investments turn their assets over to the bank to manage. Banks provide asset-management services to individuals and organizations. Assets can be grouped into three categories:

- fixed income—mostly bonds
- equities—mostly stocks
- cash equivalents—cash or investments that can be readily sold for cash, such as treasury bills or certificates of deposit

Securities are the most common investment. Bank trust departments usually have their own trading departments and are well equipped to manage securities. Trust customers allow the bank to buy and sell investments for them. Banks are paid a fee for managing the customer's investments.

Investment Banking Services

One way for a business to get money it needs for expansion is by selling shares in the company to investors. Shares in a company are also called *stock.* By selling stock in itself, the business is selling bits of ownership. Stocks may be offered only to a limited number of individuals who have strong ties to the company. Another approach is to arrange for a public offering of the stock. Investment departments in large commercial banks can help with this complicated process. The banks help determine what the starting price should be for the new stock and how many shares should be available.

Underwriting Securities

Source: Shutterstock (Goodluz)

Individuals often hire investment banks to manage their investments.

There are several ways banks generate income from investment banking. A common arrangement is for a bank to underwrite a new stock offering. In this sense, **underwriting** occurs when an investment bank buys a new stock directly from the company wanting to generate cash. The bank then sells the stock to the public. Here, the bank is acting as an intermediary, or go-between. It brings together a party that wants to get money with parties that want to invest money.

When investment banks underwrite a stock offering, they make money through the underwriting spread. The **underwriting spread** is the difference between the price paid by the investment bank and the price sold to the public. For example, an investment bank might pay \$40 per share to a company for the one million shares available for sale. If the investment bank sells the shares to the public for \$42 per share, the underwriting spread is \$2 per share. Since there are one million shares issued for sale, the investment bank will earn \$2 million in this underwriting arrangement.

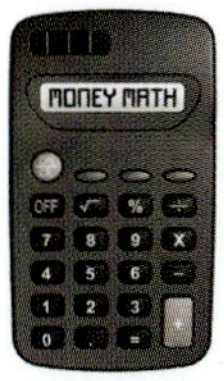

1,000,000 × $40.00 (price per share purchased from the issuing company) = $40,000,000 paid to the company

1,000,000 × $42.00 (price per share sold to the public) = $42,000,000 paid to the bank

$42,000,000 (product of public sales) – $40,000,000 (price paid to issuing company) = $2,000,000 (underwriting spread)

Underwriting arrangements carry risk for the investment bank. If the bank cannot sell the securities or must sell them at a price below what it paid for them, the bank will lose money.

BIZ TIPS

The Green Bay Packers football team is the only National Football League team that is owned by the public. The franchise issues stock for sale from time-to-time as a means for financing stadium improvements.

Mergers and Acquisitions

Mergers and acquisitions, often called *M & A,* are a big part of the investment banking business. Companies are often merging with and acquiring other companies. A **merger** takes place when two companies agree to combine. An **acquisition** happens when one company buys another company, setting itself up as the new owner. Investment bankers are experts in the M & A field and are frequently hired for this purpose. They can determine the value of each company and also negotiate the terms of the merger or acquisition. Investment bankers are paid a fee for the merger and acquisition services they provide.

International Banking

International banking services focus largely on trade. Banks offer financing and consulting services to help manage the risks involved. These services help clients conduct business beyond the borders of the US. Three types of financial institutions offer international banking services. These institutions are:

- US-based banks that do business internationally;
- foreign banks doing business in the US; and
- other international banking entities.

Some of the largest banks in the US are those that have an international presence. This has its advantages and disadvantages. One of the greatest advantages is access to more customers. A disadvantage is the exposure these banks have to the economic and political conditions of the countries where they do business. The risk to banks that do business internationally became apparent during the Great Recession, which affected people and financial institutions around the world.

The US Federal Reserve charters special financial institutions known as *Edge Act corporations.* These institutions are free from state regulations because they only work in the international arena. International airlines and shipping companies are among the clients of Edge Act institutions. The Federal Reserve also monitors and regulates branches of foreign banks doing business in the US. This is in addition to their supervision of US banks.

Source: Shutterstock (Russell Shively)

With an increase in global trade and travel, banks have seen a marked increase in international transactions.

Correspondent banks are another kind of entity engaged in international finance. They serve as a bank's agent in another country. The services of these financial institutions are needed when a bank would not otherwise be able to do business in a particular country.

Checkpoint 3.2

1. Why do people purchase insurance?
2. How do banks make money from selling insurance?
3. What are the biggest costs associated with liability cases?
4. List the major services offered by bank trust departments.
5. What is the major source of income from brokerage services?

Build Your Vocabulary

As you progress through this course, develop a personal glossary of banking terms and add it to your portfolio. This will help you build your banking vocabulary. Write out a definition for each of the following terms, and add it to your personal glossary.

risk
insurance
beneficiary
trustee
trust
estate
estate planning
probate law
treasury and cash management services
pension fund
trading
underwriting
underwriting spread
merger
acquisition

Careers in Finance
Banking and Related Services

What Does a Data Processor Do?

A **data processor** at a bank enters data into a computer, operates a variety of office machines, and performs other clerical and administrative duties. Also known as data-entry clerks, **data processors** input key financial information for a bank. Some of the activities performed by bank **data processors** include:

- entering customer financial information;
- reformatting existing data;
- editing current information; and
- proofreading new entries for accuracy.

What Is It Like to Work as a Data Processor?

A **data processor** generally works on site at a bank, but new technology allows some to work from remote locations, including home. Those working at a bank location work standard workdays, while those working at remote locations may even work after bank hours.

A **data processor** enters information about bank products, so extensive training is necessary to learn about the business. A keen eye for detail is necessary as information is keyed from hardcopy documents as well as importing information from online sources.

If you like working on the computer and the challenge of translating and entering data, a **data processor** job may be rewarding for you.

What Education and Skills Are Needed to Be a Data Processor?

- high school diploma; college degree preferred
- excellent keyboarding and computer skills
- good grammar skills
- detail oriented
- goal driven

Career Ladder

Chief Technology Officer

Information Technology Manager

Data Processor

Section 3.3
Banking Expenses

Terms
- interest expense
- interest rate
- operating expense
- profit

Objectives

After completing this section, you will be able to:

- Explain how deposits cause interest expense.
- Identify the major non-interest expense items for a bank.

Interest Expense

When the bank pays interest to customers for using their money, this is called **interest expense** for the bank. The largest expense for banks and other depository institutions is the interest paid on deposits.

Depositors often shop around for the highest interest rate they can get on their money. Banking is a competitive business. Banks want to entice customers to deposit money by offering good interest rates. By offering good rates, banks can acquire and keep customers.

The interest rates on deposits change with market interest rates and the state of the economy. If the interest rates in the market increase, banks must raise the interest rate on deposits. The **interest rate** is the percentage paid for the use of borrowed money. Paying higher interest rates to customers means that the expenses increase for the bank. However, if the interest rates drop, banks pay less in interest to their customers. This means lower operating expenses for banks.

Banks do not pay interest on all deposits. Many checking accounts do not pay interest. If they do, they generally pay a smaller amount than savings accounts and have many restrictions. For example, customers often must maintain a minimum account balance in order to receive interest. If the account balance falls below the minimum, often set at $1,000, no interest is paid.

Source: Shutterstock (Mike Truchon)

Only checking accounts with high balances are paid interest by banks.

Operating Expenses

Paying interest to customers is not the only expense for banks. Banks have a number of other expenses related to operating the bank. **Operating expenses** are those costs that are incurred to keep the bank in business. These expenses include utilities, rent, and employee wages.

Wages and salaries for employees are a major expense for banks. Bank customers may see only the tellers and loan officers when they enter a bank lobby, but there are many other employees not in public view. As the use of technology has increased in the workplace, there has been a shift in the types of careers needed for bank operations.

In addition to employee wages and salaries, banks often provide employee benefits such as health insurance and retirement plans. Banks also spend considerable amounts of money training employees. By having well-trained employees, banks hope to increase revenues.

Other operating expenses include:

- office equipment purchases and maintenance;
- security expenses; and
- advertising and marketing costs.

Banks must keep their buildings and equipment up-to-date while maintaining security. Controlling expenses is a major responsibility of bank managers to make sure that the bank is maximizing its profit. **Profit** occurs when a bank's income exceeds its expenses.

profit = total income – total expenses

Banks can increase profit by increasing income, decreasing expenses, or a combination of both. Figure 3-6 summarizes the major sources of income and expenses for banks.

Bank Income	Bank Expenses
Interest income from loans and securities	Interest paid on deposits
Gains on securities	Employee wages and salaries
Checking account fees	Employee benefits
Credit card fees	Employee training costs
ATM fees	Building and utility costs
Safe deposit box rental fees	Equipment costs
Money order fees	Security expenses
Inactivity fees	
Insurance premiums	
Trust service fees	
Brokerage commissions	
Investment banking income	

Figure 3-6.
Bank Income and Expenses

Checkpoint 3.3

1. What is the largest expense for banks?
2. What type of expense are utilities?
3. Total income minus what equals profit?
4. Why do banks pay interest to depositors?
5. How can banks increase their profits?

Build Your Vocabulary

As you progress through this course, develop a personal glossary of banking terms and add it to your portfolio. This will help you build your banking vocabulary. Write out a definition for each of the following terms, and add it to your personal glossary.

interest expense
interest rate
operating expense
profit

Chapter Summary

Section 3.1 Income from Loans and Securities

- Banks generate income through customer interest payments, interest paid on bank-owned securities, and from gains when securities are sold for a profit.
- Banks charge customers a number of fees for the different services provided.

Section 3.2 Income from Nontraditional Sources

- Premiums on insurance policies sold by banks provide income.
- Banks offer trust services, which generate revenue, for both individuals and businesses.
- Many banks now have brokerage departments that handle customer trades.
- Customers with substantial assets sometimes have banks manage the assets on their behalf.
- Commercial banks often have investment banking divisions that help businesses raise money.

Section 3.3 Banking Expenses

- The major expense for banks is the interest paid on deposits.
- Banks have a number of non-interest expenses related to operating the bank.

Check Your Banking IQ

Now that you have finished this chapter, see what you know about banking by taking the chapter post test.

www.m.g-wlearning.com
www.g-wlearning.com

Review Your Knowledge

On a separate sheet of paper or in a word processing document, match the following terms with the definition that fits best.

A. asset
B. estate
C. insurance
D. interest
E. liquidity
F. maturity
G. overdraft
H. profit
I. risk
J. trust

1. Something of value.
2. Ease with which an asset can be turned into cash.
3. Time when the initial investment and any interest become payable.
4. Sum paid to borrow money.
5. A negative balance.
6. The chance that something bad can happen.
7. A means of risk management.
8. Control, but not ownership, of assets by a third party.
9. Property and possessions of an individual.
10. Amount remaining after expenses are subtracted from income.

On a separate sheet of paper or in a word processing document, answer each of the following questions.

11. Why do riskier loans have higher interest rates?
12. Why are low interest rates on loans good for borrowers?
13. If loans are riskier than securities, why do banks prefer making loans over securities?
14. Long-term securities usually pay higher interest rates than short-term securities. Yet banks often prefer to invest in short-term securities. Why?
15. Why is a treasury bond considered risk-free, while a bond issued by a company is not?

Apply Your Knowledge

16. Research loan rates on the Internet for car loans at a bank and a credit union for 36-month, 48-month, and 60-month loans. Put your findings in the form of a table. Explain any differences you found between the rates at these two financial institutions.
17. Using the Internet, research how you can buy a treasury security directly from the government. Write a one-page paper explaining the advantages of buying directly from the Treasury over buying the security from a bank.
18. Find out what the annual premiums for a $100,000 5-year term life insurance policy would be for a 16-year-old male and a 16-year-old female. Explain any differences that you find.
19. Survey several banks and credit unions in your area to find out what interest rates they are paying on savings accounts. Put you findings in the form of a chart or table.
20. Perform an Internet search for major mergers and acquisitions in the last 20 years. Create a chart listing at least ten of these and whether each is a merger or an acquisition. Also, include any interesting details you can find about the merger or acquisition.

Working in Teams

Working with a classmate, research several banks in your area to see what checking account fees they charge. Prepare a chart that shows all the fees charged by the different banks.

G-W Learning Mobile Site

Visit the G-W Learning mobile site to complete the chapter pretest and post test and to practice vocabulary using e-flash cards. If you do not have a smartphone, visit the G-W Learning companion website to access these features.

G-W Learning mobile site: www.m.g-wlearning.com
G-W Learning companion website: www.g-wlearning.com

Common Core

College and Career Readiness

Reading. Read a magazine, newspaper, or online article about a current ethical or unethical situation that has occurred in the banking industry. Determine the central ideas and conclusions of the article. Provide an accurate summary of your reading, making sure to incorporate the *who, what, when,* and *how* of this ethical or unethical situation.

Writing. Research the history of insurance. Where did the concept of insurance originate? Write an informative report, consisting of several paragraphs to describe your findings.

EVENT PREP Role Playing and Interviews

Role playing and interviews are competitive events you might enter with your career and technical student organization (CTSO). Those who participate in a role-play will be provided information about a company or situation and given time to practice. A judge or panel of judges will review the presentations. To prepare for the role-play or interview event:

1. Read the guidelines provided by your organization. Make certain that you ask any questions about points you do not understand. It is important you follow each specific item that is outlined in the competition rules.
2. Visit the organization's website and look for role-play and interview events that were used in previous years. Many organizations post these tests for students to use as practice for future competitions. Also, look for the evaluation criteria or rubric for the event. This will help you determine what the judge will be looking for in your presentation.
3. Using previous events, write your response to the situation or questions. Time yourself to see if you are within the allotted time frame. Repeat this several times so that you are comfortable with preparing the presentation.
4. Practice in front of a mirror. Are you comfortable speaking without reading directly from your notes?
5. Ask friend or teacher to listen to your presentation. Give special attention to your posture and how you present yourself.
6. Concentrate on your tone of voice. Be pleasant and loud enough to hear without shouting.
7. Make eye contact with the listener. Do not stare, but engage the person's attention.
8. After you have made your presentation, ask for constructive feedback.

Unit 1
Summative Assessment

On a separate sheet of paper or in a word processing document, use what you have learned in this unit to answer the questions that follow.

True/False Questions

1. *True or False?* Banks can make money from interest, and they can pay interest.
2. *True or False?* Investment banks are depository institutions.
3. *True or False?* Unit banks are chartered by the Office of the Comptroller of the Currency.
4. *True or False?* Banks are one of the most important forces that drive a modern economy.
5. *True or False?* The FDIC insures financial loss due to a stock's decrease in value.

Multiple Choice Questions

6. What is a treasury security?
   A. A stock or bond traded on a stock or commodities exchange.
   B. Another term for common stock.
   C. The federal requirement that all banks must safeguard depositors' money.
   D. A kind of financial instrument backed by the US government.
7. Utilities, rent, and employee wages are examples of what?
   A. assets
   B. operating expenses
   C. asset-management categories
   D. interest expenses
8. What document details how a bank will operate and who will regulate it?
   A. charter
   B. depository institution contract
   C. the interstate banking act
   D. articles of incorporation
9. What are the two types of online banking called?
   A. Depository and non-depository.
   B. Savings and checking.
   C. Transactional and non-transactional.
   D. Mobile and on-site.
10. When a bank acts as a go-between, what role is it performing?
   A. safekeeper
   B. depository
   C. loan servicer
   D. financial intermediary

Unit 2

Money and Regulation

What You Will Learn

Safe and sound. When something is safe and sound, it is free from danger or injury. The safety and soundness of a country's financial system is central to its continued existence. To this end, financial institutions in the US are well regulated at both the federal and state levels. The word *regulate* means to control. Some of the first laws that ever existed related to financial dealings. For a long time, regulations focused on protecting the system. By the last quarter of the 20th century, laws and regulations that protected the consumer were established. In this unit, you will learn what measures are in place to help keep our money, our financial institutions, and ourselves safe and sound.

Chapter 4
Money
- Section 4.1 Money: Functions, Properties, and Types
- Section 4.2 Money Supply and Interest Rates

Chapter 5
Federal Reserve System
- Section 5.1 History of the Federal Reserve System
- Section 5.2 Structure of the Federal Reserve System
- Section 5.3 Function of the Federal Reserve System

Chapter 6
Bank Regulations
- Section 6.1 Banking Regulations
- Section 6.2 Consumer Regulations
- Section 6.3 Recent Banking

Source: Shutterstock (Petrenko Andriy)

Learn about the properties of good currency.

Source: Shutterstock (Monkey Business Images)

Discover how laws and regulations protect consumers.

Biz Kid$ in Action

The US dollar is highly recognized and respected around the world. You could in fact say it's a money superstar. However, money was not always in the form it is today. Money started out being a commodity. People would trade shells, cocoa beans, or even cows as money. But, a cow is hard to carry in your back pocket. And, what do you do if something is worth half a cow? Centuries ago, currency came to be used as money. Currency is much more portable and practical. Today, currency is often transferred electronically and can move lightening fast from one country to another.

In the past, dollars and other currencies were not well regulated. Some folks even tried to make fake currency. Imposters were rampant. Now, currency is regulated to ensure consumer confidence and that the country runs smoothly.

The Federal Reserve is an important part of currency—the dollar is money because the Federal Reserve tells everyone it is. The Federal Reserve makes sure there are just enough dollars to grow the economy, but not so many that it grows too quickly.

Banking Bits

Money was once made of precious metals like gold and silver. After a few thousand years, people started using paper notes that represented gold held in vaults. This was called the *gold standard.* This system broke down after World War II. Today, currencies are backed by—well, by nothing, except people's faith in them. Most transactions are digital, and exchange rates today are not set by authorities. They are set by markets. The only way to move an exchange rate is by buying or selling lots of a particular currency.

Quick Tip! Make sure to read the Truth in Lending statement to understand what a loan is really costing you.

Let's get started! →

Scan the code to view a Biz Kid$ video. If you do not have a smartphone, visit the G-W Learning companion website.

www.m.g-wlearning.com
www.g-wlearning.com

4

Check Your Banking IQ

Before you begin this chapter, see what you already know about banking by taking the chapter pretest.

www.m.g-wlearning.com
www.g-wlearning.com

Money

Section 4.1
Money: Functions, Properties, and Types

Section 4.2
Money Supply and Interest Rates

Shoes and socks. Peanut butter and jelly. Money and banking. Some things just go together. It's impossible to talk about banking without talking about money. They go hand in hand.

Money is the glue that holds our economy together and keeps our banking system going. In this chapter, you will be examining all of the things money does for us as well as how money is created by banks.

College and Career Readiness

Reading Prep. As you read this chapter, determine the point of view or purpose of the author. What aspects of the text help to establish this purpose or point of view?

Scan the code to view a Biz Kid$ video. If you do not have a smartphone, visit the G-W Learning companion website.

www.m.g-wlearning.com
www.g-wlearning.com

Section 4.1
Money: Functions, Properties, and Types

Objectives

After completing this section, you will be able to:

- Explain the three functions of money.
- Describe the physical properties of currency.
- Describe the types of money.

Terms

money
medium of exchange
barter
coincidence of wants
unit of account
store of value
counterfeit
divisibility
denomination
commodity
commodity money
representative money
gold standard
gold-exchange standard
fiat money
legal tender

Functions of Money

When we think of money, we usually think of what we can buy with it. However, money has more than one function. In addition to letting us buy things, money allows us to obtain things of value and helps us save for the future. In our economy, money serves three primary functions. Figure 4-1 illustrates this.

- medium of exchange—something that can be traded for goods and services
- unit of account—a measurement of the value of things
- store of value—a way to accumulate and increase usefulness

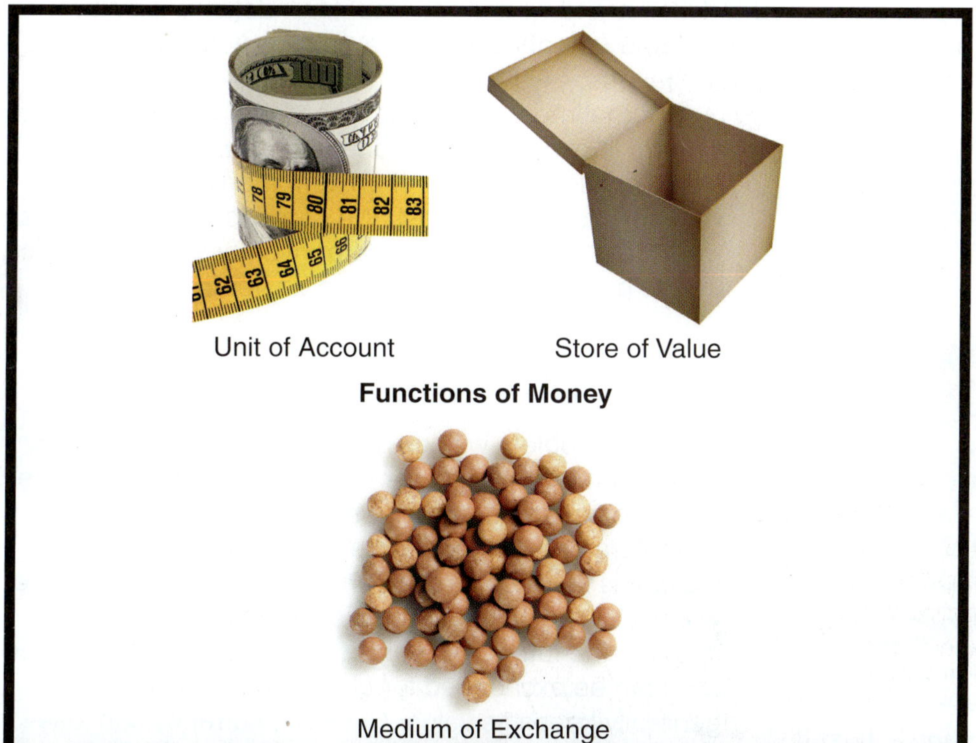

Source: Shutterstock (Lisa S., Naira, Magone)

Figure 4-1.
Functions of Money

Medium of Exchange

Money is anything of value that is accepted in return for goods or services. Throughout the history of the world, people have used beads, furs, precious metals, and other items as methods of payment for goods or services. As society evolved, paper currency and coins were created to provide a common medium of exchange. **Medium of exchange** means that we exchange money for goods and services. Money allows us to make transactions that are convenient and easy. It is the basis of our economy.

What if we did not have money? Would we still be able to get the things we need? Yes, by bartering for them. **Barter** is the exchange of one good or service for another good or service. If a horse is exchanged for a cow, that is a barter transaction. However, barter depends on a coincidence of wants. A **coincidence of wants** exists if we each want what the other has to offer. If you want what the other person is offering, but that person does not want what you are offering in return, there is no coincidence of wants.

Money does not need a coincidence of wants for a trade to occur. If a buyer has money, the cow can be purchased. Money is not only able to satisfy every party in the transaction, it is easier to transport. Although barter has some drawbacks compared to money, it has actually increased in popularity in recent years.

BIZ TIPS

Barter is becoming more popular. It is especially useful for people and businesses that don't have cash, but have something to trade for what they need. Barter websites help people match up their offerings.

Unit of Account

Money serves as a **unit of account,** which means it provides a common measure of what something is worth or what it costs. In the US, we all know what a dollar is and what it represents. A dollar is a unit of account. Using money as a unit of account is a quick way to place a cost or value on an item or service.

Sometimes, we take it for granted that the worth of an item is expressed in monetary terms. We go to the store and see the price of an item marked. This way, we know its value or cost. We can decide if the item is worth that much to us. Monetary values give us a quick way to place a cost or worth on an item.

Source: US Department of the Treasury: Bureau of Engraving and Printing

An important function of money is that it has a specific value—this bill is worth exactly 100 US dollars.

Store of Value

One problem with using some items as a currency is they can lose value over time. Money acts as a **store of value,** meaning it can be saved, or stored, to use at a future date. A good store of value is an item that maintains its value over a period of time. A good store of value must be safe and must allow you to get the item easily in the future. Money is considered a store of value as it can be exchanged for goods and services and generally keeps its value. However, currency can lose some of its purchasing power. In 2011, the US dollar lost value against currencies of other countries. This decreased the purchasing power of the dollar.

Money is not the only store of value. Gold, silver, real estate, and other similar assets can be stores of value. You can invest in these assets and trade them at a later date for goods, services, or currency. In fact, these assets may appreciate. *Appreciation* means the item is worth more in the future than the price for which it was originally purchased. Gold prices tend to be very volatile and change depending on the state of the economy. When the economy is doing well, gold prices drop. When the economy is not doing well, gold prices increase.

BIZ TIPS

When the economy takes a downturn, people see gold as a safe alternative to cash or other investments. In 2011, gold reached an all-time high, approaching $2,000 an ounce. By comparison, ten years earlier it was around $300 an ounce.

Properties of Money

You can think of currency like a brand of money. In the US, our *brand* of money is the dollar. While the dollar is our unit of currency, fractions of a dollar (coins) and multiples of a dollar (bills) are all included when we talk about currency. Money is currency plus all of the funds in a deposit account in one way or another. Money should be durable, portable, easily recognized, widely accepted, and easily divisible. US currency meets all of these standards.

Source: Shutterstock (Mark Payne)

In recent years, US currency has been enhanced to make it harder to create counterfeit money.

Durable

Money gets handled a lot. People are going to keep it for a long time as a store of value. It needs to be physically strong. US money is relatively durable. Durable means tough and long-lasting.

Our paper bills are not made out of paper. Rather, they are a special blend of cotton and linen. This blend of materials helps make the currency stronger and last longer. The average $1 bill lasts about 42 months before it becomes too worn to remain in circulation. The $100 bill is not circulated as often, so it has an average lifespan of 89 months.

US coins are currently made with a blend of metals, including copper and nickel. In previous times, some of our coins were made with gold and silver. Gold and silver are both soft metals, so eventually other metals were added in order to make the coins more durable.

BIZ TIPS

Because of the hot temperatures and salt in the air, paper currency wears out faster in tropical climates. Some countries are even switching to plastic currency to increase durability. Mexico, for instance, has issued a 20-peso note made entirely of plastic. Plastic bills look very much like paper bills, but may be a little slicker to the touch.

Portable

Money must be carried, so it needs to be portable. Paper currency has an advantage over coins because it is lighter. However, today, money is even more portable in electronic form. The credit card in your pocket can be used to access any dollar amount up to your credit limit. Some credit cards do not even have a limit.

The size of the money also affects its portability. Smaller coins take up less space and weigh less. Early US bills were larger than they are today. In 1929, our bills took their current size to fit a standard wallet.

Recognize

Good money needs to be quickly recognized. If money does not look familiar, people will be less willing to accept it. US dollars can be recognized at a glance all around the world.

Money is only good if people are willing to accept it. The US dollar is the most widely accepted currency around the world. So, it is one of the most recognizable currencies in the world. In some foreign countries, US dollars are preferred over the local currency.

Fake, or counterfeit, money is always a problem. **Counterfeit** means to make a copy of something and represent it as the real thing. It is illegal to counterfeit money. Well-designed currency tries to defeat counterfeiters. US money, both bills and coins, were redesigned in recent years. The primary purpose in changing the currency was to add features that make it more difficult to produce accurate counterfeit currency.

BIZ TIPS

To see the features and design of US paper currency, visit the Treasury Department's website at www.newmoney.com.

Acceptable

US money is so widely accepted because it has a long history of stability and value. The US political and economic systems are stable. The wide acceptance of our money reflects that.

In some countries, where there is much greater instability, people are afraid to accept their own currency as it may become worthless. After the breakup of the Soviet Union in the early 1990s, Russian rubles became almost worthless. Even when the US has an economic downturn, our government and economy keep functioning.

As with any currency, US dollars sometimes gain value and sometimes lose value. But, the ups and downs are not extreme. US dollars are accepted worldwide because they hold their value when compared to many other currencies.

Divisible

Divisibility means that money can be divided into smaller units. Money is used in exchange for goods of varying prices. Therefore, our money needs to be in denominations that work for any size of transaction. A currency's **denomination** refers to the units in which it is available. The most common US coins are in denominations that represent a fraction of a dollar:

- penny = 1/100th of a dollar
- nickel = 1/20th of a dollar
- dime = 1/10th of a dollar
- quarter = 1/4th of a dollar

The smaller its divisions, the more useful money is in handling any transaction we need to make. Paper money is in denominations that are multiples of a dollar. Denominations of US paper money currently in production are $1, $2, $5, $10, $20, $50, and $100.

Green Banking

As more transactions are handled with debit and credit cards, less cash is needed. This affects how much money is printed. The number of dollar bills rolling off the presses has been declining in recent years. Production of $5 bills has dropped to its lowest level in 30 years. No $10 bills were even printed in 2011. With less paper currency printed, the Treasury saves paper, ink, and energy. The trend toward more electronic transactions and less paper money can be good for both consumers and the environment.

Types of Money

Money has been around for centuries. As trade developed, so did the concept of money. The first form of money was commodity money. As trade and communities became more complex, money took the form of representative money. Today, US dollars are a form of fiat money. Figure 4-2 depicts the evolution of our monetary standard.

BIZ TIPS

It costs more than one cent to produce a penny due to the cost of the zinc used in its production.

Commodity Money

A **commodity** is anything that is useful or has value. Agricultural commodities are products such as wheat, corn, or oats. Oil, gold, and silver are all considered commodities. **Commodity money** is something of perceived value used as payment for something else. Beads, fur pelts, salt, cotton, and iron nails are all examples of items that have been used as commodity money.

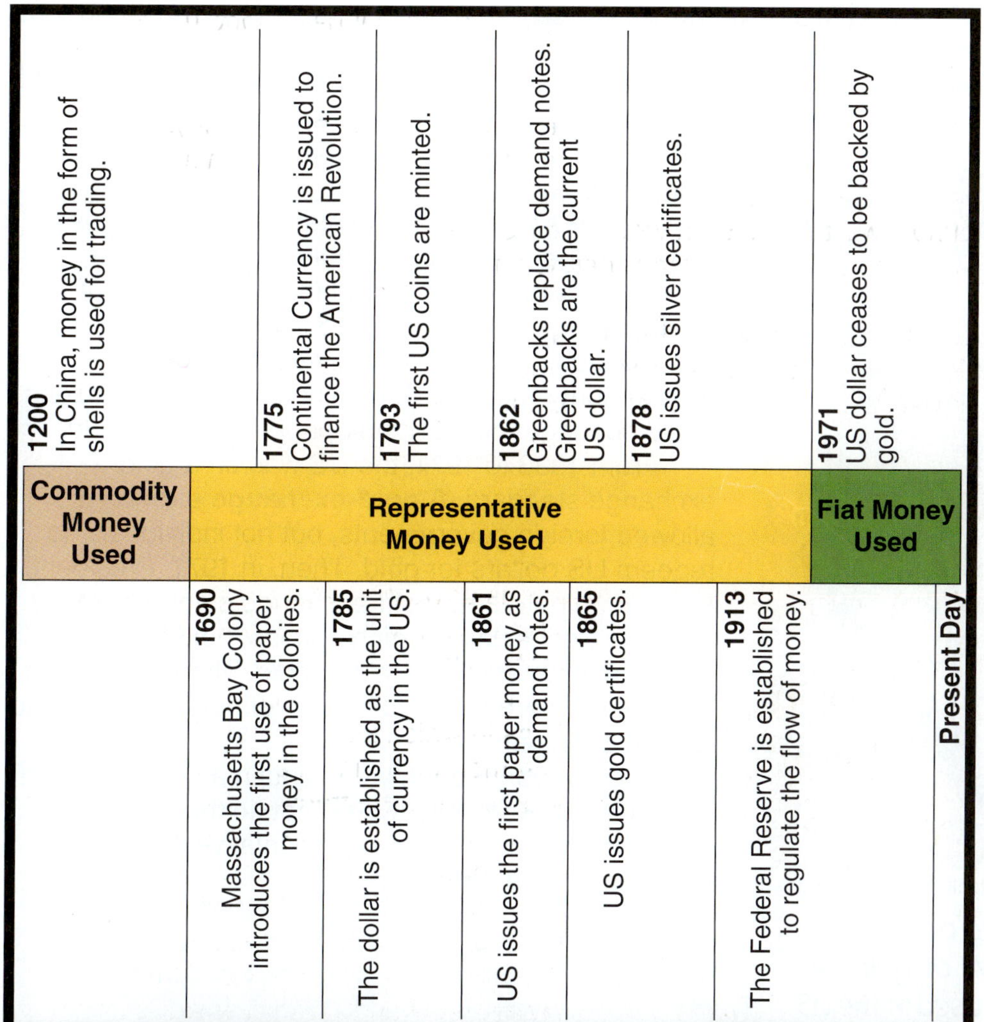

Figure 4-2.
Evolution of US Monetary Standard

Commodity money may seem like barter since in both cases goods are being exchanged for other goods. But, unlike barter, commodity money has a recognized unit of exchange. One beaver pelt might have a recognized value of $10. One beaver pelt could be used to buy $10 worth of goods. The seller of the goods would accept the beaver pelt because it could be used to buy more goods. This is unlike barter where the good would only be accepted if the other party wanted a beaver pelt. When pilgrims and early colonists encountered native peoples, they often used commodity money to trade.

Commodity money had its weaknesses. It was not very portable. Having to carry bales of cotton or animal skins around to buy things was very cumbersome. Items such as tobacco and rice would lose their value if they spoiled. Such items could only be used as money for a short time. Commodity money was useful in its day, but is rarely used in today's society.

BIZ TIPS

The expression, "not worth his salt," came from ancient Rome when soldiers were paid a ration of salt. If a soldier was not doing a good job, he was said to be, "not worth his salt." The Latin world for salt is sal, and over time this led to calling wages a salary.

Representative Money

Representative money is a bill or coin that can be exchanged for an item of value. The paper or token itself has no value, but is backed by something of value. By the beginning of the 20th century, the most economically developed countries, including the US, were issuing representative money. The money was backed by gold. This was called a gold standard.

A **gold standard** is a system that determines how much gold each paper note represents. The currency could be exchanged for a set amount of gold. The government decided to stop this practice as too much gold was being drained from the government reserves. Beginning in 1933, US citizens could no longer convert their paper dollars to gold.

From 1933 to 1971, the US was on a gold-exchange standard. A **gold-exchange standard** allowed foreign governments, but not individuals, to redeem US dollars for gold. Then, in 1971, President Nixon terminated the gold-exchange standard. Many countries, especially oil-rich nations, held US dollars and were converting them into gold. The government thought we were losing too much of our gold supply to foreign countries.

Today, even though we maintain a supply of gold at Fort Knox, Kentucky, we do not tie the dollar to gold. We no longer issue representative money. The US dollar is now fiat money.

Source: Shutterstock (Tomislav Forgo)

While US currency could once be exchanged for a set amount of gold, this gold standard is no longer used in the US.

Fiat Money

A *fiat* is a statement from an official body. **Fiat money** has value because the government says it has value. US dollars are fiat money. Fiat money is the major type of currency in the world today. Fiat money is generally in the form of coins and paper money, near money, and demand deposits. This type of money is called legal tender. See Figure 4-3 for explanations of each.

Legal tender is money that must be accepted for payment of debts or to purchase goods. The US government requires that dollars be accepted within US boundaries.

The real value of the US dollar comes from the faith people have in our government. We trust the government to control the money supply and keep a sound monetary system. If everyone in the world suddenly decided our dollars were worthless, then dollars would be worthless. This is not likely to happen since the US dollar has been universally accepted for many years. Both the Treasury Department and the Federal Reserve Bank maintain solid monetary practices that ensure US dollars will remain strong and have value.

US dollars are widely accepted because we have a stable and secure economic system. Often, when major economic or political changes occur in a country, the currency of that country loses value. Even though the value of the US dollar rises and falls over time, the dollar is a relatively stable currency.

BIZ TIPS

No major country has been on a gold standard since the 1970s.

Type of Legal Tender	Description
Coins and Paper Money	• The US Bureau of Engraving and Printing prints the paper bills. • Coins are minted by the US Mint. • US currency is no longer backed by gold and cannot be exchanged for gold.
Near Money	Funds in savings accounts and other instruments that can be cashed if needed.
Demand Deposits	Funds in checking accounts in which money is paid on demand.

Figure 4-3.
Legal Tender

Checkpoint 4.1

1. What are the three functions of money?
2. In order for a barter to occur, what is necessary?
3. What does it mean to make counterfeit money?
4. How does commodity money derive its value?
5. What is the most common type of money used today?

Build Your Vocabulary

As you progress through this course, develop a personal glossary of banking terms and add it to your portfolio. This will help you build your banking vocabulary. Write out a definition for each of the following terms, and add it to your personal glossary.

money
medium of exchange
barter
coincidence of wants
unit of account
store of value
counterfeit
divisibility
denomination
commodity
commodity money
representative money
gold standard
gold-exchange standard
fiat money
legal tender

Section 4.2 Money Supply and Interest Rates

Objectives

After completing this section, you will be able to:

- Explain how the Federal Reserve measures the money supply.
- Describe how changes in the money supply affect interest rates.
- Explain how banks create money.

Terms

money supply
aggregate
interest rate
prime rate
fractional reserve system
excess reserve
reserve
money multiplier effect
inflation

Money Supply

The **money supply** is the total amount of money available at a given time in an economy. Money supply is also known as the *money stock.* The money supply is closely watched and measured by the Federal Reserve. It has three measures, each with different data, by which it can calculate the money supply, as shown in Figure 4-4. The different measures are called **aggregates** as they represent information for a collection of data sources.

The most commonly used measure of the money supply is called M1. M1 is also known as transactions money. It is the money we use for everyday transactions. M1 is the most liquid part of the money supply, as this is money we can get to quickly. M2 is a broader measure that includes the sum of M1 plus time-related accounts that hold less than \$100,000. Time-related accounts are those that limit depositor access to funds, such as savings accounts, money market deposit accounts, money market mutual funds, and certificates of deposit.

BIZ TIPS

MZM, which stands for Money Zero Maturity, is M2 plus money market funds less time deposits. It is considered all of the money readily available for spending and consumption in the economy.

M3		
M2		
M1		
Currency (coins and bills) + Funds deposited in checking accounts	Savings account deposits < \$100,000 Money market account deposits < \$100,000 Certificates of deposit (CDs)	Savings account deposits > \$100,000 Money market account deposits > \$100,000 Institutional Money Market Mutual Funds

Figure 4-4.
Calculating the Money Supply

Ethical Banking

The Truth in Lending Act (TILA) is Title I of the Consumer Credit Protection Act of 1968. It requires that all terms of and costs related to a loan must be provided to the consumer in writing. Included must be total sale price, amount financed, annual percentage rate (APR), information related to a variable rate (if applicable), total payments, schedule of payments, prepayment policies, late payment policies, and security interest.

The Federal Reserve measures and controls our money supply. By examining these aggregates, economists can determine how much money is in circulation. An accurate measure of the money supply is important for monetary-policy decisions. The Federal Reserve can then decide if it will increase or decrease the supply.

Interest Rates

When there is a large supply of money, interest rates fall. In general, a rising money supply means lower interest rates. When the supply of money drops, interest rates go up.

The primary way banks make money is by charging interest to customers for loaning them money. Interest is the price that is paid to borrow money. The **interest rate** is the stated cost to borrow the money. The **prime rate** is the interest rate that banks give their best loan customers.

Demand is another factor that affects interest rates. If more people want loans, interest rates will rise, assuming supply stays the same. In the same way, if few people want loans, interest rates will fall.

There was a dramatic drop in demand for loans during the Great Recession of the early 21st century. During the recession, both businesses and individuals decided to borrow less. Businesses were not building new facilities, and consumers were buying fewer items for which loans were needed. This decreased demand for loans contributed to a drop in interest rates.

Creation of Money

If someone asked you how money was created in the US, what would you say? Many people would answer that money is created when the government prints money. But, the printing of money and the creation of money are two different things. Most new money is created by banks, not directly by the government. Banks create money when they make loans. When a person asks the bank for a loan, the bank simply types the amount of the loan into the person's account, and new money is created. So what prevents banks from loaning an infinite amount of money? This process is explained in the next sections.

Source: Shutterstock (fstockfoto)

The US Federal Reserve determines the reserve requirements for all US banks.

Fractional Reserve System

The **fractional reserve system** requires that banks and other depository institutions keep a fraction of their deposits in reserves. As banks make loans with the remaining funds, called the **excess reserves,** money is created. Most money that exists is just numbers in a computer.

Reserves, also known as *required reserves,* are deposits kept back, or in reserve, and not available to make loans. Reserves may be kept in a vault at the bank or deposited at a Federal Reserve district bank. Reserve requirements are set by the Federal Reserve. Generally, banks must keep 10% of deposits in reserve. Banks need some cash in the bank to make sure customers who need cash have access to their money. Most customers do not withdraw all of their money from the bank at any one time. Having 10% of deposits as cash is usually plenty to satisfy customer demands. If 10% of deposits are kept as reserves, then the other 90% is available for making loans. The amount of deposits that can be loaned out, 90% in this case, are called *excess reserves.* For example, if Victor deposits $1,500 in a bank, $150 must be set aside as required reserves. The difference can be used to make loans to other customers.

$1,500 (Victor's deposit) – $150 (10% required reserves) = $1,350 (excess reserves)

BIZ TIPS

The US Bureau of Engraving and Printing, a division of the Treasury Department, prints our paper currency. Coins are minted by the US Mint, another federal agency. Most "new" money goes to replace bills and coins that have become worn out rather than to increase the money supply.

Money Multiplier Effect

As banks make loans with the excess reserves, money is created. A new deposit into a bank makes more money available to loan to customers. As that money circulates in the economy, other banks receive deposits and also make loans. New loans turn into new deposits, which are part of the money supply. Thus, our money supply is increased by the deposit-and-loan process of banks.

As you can see in Figure 4-5, a new deposit increases the money supply by more than the original deposit. This phenomenon is known as the **money multiplier effect.** A small increase in deposits can lead to a much larger increase in the money supply. The Federal Reserve increases bank deposits by purchasing securities. When the Federal Reserve increases deposits by a small amount, it is counting on the multiplier effect to increase the money supply by a larger amount.

With a 20% reserve requirement:

$500 (increase in deposits) ÷ .20 (percent of reserve requirement) = $2,500 (potential increase in money supply)

The money multiplier also works with a decrease in deposits. If deposits leave banks, there will be less money to make loans. So, the money supply will decrease. When the Federal Reserve sells securities and receives money from bank customers, bank deposits fall. As a customer's account declines, the bank loses the potential for making loans with that money. For example, if bank deposits fall by $500 initially and the reserve requirement is 10%, the potential decrease in the money supply is $5,000 (500/.10).

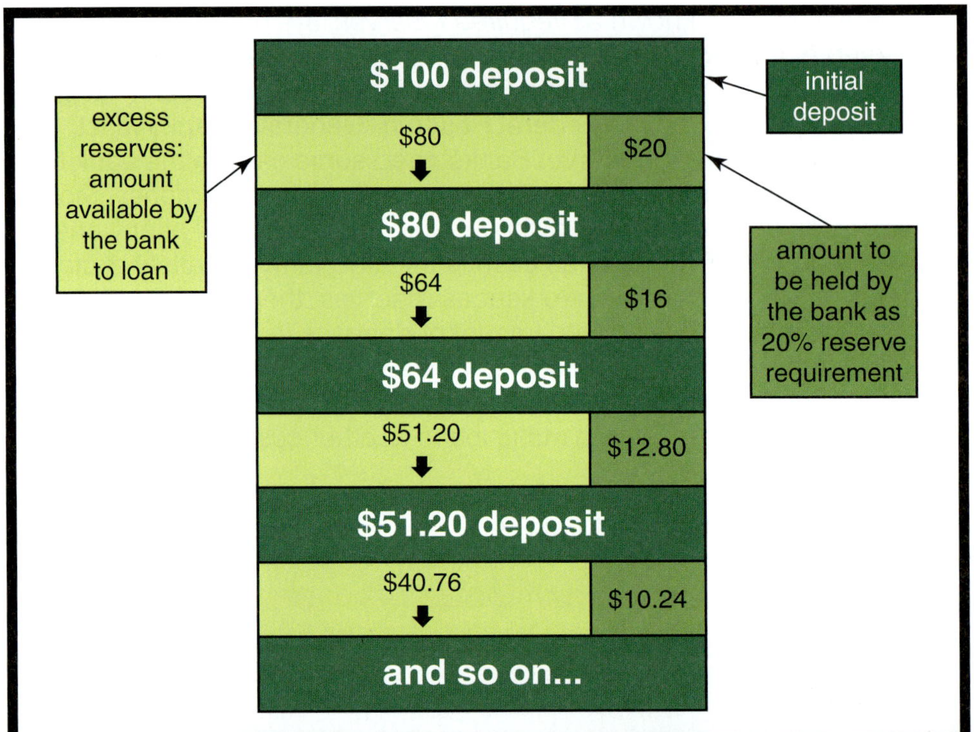

Figure 4-5.
Money Multiplier

With a 10% reserve requirement:

$500 (decrease in deposits) ÷ .10 (percent of reserve requirement) = $5,000 (potential decrease in money supply)

When the economy slows down or enters a recession, the Federal Reserve tries to stimulate the economy. It does this by increasing the money supply. As the money supply grows, interest rates will fall. Low interest rates are good for an economy in recession as they encourage businesses and individuals to borrow. In 2008, the Federal Reserve took action to greatly increase the money supply in response to the financial crisis that would come to be called the Great Recession.

When there is a threat of inflation, the Federal Reserve typically decreases the money supply. Too much money in the economy can lead to rising prices, which is called **inflation.** The Federal Reserve is always trying to balance the need for money to grow the economy with the need to keep inflation low. In some ways, the Federal Reserve is like Goldilocks, looking for the porridge (or amount of money) that is not too hot or too cold, but just right.

Checkpoint 4.2

1. The Federal Reserve uses which three measures to calculate the money supply?
2. What is the fractional reserve system?
3. What are reserves?
4. How is money created?
5. If a bank's deposits increase initially by $2,500 and the reserve requirement is 10%, what is the potential increase in the money supply?

Build Your Vocabulary

As you progress through this course, develop a personal glossary of banking terms and add it to your portfolio. This will help you build your banking vocabulary. Write out a definition for each of the following terms, and add it to your personal glossary.

money supply
aggregate
interest rate
prime rate
fractional reserve system
excess reserve
reserve
money multiplier effect
inflation

Careers in Finance
Banking and Related Services

What Does a Title Abstractor Do?

A **title abstractor** searches real estate records and examines titles to property to locate and verify information related to mortgage loans. Title examiner and title officer are other terms used for this position. Some of the activities performed by **title abstractors** include:

- preparing lists of all legal instruments applying to a specific piece of land;
- examining documentation to verify the property's legal description and owner;
- copying or summarizing recorded documents such as mortgages and deeds;
- preparing reports describing any actions needed to clear title; and
- verifying accuracy and completeness of land-related documents.

What Is It Like to Work as a Title Abstractor?

Title abstractors often work in courthouse record locations or other places where legal documents are kept. The working conditions are typical office surroundings with adequate light and room to work.

A solid knowledge of legal documents and procedures is necessary for **title abstractors**. Knowledge of real estate descriptions and procedures is also required. Good computer and research skills are necessary to uncover facts and figures for the documents.

If you like the legal profession, enjoy detailed work, and are able to maintain a high degree of accuracy, a career as a **title abstractor** might suit you.

What Education and Skills Are Needed to Be a Title Abstractor?

- college degree in real estate, banking, law, or business administration
- eye for detail
- research skills

Career Ladder

Underwriter

Real Estate Sales Agent

Title Abstractor

Chapter Summary

Section 4.1 Money: Functions, Properties, and Types

- The three functions of money are to act as a medium of exchange, unit of account, and store of value.
- The five properties of good money are currency that it is durable, portable, easily recognizable, acceptable, and divisible.
- The three types of money are commodity money, representative money, and fiat money.

Section 4.2 Money Supply and Interest Rates

- The Federal Reserve uses various aggregates to measure the money supply at any given time.
- The supply of money is a major factor affecting interest rates.
- Banks create money by loaning out excess reserves.

Check Your Banking IQ

Now that you have finished this chapter, see what you know about banking by taking the chapter post test.

www.m.g-wlearning.com
www.g-wlearning.com

Review Your Knowledge

On a separate sheet of paper or in a word processing document, match the following terms with the definition that fits best.

A. unit of account
B. store of value
C. denomination
D. commodity
E. representative money
F. gold-exchange standard
G. aggregate
H. interest rate
I. excess reserve
J. inflation

1. Once allowed foreign governments to exchange US dollars for gold.
2. Units in which currency is available.
3. Used by banks to provide loans and create money.
4. Something that is useful or has value.
5. Common measure of what something is worth.
6. Measures by which the Federal Reserve can calculate the money supply.
7. Increased prices.
8. Bill or coin that has no value, but is backed by something of value.
9. Maintains its value over a period of time.
10. Cost of borrowing money.

On a separate sheet of paper or in a word processing document, answer each of the following questions.

11. What is a disadvantage of gold compared to money?
12. What gives representative money its value?
13. Why is it important for money to be divisible?
14. If the supply of money increased and demand for money stayed the same, what would be the expected effect on interest rates?
15. How are printing money and creating money not the same things?

Apply Your Knowledge

16. What features of US dollars make it clear that they are a *brand* of money? Write a few paragraphs identifying the features and explaining how they contribute to the brand.
17. Use the Internet to find some barter websites. Explain how they work and list a few advantages and disadvantages.
18. Research the new US bills and describe the special features that have been introduced to reduce counterfeiting.
19. Why do you think the US now uses fiat money instead of representative money? Write a few paragraphs explaining your position.
20. Explain how lower interest rates help borrowers, but hurt depositors.

Working in Teams

Working with a classmate, research the various denominations in which US currency has been made over the years. Which denominations are no longer produced? Are there denominations that have been created in recent years? Are there any denominations not in existence that you think should be included in the money supply? Prepare a presentation in which you decide which denominations should be included in the US money supply and why. Present your findings to the class.

G-W Learning Mobile Site

Visit the G-W Learning mobile site to complete the chapter pretest and post test and to practice vocabulary using e-flash cards. If you do not have a smartphone, visit the G-W Learning companion website to access these features.

G-W Learning mobile site: www.m.g-wlearning.com
G-W Learning companion website: www.g-wlearning.com

Common Core

College and Career Readiness

Listening. Perform an Internet search on President Nixon's termination of the gold-exchange standard. Look for opinions for and against the issue. After reading a few expert opinions on this controversial decision, use this information to form your own opinion. Discuss your findings and reasoning with the class. As you listen to your classmates' stances on this issue, evaluate your own position. How does their reasoning contribute to your understanding of President Nixon's decision? Does your opinion change or is it strengthened?

Speaking. Research the features of some of the currencies used around the world. Compile information about the aspects of each type of currency that help to prevent counterfeiting, the denominations that are made available, the materials used in making the currency, the features of the currency that help to identify the country it represents, and any other interesting information you find. Use this information, along with what you already know about the features of US currency, to create a *world currency.* Using various elements (visual displays, written handouts, technological displays), present your currency to the class. Explain why you chose the features you did.

EVENT PREP

Banking Concepts

Banking concepts is a competitive event you might enter with your career and technical student organization (CTSO). The banking concepts competitive event may include an objective test that covers multiple topics. Participants are usually allowed one hour to complete the event. One of the topics that may be included on the test is basic banking concepts. To prepare for the concepts portion of the banking test:

1. Review the checkpoint activities at the end of each section of the text.
2. Review the end-of-chapter activities for additional practice.
3. Ask your instructor to give you practice tests for each chapter of this text. It is important that you are familiar with answering multiple choice and T/F questions. Have someone time you as you take a practice test.

Check Your Banking IQ

Before you begin this chapter, see what you already know about banking by taking the chapter pretest.

www.m.g-wlearning.com
www.g-wlearning.com

5

Federal Reserve System

As you have read in previous chapters, the supply of money in a system has a great deal to do with whether or not the economy will grow. The actions taken by a government to control its money supply will determine how much that dollar in your pocket is worth. Every day, the value of a dollar changes. Prices and interest rates go up and down. The Federal Reserve System is the means for making sure the value of the dollar remains stable and your savings are protected.

College and Career Readiness

Reading Prep. In preparation for this chapter, research the US Supreme Court case of *McCulloch v. Maryland.* As you are reading the chapter, keep in mind the reasoning used by the court in this decision.

Scan the code to view a Biz Kid$ video. If you do not have a smartphone, visit the G-W Learning companion website.

www.m.g-wlearning.com
www.g-wlearning.com

Section 5.1 History of the Federal Reserve System

Terms

central bank
era of free banking
National Currency Act
Office of the Comptroller of the Currency (OCC)
National Banking Act
bank note
bank panic
bank run
bond

Objectives

After completing this section, you will be able to:

- Describe the first two central banks in the US.
- Explore the problems caused by the lack of a central bank.
- Explain how the Federal Reserve System solved the nation's financial problems.

Central Bank in the US

The first secretary of the Treasury, Alexander Hamilton, advocated and developed the First Bank of the United States. A **central bank** is the organization that oversees a nation's monetary system. Hamilton believed that a central bank would make the country stronger. The First Bank, chartered in 1791, was considered a central bank and:

- assumed the debts of the individual states;
- made commercial loans;
- held federal funds; and
- issued payments.

Although the bank performed well, its charter was allowed to expire in 1811. Rural interests, as voiced by Thomas Jefferson, did not like the idea of a central bank. Opponents believed it took power away from the states and put it into the hands of eastern bankers.

Congress again saw a need for a central bank and chartered the Second Bank of the United States in 1816. The Second Bank was very similar to the First Bank, but it was much larger. The First Bank began with $10 million on deposit and eight branches. The Second Bank started with $35 million and 25 branches. From the beginning, the bank's existence was challenged. Farmers from the South and West strongly opposed it.

Source: Shutterstock (ChipPix)

The idea of a central bank in the US was controversial because rural farmers felt it favored urban populations.

States tried to do what they could to undermine the authority of the bank. This led to a Supreme Court challenge to its constitutionality. In the case of *McCulloch v. Maryland* (1819), the court ruled that the creation of a central bank was within the power of Congress. The court's decision did not make the idea more popular, however.

While campaigning for president, Andrew Jackson promised to do away with the bank. He believed that a central bank was un-American. Once Jackson became president, he ordered that all government funds be withdrawn from the bank. In 1836, he vetoed the bill that renewed the bank's charter. The period of time from 1837 to 1863 is known as the **era of free banking.** During this time, all bank functions were handled by state banks. Federal funds were held in the US Treasury.

Green Banking

The Environmental Bankers Association (EBA) is a nonprofit organization that supports financial institutions, such as banks, to promote social responsibility in the industry. The EBA helps protect the assets and income of financial institutions from environmental exposure and liability.

Banking Without a Central Bank

Without consistent regulation, many banks failed. This presented a problem for the federal government. The government needed a system of strong and reliable banks from which it could get financing for the Civil War. The **National Currency Act** created the Office of the Comptroller of the Currency (OCC) in 1863. The **Office of the Comptroller of the Currency (OCC)** created a uniform national currency and a system of national banks. Today, the OCC still charters and supervises national banks.

In 1864, the National Currency Act was modified and became known as the National Banking Act. The **National Banking Act** allowed the federal government to charter private banks. These new banks issued bank notes. **Bank notes** are intended to be used as currency and promise immediate payment by the bank that issued the note. Each note was backed by a government bond. The act also provided that notes issued by state banks would be charged a 10% tax. This persuaded most state banks to seek national charters. A national charter came with strict rules. Among other things, a minimum cash reserve was required.

In the late 19th century, the number of state-chartered banks increased. Because state banks were not subject to the same strict rules as were national banks, many state banks failed. This led to bank panics in 1873, 1893, and 1907. A **bank panic** occurs when there is a widespread worry that banks do not have enough money to cover customer demands for withdrawals. A bank panic is usually started by a run on a single bank. A **bank run** is when depositors fear their money is not safe in the bank in which it was deposited. The depositors arrive in great numbers at the same time to withdraw their money from the bank.

In addition, currency shortages arose when the federal government reduced its debt. Reducing the debt meant reducing the number of government bonds available to back bank notes. Bonds represent debt. In this case, a **bond** represents money the federal government has borrowed from the bondholder.

After the bank panic that occurred in 1907, the idea of a central bank began to take hold. In 1913, the Federal Reserve System was established.

BIZ TIPS

You can probably identify national banks in your community. A national bank must have the word *National* or the abbreviation *N.A.* (National Association) in its name.

Creation of the Federal Reserve System

President Woodrow Wilson signed the Federal Reserve Act in 1913. Its development was affected by events and failures in the two previous central banks as well as the development of the country. Figure 5-1 illustrates historical events in relationship to the development of the US central bank.

BIZ TIPS

The idea of a central bank is not a modern one. The Bank of England, which is the central bank for the United Kingdom, was founded in 1694. Other nations also had central banks centuries ago.

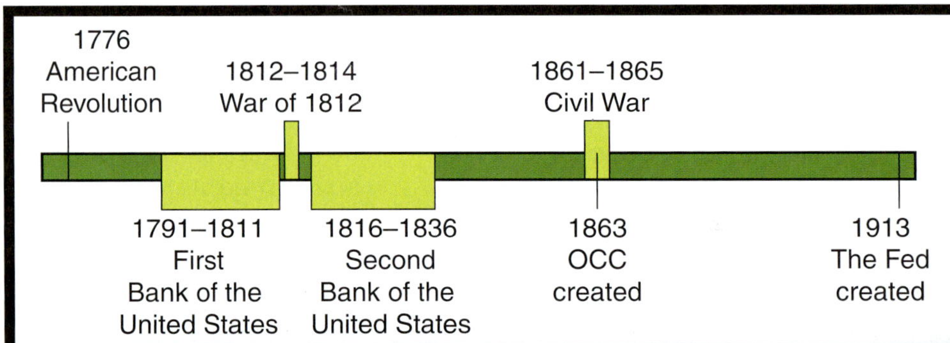

Figure 5-1.
Timeline of US Central Banks

Checkpoint 5.1

1. Why were rural citizens opposed to the First Bank of the United States?
2. What did the US Supreme Court decide in *McCullough v. Maryland?*
3. Why is the time from 1837 to 1863 known as the era of free banking?
4. What two things did the Office of the Comptroller of the Currency accomplish when it was first created?
5. How does a bank panic usually start?

Build Your Vocabulary

As you progress through this course, develop a personal glossary of banking terms and add it to your portfolio. This will help you build your banking vocabulary. Write out a definition for each of the following terms, and add it to your personal glossary.

central bank
era of free banking
National Currency Act
Office of the Comptroller of the Currency (OCC)
National Banking Act
bank note
bank panic
bank run
bond

Section 5.2
Structure of the Federal Reserve System

Objectives

After completing this section, you will be able to:

- Explain how the Federal Reserve System is structured.
- Describe how decentralization affected the location of the Federal Reserve Banks.
- Identify the roles of the Federal Reserve's Board of Governors and Federal Open Market Committee.

Terms

Federal Reserve System
Fed
monetary system
decentralization
Federal Reserve Bank
Board of Governors (BOG)
Federal Open Market Committee (FOMC)

Structure of the Federal Reserve

The **Federal Reserve System,** also known as the **Fed,** is the central bank for the United States. It is responsible for the country's monetary system. A **monetary system** is the mechanism a nation uses to provide and manage money for itself. Having control over a nation's monetary system is a lot of power. When an organization has so much power, it must have controls in place. The structure of the Fed is meant to safeguard against corruption. The location and organization of the Federal Reserve System reflect this need. This setup made it different from its predecessors in the US and central banks in other countries.

Location of the Federal Reserve

Decentralization was one of the driving forces that determined how the Fed would be organized and located. **Decentralization** occurs when a central authority shares power with regional and local authorities. The Fed is composed of 12 regional central banks, which are known as **Federal Reserve Banks.** Multiple Federal Reserve Banks were created to avoid establishing a single central bank in a single location. In particular, the Fed's designers did not want the Fed to be located only in New York. New York was, and continues to be, the home of Wall Street and many high-powered financial institutions. Many feared that the Fed would be affected by the needs of the stock market and financial institutions in New York.

Source: Shutterstock (Vacclav)

The Federal Reserve System is decentralized so that institutions like Wall Street do not have too much power.

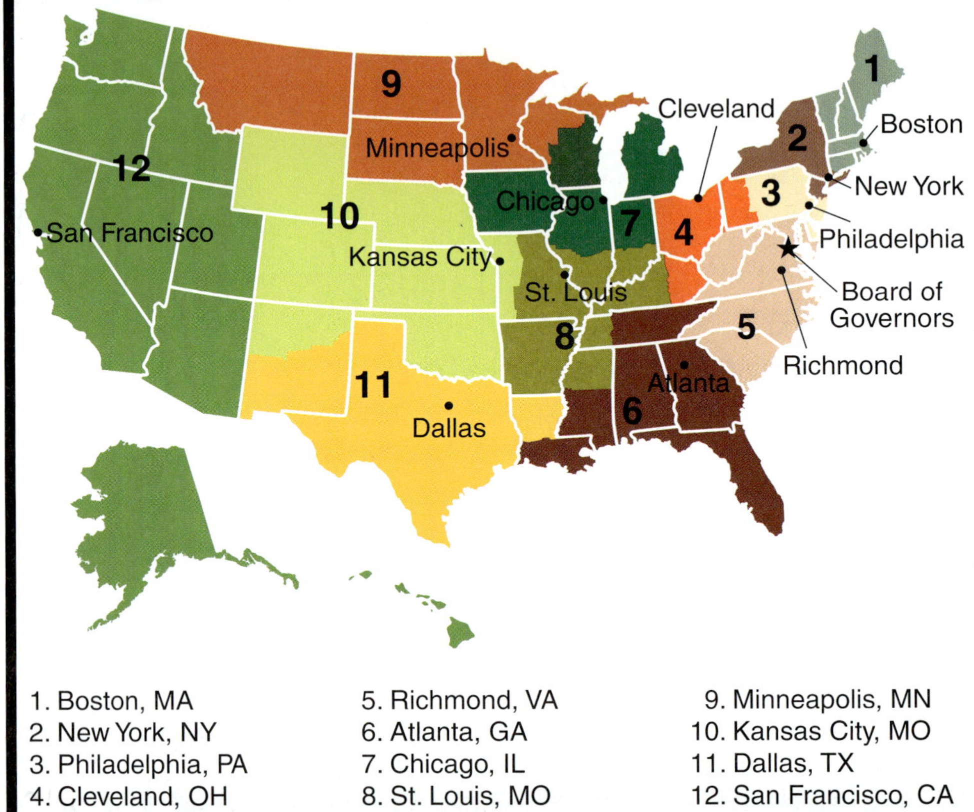

Source: www.federalreserve.gov

Figure 5-2.
District Reserve Banks

BIZ TIPS

In today's world of Internet access and high-speed travel, concern about the physical location of the Fed might be difficult to understand. However, in the early 1900s when the Fed was created, trading stock required you or your representative to be physically present to make the trade.

By examining the districts shown in Figure 5-2, you can see that the sizes of Federal Reserve Bank districts vary. Districts with a denser population and greater financial activity are smaller in area than districts more sparsely populated and with less financial activity. For example, the district based in New York City is geographically much smaller than the district based in Kansas City.

The Fed identifies each district by number and the name of the city where the Federal Reserve Bank is located. Within each district, the Federal Reserve Bank may have one or more branches. Today, all of the cities containing Federal Reserve Banks are considered major cities.

Organization of the Federal Reserve

Each Federal Reserve Bank governs itself and supervises the member banks in its region. Figure 5-3 shows the structure of the Federal Reserve, which includes the Board of Governors and the Federal Open Market Committee.

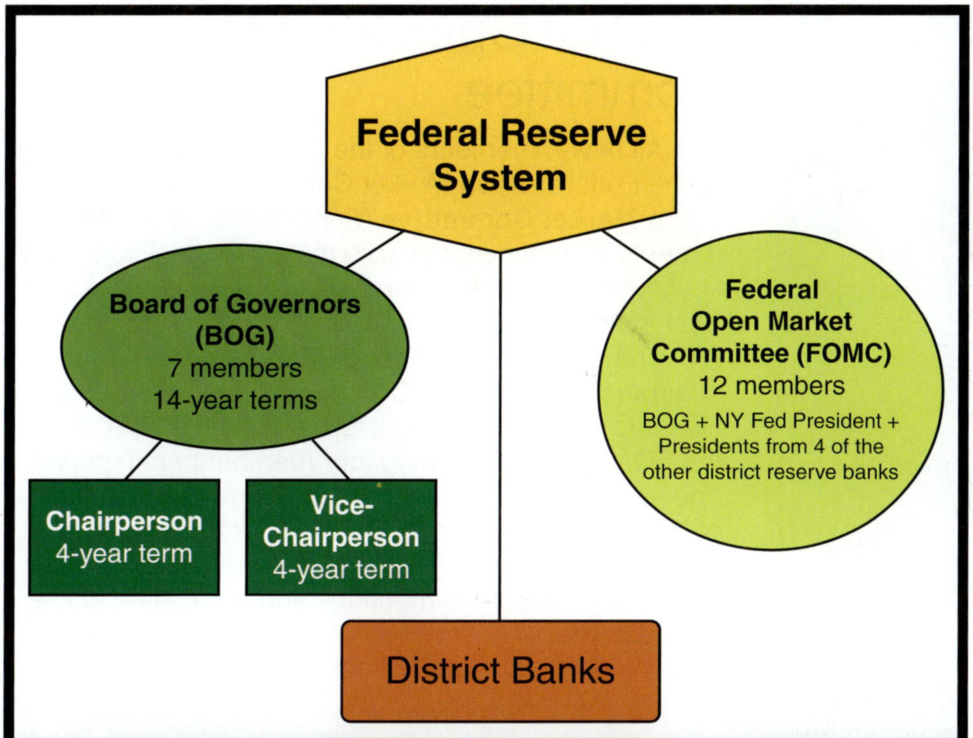

Figure 5-3.
Structure of the Fed

Board of Governors

The **Board of Governors (BOG)** is the governing body of the Federal Reserve System. Although the BOG is a federal governmental agency, the Federal Reserve System is considered an independent central bank. It does not report to the US president or any other member of the executive branch. However, the Fed reports to the US Congress.

The Fed's actions should be in-line with the government's economic goals. Twice a year, the Fed chairperson reviews the Fed's recent actions and its economic predictions and presents these to Congress. If legislation related to banking and finance is under consideration, Congress often requests additional presentations.

All of the members of the BOG are appointed by the US president and confirmed by the Senate. Five members serve 14-year terms. The chairperson and vice-chairperson each serve four-year terms. Each district can have no more than one member on the BOG. The chair of the Board of Governors is usually referred to as the Fed chair.

There have only been 15 chairs since the Fed's founding in 1913. The longest serving Fed chair was Alan Greenspan. He served from 1987 to 2006. He was first appointed by President Reagan and went on to serve during the terms of three more presidents. Greenspan is thought to be a genius by some and the architect of the Great Recession by others. In 2006, President George W. Bush appointed Ben Bernanke as Fed chair. He was reappointed by President Obama four years later. Although the Fed chair has a very visible role, the Federal Open Market Committee is the body responsible for making monetary policy.

Ethical Banking

Those working for the Federal Reserve are held to very high ethical standards. Each district bank has its own code of ethical conduct. Many of the codes are very specific, going so far as to ban Fed employees from eating meals with employees of banks they regulate. The absolute purity of the Fed is central to its mission.

Source: Shutterstock (Albert H. Teich)

In 2006, Ben Bernanke was appointed the chair of the Board of Governors of the Federal Reserve System.

Federal Open Market Committee

All seven members of the BOG are also members of the Federal Open Market Committee. The **Federal Open Market Committee (FOMC)** has 12 members. It meets eight times a year to make key decisions that set US monetary policy and allow the Federal Reserve System to carry out its functions.

The chairperson of the BOG is also the chairperson of the FOMC. The president of the Federal Reserve Bank in New York is always a member of the FOMC. The remaining four members each serve one-year terms. They are chosen from the presidents of the other 11 Federal Reserve Banks. Presidents of the Federal Reserve Banks who are not on the FOMC still attend the meetings and participate in the discussions.

Checkpoint 5.2

1. How is the Federal Reserve System set up differently than its predecessors?
2. Why did the Fed's designers want to avoid making the Fed a single bank in New York?
3. How are members of the Board of Governors selected?
4. What is the Federal Open Market Committee responsible for?
5. Who are the members of the FOMC?

Build Your Vocabulary

As you progress through this course, develop a personal glossary of banking terms and add it to your portfolio. This will help you build your banking vocabulary. Write out a definition for each of the following terms, and add it to your personal glossary.

Federal Reserve System
Fed
monetary system
decentralization
Federal Reserve Bank
Board of Governors (BOG)
Federal Open Market Committee (FOMC)

Section 5.3
Function of the Federal Reserve System

Objectives

After completing this section, you will be able to:

- List the Fed's core functions.
- Define monetary policy and how the Fed conducts it.
- Describe how the Fed regulates and supervises its member banks.
- List the financial services the Fed provides for its member banks and the US government.
- Identify the tools the Fed uses to make the financial system stable.

Terms

monetary policy
discount rate
prime rate
reserve requirement

Core Functions

The Fed's functions allow banks, businesses, and individuals to conduct business. Buying, selling, saving, and spending are all affected by the Fed. The Federal Reserve System has four primary functions:

- establishing the nation's monetary policy, which affects the monetary and credit conditions in the economy
- supervising and regulating banking institutions
- providing financial services to depository institutions, the US government, and foreign official institutions, including operating the nation's payments system
- maintaining the stability of the financial system

Monetary Policy

Devising and carrying out monetary policy is not an easy task. **Monetary policy** is the regulation of a country's money supply to achieve economic goals and stability. The Fed uses tools to control the interest rate charged for loans and the amount of reserves banks must maintain. If banks are instructed to maintain higher reserves, the interest rate borrowers must pay drops. This causes the economy to grow. For example, you may need a loan to buy a new car. It is more attractive to buy a car when the interest rate is 2% than if the interest rate is 5%. This is because your monthly payments and the interest you pay would be less at 2% than 5%.

Source: Shutterstock (Juriah Mosin)

Interest rates, which affect the total price you pay on a car loan, are regulated by the Federal Reserve System.

$299.70 (payment per month on a $10,000 loan at 5%) × 36 (term of the loan in months) = $10,789.20

$286.42 (payment per month on a $10,000 loan at 2%) × 36 (term of the loan in months) = $10,311.12

$10,789.20 (total paid for car with 5% interest) – $10,311.12 (total paid for car with 2% interest) = $478.08 (difference paid over the life of the loan)

The BOG and the FOMC have three basic tools they use to conduct monetary policy:

- open market operations
- the discount rate
- reserve requirements

Together, these tools enable the Fed to effectively carry out the nation's monetary policy.

The FMOC supervises the purchase and sale of long-term loans issued by the government to raise money. This is an application of the open market operations tool.

The **discount rate** is the interest banks pay to borrow money from a Federal Reserve Bank. This rate affects the interest rate that the banks charge customers to borrow money. The FOMC sets the discount rate every two weeks. The BOG then approves the new rate. The discount rate is an important factor in monetary policy. Businesses borrow money if they need funds to expand or survive an economic downturn. A change in interest rate, either up or down, might affect the number of people a business can afford to employ.

If your employer cannot afford to borrow money because interest rates are high, it may need to reduce staff and your job may be cut. On the other hand, if your employer can borrow money to grow the business because interest rates are low, it may be able to hire more employees. This is the effect the Fed can have on employment.

The discount rate also affects the interest you pay to purchase something on credit, as shown in Figure 5-4. You and the businesses in your area may borrow money from your local bank. If necessary, your local bank borrows money from the Federal Reserve Bank in its district to make the loan. The interest rate the bank charges you when you borrow money is based on the discount rate charged by the Federal Reserve Bank. The interest rate you pay is tied to the prime rate. The **prime rate** is the interest rate that banks charge their best commercial customers.

Reserve requirements also play a big role in monetary policy. The BOG sets the amount of money each bank must keep in its vaults or at a Federal Reserve Bank. This value is rarely changed.

The Fed also dictates reserve requirements. A **reserve requirement** is the amount of money a bank must keep and not invest or loan out. The amount of the reserve requirement has a big impact on the money supply.

Bank Regulation and Supervision

All national banks and some state-chartered banks are members of the Federal Reserve System. The Fed issues regulations that affect how member banks conduct business. For example, regulations determine

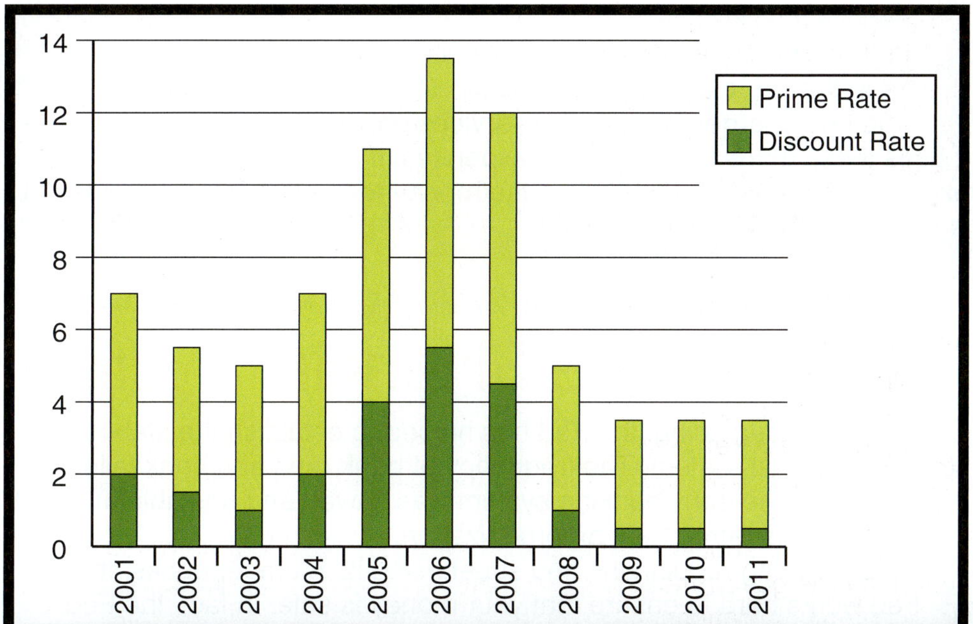

Figure 5-4.
Discount Rate and Prime Rate

how member banks use personal customer information that is not publicly available. Many regulations are issued to implement laws passed by Congress that affect the banking industry.

In addition to making regulations, the Fed supervises its member banks to evaluate their soundness. Bank examiners conduct on-sight audits of member banks. The Fed also uses software to screen the activities of member banks for negative trends and possible problems.

Financial Services

The Federal Reserve provides several services to its member banks. In addition to providing short-term loans to banks as discussed above, Federal Reserve Banks offer services:

- collecting and paying funds when two member banks use checks to transfer funds between them
- transferring funds almost immediately
- offering customer services such as depositing a payroll check directly into a bank account and automatic payment of some bills, such as a car or house payment, directly from the customer's account
- holding the reserves that member banks are required to maintain

The Fed provides necessary services to the US government as well. These activities make it the nation's bank. In this area, the Fed:

- holds all of the checking accounts owned by the US government from which tax refunds and Social Security benefits are paid;
- monitors the value of the dollar compared to the currency issued by other nations; and

- negotiating skills
- buys and sells the dollar and currency issued by other countries to keep the value of the dollar stable.

The Fed charges fees for the services provided to its member banks. It uses these funds to pay its own expenses. If any funds remain after expenses are paid, the Fed gives the money to the US Treasury, where it is applied to the US national debt.

Source: Shutterstock (Michael G. Smith)

After the Fed pays its expenses, it gives the extra money to the US Treasury, where it is applied to the national debt.

Stability of the Financial System

From the beginning, the Fed has helped to establish the stability of the US financial system. The frequency of bank runs and bank failures showed that the early banking system was flawed and unstable. It relied on individuals rather than an organization.

By issuing regulations and supervising its member banks, the Fed works hard to ensure that your money is safe. In fact, the Fed supervises every aspect of your bank's activities. Today, the Fed uses its entire toolset to maintain the stability of the financial system. It monitors the economy, supervises and regulates member banks, and serves as the nation's bank. In every way possible, the Fed works to maintain the nation's economic stability and provide an environment that promotes the growth and success of American individuals and businesses.

Checkpoint 5.3

1. How does the Fed conduct monetary policy?
2. When is the discount rate set?
3. What are some customer services offered by Federal Reserve Banks?
4. What does the Fed do with the money it earns?
5. How does the Fed use its entire toolset to maintain the stability of the financial system?

Build Your Vocabulary

As you progress through this course, develop a personal glossary of banking terms and add it to your portfolio. This will help you build your banking vocabulary. Write out a definition for each of the following terms, and add it to your personal glossary.

monetary policy
discount rate
prime rate
reserve requirement

Careers in Finance
Banking and Related Services

What Does a Bank Examiner Do?

A **bank examiner** reviews the financial assets and documents of banks to ensure compliance with state and federal regulations. **Bank examiners** can work for federal and state regulatory agencies and Federal Reserve Banks. Those working in the Office of the Comptroller of the Currency may even work in many different specialty areas. Some of the activities performed include:

- using word processing, spreadsheet, and database software to collect and present data;
- leading audits of banking institutions, including verifying cash on hand, loan documentation, and loan collateral and investments;
- making presentations to committees and bank regulators;
- evaluating a bank's investment and loan decisions; and
- recommending and implementing corrective actions in the event of bank weaknesses or deficiencies.

What Is It Like to Work as a Bank Examiner?

Bank examiners are constantly traveling to different financial institutions to conduct audits. The work conditions of a **bank examiner** can be very stressful, as he or she has a great deal of responsibility and is charged with enforcing laws and regulations.

Bank examiners audit all of the financial transactions of an institution, so previous experience in financial services and high ethical standards are necessary for success in this position. While **bank examiners** receive highly specialized training, they are also expected to stay up to date on new laws and regulations affecting the financial services.

If you enjoy working with numbers and on your own, a career as a **bank examiner** might suit you.

What Education and Skills Are Needed to Be a Bank Examiner?

- college degree in accounting, banking, business administration, or economics
- prior experience in financial services, such as bank lending or management
- strong verbal and written communication
- good organization skills

Career Ladder

Compliance Officer

Bank Examiner

Internal Auditor

Chapter Summary

Section 5.1 History of the Federal Reserve System

- Twice, the US created a central bank, which lasted from 1791 to 1811 and 1816 to 1836.
- Without a central bank, the US established a standard currency and national banks to fight economic instability.
- The Federal Reserve System (Fed) was established in 1913.

Section 5.2 Structure of the Federal Reserve System

- The Fed's structure reflects the need to keep it free of corrupting influences.
- The Fed is composed of 12 regional central banks.
- The Fed's organization includes the Board of Governors (BOG) and the Federal Open Market Committee (FOMC).

Section 5.3 Function of the Federal Reserve System

- The Fed's primary functions enable the US economy to thrive.
- The Fed uses financial tools to make and carry out US monetary policy.
- Bank regulation and supervision ensures that member banks are stable.
- The Fed provides financial services to its member banks and the US government.
- The Fed maintains the nation's economic stability.

Check Your Banking IQ

Now that you have finished this chapter, see what you know about banking by taking the chapter post test.

www.m.g-wlearning.com
www.g-wlearning.com

Review Your Knowledge

On a separate sheet of paper or in a word processing document, match the following terms with the definition that fits best.

A. decentralization
B. discount rate
C. monetary system
D. National Banking Act
E. bank run
F. prime rate
G. central bank
H. reserve requirement
I. Federal Open Market Committee (FOMC)
J. era of free banking

1. Amount of money a bank must keep on hand and not invest or loan out.
2. Allowed the government to charter private banks.
3. Central authority shares power with regional and local authorities.
4. Depositors come in great numbers at the same time to get their money out of the bank.
5. Time period when all bank functions were handled by state banks.
6. Affects the interest rate that the bank charges customers to borrow money.
7. Interest rate that banks charge their best commercial customers.
8. The President of the Federal Reserve Bank in New York is always a member.
9. Mechanism a nation uses to provide and manage money for itself.
10. Alexander Hamilton believed this would make the country stronger.

On a separate sheet of paper or in a word processing document, answer each of the following questions.

11. Identify the three US politicians who were involved in establishing the first two central banks in the US.
12. In what way was the Second Bank of the US different than the First Bank?
13. What feature of the Federal Reserve System ensures that it is a decentralized banking system?
14. How does the Fed report to the US Congress?
15. What are the four primary functions of the Fed?

Apply Your Knowledge

16. Research the Federal Reserve Bank in your district. Write a summary including its location, the various areas or states that it covers, and any interesting facts you find.
17. Perform an Internet search on the current condition of the US economy. Write a summary of your findings, citing specific evidence to support your analysis.
18. Research the current discount rate. How long has it been in effect? Explain why you think it has or has not changed recently.
19. Visit www.federalreserve.gov. Write a report in which you identify the BOG members and describe their education and experience. Include a possible career plan for a high school senior planning to become a member of the BOG.
20. Research the national banks in your area. Create a chart in which you list each bank and the services that it provides due to its membership in the Federal Reserve System. If there are any differences between banks, consider some possible explanations for the discrepancy.

Working in Teams

Working with two or three classmates, research the Bank Panic of 1907. Use the information that you find to prepare a presentation to the class in which you explain the following: how the bank panic started, what factors made the panic worse or better, the major financial or political factors, some consequences of the bank panic, and how the situation was eventually solved. Present your findings to the class, making sure to include time at the end of your presentation for questions.

G-W Learning Mobile Site

Visit the G-W Learning mobile site to complete the chapter pretest and post test and to practice vocabulary using e-flash cards. If you do not have a smartphone, visit the G-W Learning companion website to access these features.

G-W Learning mobile site: www.m.g-wlearning.com
G-W Learning companion website: www.g-wlearning.com

Common Core

College and Career Readiness

Reading. Using independent research and the information contained in the text, write a report in which you analyze how the founders of the US responded to the idea of a central bank. Why did they support or oppose it? How do these reasons connect with other important events or ideas that were influential at this time in our country's history? Cite specific evidence from the text and your research to support your understanding of this issue.

Writing. Conduct a short research project to answer the question, "How does the Fed protect me as a consumer?" Using information from multiple sources, write a report on your response to this question.

EVENT PREP

Community Service Project

A community service project is a competitive event you might enter with your career and technical student organization (CTSO). This project is usually carried out by the entire CTSO chapter and spans an extensive number of months. There will be two parts of the event: written and oral. The chapter will designate several members to represent the team at the competitive event. To prepare for a community service project:

1. Contact the association immediately at the end of the state conference to prepare for next year's event.
2. Go to the website of your organization for specific information. Visit the site often as information changes quickly.
3. Print a copy of the event so that you may highlight important information.
4. Read all the guidelines closely. These rules and regulations must be strictly adhered to or disqualification can occur.
5. Ask your instructor for guidance in assigning roles to team members in order to execute the community project.
6. During regular chapter meetings, the plan for the project should be created based on direction from the CTSO.

6

Check Your Banking IQ

Before you begin this chapter, see what you already know about banking by taking the chapter pretest.

www.m.g-wlearning.com
www.g-wlearning.com

Bank Regulations

Regulations have a major impact on how banks are managed, how they deal with customers, the types of products they can offer, and the amount of risk they can take on. Compared to most industries, banking is heavily regulated. In banking, as in other industries, regulations often follow a crisis. Laws are passed to try to avoid the same mistakes that caused the crisis. Bank regulations are meant to prevent bank failures and protect bank customers, while allowing banks to be competitive.

College and Career Readiness

Reading Prep. As you read the chapter, think about the advantages and disadvantages of banking regulations. Do you think regulations help or hurt the banking industry? Use examples from the text to support your opinion.

Scan the code to view a Biz Kid$ video. If you do not have a smartphone, visit the G-W Learning companion website.

www.m.g-wlearning.com
www.g-wlearning.com

Section 6.1
Banking Regulations

Objectives

After completing this section, you will be able to:

- Explain the conditions that existed in the banking industry during the 1920s and 1930s.
- Describe the provisions of the Glass-Steagall Act.
- Explain why the legislation that created FIRREA and FDICIA was needed.
- Describe how the Sarbanes-Oxley Act increases transparency and accountability in banking.

Terms

bank run
Emergency Banking Act of 1933
Glass-Steagall Act
interest rate ceiling
Federal Home Loan Bank Board
Financial Institutions Reform, Recovery, and Enforcement Act (FIRREA)
Federal Depository Insurance Corporation Improvement Act (FDICIA)
Sarbanes-Oxley Act (SOX)

Setting the Stage for Failure

During the Great Depression, there were huge numbers of bank failures. Over 9,000 banks closed their doors during this time. In 1933 alone, some 4,000 banks failed. Figure 6-1 shows the number of bank failures throughout the 19th and 20th century. Why did so many banks fail? There were several contributing factors, including crop failures in the

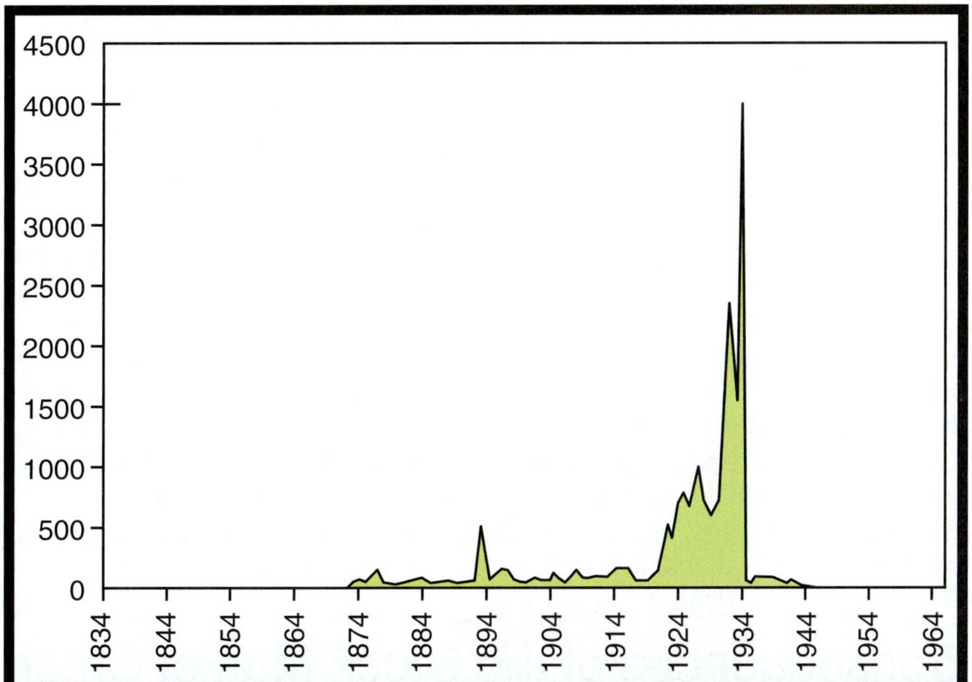

Source: The Federal Reserve

Figure 6-1.
Number of Bank Failures

Cause	Effect
Crop failures during the 1920s	Small banks in farming areas were affected as farms were foreclosed.
Contagion	Lack of faith in the soundness of banks spreads like the common cold.
Branching	• State banks were largely prohibited from opening branches in other locations. • National banks opened branches that provided stiff competition to unit banks.
Number of banks	The number of banks increased more than the population's need for banks did.
Reduced travel costs	• Because it was too difficult or too expensive to travel far, people banked locally. • Cars and train travel became less expensive, which allowed people to travel outside of their town to do their banking.
Stock market crash	Banks had invested in the stock market and lost much of their assets during the crash.

Figure 6-2.
Causes of Bank Failures during the 1920s and 1930s

1920s, changes in branch banking regulations, the stock market crash, and the already large number of banks. Figure 6-2 outlines the many factors that caused widespread bank failures during the Great Depression.

During the 1920s, there were widespread crop failures. Because most farming operations, both then and now, relied heavily on credit, farmers were unable to repay loans they took out to plant the crops that were never harvested. As a result, many small banks that served the needs of farmers were forced to close.

State-chartered banks tended to be smaller than nationally chartered institutions. When regulations regarding branch banking were changed, national banks were free to open branches that directly competed with the state and unit banks that were still largely prohibited from branch banking. The competition forced many smaller banks out of business. When one bank closed, it frequently made customers lose faith in the stability of their own banks. These customers often immediately went to the bank to demand their money. When many depositors did this at the same time, a bank run occurred. To meet the demands of the depositors, the banks were forced to sell their assets to get cash, which frequently resulted in tremendous losses. What began as a healthy bank ultimately failed because of the irrational fears of its depositors.

Consequences of the Stock Market Crash

The stock market crashed in October of 1929 and did not recover for years. Banks and investment banking operations that owned securities lost most of their investments. Unemployment was quite high during the

Great Depression. Many individuals and businesses could not make loan payments, which caused these customers to *default* on loans. When a bank does not receive loan payments, it cannot meet its own financial obligations. Some banks were paying high interest rates to attract depositors so they would have funds to make more loans. Because banks were paying high interest rates to some customers and were not receiving loan payments from other customers, loans became unprofitable.

Bank Run

A **bank run** occurs when a large number of depositors withdraw all of their money from the bank at the same time. Bank deposits were not insured at the beginning of the Great Depression. If a bank failed, depositors would lose all of the money they had in the bank. Often, a rumor about a bank failing would be enough to send depositors running to the bank to take out their money. If enough depositors withdrew money, the bank would actually fail. Many depositors felt banks were unsafe and started keeping their money at home. In addition, there were many more banks at that time than there are today, as shown in Figure 6-3. The number of banks exceeded customer needs.

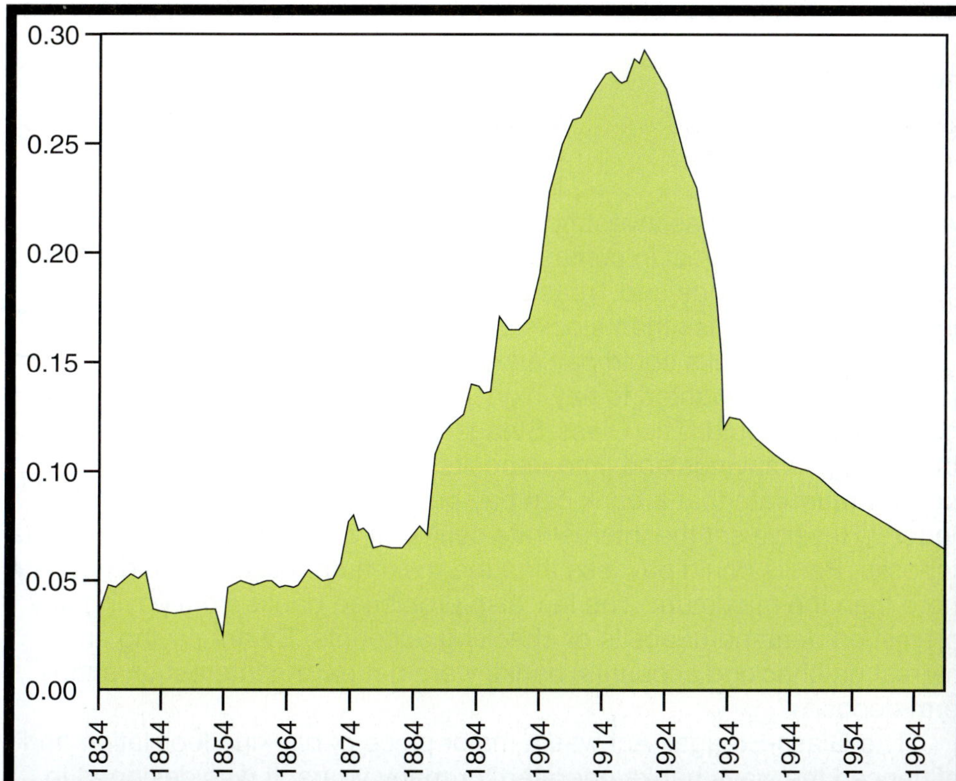

Source: The Federal Reserve

Figure 6-3.
Number of Banks per Thousand Persons

Glass-Steagall

To prevent massive bank failures from happening in the future, Congress passed the Emergency Banking Act of 1933.The **Emergency Banking Act of 1933,** also known as the **Glass-Steagall Act,** had several provisions designed to not only keep banks safe, but also to give the public confidence in our banking system. Perhaps the best known provision of this law is that it established the Federal Deposit Insurance Corporation (FDIC). By having deposits insured, depositors felt that money deposited in a bank was safe. As a result, bank runs rarely occurred. The creation of the FDIC was a major factor in restoring consumer confidence in banks.

Many economists believed that banks took on too much risk with depositors' money by investing in common stocks. When the stock market crashed, bank assets and depositors' money was lost as well. The Glass-Steagall Act separated investment and commercial banking. Prior to the Glass-Steagall Act, commercial banks could also be investment banks. The Glass-Steagall Act prohibited commercial banks from engaging in investment banking activities. Congress felt that banks would have less risk if they were not also acting as investment bankers. In addition, banks were no longer allowed to invest in common stock. They were only allowed to invest in certain bonds and Treasury securities, as these securities are generally less of a risk than stocks.

Previously, banks could pay any interest rate they wanted on deposits. If banks wanted to pay high interest rates to attract money into the bank, they could. The Glass-Steagall Act established an interest rate ceiling on savings and time deposits. An **interest rate ceiling** is the maximum rate that a bank can pay on certain deposits. In 1933, the Federal Reserve set the interest rate ceiling at 3% on all savings and time deposits. Banks could pay less than the maximum rate, but could not pay more than the maximum. The law also prohibited banks from paying any interest on demand deposits or checking accounts. By not paying any interest on checking accounts, banks were not paying interest on short-term deposits.

The Glass-Steagall Act was a major piece of banking legislation and influenced the ways banks operated for many years. It was designed to keep bank failures low and, by that standard, it worked well. In 1934, the first year the FDIC was in operation, there were only nine bank failures. After 1942, the number of bank failures per year was never above 10 until 1975 when it hit 13. However, since the start of the Great Recession in 2008, over 300 banks have failed.

Green Banking

Not long ago, the banking world had few environmental regulations. But, times have changed. As environmental problems have increased, the number of green regulations has also increased. Both India and China have enacted laws that banks and other businesses must follow to reduce their carbon footprints. In Australia, many banks have signed the Equator Principles, which require participating countries to serve as regulators of environmental standards in developing countries. The banks that signed the Equator Principles agreed to make sure borrowers follow very strict rules that will protect the environments of developing countries.

BIZ TIPS

The Bank Holding Company Acts of 1956 and 1970 opened the regulatory door. It let banks do business through holding companies that would have otherwise been banned.

Relaxing Depression-Era Regulation

Many regulations on depository institutions were lifted in the early 1980s. Savings associations were allowed to operate much as banks did. Regulatory agencies, especially the Federal Home Loan Bank Board and the Federal Savings and Loan Insurance Corporation (FSLIC), relaxed their rules and procedures. The **Federal Home Loan Bank Board** chartered and examined savings associations. The FSLIC insured the deposits of savings associations.

In the early 1980s, interest rates rose due to inflation. With no interest rate ceiling, banks and savings associations were paying very high interest rates to keep and attract deposits. Depository institutions faced increasing competition from non-depository institutions for deposits.

A major recession began in 1980 and lasted into 1982. With a falling economy, banks and other lenders saw low demand for loans as well as increased losses from loans. Real estate values also dropped in the mid-1980s, especially in southwestern states.

Many banks and savings associations began losing money and a large number failed. Almost half of all savings associations failed in the 1980s, along with about 1,000 banks. Two federal deposit insurance agencies, the FDIC and the FSLIC, ran out of money to pay depositors in failed institutions. By the late 1980s, both the banking and savings-association industries were in deep trouble.

FIRREA was enacted following the savings and loan crisis of the late 1980s. The **Financial Institutions Reform, Recovery, and Enforcement Act (FIRREA)** was designed to reduce the risk of depository institutions and change the structure of banking agencies. FIRREA is commonly known as the *S & L bailout bill* because government funds were used to resolve the crisis.

FIRREA had two aims: to strengthen banks and savings associations and to clean up the large number of failed institutions. The major provisions of FIRREA were to:

- abolish the FSLIC;
- give the FDIC responsibility for insuring savings associations' deposits;
- replace the Federal Home Loan Bank Board with the Office of Thrift Supervision;
- increase regulations regarding lending, investments, and capital requirements for banks and savings associations;
- create the Resolution Trust Corporation (RTC) to sell assets of failed banks and savings associations; and
- authorize additional funds for the FDIC to pay depositors of failed banks and savings associations.

It took several years after FIRREA for banks and savings associations to gain a solid footing. Today, FIRREA is considered a success because few savings associations have failed since it was set up.

Source: Library of Congress

Depositors gather at a failing bank during a bank run.

The FDIC did not perform as well as it should have during the S & L crisis. To make sure this was not repeated, the FDICIA was passed by Congress in 1991. The major purpose of the **Federal Depository Insurance Corporation Improvement Act (FDICIA)** was to provide additional funding for the FDIC. The act required banks and savings associations that were considered riskier to pay higher insurance premiums for deposit insurance from the FDIC. It also included specific actions the FDIC must take when banks and savings associations start having problems.

Sarbanes-Oxley Act

In 2001, several major corporations failed, which triggered another financial crisis. The failed companies included Enron, Tyco, Arthur Andersen, and WorldCom. These were large businesses that had many investors and employees, all of which appeared quite successful just a few months before they failed. However, after they failed, it was discovered that these companies were using unusual accounting methods. This was done to make the companies look more profitable than they actually were. As a result, it was difficult for investors and others to determine the companies' true financial conditions.

The **Sarbanes-Oxley Act (SOX)** was passed in 2002 to ensure more accurate disclosure of a company's financial information. By mandating greater transparency and accountability, Congress sought to stop the potential recurrence of major corporate failures. Accountants must now follow very strict standards in preparing financial statements. The law requires financial reports to be prepared by outside accountants that have no other ties to the company. It also increases the penalties for anyone who distorts accounting statements or misleads investors.

Although banks were not the target of the Sarbanes-Oxley Act, they are still affected by the law. Most banks are corporations, and all corporations must comply with the provisions of Sarbanes-Oxley. Some believe that it makes it much easier for an investor or a customer to judge the financial strength of a bank. Others believe the act has little benefit and results in unneeded work for corporations.

Ethical Banking

Today, many banks are increasing the number of independent directors who do not work for the bank or borrow from it. They are more likely to question management decisions and take action if needed. Although many banks had capable directors prior to Sarbanes-Oxley, this act pushed many banks into having a more ethical and responsible board of directors.

Checkpoint 6.1

1. List four factors that lead to the many bank failures during the Great Depression.
2. What were two goals of the Glass-Steagall Act?
3. How did the Glass-Steagall Act affect interest rates?
4. Name two federal agencies that were eliminated under the FIRREA.
5. What is the major purpose of the Sarbanes-Oxley Act?

Build Your Vocabulary

As you progress through this course, develop a personal glossary of banking terms and add it to your portfolio. This will help you build your banking vocabulary. Write out a definition for each of the following terms, and add it to your personal glossary.

bank run
Emergency Banking Act of 1933
Glass-Steagall Act
interest rate ceiling
Federal Home Loan Bank Board
Financial Institutions Reform, Recovery, and Enforcement Act (FIRREA)
Federal Depository Insurance Corporation Improvement Act (FDICIA)
Sarbanes-Oxley Act (SOX)

Section 6.2
Consumer Regulations

Objectives

After completing this section, you will be able to:

- Describe the regulations that govern consumer credit.
- Explain the need for regulations that focus on fair access to credit.

Terms

Consumer Financial Protection Bureau (CFPB)
Consumer Credit Protection Act
Truth in Lending Act (TILA)
annual percentage rate (APR)
finance charge
Fair Credit Reporting Act (FCRA)
Fair Credit Billing Act (FCBA)
Credit CARD Act
Community Reinvestment Act (CRA)
redlining
Home Mortgage Disclosure Act (HMDA)
Equal Credit Opportunity Act (ECOA)

Protecting Borrowers

The Dodd-Frank Wall Street Reform and Consumer Protection Act of 2010 created a new consumer-protection agency as part of the Department of the Treasury. The **Consumer Financial Protection Bureau (CFPB)** was created to protect the interests of consumers by making sure federal consumer-protection laws are enforced. In addition, the CFPB is charged with promoting financial literacy, watching for market trends that might have a negative effect on consumers, and encouraging fair lending practices.

Truth in Lending Act

A major consumer-protection law, the **Consumer Credit Protection Act,** was enacted in 1968. Today, this law is known as the **Truth in Lending Act (TILA).** It requires every lender to provide the borrower with information about the cost of credit. This act applies not only to banks, but also to all lenders who extend credit to consumers, such as retail stores. An amendment to TILA is called the *Fair Credit and Charge Card Disclosure Act.* It requires direct mail or telephone offers for credit cards to include specific information regarding fees. The Consumer Financial Protection Bureau enforces the provisions of the Truth in Lending Act.

The two most important disclosures required by the Truth in Lending Act are the annual percentage rate and the total finance charges on a loan. The purpose of these disclosures is to increase the borrower's awareness of the true cost of getting a loan. Figure 6-4 shows what a

Annual Percentage Rate	Finance Charge	Amount Financed	Total Payments
The cost of your credit at a yearly rate	The dollar amount the credit will cost you	The amount of credit provided to you or on your behalf	The amount you will have paid after you have made all payments as scheduled
%	$	$	$

Figure 6-4.
Truth in Lending Act Disclosure Form

standard disclosure form looks like. If consumers have this information, they can shop more wisely for credit and obtain credit at the lowest rate. The Truth in Lending Act makes it possible for borrowers to compare loans from different lenders. The annual percentage rate, often referred to as APR, can be one such point of comparison for consumers.

Annual Percentage Rate

The **annual percentage rate (APR)** is the actual or true rate of interest paid over the life of a loan. APR is calculated on single-payment loans using the formula shown in Figure 6-5.

It is easy to compare loans on the basis of APR, even if the loans are for different terms. Suppose you want to borrow $1,000.

- Bank A will loan you the $1,000 for six months (180 days), and you must repay the $1,000 plus $50 interest at the end of the six months.
- Bank B will loan you the $1,000 for three months (90 days), and you must repay the $1,000 plus $27.50 interest at the end of the term.

At first glance, it looks as though Bank B is the best deal as you pay less interest. But compare the APRs of the two loans.

Bank A

$$\text{APR} = \frac{\$50}{1{,}000} \times \frac{360}{180} = .05 \times 2 = .10 = 10\%$$

Bank B

$$\text{APR} = \frac{\$27.50}{1{,}000} \times \frac{360}{90} = .0275 \times 4 = .11 = 11\%$$

APR allows borrowers to quickly see which loan really has the lowest actual interest rate. In this case, the loan from Bank A has the lowest APR. Borrowers do not have to calculate APR for themselves. All loan contracts must state the APR.

Finance Charges

Finance charges must also be disclosed under the Truth in Lending Act. **Finance charges** are the total dollar amount of interest and any other fees paid on the loan. Fees include late-payment fees, pay-by-phone fees, skip-a-payment fees, or any other fee associated with the agreement. Another way to compare loans is by comparing the finance charges. Some borrowers like knowing the total amount of money they will pay to get a loan rather than the effective interest rate.

$$\text{APR} = \frac{\text{Total interest paid}}{\text{Loan amount}} \times \frac{\text{360 days}}{\text{Length of loan in days}}$$

Note: Although there are 365 days in a year, the figure 360 is more commonly used in financial calculations because all months are considered to have 30 days.

Figure 6-5.
Calculating APR

In addition to APR and finance charges, the Truth in Lending Act requires other items be disclosed to the borrower:

- total sales price
- amount financed
- total payments
- schedule of payments
- prepayment policies
- late payment policies

The Truth in Lending Act requires that APR and finance charges can be easily located within loan documents. Generally, APR and finance charges are in bold print and have boxes around them to be quickly located by borrowers.

BIZ TIPS

Usury is charging extremely high interest rates. It is unethical and illegal. The legal limit on interest rates varies by state and situation.

Fair Credit Reporting Act

To apply for credit, consumers must provide private and sensitive information to lenders. The **Fair Credit Reporting Act (FCRA),** passed in 1970, protects consumer credit information. The rights of consumers must be balanced with the needs of those who use consumer-credit information to make credit decisions. The FCRA establishes these consumer rights concerning credit information:

- Individuals must be told what information a credit bureau has and who has access to it.
- Individuals must be told of information that has been used to deny them credit.
- Individuals can dispute any information a credit bureau retains that is false or inaccurate.
- Inaccurate information must be corrected or deleted.
- Information reported by credit bureaus must be no more than seven years old, or, in the case of bankruptcies, no more than ten years old.
- Access to credit information kept by credit bureaus is strictly limited to certain entities and for certain purposes.
- Employers can only receive credit information and reports containing medical information if authorized by the individual.

Fair Credit Billing Act

The **Fair Credit Billing Act (FCBA)** of 1974 protects consumers from unfair billing practices and provides a way to correct billing errors. It was passed in response to increasing problems in credit card accounts. For example, in the early days of credit cards, many banks sent unsolicited cards to customers. If these cards were stolen, the person whose name was on the card was still responsible for any charges the thief made.

The FCBA allows consumers to dispute billing errors by sending a written notice to the creditor. If there is an error on an account statement, the customer has 60 days to dispute the error and notify the creditor. Examples of billing errors include:

- charges not made by the customer;
- charges in the wrong amount;
- charges for goods not received;

Source: Shutterstock (AVAVA)

There are many regulations in place to protect consumers and their money.

- charges for goods that were damaged on delivery;
- failure to properly reflect payments made on an account; and
- calculation errors.

After receiving notice of a dispute by a customer, the creditor must acknowledge the dispute within 30 days. Any error must be corrected within 90 days. If there is no error, the consumer must be notified within 90 days. The FCBA contains additional regulations, including:

- banks may not use money in checking or savings accounts to pay a delinquent credit card with the same bank; and
- customers may withhold payment if goods are damaged upon receipt.

Credit CARD Act

In 2009, Congress passed the Credit Card Accountability, Responsibility, and Disclosure Act, commonly known as the Credit CARD Act. The **Credit CARD Act** protects consumers from unfair and deceptive credit card practices. The act also gives credit cardholders additional rights as well as more disclosure of important information. The key elements of the Credit CARD Act provide that credit card issuers must:

- not increase rates on existing balances except for a few exceptions;
- give cardholders a reasonable time to pay the monthly bill, at least 21 days from time of mailing;
- calculate interest fairly;
- receive customer approval for transactions that place the account over the credit limit;
- state account terms and statement information clearly and display this information in highly visible locations;
- disclose how long it will take to pay off the existing balance and total interest cost if only the minimum payment is paid each month;
- state what monthly payment amount is necessary to pay off the existing balance in 36 months and the total interest cost to the cardholder;
- disclose connections between card issuers and colleges;
- not offer gifts to college students for signing up for credit within 1,000 feet of campus; and
- limit the ability of those younger than 21 to receive credit cards.

This act provides greater access to credit card information and ensures greater accountability by card issuers.

BIZ TIPS

Most credit cards are issued by banks or other depository institutions. Although credit cards may bear the logo of Visa or MasterCard, they are actually issued by banks. The leading banks in the US for issuing credit cards are Bank of America, Chase, Citigroup, Capital One, and HSBC Bank.

Source: Shutterstock (Elzbieta Sekowska)

It is illegal for lenders to discriminate against credit applicants based on gender, race, age, or other factors.

Promoting and Ensuring Fair Access to Credit

The **Community Reinvestment Act (CRA),** passed in 1977, prevents redlining. **Redlining** occurs when a lender draws an imaginary red line on a map around one part of a community and does not make loans in that area. Under the CRA, banks and other depository institutions must be able to show that they are serving the credit needs of all people in their market area. Prior to this act, some lenders were taking in deposits in one location, often a poor area, and using those deposits to make loans in another location, often a more prosperous area.

The law does not require a specific number of loans to be made in a community, but looks at each bank's individual situation. Nor does the CRA require a bank to make higher-risk loans in certain areas. Instead, a bank should make as many good loans as possible within its service area.

The **Home Mortgage Disclosure Act (HMDA)** requires most mortgage-lending institutions to report data related to mortgage loans. No provision of this act requires loans be made in a particular area. Instead, it allows for greater transparency in lending.

In 1974, Congress passed the Equal Credit Opportunity Act. The **Equal Credit Opportunity Act (ECOA)** makes it illegal for any lender to use these factors when determining whether someone should get a loan:

- gender
- marital status
- race
- religion
- age
- national origin
- whether an individual's income is from public assistance benefits

In addition, lenders cannot use this information when setting the terms of a loan. For example, it is illegal to charge Wanda a higher interest rate than Philip would be charged simply because she is a woman. All credit decisions must be based solely on financial information such as income and credit history. The Consumer Financial Protection Bureau enforces the ECOA.

Under the act, you must be notified within 30 days after you file a completed credit application if your application was rejected or accepted. In addition, you have the right to know why you have been denied credit. Creditors must notify you of the reason for your rejection within 60 days of your application. You are also entitled to a free credit report if you are turned down for a loan.

While you must still pass the creditor's tests of creditworthiness to receive credit, the Equal Credit Opportunity Act ensures that a lender's credit tests are applied fairly and based on solid financial reasons.

BIZ TIPS

Under the Dodd-Frank Wall Street Reform and Consumer Protection Act of 2010, loan customers can now get their credit score along with a free credit report if they are denied a loan. A credit score is often used as a factor when granting a loan. A borrower can now see what his or her credit score is and what items are affecting it.

Careers in Finance
Banking and Related Services

What Does a Compliance Officer Do?

A **compliance officer** is a very important position in the operations of a bank. The **compliance officer** serves as the advisor to the bank to make sure that policies and procedures follow all federal and state regulations. Some of the activities performed by **compliance officers** include:

- recommending bank policy changes to meet changes in federal bank regulations;
- reviewing a bank's policies, procedures, records, and reports to confirm bank compliance;
- preparing reports on a bank's operations; and
- providing training for employees within the bank to ensure bank regulations are met.

What Is It Like to Work as a Compliance Officer?

Compliance officers generally work in the corporate headquarters of a bank, rarely in branch locations. They must be able to understand complex legal requirements as well as accounting statements. Attention to detail is critical.

Compliance officers are often considered part of top management and are well compensated. As part of the management team, long hours may be required.

If you possess strong communication skills, enjoy performing research, and like the prospect of conducting detailed investigations, a career as a **compliance officer** might suit you.

What Education and Skills Are Needed to Be a Compliance Officer?

- bachelor degree in finance or a related field; master degree in business administration is frequently required
- certification such as Certified Bank Compliance Officer (CBCO) or Certified Regulatory and Compliance Professional (CRCP).
- ability to lead and make sound decisions

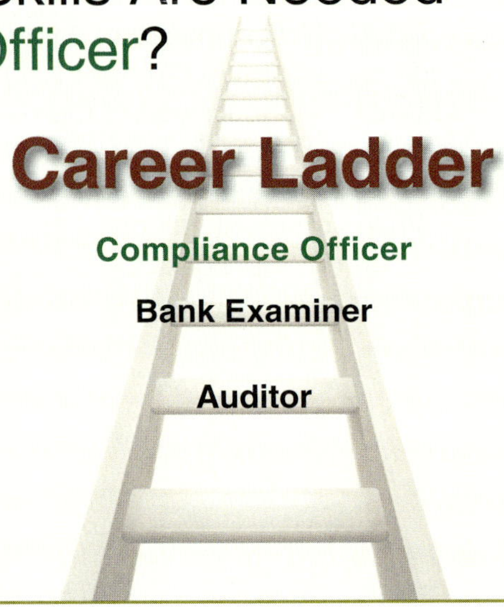

Checkpoint 6.2

1. What are the two most important disclosures that are required under the Truth in Lending Act?
2. What is the purpose of the Fair Credit Reporting Act?
3. According to the Fair Credit Billing Act, how long does a consumer have to dispute an error on his or her account statement?
4. Which law requires that credit card issuers state the monthly payment amount necessary to pay off a cardholder's existing balance in 36 months?
5. Under the Equal Credit Opportunity Act, lenders may not discriminate against potential borrowers based on what factors?

Build Your Vocabulary

As you progress through this course, develop a personal glossary of banking terms and add it to your portfolio. This will help you build your banking vocabulary. Write out a definition for each of the following terms, and add it to your personal glossary.

Consumer Financial Protection Bureau (CFPB)
Consumer Credit Protection Act
Truth in Lending Act (TILA)
annual percentage rate (APR)
finance charge
Fair Credit Reporting Act (FCRA)
Fair Credit Billing Act (FCBA)
Credit CARD Act
Community Reinvestment Act (CRA)
redlining
Home Mortgage Disclosure Act (HMDA)
Equal Credit Opportunity Act (ECOA)

Section 6.3
Recent Banking

Terms

deregulation
Depository Institutions Deregulation and Monetary Control Act (DIDMCA)
negotiable order of withdrawal (NOW) account
Garn-St. Germain Act
money market deposit account (MMDA)
Interstate Banking Act
branching
McFadden Act
Gramm-Leach-Bliley Act
dual banking system
e-compliance

Objectives

After completing this section, you will be able to:

- Compare and contrast deregulation laws.
- Explain the importance of compliance in the banking industry.

Deregulation

As you have read, many bank regulations initially focused on keeping banks from failing. But, in the late 1970s, banks started failing again. Many consumers blamed excessive regulation because they thought it made banks less competitive by restricting their business. As a result, a movement was started to deregulate the banking industry. **Deregulation** is the act of removing regulations and emphasizing less governmental control.

Due to deregulation, the banking industry had increased flexibility in the:

- services it offered;
- locations where banks operated; and
- rates paid to depositors.

Banks were also able to engage in new ventures that were previously prohibited, such as selling insurance products.

Deregulation is a double-edged sword. It has created more opportunities for banks to make money, but has also allowed more risk into the financial system. Many of the products and services now open to banks carry a higher risk than traditional banking activities. In addition, banks are now entering areas in which they have less expertise, which also increases their risk.

Source: Shutterstock (Yuri Arcurs)

Today, banks are offering more services due to deregulation of the industry.

Depository Institutions Deregulation and Monetary Control Act (DIDMCA)

For many years, Congress, the regulatory agencies, and the banking industry discussed reducing bank regulations. In 1980, the **Depository Institutions Deregulation and Monetary Control Act (DIDMCA)** was enacted to reduce regulations on depository institutions. The law removed many of the regulations that were passed during the Great Depression. Interest rate ceilings on savings and time deposits were phased out, allowing depository institutions to pay whatever interest rate they chose. Checking accounts that could earn interest were also allowed. **Negotiable order of withdrawal (NOW) accounts** are checking accounts that can pay interest.

The DIDMCA allowed depository institutions to make more types of loans and investments. Savings associations, for example, could now make some consumer loans and offer credit cards.

Federal deposit insurance, offered by the FDIC, FSLIC, and National Credit Union Association (NCUA), was increased from $40,000 to $100,000 per depositor. Many customers had taken some of their money out of depository institutions prior to the DIDMCA to keep it safe. Now, they could deposit more money in the bank and not worry about losing any if the bank failed.

Initially, there was great praise for the DIDMCA. Banks and other depository institutions saw an increase in deposits as well as profits from new products offered. However, the new products brought new risk. By the end of the 1980s, bank failures increased and many felt that the DIDMCA had gone too far in reducing regulation.

Garn-St. Germain Act

Banks and other depository institutions were further deregulated in 1982 with the Garn-St. Germain Act. The law came at a time when a number of savings associations were having severe financial problems. The **Garn-St. Germain Act** reduced bank regulations further and made it easier to save failing banks and savings associations.

A key provision of the act allowed depository institutions to offer **money market deposit accounts (MMDAs).** These deposit accounts are nearly the same as money market mutual funds (MMMFs), except MMDAs are FDIC-insured. Both of these types of deposit accounts are a combination of checking and savings accounts. They:

- offer some check writing privileges (usually limited to three checks per month);
- have no maturity;
- pay interest like a savings account, but often offer higher interest rates than regular savings accounts; and
- may require higher minimum amounts to open the account, often $2,500.

At the time of the passage of the Garn-St. Germain Act, many people were pulling money out of savings accounts and putting it in money market mutual funds. Many MMMFs were offering rates over 15% in 1982. Individuals could get higher rates and the convenience of writing checks on these accounts. MMDAs were designed to compete with money market mutual funds so customers would leave their money in depository institutions.

The Garn-St. Germain Act also allowed depository institutions to acquire other depository institutions that were failing, regardless of where they were located. Prior to the law, many states did not let outside institutions operate within the state. For example, if a Louisiana bank was failing and a Texas bank wanted to acquire it, the Texas bank would have been unable to take it over, because it was located outside of Louisiana. Under the Garn-St. Germain Act, state laws that prevented failing banks from being acquired by banks outside of the state they operated in

Source: Shutterstock (Valvua Vitaly)

Online banking has made issues related to branch banking less relevant.

were abolished. This allowed for more mergers and acquisitions and ensured that more failing institutions could be saved.

Interstate Banking and Branching Efficiency Act

In 1994, Congress passed the Riegle-Neal Interstate Banking and Branching Efficiency Act, commonly known as the Interstate Banking Act. The **Interstate Banking Act** eliminates most restrictions on interstate bank branching. **Branching** is opening banking facilities away from a bank's home office. The law effectively overrode the 1927 McFadden Act. The **McFadden Act** gave individual states the right to set their own rules regarding out-of-state banks coming into the state. From 1927 to 1994, the federal government stayed out of the branching laws of states, except for allowing some mergers under the Garn-St. Germain Act.

Many states had laws that did not allow any outside banks to conduct business within the state. Some states only allowed an out-of-state institution to enter the state if the arrangement was reciprocal. A *reciprocal agreement* means that out-of-state banks will be permitted if both states allow it. For instance, if Georgia permits Florida banks to operate in Georgia only if Florida permits Georgia banks to operate in Florida, this is a reciprocal agreement.

In 1994, there were still 36 states that had some restrictions on allowing out-of-state banks to open branches in the state. The Interstate Banking Act essentially eliminated all barriers to interstate banking. It allowed banks to open branches anywhere in the United States.

BIZ TIPS

After the Interstate Banking Act was passed, the first truly national US bank emerged. In 1998, NationsBank, which was based in North Carolina, acquired BankAmerica Corp, which started in California. The new bank took the name Bank of America and is headquartered in Charlotte, North Carolina. Bank of America has branches all across the country.

Gramm-Leach-Bliley Act

In 1999, Congress passed the Financial Services Modernization Act, known as the Gramm-Leach-Bliley Act. The act repealed several key provisions of the Glass-Steagall Act. The **Gramm-Leach-Bliley Act** allows banks to engage in almost any financial activity, including investment banking, insurance, and securities trading.

Although banks were allowed to participate in investment banking, insurance, and securities in a limited fashion before the Gramm-Leach-Bliley Act, this law increased the degree to which banks can offer these services. Banks now have relatively unlimited access to any financial area. Banks benefit from being involved in other financial services in three ways:

- the ability to better serve customer needs
- increased profitability as insurance, investment banking, and securities trading are often good sources of income
- reduced risk through diversification, since a bank is not tied to one activity

Now that banks have more freedom to pursue these activities, more consolidation is occurring between banks, securities firms, and insurance companies. Since the law was passed, many large banks have either acquired or merged with other financial companies. As a result, banks are getting larger as they offer other financial services in addition to their traditional banking business.

The Gramm-Leach-Bliley Act also required banks to safeguard the private financial information of all of their customers. Banks must disclose their policies for sharing information with other institutions. Customers may limit the access of third parties to their information in some cases.

BIZ TIPS

The Bank Secrecy Act and USA Patriot Act require banks to report suspicious customer activities that might signify criminal activities, such as money laundering or tax evasion.

Compliance

Our bank regulatory system is often referred to as a **dual banking system** because both states and the federal government pass and enforce bank laws. Regulatory change comes from legislation. There are several federal agencies that enforce bank laws and conduct bank examinations on a regular basis. The Federal Reserve, FDIC, Office of the Comptroller of the Currency, and the National Credit Union Association are all actively engaged in overseeing depository institutions. In addition, each state has a state banking agency that enforces state laws and may also examine banks.

Banks spend a great deal of time and money to ensure they comply with bank regulations, many of which are quite complex. Customers do not see the amount of effort banks expend to keep the bank in compliance with all of the banking laws in effect today. Functional areas of compliance for banks include:

- advertising;
- anti-money laundering;
- the Bank Secrecy Act;
- depository operations;
- lending;
- loan servicing; and
- loss prevention.

Source: Shutterstock (Goodluz)

Though banking has been deregulated, banks strive to comply with the regulations that are still in place.

Keeping the bank in compliance with so many regulations requires a strong compliance plan. Such a plan should:

- identify areas of high risk;
- establish internal controls;
- provide for an audit of the system by an outside source on an ongoing basis;
- assign someone in the organization to manage all compliance matters, usually called a compliance officer;
- provide training to all staff working in areas where compliance is an issue; and
- set up a system to verify bank customer identity.

After the terrorist attacks on September 11, 2001, bank compliance regulations were greatly increased.

Another factor that has affected banks is the extent to which transactions take place in an electronic environment. Managing risk associated with this environment is called **e-compliance.** Privacy, record keeping and storage, and protection from hackers are among the areas with which e-compliance is concerned.

Checkpoint 6.3

1. Why did a movement to deregulate banks start in the 1980s?
2. How much was federal deposit insurance under DIDMCA?
3. What is the difference between money market deposit accounts (MMDAs) and money market mutual funds (MMMFs)?
4. Which law did the Interstate Banking Act override?
5. What are the functional areas of bank compliance?

Build Your Vocabulary

As you progress through this course, develop a personal glossary of banking terms and add it to your portfolio. This will help you build your banking vocabulary. Write out a definition for each of the following terms, and add it to your personal glossary.

deregulation
Depository Institutions Deregulation and Monetary Control Act (DIDMCA)
negotiable order of withdrawal (NOW) account
Garn-St. Germain Act
money market deposit account (MMDA)
Interstate Banking Act
branching
McFadden Act
Gramm-Leach-Bliley Act
dual banking system
e-compliance

Chapter Summary

Section 6.1 Banking Regulations

- Many conditions and circumstances led to a collapse of the banking system at the beginning of the Great Depression.
- The Glass-Steagall Act was designed to prevent large-scale bank failures, as was seen in the Great Depression.
- The FIRREA and FDICIA restructured regulatory agencies of savings associations as well as the FDIC.
- The Sarbanes-Oxley Act provides for complete and accurate financial information about a company so investors, employees, and others can make informed decisions.

Section 6.2 Consumer Regulations

- The Truth in Lending Act gives borrowers the true cost of loans and a way to compare loans.
- The Equal Opportunity Act made sure that lenders did not discriminate when granting credit to borrowers.

Section 6.3 Recent Banking

- The DIDMCA eliminated many provisions of the Glass-Steagall Act to make banks more competitive.
- Maintaining compliance with bank regulations is a major concern of banks.

Check Your Banking IQ

Now that you have finished this chapter, see what you know about banking by taking the chapter post test.

www.m.g-wlearning.com
www.g-wlearning.com

Review Your Knowledge

On a separate sheet of paper or in a word processing document, match the following terms with the definition that fits best.

A. Consumer Financial Protection Bureau (CFPB)

B. negotiable order of withdrawal (NOW) account

C. Federal Home Loan Bank Board

D. dual banking system

E. Federal Depository Insurance Corporation Improvement Act (FDICIA)

F. redlining

G. Banking Act of 1933

H. Home Mortgage Disclosure Act (HMDA)

I. e-compliance

J. McFadden Act

1. Allowed under DIDMCA.
2. Prevented by the Community Reinvestment Act of 1977.
3. Created by the Dodd-Frank Wall Street Reform and Consumer Protection Act of 2010.
4. Managing risk associated with banking transactions that occur in an electronic environment.
5. The Glass-Steagall Act.
6. Provided additional funding for the FDIC.
7. Chartered and examined savings associations.
8. Overrode by the Interstate Banking Act.
9. Requires most mortgage lending institutions to report data related to mortgage loans.
10. Both states and the federal government pass and enforce bank laws.

On a separate sheet of paper or in a word processing document, answer each of the following questions.

11. In addition to the APR and total finance charges of a loan, what other information must be revealed to borrowers under the Truth in Lending Act?
12. How can a bank run cause a bank to fail?
13. What is redlining, and why did Congress outlaw it under the CRA?
14. Under the Credit CARD Act, when can credit card issuers allow over-limit transactions?
15. What are four components of a strong compliance plan for a bank?

Apply Your Knowledge

16. Using the FDIC website, research how many banks failed last year. Prepare a chart listing the name of the bank, the amount of total assets, the amount of total deposits, and, if the bank was taken over, what entity assumed all of its deposits.
17. Working in teams, research your state banking agency. Prepare a summary listing the major responsibilities of the agency and a graphic organizer showing the structure of the agency.
18. The Credit CARD Act requires credit card issuers to disclose how long it will take the cardholder to pay off the current balance if only the minimum payment is made. Write a paragraph describing what effect you think this requirement has on cardholders, if any, and why.
19. Decide if you are in favor of bank deregulation or not. Outline the main reasons for your position. Be prepared to defend your position in a group or class discussion.
20. Create a flowchart tracking the major developments in banking regulations. Make sure your flowchart covers the years from the Great Depression to the present time and includes at least five main points.

Working in Teams

Working with a classmate, discuss the regulations that apply to banks today. Using the guidelines provided in the text, develop a compliance plan for a bank. Prepare a document explaining your compliance plan, and present it to the class, allowing your classmates to comment on the effectiveness of your plan.

G-W Learning Mobile Site

Visit the G-W Learning mobile site to complete the chapter pretest and post test and to practice vocabulary using e-flash cards. If you do not have a smartphone, visit the G-W Learning companion website to access these features.

G-W Learning mobile site: www.m.g-wlearning.com
G-W Learning companion website: www.g-wlearning.com

Common Core

College and Career Readiness

Listening. Research the positives and negatives of abolishing the Federal Reserve. Using the Internet, find video footage of at least three speeches or news broadcasts that discuss this topic. Compare and contrast the speakers' information, points of view, and opinions. How are they similar and different? Using the information presented, decide whether you are for or against abolishing the Federal Reserve System.

Speaking. Working in small groups, develop a list of regulations that you would like to have in your classroom and your reasoning for each one. Develop a presentation in which you attempt to persuade your classmates to adopt your regulations. Then, develop a separate presentation in which you attempt to persuade your teacher, acting as a member of the school board, to adopt your regulations. How will you alter your presentations for these two different audiences?

EVENT PREP Job Interviewing

Job interviewing is a competitive event you might enter with your career and technical student organization (CTSO). By participating in the job interview, you will be able to showcase your presentation skills, communication talents, and ability to actively listen to the questions asked by the interviewers. For this event, you will be expected to write a letter of application, create a résumé, and complete an application. You will also be interviewed by an individual or panel. To prepare for a job interviewing event:

1. Visit the Career and Technical Student Organizations (CTSOs) for guidelines on topics that may be selected. This is usually a timed event you can prepare for before the competition. You will have time to research, prepare, and practice before going to the competition. Review the specific guidelines and rules for this event for direction as to topics and props you will be allowed to use.
2. Review the interviewing techniques presented in this chapter.
3. Write your letter of application, create your résumé, and complete the application (if provided for this event).
4. Solicit feedback from your peers, teachers, and parents.
5. Make certain that each piece of communication is complete and free of errors.

Unit 2
Summative Assessment

On a separate sheet of paper or in a word processing document, use what you have learned in this unit to answer the questions that follow.

True/False Questions

1. *True or False?* The Federal Open Market Committee (FOMC) is the governing body of the Federal Reserve System.
2. *True or False?* Both states and the federal government pass and enforce bank laws.
3. *True or False?* The exchange of money requires a coincidence of wants.
4. *True or False?* Over 9,000 banks failed during the Great Depression.
5. *True or False?* The prime rate is the rate that banks pay to borrow money from a Federal Reserve Bank.

Multiple Choice Questions

6. Which of the following does not apply to the Second Bank of the US?
   A. Much larger than the First Bank.
   B. Chartered in 1791.
   C. The bank's existence was challenged from the beginning.
   D. Started with $35 million and 25 branches.
7. Which type of currency do we currently use in the US?
   A. Commodity money.
   B. Representative money.
   C. Fiat money.
   D. None of the above.
8. Which of the following is not an example of the money multiplier effect?
   A. A small increase in deposits leading to a much larger increase in the money supply.
   B. The Federal Reserve purchases a small amount of securities, hoping they will increase the money supply by a larger amount.
   C. The Federal Reserve sells some securities, but loses the potential for making loans with that money.
   D. The Federal Reserve stimulates the economy by increasing the money supply.
9. Which of the following does not apply to money market mutual funds (MMMFs)?
   A. Offer some check writing privileges and have no maturity.
   B. Insured by the FDIC.
   C. Pay interest like savings accounts, but often with higher interest rates than regular savings accounts.
   D. May require a higher minimum amount to open an account.
10. A uniform national currency was created by the _____.
    A. Office of the Comptroller of the Currency (OCC)
    B. Sarbanes-Oxley Act (SOX)
    C. National Bank Act
    D. Federal Deposit Insurance Corporation (FDIC)

Unit 3

Customer Services

What You Will Learn

Savings, Lending, and Payments are not only the chapter titles for this unit—they are also the activities that financial institutions help consumers to carry out. In this role, banks act as intermediaries. They take in money to safeguard and grow it. They lend the money they receive in deposits to worthy borrowers so that they can pay interest to depositors. Powered by technology, financial institutions help consumers make payments and ensure vendors are paid. In this unit, you will learn how financial institutions carry out these important functions.

Source: Shutterstock (mangostock)

Explore what you can do with the money you earn.

Source: Shutterstock (oliveromg)

Discover how saving money can help you accomplish a goal.

Biz Kid$ in Action

Student Steve has enjoyed banking with his local bank ever since he opened his first savings account at the age of seven. The customer service has always been terrific, and his questions have always been answered. The branch manager even knows him by first name!

Student Steve has tried hard to save enough to finish college, using his savings account and then transferring money to CDs and other investments that yield higher interest. The bank has always been there to help him make the right choice. However, he does not quite have enough to finish college, so he asked his bank for a student loan. Luckily, due to his long-term relationship with the bank, the bank knows Steve is prudent with his money.

The bank has even counseled Student Steve on the smart use of credit. After Steve saw his sister destroy her credit score by being careless, he knows he needs to be more careful with his own finances. Securing this student loan and paying it off on time will help him build a good credit score.

Banking Bits

Shopping for a bank is just like shopping for anything else. Different lenders charge different fees and interest rates. Nowadays, it is pretty easy to comparison shop for credit cards and loans using sites like www.cardratings.com and www.bankrate.com. Read the fine print and make sure you know what you are getting into. Also, be aware that credit unions often provide better rates than commercial banks.

Quick Tip! Don't apply for more credit cards than you need. Having too many credit cards, even if you don't use them, negatively impacts your credit score.

Let's get started! ⟶

Scan the code to view a Biz Kid$ video. If you do not have a smartphone, visit the G-W Learning companion website.

www.m.g-wlearning.com
www.g-wlearning.com

7

Check Your Banking IQ

Before you begin this chapter, see what you already know about banking by taking the chapter pretest.

www.m.g-wlearning.com
www.g-wlearning.com

Savings

Everyone faces the same question every day for every dollar in their hands: save it or spend it? Companies must answer the same question for larger amounts of money: save it or spend it? If a consumer chooses to save money, banks can offer a wide variety of options. Matching the customer's needs to the products a bank offers benefits the customer and the bank.

College and Career Readiness

Reading Prep. Think of some of your life goals. How are these goals affected by your personal finances? As you read the chapter, focus on how goals affect the savings habits of consumers.

Scan the code to view a Biz Kid$ video. If you do not have a smartphone, visit the G-W Learning companion website.

www.m.g-wlearning.com
www.g-wlearning.com

Section 7.1
Why Do Customers Save?

Objectives

After completing this section, you will be able to:

- Define savings goals.
- Explain how interest is earned.

Terms

savings
liquidity
interest
deposit
compound interest
principal
accrued interest
annual percentage yield (APY)

Savings Goals

Savings is the portion of income that is not spent. Why would a customer choose to save rather than spend? After all, the money is right there, just waiting to be spent. Customers save money to achieve a goal. The customer's goals determine how his or her income should be saved.

One aspect of a savings goal is the length of time that the customer will save the funds. Goals can be classified as short term or long term.

Source: Shutterstock (mangostock)

Buying a car is a short-term goal for many people.

Short-Term Savings Goals

Sometimes, customers are saving for a short-term goal. Jorge might choose to save money from each paycheck so he can pay his rent at the end of the month. Julia might save her money to buy a car in six months. The XYZ Company could be saving money for new equipment. Goals that can be accomplished in less than a year are short-term goals.

Customers saving for short-term goals will be interested in products that are safe and do not charge fees. If the customer loses money or pays a lot of fees, it will increase the length of time he or she will need to save. This could mean failing to accomplish the short-term savings goal.

Liquidity is the ability of a financial asset to be quickly converted into cash without any financial loss. Liquidity is important to those saving for a short-term goal. While a car is an asset, it is not liquid. It might take some time to find a buyer. On the other hand, if you put your money in a savings account, you are able to access your money quickly and without any loss to your initial investment. You may even make money in interest.

Convenience identifies the ease in getting money. Customers might want to stop by the bank or use an automatic teller machine (ATM) to access their cash. They do not want to fill out long forms or wait weeks to receive their cash.

BIZ TIPS

Losing money in a money market mutual fund is very rare. One share in these funds is valued at one dollar. However, if the fund's assets cannot cover the share price, because, for example, interest rates fall to a very low level, the fund "breaks the buck" and the share price falls below one dollar.

Interest is an amount charged to borrow money. In the case of savings, the bank is borrowing the money deposited by customers, so it pays interest to the account owners. Because a bank is a business that must earn more than it spends, it pays a lower interest rate to its account owners than customers pay to borrow money from the bank. To somebody saving for a short-term goal, the amount of interest earned is less important than liquidity. It is more important to the customer to keep the money safe and be able to access it quickly when it is needed.

Source: Shutterstock (hxdbzxy)

Long-term savings goals help consumers afford large expenses, such as going to college.

Long-Term Savings Goals

Customers also save for long-term goals. These are goals that take more than one year to accomplish. Long-term goals for individuals could include buying a house, retiring, and paying for a college education. Businesses might save to expand the business, open a new location, or help their employees retire.

Safety is not as important to customers with a long-term goal. Of course, no one wants to lose money, especially if it took a long time to save. However, if the goal is years away, the customer does not need immediate or frequent access to the funds. For a higher interest rate, a customer can agree to give up immediate access and leave the money untouched for a long period of time. This sacrifices some liquidity because he or she must pay a penalty fee to access the money early. If a customer's car breaks down and he or she has to withdraw money to get it fixed, part of the principal or earnings may be lost. This makes an early withdrawal a potentially expensive decision.

Liquidity is not as important when saving for a long-term goal. Because the customer is saving for a goal that will not occur for a long time, it is not necessary to access the funds until that time. If you begin saving for retirement when you are 20 years old and you plan to retire when you are 60 years old, you have 40 years to save before you need the money.

The convenience of getting your money is also less important for long-term savings goals. The ability to access the funds is not important if the customer does not plan to use the money for several years. For long-term savers, the ease of making deposits is more important than the convenience of withdrawing money.

The interest rate is more important to long-term savers because the account will earn interest for a long time. The interest earned makes the amount saved grow without any additional effort. A higher interest rate makes the amount grow more, which is obviously desirable over a long period of time.

When selecting a bank product, customers should consider their savings goals. Depending on the length of time they plan to save, customers will emphasize safety, liquidity, convenience, or interest earned, as shown in Figure 7-1.

Characteristics	Priorities	
	Short-term savings goals (less than one year)	Long-term savings goals (more than one year)
Safety	✓	✓
Liquidity	✓	
Convenience	✓	
Interest earned		✓

Figure 7-1.
Savers' Priorities

Interest Earned

When a customer makes a **deposit,** transferring money into the bank, it is not stored in a big, dark box until the customer comes back to claim it. The bank uses the customer's money to earn more money for itself. In order to use a customer's money, the bank pays a fee, which is known as interest. A major reason people use banks is because they can earn money while keeping their money safe. **Compound interest** is interest paid on interest. For example, if you open a bank account that pays an annual interest rate of 5% with an initial deposit of $500, after one year you will have $525 in your account, assuming you did not take out any of the money. The next year, interest is not only earned on **principal,** or your initial deposit, it is earned on the principal plus interest earned the previous year.

Compound interest is a powerful savings tool that uses accrued interest. **Accrued interest** is the amount added to the principal at regular time periods. The bank states its interest rate as an **annual percentage yield (APY),** the rate of return on an investment for a one-year period. You can use the APY to compare different interest rates at different financial institutions, regardless of any differences in when interest is accrued or compounded.

BIZ TIPS

Simple interest is interest paid only on the principal, not on the principal and accrued interest, as is the case with compound interest.

MONEY MATH

Year One

$500 (initial deposit) + $25 (5% interest earned after one year) = $525 (balance after one year)

Year Two

$525 (principal + accrued interest) + $26.25 (5% interest earned after one year) = $551.25

[$500 (principal) + $51.25 (accrued interest)] – $500 (initial deposit) = $51.25 (interest earned after two years at 5%)

Without making any additional deposits, the customer's money grew significantly. That is the power of compound interest. When you look at a time period this short, the power of compounding interest is not as impressive as it is over a longer term. Therefore, customers with short-term savings goals do not think the interest rate is as important as liquidity and convenience.

If the customer has long-term savings goals, the interest rate is more important. Banks usually offer higher interest rates on savings products for long-term savings. In most accounts, interest is compounded at least twice a year. It might be compounded monthly. The formula for calculating the result of compound interest when interest is compounded *annually* is shown in Figure 7-2.

Final amount → F; Rate of interest → r

$$F = P(1+r)^t$$

Principal → P; # of times compounded → t

Figure 7-2.
Compound Interest

Checkpoint 7.1

1. How long does it take to achieve a short-term goal?
2. What factors are most important to savers with short-term goals?
3. What factor is most important to savers with long-term goals?
4. Name the fee a bank pays to use a customer's money.
5. How often is interest compounded at most banks?

Build Your Vocabulary

As you progress through this course, develop a personal glossary of banking terms and add it to your portfolio. This will help you build your banking vocabulary. Write out a definition for each of the following terms, and add it to your personal glossary.

savings
liquidity
interest
deposit
compound interest
principal
accrued interest
annual percentage yield (APY)

Section 7.2
Savings Products

Objectives

After completing this section, you will be able to:

- Identify the types and characteristics of savings accounts.
- Describe the characteristics of a certificate of deposit.
- Explain the difference between savings accounts and certificates of deposit.

Terms

savings account
passbook
custodial account
money market account
certificate of deposit (CD)
time deposit
fixed deposit
mature
penalty
jumbo CD

Savings Accounts

Most banks offer savings accounts. A **savings account** is a deposit account at a depository institution that pays interest to the account owner. All savings accounts earn a low rate of interest. Customers can add money, withdraw money, or close the account at any time. The FDIC protects account owners from losses up to $250,000. Other characteristics, such as the amount of interest earned, how the customer accesses the account, and other minor details will differ among institutions and even among different types of savings accounts at the same institution.

A savings account is not a good choice for long-term savings because the interest rate is low. In 2011, an interest rate of .01% was common for savings accounts. However, a basic savings account is a safe, stable option to hold money before it is used for a short-term goal or moved to an account that earns more interest.

BIZ TIPS

There are no fundamental differences between business and personal savings accounts. The account types and interest rates are similar.

Types of Savings Accounts

Four basic types of savings accounts are offered at most banks: passbook savings accounts, online savings accounts, custodial accounts, and money market accounts.

Passbook Savings Accounts

A passbook savings account is the traditional savings account. It is known as a passbook account because the account owner is given a passbook when the account is opened. A **passbook** is a small book kept by the account owner. When the account owner comes into the bank to make a deposit or withdrawal, the transaction is recorded in the passbook.

Few banks or account owners rely on a passbook today. Instead, banks mail or e-mail a list of all transactions to the account owner at regular intervals. Account balances can also be viewed at automated teller machines (ATMs).

Source: Shutterstock (michaeljung)

Knowing how you want to use your money will help you choose the right account.

Online Savings Accounts

An online savings account is opened and used without visiting a physical location. The account owner visits a website, fills out some electronic forms, and transfers money into the account. Because the account owner never visits a physical location, all communication is done through the Internet or mail.

Online savings accounts allow customers to open accounts in other states or at a local bank. Thanks to the Internet, the locations of the bank and the customer do not matter. Banks now compete not only with other banks in the area, but with banks thousands of miles away.

Custodial Accounts

Custodial accounts are managed by an adult for a minor who is younger than 18 or 21 years old. Age requirements depend on the state's laws. The adult is usually a parent, grandparent, or legal guardian.

These accounts are often intended to teach children about the benefits of saving. The minor cannot withdraw money or close the account without the custodian present. The account's custodian must approve all transactions.

Money Market Accounts

A **money market account** is a savings account that pays a higher interest rate than a traditional savings account. The financial institution uses money from money market accounts to buy a variety of financial products. Because some of these purchases can be a little risky, the bank can earn more money on them.

A money market mutual account has restrictions on the number of withdrawals. There is also a minimum amount that must be kept in the account. This gives the bank more options for using the money to make a profit for itself. In some cases, banks offer accounts with a higher minimum balance in exchange for providing a higher interest rate on the account.

Savings Account Features

Banks compete for customers. In doing so, they offer products, like savings accounts, that offer features designed to attract deposits. Figure 7-3 outlines some common features and fees associated with savings accounts.

Green Banking

As environmental issues become more important in our society, banks have increased restrictions for loans that might involve environmental risks. When banks make loans to both individuals and corporations, background checks are completed to ensure there are no potential risks to the environment. These risks could impact the customer's ability to repay a loan, which means the bank would lose money.

Certificates of Deposit

For long-term goals, an account owner can purchase a **certificate of deposit (CD),** which requires that a specific amount of money be held on deposit for a specific amount of time. Because the length of time

Feature	Description
ATM fee	Customers may be charged if they use an automated teller machine belonging to an institution other than where they have their account.
Insured balance	A certain amount in an account owner's balance, in each bank, is insured by the FDIC.
Limited number of transactions	Transactions per a given period are limited.
Linked accounts	Connects the savings account to another account.
Minimum balance	The lowest amount of money needed to keep an account open. Banks will often charge fees if an account's balance drops below this amount.
Minimum deposit to open account	The lowest amount of money that can be used to open an account. The amount is usually $25 or more.
Monthly fee	Amount paid to the bank for account maintenance, which is often waived if the account does not fall below a minimum balance.
Online banking	Allows the account owner to access account information and make financial transactions on the Internet.
Transaction fee	Amount paid to the bank every time a transaction is made.

Figure 7-3.
Savings Accounts—Features and Fees

and amount are specified, or fixed, a CD is also known as a **time deposit** or a **fixed deposit.** When the fixed term expires, the CD is **mature.** After this time, the owner can withdraw his or her money without paying a **penalty,** a fee for breaking the account's terms.

A certificate of deposit pays the account owner a higher interest rate than a savings account because the bank knows exactly how much money is available for exactly how long. This is a big advantage to the bank because it can plan how it will earn the most profit by using the money. The higher interest rate paid to the customer is justified because the customer cannot access his or her money for months. Like money in a savings account, the money in a CD is insured by the FDIC. Therefore, it is considered to be a safe option for savers with a long-term goal.

As a savings tool, CDs are an attractive option for many reasons. Many of those reasons are similar to those of savings accounts. Others are unique to CDs or differ slightly:

- The interest rate is higher than that of a savings account.
- The balance, up to $250,000, is insured by the FDIC.
- The length of the deposit is fixed.
- A specified amount is needed to purchase.
- A fee is charged if a withdrawal is made before the date of maturity.

Terms, Amounts, and Interest Rates

As you might expect, the interest rate paid to customers is based on three things:

- the amount deposited
- the length of time
- competitors' interest rates

Customers should only purchase CDs if they have a significant amount of money that they are positive will not be needed for a long period of time. CDs usually require deposits of at least $1,000. Some institutions offer one-month CDs, but the shortest time period is usually about six months. The longest time period is about five years.

In 2011, a six-month CD paid a rate of 0.55% on average. That may not seem like a high rate. But, from a customer's perspective, it is much better than the .01% paid on a savings account.

Because a customer does not regularly access a CD, individuals and businesses often shop for the best interest rates. Customers can easily check rates on the Internet. To attract more deposits, banks offer interest rates that are similar to those of competing banks.

Source: Shutterstock (Supri Suharjoto)

Shopping around will help you find the best interest rates.

Jumbo CDs

A jumbo CD is just like it sounds, it is a big CD. A **jumbo CD** is a CD for a large amount of money, usually $100,000 or more. Because the amount is larger, interest rates are higher. In every other way, jumbo CDs are just like regular CDs.

Everyone does not have jumbo amounts of cash to place in CDs. Many customers purchasing jumbo CDs are businesses. They have large amounts of cash saved for a specific length of time. A jumbo CD is a safe option for them.

Essentially, CDs offer a higher interest rate to customers in exchange for the right to use the customer's money for a predefined length of time. This gives advantages to the bank and the customer. However, the customer is heavily penalized if he or she needs to break the terms of the agreement.

BIZ TIPS

The bank issuing the CD can redeem it, or *call it away,* before the CD matures. The CD's owner does not have this ability. A bank might call a CD if the interest rate drops before the CD matures. This enables the bank to issue the same CD to a different customer and pay a lower interest rate.

Comparing Savings Accounts and CDs

No savings account or CD is the perfect savings option for all people all of the time. Understanding the options your bank offers will improve your recommendations to customers and might improve your own financial status. Figure 7-4 compares the features of different types of savings accounts and CDs.

		Products					
		Passbook	**Online**	**Custodial**	**Money Market**	**CD**	**Jumbo CD**
Characteristics	**Interest rate**	Low	Low	Low	Medium	High	Highest
	Amount	Any amount	Any amount	Any amount	Minimum balance	Fixed	Fixed
	Time period	Short term	Short term	Short term	Short term	Fixed	Fixed
	Access	Any time	Any time	Any time	Limited	None	None

Figure 7-4.
Savings Vehicles

Checkpoint 7.2

1. Name three characteristics of a savings account.
2. What is the main advantage of an online savings account?
3. Why does a money market account earn more interest than a passbook savings account?
4. Why is a CD also known as a time deposit or a fixed deposit?
5. How is a jumbo CD different from a regular CD?

Build Your Vocabulary

As you progress through this course, develop a personal glossary of banking terms and add it to your portfolio. This will help you build your banking vocabulary. Write out a definition for each of the following terms, and add it to your personal glossary.

savings account
passbook
custodial account
money market account
certificate of deposit (CD)
time deposit
fixed deposit
mature
penalty
jumbo CD

Section 7.3
Retirement Accounts

Terms

retirement
Social Security
pension
defined benefit plan
individual retirement account (IRA)
compensation
contribution
distribution
benefits
defined contribution plan
Simplified Employee Pension (SEP)
SIMPLE IRA plan
401(k) plan

Objectives

After completing this section, you will be able to:

- Explain why it is necessary to save money for retirement.
- Describe the characteristics of an IRA.
- Differentiate among employee options for retirement planning.

Source: Shutterstock (Yuri Arcurs)

It's important to plan for retirement early.

Saving for Retirement

Does the idea of sitting on the beach watching the sun go down appeal to you? When you are studying and planning to start a new career, it is hard to believe that you will retire someday. If you are like most people, you will work for many years before you can retire. Saving and planning can make retirement a time to anticipate and enjoy. Banks and other financial institutions can help consumers reach their retirement goals.

Expectations

Retirement is a person's withdrawal from active participation in a job or business. A child born in the United States in 2011 has a life expectancy of 78 years. Most people quit working a full-time job long before they are 78 years old. But, if you stop working, how do you pay your bills? Without saving and planning, you will not be able pay for dinner, much less a view of the beach.

Historical Solutions

Social Security is a federal program that includes financial benefits intended to supplement retirement savings for Americans. The amount received depends on the income the retiree earned while working, the year when he or she was born, and the age he or she started to receive benefits. Social Security was enacted in 1935. Prior to this time, all of the money a person needed for retirement had to come from his or her own savings or from the company for which he or she worked.

In the past, employees often worked for the same company their entire career. As a reward for the employee's loyalty, many companies provided pensions. A **pension** is a fixed sum of money a company provides for its retired employees. Pensions are known as **defined benefit plans** because the money provided is a fixed amount defined by qualifications, such as years of service, not by company profit.

Today, the future of the Social Security program is debated. People do not work for the same company for their entire career. Fewer and fewer businesses provide pensions. People need to look for other solutions to ensure a comfortable retirement.

Ethical Banking

Social networking media is commonly used by banks to reach existing customers and find new ones. Because it is so available and easy to use, those who are writing communication for the organization must be ethical when using websites such as Facebook® or Twitter® for business purposes.

Individual Retirement Accounts (IRAs)

An **individual retirement account (IRA)** is a savings account in which income taxes are deferred on some deposits and all interest until all or part of the balance is withdrawn at retirement age. It is an interest-earning account that provides tax advantages. To open a traditional IRA and make deposits, customers must meet two legal requirements:

- The customer or the customer's spouse must have taxable compensation that year.
- The customer cannot be 70 1/2 years old by the end of the year the account is opened.

Compensation is the wages and financial benefits earned by working. It includes income from sources such as salary and income earned by owning a business. It does not include some income, such as interest earned or income that cannot be taxed.

For an IRA, deposits are known as **contributions.** Only a certain amount can be contributed each year. The money contributed can be deducted from your income before it is taxed. This is an important advantage because it reduces your income, which reduces the amount of income tax you pay. Before retirement, you make contributions to an IRA. Withdrawals from an IRA are known as **distributions.** The account owner *must* begin receiving cash from the IRA by April 1 the year after reaching the age of 70 1/2 years. If taken before age 59 1/2, there is a 10% penalty paid to the Internal Revenue Service (IRS). The money contributed to an IRA is not taxed at the time it is contributed.

Source: Shutterstock (Rob Marmion)

Contributions to IRAs are made prior to retirement

Roth IRA

A Roth IRA is similar to a traditional IRA. The long-term goal of saving money for retirement is identical, but the characteristics differ slightly and there are some restrictions to investigate. Contributions are not deducted from your income. Instead, contributing to a Roth IRA is just like any other expense. You can withdraw money from your Roth IRA if you are 59 1/2 years old and the Roth IRA has been open for at least five years.

The money placed in a Roth IRA is taxed when it is earned, rather than when it is distributed. You can continue to make contributions to a Roth IRA after you are 70 1/2 years old. A Roth IRA has a bonus feature, as well. You can withdraw money from a Roth IRA to buy a first home or pay for college tuition. However, this is not a good idea, because an IRA is a long-term savings vehicle. However, the flexibility this option offers can be valuable.

BIZ TIPS

The Roth IRA was established in the Taxpayer Relief Act of 1997. The IRA is named after Senate Finance Committee Chairman, Senator William V. Roth, Jr. The Taxpayer Relief Act of 1997 was intended to reduce tax rates and provide tax credits for all taxpayers.

Retirement Accounts Provided by Employers

Although most companies no longer provide pensions directly to retired employees for their entire lifetime, many provide benefits. **Benefits** are services or rights an employer provides for its employees. Benefits differ from company to company and employee to employee. Benefits are an important way to attract and retain good employees. The most common retirement benefits include Simplified Employee Pension (SEP), SIMPLE IRA, and 401(k). All of these can be provided by a financial institution.

These plans are considered **defined contribution plans,** because there is a fixed maximum amount that can be contributed each year. The contribution is not based on qualifications such as years of service or the expected retirement benefit.

Simplified Employee Pension (SEP)

A **Simplified Employee Pension (SEP)** is a retirement plan established by a business for its employees or owners. Self-employed individuals can set up an SEP for themselves.

In an SEP, the business makes contributions directly to the participants' SEP-IRAs. An SEP-IRA has the characteristics of a traditional IRA. An SEP-IRA cannot be a Roth IRA. A simple three-step process is required to establish an SEP:

1. The business must execute a formal written agreement to provide an SEP for all eligible employees.
2. The business must provide specific information to each eligible employee.
3. Each eligible employee must have an SEP IRA set up by the business or the employee.

Employees' SEP-IRAs can be established at any financial institution that provides this type of account. The business sends contributions directly to the financial institution.

An SEP provides advantages to the employer as well as the employee. Contributions are tax deductible. The cost to administer the SEP is low. The business does not have to make contributions every year. Contributions to each employee's SEP-IRA cannot exceed 25% of the employee's salary or the legal limit, whichever is less. In 2011, the maximum amount was $49,000.

Source: Shutterstock (Blend Images)

Saving money is the key to retirement planning.

Employees cannot take loans from an SEP-IRA. They can move the funds to a different IRA or withdraw cash. If they make a withdrawal, they must pay taxes on it. If they are not 59 1/2 years old, an additional tax can be applied. Like a traditional IRA, distributions must begin when the employee is 70 1/2 years old.

SIMPLE IRA Plans

A **SIMPLE IRA plan** is an IRA-based plan that gives small employers a simplified method to make contributions toward their employees' retirement. An employer can establish a savings incentive match plan for employees' SIMPLE IRA plan if it meets two criteria. The business:

- must have no more than 100 employees; and
- cannot have any other retirement plan.

Employee contributions are subtracted from their paychecks. Employees can choose to contribute any amount, up to the legal maximum. In 2011, the maximum was $11,500. Employees can stop contributing at any time.

Businesses have two options when contributing to the employees' SIMPLE IRA. An employer can:

- match the employee's contribution, up to a maximum of 3% of the employee's contribution; or
- make contributions to every employee, regardless of whether the employee contributes or not.

Employees cannot take loans from a SIMPLE IRA. They can move the funds to a different IRA or withdraw cash. If they make a withdrawal, they must pay taxes on it. If they withdraw cash within the first 2 1/2 years, employees must pay an additional tax. Like a traditional IRA, distributions must begin when the employee is 70 1/2 years old.

Traditional 401(k) Plan

A traditional 401(k) plan offers flexibility in retirement savings. A **401(k) plan** enables employees to make tax-deferred or taxed contributions through payroll deductions. Employers can:

- match employee contributions;
- make contributions to every employee, regardless of whether the employee contributes or not; or
- perform a combination of these types of contributions.

The funds in a 401(k) account can be managed by the employer or the employee, depending on how the employer set up the plan.

Employers are not required to contribute to employees' 401(k). In a 401(k), the amount contributed is limited to the lesser of two options: 100% of the employee's compensation, or the legal maximum amount. In 2011, the limit was $11,500. Distributions from a 401(k) can be moved to another retirement account. Distributions made before the employee is 59 1/2 years old are taxed an additional 10%.

Many 401(k) plans enable employees to make a withdrawal based on financial hardship. Hardship distributions are generally limited to the amount that the employee contributed to the 401(k). When the economy is poor, hardship withdrawals from 401(k) plans increase.

BIZ TIPS

The 401(k) plan was named for the location of the plan description in a document produced by the Internal Revenue Service.

Checkpoint 7.3

1. Historically, how did individuals pay for retirement?
2. What is the main difference between a traditional IRA and a Roth IRA?
3. Why does a company provide benefits?
4. How does a business qualify to provide a SIMPLE IRA?
5. When can an employee make an early withdrawal from his or her 401(k)?

Build Your Vocabulary

As you progress through this course, develop a personal glossary of banking terms and add it to your portfolio. This will help you build your banking vocabulary. Write out a definition for each of the following terms, and add it to your personal glossary.

retirement
Social Security
pension
defined benefit plan
individual retirement account (IRA)
compensation
contribution
distribution
benefits
defined contribution plan
Simplified Employee Pension (SEP)
SIMPLE IRA plan
401(k) plan

Careers in Finance
Banking and Related Services

What Does a Retirement Planning Specialist Do?

A **retirement planning specialist** helps businesses manage their employee benefit programs and educates employees on their benefits options. Some of the activities performed by **retirement planning specialists** include:

- reviewing current retirement plans and making recommendations to management;
- conducting research on the pricing and features of related competitors' retirement programs;
- developing and presenting marketing plans for various retirement programs; and
- educating current and future employees about retirement program options.

What Is It Like to Work as a Retirement Planning Specialist?

Retirement planning specialists work for insurance companies, financial institutions, and consulting firms. They often work a standard workweek in an office environment, although occasional travel may be required.

A **retirement planning specialist** is responsible for many administrative duties, and therefore must be organized and comfortable using a computer. Because a **retirement planning specialist** also plays a large role in marketing retirement products and educating employees, public speaking skills and a managerial spirit are essential in this position.

If you enjoy performing research, presenting information, and working with people, a career as a **retirement planning specialist** might suit you.

What Education and Skills Are Needed to Be a Retirement Planning Specialist?

- college degree in business, economics, finance, or human resources
- various voluntary or state certifications may be required
- experience in marketing or sales may be beneficial
- excellent verbal and written communication skills

Career Ladder

Director of Corporate Retirement Plans

Retirement Planning Specialist

IRA Accounts Officer

Section 7.4
Opening and Maintaining an Account

Terms

account holder
deposit slip
remote deposit capture
statement

Objectives

After completing this section, you will be able to:

- Explain the process of opening a new account.
- Describe the process of maintaining an account.

Opening an Account

Regardless of the type of account a customer opens, the process for opening an account is similar. The customer fills out an application and deposits at least the minimum amount. The financial institution checks the information. The account and its funds become available for use.

Generally speaking, accounts can be opened and maintained by individuals, groups of individuals, and businesses. An **account holder** is anyone authorized to perform transactions in an account. Spouses, family members, and business partners are frequently account holders who share responsibilities for an account.

Completing an Application

Account applications vary from one financial institution to another. Even within the same financial institution, applications for different types of accounts might vary slightly. The basics of each application remain the same, though.

To complete an application, the customer will need to provide specific information:

- Social Security number
- driver's license or state-issued ID
- contact information
- an opening deposit

Personal Information

To begin the application process, the customer provides personal information, as shown in Figure 7-5. Federal law requires that the financial institution obtain this information to verify the customer's identity.

When the customer completes the application form, he or she should use information that can be verified. For example, the name on the application should match the name on his or her legal identification. Financial institutions in the US collect information to assist government agencies in detecting and preventing financial crimes. Occupation is an example of information collected for this purpose.

Personal Information

Please tell us about yourself and provide your contact information so that we may deliver important information about your new account(s).

Name — Title | First Name | Middle Name | Last Name | Suffix

Home Address — Address 1 (PO Boxes are not acceptable) | Address 2 (Apartment/Suite (e.g., 11G))

City | State | Zip Code - +4 Code

Home Phone ___ - ___ - ___

Mobile Phone ___ - ___ - ___

E-mail Address (e.g., JLWebb@yahoo.com)

Occupation

Figure 7-5.
Personal Information Section of an Account Application

Security Information

Security information helps financial institutions identify their customers. When the customer contacts the financial institution later, this information helps the bank confirm the customer's identity. Mother's maiden name is a common security question.

Accurate personal information for customers is required by federal law. Date of birth is an example of information that must be recorded for account owners. The account holder's Social Security number is required because it is used to report financial information for taxation. The financial institution must protect this information from theft or misuse.

Depositing an Opening Amount

A deposit is usually required to open an account. The deposit can be cash, or it can be transferred from another account in the same bank or in a different bank. Generally, the funds for the opening deposit are held by the bank for several days. This ensures that the funds are available before the customer tries to make a withdrawal.

Maintaining an Account

After an account becomes active, customers can interact with the account. He or she can make deposits and withdrawals, check an account balance, and verify that an account balance is accurate.

Depositing Funds

Hopefully, customers will make frequent deposits. If customers come into the bank to make a deposit, they will need to fill out a **deposit slip** to record the deposit information, as shown in Figure 7-6. If they bank online, they will provide similar information to electronically transfer money to an account.

The information that the customer enters on a deposit slip is important in several ways. It identifies the date the deposit was made, the account receiving the deposited funds, the tracking numbers for any checks deposited, the amount of cash the customer will receive from the deposit, and the customer's signature if he or she receives any cash from the deposit.

If customers make deposits online, they will complete an electronic form. The information they enter is similar. Some banks allow customers to scan checks for deposit electronically. This **remote deposit capture** records the information the customer would otherwise have to enter.

Withdrawing Funds

To withdraw funds in person, the account holder fills out a withdrawal slip. The slip records the date, amount, account number, and the account holder's signature. The signature identifies the individual who made the withdrawal. It is the bank's responsibility to verify that the individual is an account holder for the account.

Account holders can also withdraw funds through an automated teller machine (ATM). In this case, the account holder must be able to enter the secret code to make the withdrawal.

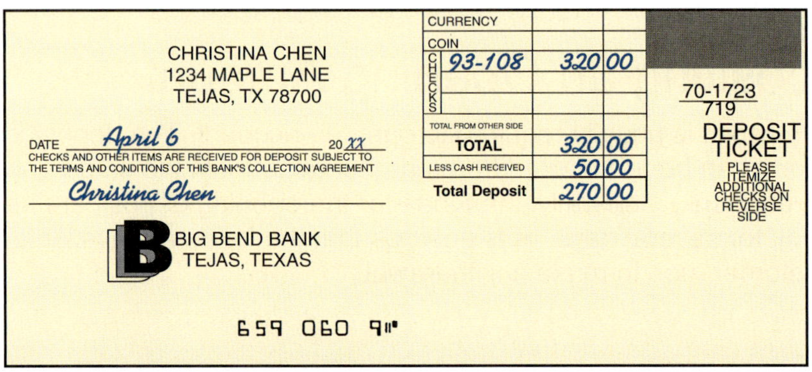

CHRISTINA CHEN
1234 MAPLE LANE
TEJAS, TX 78700

DATE April 6 20 XX
CHECKS AND OTHER ITEMS ARE RECEIVED FOR DEPOSIT SUBJECT TO THE TERMS AND CONDITIONS OF THIS BANK'S COLLECTION AGREEMENT

Christina Chen

BIG BEND BANK
TEJAS, TEXAS

659 060 9

CURRENCY		
COIN		
CHECKS 93-108	320	00
TOTAL FROM OTHER SIDE		
TOTAL	320	00
LESS CASH RECEIVED	50	00
Total Deposit	270	00

70-1723
719

DEPOSIT TICKET

PLEASE ITEMIZE ADDITIONAL CHECKS ON REVERSE SIDE

Figure 7-6.
Deposit Slip

Big Bend Bank
234 Southside St.
Tejas, TX 78700

Statement June 20--

Checking Account

Posting	Description/Transaction	Debits	Credits	Balance
JUN 1	Beginning Balance			817.02
JUN 13	CHECK NO. 500	68.79		748.23
JUN 13	CHECK NO. 502	148.00		600.23
JUN 15	CHECK DEPOSIT		440.02	1040.25
JUN 20	CHECK DEPOSIT		1500.00	2540.25
JUN 20	WITHDRAWAL	100.00		2440.25
JUN 25	CHECK NO. 503	1895.00		545.25
JUN 25	CHECK NO. 504	49.83		495.42
JUN 26	ATM WITHDRAWAL	60.00		435.42
JUN 28	CHECK NO. 506	10.13		425.29
JUN 30	Check Fees	1.25		424.04
JUN 30	Closing Date...Ending Balance			424.04

Savings Account

Posting	Transaction	Debits	Credits	Balance
JUN 1	Beginning Balance			1102.00
JUN 11	Deposit		100.00	1202.00
JUN 25	Deposit		100.00	1302.00
JUN 30	Interest Earned (1.5%)		19.53	1321.53

Figure 7-7.
Bank Statement

Understanding a Bank Statement

At regular intervals, a financial institution sends a statement to the account holder. The **statement** shows all of the activity that has occurred during the covered time period. The time period covered in a statement is usually a month, but could be longer depending on how the account is set up.

All of the account holder's withdrawals, deposits, and interest earned are recorded for the account. Figure 7-7 provides an example. The statement gives the account holder an opportunity to verify that his or her records agree with the bank's records. Knowing how much money is in an account helps the account holder avoid spending more money than is in the account.

Checkpoint 7.4

1. What is the basic process for opening an account?
2. Why is security information collected on an account application?
3. Why does a financial institution record a customer's Social Security number?
4. What information is reported on a deposit slip?
5. How long is the time period usually covered by a bank statement?

Build Your Vocabulary

As you progress through this course, develop a personal glossary of banking terms and add it to your portfolio. This will help you build your banking vocabulary. Write out a definition for each of the following terms, and add it to your personal glossary.

account holder
deposit slip
remote deposit capture
statement

Chapter Summary

Section 7.1 Why Do Customers Save?

- Customers save for short-term goals, which can be achieved in less than a year. Customers also save for long-term goals, which take longer than a year to achieve.
- Customers save to earn interest on their money while keeping it safe.

Section 7.2 Savings Products

- Savings accounts include passbook savings accounts, online savings accounts, custodial accounts, and money market accounts. Banks compete by offering different interest rates and account features.
- CDs and jumbo CDs allow customers to save a fixed amount of money for a fixed length of time.
- Different savings accounts and CDs fit the needs of different customers.

Section 7.3 Retirement Accounts

- Social Security is intended to supplement an individual's own retirement savings, which may be, in part, from a company's benefit plan.
- Traditional IRAs allow customers to save for retirement through tax-deferred contributions that are taxed at distribution.
- Roth IRAs allow customers to save for retirement through contributions that are taxed at contribution.
- Employers can provide benefits that include retirement savings such as a simplified employee pension (SEP) plan, SIMPLE IRA plan, and a traditional 401(k) plan.

Section 7.4 Opening and Maintaining an Account

- To open an account, the customer fills out an application and deposits at least the minimum amount. The financial institution then verifies the information.
- Maintaining an account includes tracking deposits, withdrawals, and interest, which are reported in the account's statement at regular intervals.

Check Your Banking IQ

Now that you have finished this chapter, see what you know about banking by taking the chapter post test.

www.m.g-wlearning.com
www.g-wlearning.com

Review Your Knowledge

On a separate sheet of paper or in a word processing document, match the following terms with the definition that fits best.

A. contribution
B. individual retirement account (IRA)
C. custodial account
D. liquidity
E. remote deposit capture
F. Simplified Employee Pension (SEP)
G. compound interest
H. fixed deposit
I. distribution
J. penalty

1. Interest paid on interest.
2. Savings account in which income taxes are deferred on some deposits and all interest until all or part of the balance is withdrawn.
3. Deposit into an IRA.
4. Allows customers to scan checks for deposit electronically.
5. Withdrawal from an IRA.
6. Retirement plan established by a business for its employees or owners.
7. Managed by an adult for a minor who is younger than 18 or 21 years old.
8. Fee for breaking the account's terms.
9. Ability of a financial asset to be converted into cash quickly without any financial loss.
10. Length of time and amount are specified.

On a separate sheet of paper or in a word processing document, answer each of the following questions.

11. Why is APY useful?
12. What are the four basic types of savings accounts?
13. When is a basic savings account a good option for a consumer?
14. In a Roth IRA, when can a retiree begin to take distributions?
15. What does a customer need to complete an account application?

Apply Your Knowledge

16. Make a list of three short-term goals and three long-term goals. If a bank customer asked you for financial recommendations to help him or her achieve these goals, what types of accounts would you recommend?
17. Use the Internet to investigate the current rates for CDs. Compare the rates at five banks. Create a table comparing your results. Be prepared to present your results to the class.
18. Select a local business. Contact the Human Resources department. Ask for information about any retirement savings options the company offers to employees. Evaluate the plan. Be prepared to present your results to the class.
19. Use the Internet to investigate the information a bank must tell its customers before they purchase a CD. To find the information, go to a bank's website and search for *disclosures* or *conditions.* Summarize the information in a few written paragraphs. Evaluate the difficulty of understanding the information.
20. Visit a local bank. Ask a bank employee to walk you through the process of opening any of the account types discussed in this chapter.

Working in Teams

Working with a partner, select three local banks and two online banks. Identify and compare the interest rates and features offered with a savings account. Create a table comparing each bank's savings account features.

G-W Learning Mobile Site

Visit the G-W Learning mobile site to complete the chapter pretest and post test and to practice vocabulary using e-flash cards. If you do not have a smartphone, visit the G-W Learning companion website to access these features.

G-W Learning mobile site: www.m.g-wlearning.com
G-W Learning companion website: www.g-wlearning.com

Common Core

College and Career Readiness

Reading. Research the Social Security issues that are currently being debated across the US. What are the most common opinions of the Social Security system? Using multiple media outlets (print and online news articles, speeches, official documents, opinions), write a report in which you discuss the controversies surrounding the Social Security system and your stances on these issues.

Speaking. Imagine you are a business owner. Using information presented in this chapter and your personal research, create a presentation in which you develop a benefits plan for your employees. What types of retirement plans will you offer to them and why? Present your benefits plan to your class as a business owner presenting to his or her employees. Allow time at the end for employee questions.

EVENT PREP

Team Presentation

Team presentation is a competitive event you might enter with your career and technical student organization (CTSO). This activity is an industry scenario for which your team will provide a solution. You may be asked to interact with the judges as they ask you questions about the case. However, you may be asked to role-play, in which you will be assigned a specific part to play.

This event will demonstrate your team's knowledge of banking concepts and operations, as well as persuasive skills and oral presentation abilities. To prepare for a team presentation event:

1. Read the guidelines provided by your organization. Make certain that you ask any questions about points you do not understand. It is important you follow each specific item that is outlined in the competition rules.
2. Do an Internet search for *banking case studies.* Your team should select a case that seems appropriate to use as a practice activity. Look for a case that is no more than one page long.
3. Read the case and discuss with your team members. What are the important points of the case?
4. To practice your note-writing techniques, each team member should have two index cards. Make important notes on the card that will help with a presentation.
5. Team members should exchange note cards so that each can evaluate the other person's notes. Are your cards accurate enough to help as you are presenting?
6. Assign each team member a role for the presentation. Ask your teacher to play the role of competition judge as your team reviews the case.
7. Ask a fellow student to be the timekeeper as the presentation is made.
8. Each team member should introduce themselves, review the case, make suggestions for the case, and conclude with a final summary.
9. After the presentation is complete, ask for feedback from your teacher. You may consider having a student audience to listen and give feedback.

Check Your Banking IQ

Before you begin this chapter, see what you already know about banking by taking the chapter pretest.

www.m.g-wlearning.com
www.g-wlearning.com

8

Lending

Around 1600, William Shakespeare wrote, "Neither a borrower nor a lender be." Regardless of Shakespeare's advice, most people are borrowers and lenders in today's world. Whether you borrow money from a friend to pay for gas or from the bank to buy a house, you are a borrower. If you loan your friend lunch money or deposit money in a bank, you are a lender. Few people make it through life without borrowing or lending at some point. In fact, individuals often owe several financial institutions at the same time. Banks make loans to many people and businesses.

College and Career Readiness

Reading Prep. As you read the chapter, think about the safeguards that lenders use to protect their businesses from financial loss. Using what you've learned so far about the history of banking and regulations, evaluate the safety of the lending process most banks use today.

Scan the code to view a Biz Kid$ video. If you do not have a smartphone, visit the G-W Learning companion website.

www.m.g-wlearning.com
www.g-wlearning.com

Section 8.1 Loans

Terms

loan
principal
loan policy
consumer loan
commercial loan
open-ended loan
closed-end loan
installment loan
secured loan
collateral
unsecured loan
signature loan
Small Business Administration (SBA)
Export-Import Bank of the United States
Farm Service Agency (FSA)
World Bank Group (WBG)

Objectives

After completing this section, you will be able to:

- Describe the different types of loans.
- Explain the types of financing assistance provided to businesses.

Loan Characteristics

A **loan** is money temporarily transferred to a borrower in exchange for repayment and interest. The **principal** is the amount that a bank loans to a customer. When a bank loans money to a customer, it expects the customer to repay the principal *and* pay an additional sum of money for using the principal. The additional money paid to borrow the principal is called the *interest*. Loans can be classified in a variety of ways, including consumer or commercial, open-ended or closed-end, and secured or unsecured.

Individuals and businesses that borrow money from a bank generally use the money to make a purchase or improve their current situation. This benefits the entire community. For example, Shula might borrow money from the bank to buy a new car. This purchase provides income for the car dealership, the gas station, and eventually, a car repair shop. Shula's Deli might borrow money from the bank to purchase new kitchen equipment and redecorate. This provides income for her employees, the equipment manufacturers, the interior designers, and the workers who install the new items. Thus, a loan ends up providing income for individuals and companies that sell goods and services in the community, as well as for the bank granting the loan.

Source: Shutterstock (s_oleg)

Consumer loans allow an individual to make large purchases, which stimulate the economy.

Loan Policy

A lending institution's risk tolerance is balanced with the need to make loans that will help the bank generate money through the interest charged. The riskiest loans are made to borrowers who may or may not pay back the money. These loans charge a higher interest rate because the chance the loan will not be repaid is greater. Any lending institution must balance the need to make money with the risk involved. To keep things in balance, lenders have **loan policies** they follow. Certain guidelines are included in these policies:

- portfolio mix
- rate of interest
- risk diversification

Portfolio mix refers to selecting loans from different sectors. *Rate of interest* refers to the interest earned on loans relative to collection costs for the loans. *Risk diversification* refers to a balance between safe and risky loans.

Loan policies are developed by the institution's loan committee. The committee does not give a thumbs up or thumbs down to individual loans. Instead, the committee establishes the guidelines from which each policy takes shape. A loan committee:

- reviews loan policy on an ongoing basis;
- explores the development of new loan products;
- looks for trends that will affect profitability or exposure to risk; and
- makes suggestions for changes to the policy, which usually take place once a year.

BIZ TIPS

The Truth in Lending Act (TILA) of 1968 protects the consumer when borrowing money. The law requires that the lender reveal all information about a loan to the consumer, including rates, terms, and the final cost of the loan.

Consumer and Commercial

The first characteristic used to classify loans is based on who borrows the money. A **consumer loan** is when an individual borrows money for his or her own use. The borrowed money is usually used for personal, family, or household needs, such as repairs or improvements.

A **commercial loan** is when a company borrows money. Commercial loans are usually used to purchase equipment, machinery, or inventory. Commercial loans are short-term loans because they are usually repaid within a year after the loan is made. There are many types of commercial loans, including acquisition, acquisition and development, asset based, bridge, construction, development, construction improvement and rehab, and Small Business Association (SBA). Figure 8-1 provides an overview of these products.

Type of Loan	Uses
Acquisition	Purchase property or another company
Acquisition and development	Purchase and improve property
Asset-based	For any reason; collateral is held
Bridge	Temporary funds to use before long-term financing is acquired
Construction	Building things such as factories, retail stores, and office buildings
Construction improvement and rehab	Purchase an existing property that is then repaired and/or remodeled
Development	Property developers improve a property, such as adding new houses to a subdivision
Refinancing	Pay off debt
Small Business Administration (SBA)	Help small businesses get started

Figure 8-1.
Overview of Commercial Loan Products

Open and Closed

The second characteristic used to classify loans is based on repayment of the loan. An **open-ended loan** is a loan that does not have to be paid in full by a specific date. A credit card is a good example of an open-ended loan. As long as the borrower makes regular payments, the principal does not have to be paid in full.

In an open-ended loan, the borrower makes a payment each month. That payment is applied to the principal and the interest. If the principal and interest are not paid in full, interest continues to be applied. Next month, the borrower pays interest on the interest and principal he or she did not pay off in the previous months.

A **closed-end loan** must be paid in full on a specific date. Some closed-end loans cannot be paid in full before that date without a penalty. A closed-end loan benefits the bank because it knows how much interest it will earn from making the loan and when this interest will be received.

Most bank loans are installment loans. These are a type of closed-end loan. An **installment loan** is a loan for a large amount of money that is repaid in smaller amounts over a specified period of time. Closed-end installment loans may be granted for a variety of purposes, such as buying a home or a car.

BIZ TIPS

The bank usually requires the borrower to insure the financed item. This protects the bank from financial loss based on the item's loss. After all, if the item is destroyed, the bank will not be paid.

Secured and Unsecured

Security means safety. From the bank's perspective, a secured loan is safer than an unsecured loan because the bank is protected from financial loss. A **secured loan** is a loan backed by the borrower's property. **Collateral** is the borrower's property that is pledged to secure the loan. When the bank makes a secured loan, the bank has the right to take the borrower's collateral if the borrower cannot repay the loan. The bank can then sell the property to replace the money lost by the borrower's failure to repay.

A loan used to purchase a car is a secured loan. If the borrower does not repay the loan, the bank takes ownership of the car.

An **unsecured loan** is less safe for the bank because it is not backed by collateral. If the borrower does not repay the loan, the bank cannot automatically take possession of the borrower's property. The loan is backed only by the borrower's promise to pay. An unsecured loan is also known as a **signature loan,** because the borrower's promise to pay is shown by his or her signature on the loan agreement.

Because the bank is less confident that an unsecured loan will be repaid, it takes several measures to protect itself from financial loss when issuing an unsecured loan:

- The interest rate for an unsecured loan is usually higher than the interest rate for a secured loan.
- If a payment is late, additional fees are applied to the loan.
- The bank can sue the borrower for failing to repay the loan.

Green Banking

Many banks, as well as other corporations, use green cleaning products in their facilities. The crews that clean the building use green products rather than those that contain toxic chemicals. Toxic chemicals in cleaning products can pollute water sources and damage equipment and other business assets.

Financial Assistance to Businesses

Many economists believe helping businesses is the best way to help the economy as a whole. Many organizations and agencies exist to provide financial assistance and support to businesses, both large and small. These organizations include the Small Business Administration, the Export-Import Bank of the US, the Farm Services Agency, and the World Bank Group.

Small Business Administration

The **Small Business Administration (SBA)** was created in 1953 as an independent agency of the federal government. Its purpose is to help Americans start and grow businesses. Much of this help comes in the form of loans. Banks and other lenders function as intermediaries between the SBA and the borrower. The loan programs and their respective characteristics are shown in Figure 8-2.

Loan Program	Characteristics	Eligibility
7(a) Loan Max: $2 million Loan Duration: Long term, up to 25 years	• most common SBA program • money from the loan can be put to nearly any legitimate business purpose	• existing or new business
7 (m) Microloan Loan Max: $50,000 Loan Duration: Short term	• average loan is $13,000 • working capital • inventory, supplies, or fixtures • equipment and machinery	• must be a for-profit business or a certain kind of non-profit child care center • cannot be used to pay existing debts
Certified Development Company/504 Loan Max: $1.5 million Loan Duration: Long term	• may be used to purchase land, buildings, or machinery; to improve land; or modernizing business facilities • cannot be used for speculation or investment in rental properties	• have < $7.5 million in net worth • must be a for-profit company • 10% of cost must be assumed by the borrower, 50% from a private lender, and 40% from a CDC.
Disaster Loan Loan Max: $200,000 for homeowners $2 million for businesses Loan Duration: Long term	• repair or replace buildings, personal property, machinery, inventory and business assets that have been damaged or destroyed in a declared disaster. • low interest	available to qualifying homeowners, renters, for-profit and nonprofit organizations large and small

Figure 8-2.
SBA Loan Programs

Export-Import Bank of the United States

The **Export-Import Bank of the United States** is better known as Ex-Im Bank. The purpose of this independent federal agency is to help businesses export American goods and services to foreign countries. It was created by a presidential decree in 1934. It has changed over time in response to increased globalization. Ex-Im Bank provides loans, loan guaranties, and insurance to small and large companies to support export ventures to 175 other countries.

Farm Service Agency

The **Farm Services Agency (FSA)** provides financial and logistical support to commercial farms and is part of the US Department of Agriculture (USDA). The FSA makes some loans and provides guaranties for others. The USDA itself does not make loans, but it makes grants to provide financial assistance that does not need to be repaid.

World Bank Group

In 1944, the International Bank for Reconstruction and Development (IBRD) was created to help rebuild countries after World War II. Since that time, it has joined with four other international organizations as part of the World Bank Group. The mission of the **World Bank Group (WBG)** is to ease poverty around the world. Businesses can benefit from the loans and grants the WBG makes to developing countries by selling goods and services that development organizations use WBG loans to purchase. Companies that meet WBG requirements can benefit from the connections that the organization provides.

Checkpoint 8.1

1. What is a lending institution balancing when it makes a loan? Name two things.
2. List the types of commercial loans.
3. A credit card is considered what type of loan? Why?
4. Why is collateral important to the bank when granting a loan to customers?
5. Why is an unsecured loan also known as a signature loan?

Build Your Vocabulary

As you progress through this course, develop a personal glossary of banking terms and add it to your portfolio. This will help you build your banking vocabulary. Write out a definition for each of the following terms, and add it to your personal glossary.

loan
principal
loan policy
consumer loan
commercial loan
open-ended loan
closed-end loan
installment loan
secured loan
collateral
unsecured loan
signature loan
Small Business Administration (SBA)
Export-Import Bank of the United States
Farm Service Agency (FSA)
World Bank Group (WBG)

Section 8.2
Real Estate Loans

Terms

real estate
mortgage loan
mortgage-backed securities (MBSs)
government-sponsored enterprise (GSE)
fixed-rate mortgage
adjustable-rate mortgage (ARM)
cap
term
closing costs
equity
equity loan

Objectives

After completing this section, you will be able to:

- Describe the characteristics of a mortgage loan.
- Explain a home-equity loan.

Source: Shutterstock (Joe Belanger)

Purchasing real estate often requires a mortgage loan.

Mortgage Loans

The most expensive thing that most people will ever buy is a house. In May 2011, the average sales price of a new home in the US was $266,400. You can see why consumers need a loan to pay for a house.

Real estate is a section of land, the air above it, the ground itself, and any buildings on the land. A **mortgage loan,** typically known as a *mortgage,* is a loan made to purchase real estate. A mortgage is a secured loan because the lender can take ownership of the real estate if the mortgage is not repaid. When the real estate is sold by the borrower, the mortgage must also be paid in full.

Government-Backed Mortgage Programs

The Federal Housing Administration (FHA) guarantees home loans with down payments of 3% or less. The borrower pays a mortgage insurance premium that helps support the program. The FHA does not make loans. Instead, it backs the loans lenders make. The Veteran's Administration (VA) also provides loan guarantees to lenders that make mortgage loans to qualifying veterans. The Government National Mortgage Association, now known as Ginnie Mae, is a government-owned corporation that backs the loans made by the FHA and VA. Ginnie Mae puts together a group of FHA loans, for example, and sells them as bonds that are guaranteed by the US government. These bonds are **mortgage-backed securities (MBSs).**

Fannie Mae and Freddie Mac are government-sponsored enterprises. **Government-sponsored enterprises (GSEs)** are chartered and supported by the government to promote a public interest. In this case, the public interest is in increasing homeownership and affordable rental housing. Each is a publicly traded-company owned by stockholders. Both of these GSEs provide a market for the sale of mortgages. Without a place to sell the mortgages they make, lenders would be more reluctant to make certain mortgages. They keep some of the mortgages they purchase and assemble others as mortgage-backed securities that are resold. Unlike the mortgage-backed securities issued by Ginnie Mae, these are not backed by the government.

Nature of Mortgage Loans

Mortgage loans can be consumer or commercial. They vary by interest rate, time period, and fees. Most of these features can be negotiated by the borrower and the lender, making each loan unique. The mortgage contract signed by the borrower and the lender will identify all of the features of a specific mortgage loan.

Consumer and Commercial

An individual who seeks a mortgage loan is buying a home. This is a consumer loan because it is provided for an individual. The mortgage generally applies to land and a house. Additional buildings, such as a barn, garage, or carriage house could be included in the real estate.

A business or organization that seeks a mortgage loan is looking for a business location. The type of business and the way the business intends to use the property determine the type of buildings and structures that could be included in the real estate. For example, a company that makes baby strollers might need a factory to build the strollers and a warehouse to store them. A business that takes tourists on fishing expeditions might need waterfront property, a boathouse, and a dock.

An individual can purchase real estate for commercial purposes, making it a commercial loan. For example, a house can be rented to residents or serve as an office for a small business.

Mortgage Interest Rates

Borrowers cannot use the bank's money for free. They pay interest, which is an important source of the bank's income. A bank usually advertises the interest rate it charges for a mortgage loan. However, there is usually room for negotiation. Several factors are considered when the interest rate for a mortgage loan is determined:

- interest rates offered by competing banks
- whether the borrower already has an account with the bank or is willing to open an account
- the length of time before the loan will be repaid

A loan's interest rate may remain the same or change throughout the loan's lifetime. This depends on how the loan is structured.

Source: Shutterstock (Frontpage)

A shared goal of Fannie Mae and Freddie Mac is to increase homeownership in the US.

In a **fixed-rate mortgage,** the interest rate stays the same (fixed) for the entire term of the loan. The borrower knows exactly how much he or she will pay this month, next month, and every month after that until the loan is paid off. The benefits for the borrower and the bank are related. The bank knows how much it will earn and when the money will arrive. Likewise, the borrower knows exactly how much each payment will be until the loan is paid in full. The interest rate on a fixed-rate mortgage is often higher than the initial interest rate of an adjustable-rate mortgage.

In an **adjustable-rate mortgage (ARM),** the interest rate may change over the life of the loan. The changes to the interest rates are based on many factors, including interest rates in general and the profit the bank wants to earn for each loan it makes.

The interest rate for an ARM is usually fixed for a certain length of time after the ARM is created. The initial interest rate can remain the same for one month or several years. The initial interest rate is usually lower than the interest rate for a fixed-rate mortgage, making it an attractive option for many borrowers. This initial low interest rate is often called a *teaser rate.*

After the initial fixed period, the interest rate and monthly payment may change at regular intervals. Common intervals are one month, three months, one year, three years, or five years. The loan is often known by how often its rate can change. For example, the interest rate can change annually in a one-year ARM. If a loan is fixed for several years and then adjusts, it is known by the length of time it is fixed and the frequency that it is adjusted. For example, a 3/1 ARM has a fixed rate for three years. Then, it is adjusted annually.

Borrowers also look for a cap in an ARM contract. A **cap** identifies the maximum increase that can be applied to a monthly payment or the maximum interest rate increase when the rate is adjusted. Most ARMs set a cap for the lifetime of the loan.

BIZ TIPS

In addition to principal plus interest, a borrower must also pay for insurance and real estate taxes on a home. Together, this is known in the banking business by the acronym PITI (principal, interest, taxes, and insurance).

Term and Fees

The mortgage **term** is the number of years a loan will exist. Most mortgage loans are long-term loans. Most banks advertise rates for 15- and 30-year loans. Other loan terms may be available as well.

Generally, banks earn the most interest on a loan with a longer term. For example, a $200,000 mortgage loan at 5% interest for 30 years means a monthly payment of $1,073.64. A lot of that monthly payment is interest, which is profit for the bank. However, toward the end of the loan, most of the payment is principal, so the bank earns less at that point in the loan.

If the same loan is created for a 15-year term, the monthly loan payment is $1,581.59. The larger monthly payment pays for the $200,000 loan in half the time—15 years instead of 30 years. Like the 30-year loan, part of the payment is interest, so the bank still earns a profit. Because the term is shorter, the bank might earn less interest over the life of the loan. It is important to note that 15-year mortgages carry a lower interest rate than do 30-year mortgages. For purposes of comparison, Figure 8-3 shows the difference in interest between these two terms. In this example, the borrower pays $1,824.20 more in interest for a mortgage with a 30-year term.

$86,510.40 (interest paid over 30 years) – $84,686.20 (interest paid over 15 years) = $1,824.20 (difference paid with 30-year term)

Loan Term	Number of Payments	Payment per Month	Interest Paid Over the Course of the Loan
15 years	180	$1,581.59	$84,686.20
30 years	360	$1,073.64	$186,510.40

Figure 8-3.
Comparing Loan Terms for a $200,000 Mortgage at 5% Interest.

For the borrower, it is better to pay off a loan faster at a lower rate. For the bank to maximize its profit, it needs to use its money as efficiently as possible. If the borrower repays a loan quickly, the bank needs to immediately put its profit to work earning more profit—perhaps by making additional loans.

Several fees, known as **closing costs,** are applied when a mortgage is signed. The fees and the amounts vary from lender to lender. Some lenders allow the closing costs to be included in the mortgage loan rather than paid directly at signing.

Applying for a Mortgage

Before applying for a mortgage, the potential buyer must make sure his or her finances are in order. Once that is done, the buyer must fill out a mortgage application. As part of the application process, the potential borrower will be asked to provide information and supporting documents. These documents will include proof of income and assets. The lender will also order a credit report to make sure the borrower's credit history shows that he or she can handle additional credit. Once the buyer has provided the information and signed the application, processing begins.

Depending on how many applications are submitted at the same time, the processing time varies, but usually takes one to three business days. During this time, the lender makes certain that all the needed information has been provided. The lender must provide a *good faith estimate* to the buyer, disclosing all of the costs associated with making and closing the loan. The application then goes to the underwriter.

The underwriter applies the lender's guidelines and the law to approve or deny the loan. The underwriting process usually takes another [illegible] three business days. Sometimes before making a decision, the un[illegible] needs more information. If the loan is approved, it is set for closing[illegible] *closing,* or settlement, the transfer of ownership takes place.

Mortgage-Related Laws

Many federal consumer-protection laws deal with mortgage [illegible] The Truth in Lending Act (TILA) requires lenders to plainly show [illegible] cost of any loan, including mortgage loans. The Community Rein[illegible] Act (CRA), the Home Mortgage Disclosure Act (HMDA), and the [illegible] Credit Opportunity Act (ECOA) are meant to promote fair access [illegible] Each of these laws is discussed in detail in Chapter 6.

srcg STRIDE RITE CHILDREN'S GROUP A DIVISION OF WOLVERINE WORLDWIDE
The TILA requires lenders to plainly show the true cost of any loan, including mortgage loans. The CRA, HMDA, and the ECOA are meant to promote fair access to credit

The Real Estate Settlement Procedures Act (RESPA) was passed in 1974. It requires lenders to provide borrowers with a good faith estimate of all costs related to the mortgage and closing costs. Since 2011, the Consumer Financial Protection Bureau has enforced RESPA rules.

In 1994, the Home Ownership and Equity Protection Act (HOEPA) was passed. HOEPA applies to high-interest loans. It requires that lenders verify borrowers' assets and determine if they are capable of repaying the loan. It also removes any penalties for early loan payments that take place after two years. Usually, real estate taxes and homeowners insurance must be held in an escrow account set up by the lender. An *escrow account* is an account in the name of the borrower and is separate from the mortgage account.

Buyers who finance more than 80% of a property's value are required to pay *private mortgage insurance (PMI).* PMI is an insurance policy that pays the lender if the borrower defaults on his or her loan. The Homeowners Protection Act of 1998 applies to mortgages for homes the borrower lives in. The law requires lenders to tell borrowers when they no longer have to pay PMI.

Equity Loans

Real estate has value. The value is based on the amount someone will pay for the property. **Equity** is the difference between the real estate's value and the amount owed for the real estate. Equity belongs to the owner. If the owner sells the real estate, he or she pays off the loan first. The amount of money left is the equity.

Figure 8-4 shows the relationship between the value of the real estate and the owner's equity. In this example, the owner owes $160,000

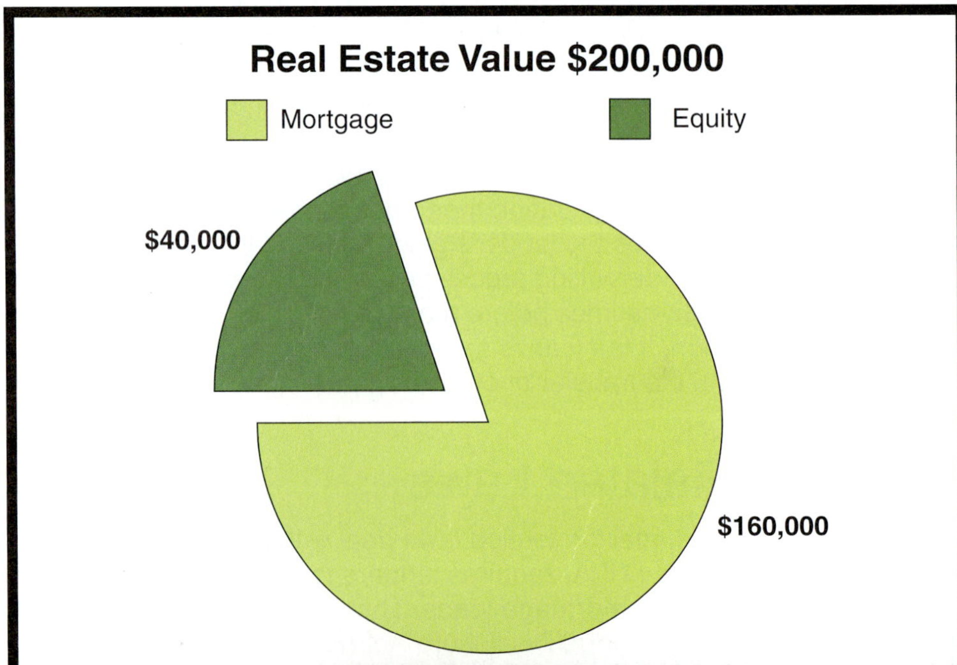

Figure 8-4.
Relationship Between Equity and Value

for the mortgage. If the owner sold this real estate for $200,000, he or she will pay $160,000 to the bank and keep $40,000. To calculate the equity, simply subtract the mortgage loan's balance from the value of the real estate. Hopefully, the homeowner owes less than the real estate value, but this is not always the case.

An **equity loan** is a loan that temporarily transfers cash to the borrower. It is secured by the owner's equity. Because the equity belongs to the owner, it is collateral for the loan.

For the borrower, an equity loan is a source of cash. However, it risks his or her real estate because it serves as collateral.

For the lender, an equity loan is a second way to earn money on the same real estate. Lenders earn interest and fees on the first mortgage and then earn interest and fees on the equity loan.

BIZ TIPS

If a consumer uses his or her home as collateral for a home-equity loan, federal law gives him or her three business days after signing the loan papers to cancel the deal, for any reason, without penalty.

Equity Loan Characteristics

The characteristics of an equity loan are so similar to a mortgage loan that an equity loan is often known as a *second mortgage.* In fact, if the owner fails to repay a mortgage loan, the real estate is sold. The profits are used to repay the mortgage loan first, and the equity loan is repaid second. Like a mortgage loan, many characteristics of an equity loan can be negotiated before a loan contract is signed.

Consumer and Commercial

Home-equity loans are common. The borrower pledges the equity in his or her home in exchange for cash. The cash can be used in many ways. For example, a consumer could pay off credit cards, improve the real estate, or pay education costs.

Commercial equity loans pledge the borrower's equity in a business in exchange for cash. Commercial equity loans are used to improve a business. For example, the borrower could purchase additional equipment or inventory, repair or improve existing equipment, or expand the business in other ways.

Source: Shutterstock (RonGreer.Com)

A home-equity loan can be used to get the money needed for home improvements.

Interest Rates

The interest rate on an equity loan is usually higher than a mortgage loan's interest rate, but less than a credit card's interest rate. The reason the rate on an equity loan is higher than on a mortgage is because the equity loan is riskier:

- The same property is being used to secure two different loans.
- The first loan (mortgage) is paid before the second loan (equity loan).

Many consumers use a home-equity loan to pay off credit card debt. They will still owe the same amount if they transfer the debt from a credit card to an equity loan. However, the interest rate for an equity loan is lower, so they will pay less interest.

Term and Fees

Equity loans can have a term of 5 to 30 years. In some cases, a penalty might be charged if the borrower pays off the loan early. Like a mortgage loan, closing costs are associated with signing an equity loan. The fees and amounts vary from lender to lender.

Checkpoint 8.2

1. Why is a mortgage a secured loan?
2. What public interest are Fannie Mae and Freddie Mac chartered to promote?
3. How does a fixed rate loan benefit the lender?
4. How do you calculate the owner's equity if he or she has a mortgage loan?
5. Why would a consumer use a home-equity loan to pay off credit card debt?

Build Your Vocabulary

As you progress through this course, develop a personal glossary of banking terms and add it to your portfolio. This will help you build your banking vocabulary. Write out a definition for each of the following terms, and add it to your personal glossary.

real estate
mortgage loan
mortgage-backed securities(MBSs)
government-sponsored enterprise (GSE)
fixed-rate mortgage
adjustable-rate mortgage (ARM)
cap
term
closing costs
equity
equity loan

Section 8.3
Granting Loans

Objectives

After completing this section, you will be able to:

- Describe the five C's of credit.
- Explain how commercial loans are evaluated.
- Describe the steps in applying for a loan.

Terms

creditworthiness
character
capacity
capital
conditions
credit score
risk
credit bureau
FICO score
debt ratio
cosigner
underwriting
subprime loan

Five C's of Credit

A friend stops you in the hall and asks, "Hey, can I borrow money for lunch?" What are you thinking before you respond?

- She always borrows lunch money, but she always repays me the next day.
- If I loan her lunch money, that is $10 I will never see again.

Banks go through the same process when considering a loan. When a consumer applies for a loan, the bank looks at the customer's creditworthiness. **Creditworthiness** is an assessment of a borrower's ability to repay a loan. As shown in Figure 8-5, lenders start with the five C's of credit: character, capacity, capital, collateral, and conditions. These criteria apply to both commercial and consumer loans.

Figure 8-5.
Five C's of Credit

Careers in Finance
Banking and Related Services

What Does a Loan Officer Do?

A **loan officer** finds potential loan applicants and helps them apply for loans. The **loan officer** provides information and guides the applicant to the right loan product. The **loan officer** may help the applicant complete the application process and explain the loan's language to ensure that the applicant knows and understands the specific characteristics of the loan. After the application is complete, the **loan officer** may request additional information and begin verifying the information in the application. **Loan officers** generally specialize in one type of loan:

- Commercial **loan officers** may focus on contacting businesses to identify any loan needs they may have.
- Consumer **loan officers** work with individual consumers to identify their loan needs.
- Mortgage **loan officers** form working relationships with local realtors who might notify them when real estate is sold.

What Is It Like to Work as a Loan Officer?

Many **loan officers** spend time out of the office, meeting with potential applicants. A position as a **loan officer** can include a lot of time traveling to meetings. Some **loan officers** travel among bank branch offices, meeting clients at one branch several days a week and at a different branch on other days. Other **loan officers** work at a single location all of the time.

If you enjoy working with people and have sales experience, a career as a **loan officer** might suit you.

What Education and Skills Are Needed to Be a Loan Officer?

- college degree preferred
- may require licensure in specialty areas
- sales abilities
- highly motivated

Career Ladder

Bank Manager

Loan Officer

Loan Processor

Before granting a loan, the bank must evaluate the applicant's complete financial picture. Lenders review the applicant based on the five C's. Skipping this review can mean approving a loan that is not profitable for the lender because the borrower is not able to repay the loan. In turn, the lender loses money, which reduces its income.

Character

Character is a loan applicant's honesty and integrity as shown by how he or she handles debt. Consistent and timely debt payment is positively viewed by banks. A pattern of late or missed payments will seriously hurt an applicant's chances for credit approval. The lender asks the applicant questions that reveal these characteristics:

- Have you used credit in the past?
- Have all of your bills been paid on time?
- How long have you had your current job?
- How long have you lived at your current address?

The answers to these questions help the lender determine an applicant's attitude toward debt and his or her priorities when dealing with a loan. Lenders want applicants who have experience as borrowers, pay bills on time, and demonstrate stability in home and work arrangements.

A business also has character. Its character is based on how it handles debt. Businesses with good character pay bills on time and have been in the same type of business for several years. New businesses may not have character because of their short record of handling debt.

BIZ TIPS

The Equal Credit Opportunity Act (ECOA) of 1974 protects consumers against discrimination when applying for a loan. The loan must be based on credit qualifications only.

Capacity

Capacity is a loan applicant's ability to pay debts as shown by cash flow. Therefore, sometimes this C is known as cash flow. The lender looks at the amount of money going out (expenses) and the amount of money coming in (income). The lender asks the applicant questions that reveal their capacity for credit:

- What are your current expenses?
- How much money do you owe?
- What is your current income?
- Is your income steady?

Lenders look for steady employment and a salary that can cover expenses and debt before loaning money to an individual. Businesses with good capacity demonstrate steady profit over time.

Capital

Capital is a loan applicant's money, property, and other valuables. If a borrower owns items of value, those items can be used as collateral for a loan. If the borrower has little or no capital, then the loan may represent a greater risk for the bank.

Collateral

Collateral is used to back up a loan. If the borrower's income ends, resources must be available to repay the loan. The less collateral a borrower has, the riskier the loan is for the bank. A bank will only consider certain assets as collateral. An asset must be easily liquidated to be considered collateral. In some cases, the asset must be appraised to determine its value. For example, when buying a house, its appraised value must be at least equal to the loan amount.

Conditions

Conditions involve the overall environment in which the loan will be given. The bank needs to be sure the conditions are such that the loan can be repaid. For example, if you are applying for a mortgage, but the house is located in an area that has seen double-digit decreases in housing values each of the past five years, the bank may not be willing to offer a loan for the appraised value. If you are employed in an industry that has had widespread layoffs, this may be a factor that the bank deems too great of a risk for offering the loan. On the other hand, if you have been a customer with the bank for the past 30 years and have never bounced a check or defaulted on any other loans, this may change the conditions in your favor.

Source: Shutterstock (Tyler Olson)

Lenders will consider many factors when determining risks, such as the industry in which the borrower works.

Credit Scores

When banks grant loans to customers, they not only evaluate the applicant's creditworthiness by using the five C's, they evaluate the applicant's credit score. A **credit score** is a measure of risk based on the borrower's credit history. **Risk** is the likelihood of financial loss caused by a borrower failing to repay the principal and interest as specified in a loan.

Like a grade on a school assignment, higher is better. A high credit score means the customer is a lower risk and will probably pay debts in a timely manner. The loan should be approved. A low credit score means the customer is a higher risk and may not meet the requirements of the loan. The lender should reconsider the loan application because the risk is high.

Generally, applicants with high credit scores are more likely to be approved for loans than applicants with low credit scores. If both applicants are approved, the applicant with the higher credit score may be offered a lower interest rate than the applicant with the lower credit score. The difference in interest rates occurs because the lender must earn money quicker on the riskier loan because it might not be paid off.

A **credit bureau** is a company that gathers, analyzes, and summarizes credit-related information on consumers. The three national credit bureaus are Equifax, Experian, and TransUnion. Consumers can receive a free copy of their credit reports every 12 months. However, these credit reports are provided for information only. Most lenders use the FICO score.

The **FICO score** is a credit rating used by lenders to predict an applicant's ability and willingness to repay loans. The FICO score was created by the Fair Isaac Corporation. It is composed of five elements—payment history; amount owed, or outstanding debt; length of credit history; new credit; and types of credit used, as shown in Figure 8-6. Though all the elements contribute to an applicant's overall FICO score, some elements play a larger role than others. Payment history is the largest part of the score and, therefore, one of the most important components.

A FICO score ranges from 300 to 850. The FICO score is not permanent. A consumer's credit score changes over time as the consumer gets new loans and pays off debt. Consumers who have low credit scores will likely pay more for things such as loans and insurance. If a consumer's credit score is too low, credit may be denied altogether.

BIZ TIPS

The Fair Credit Reporting Act (FCRA) makes certain that credit bureaus collect and distribute information in a fair and legal manner. It also provides processes for correcting any errors that may be on a credit report.

Credit for Commercial Loans

Whether a loan is being made to an individual or a business, the lender has to look at the risk posed by making the loan. To assess the risk involved with commercial loans, lenders look at the company or organization's balance sheet, cash flow, and collateral. By evaluating a company's balance sheet, the lender can determine a company's assets.

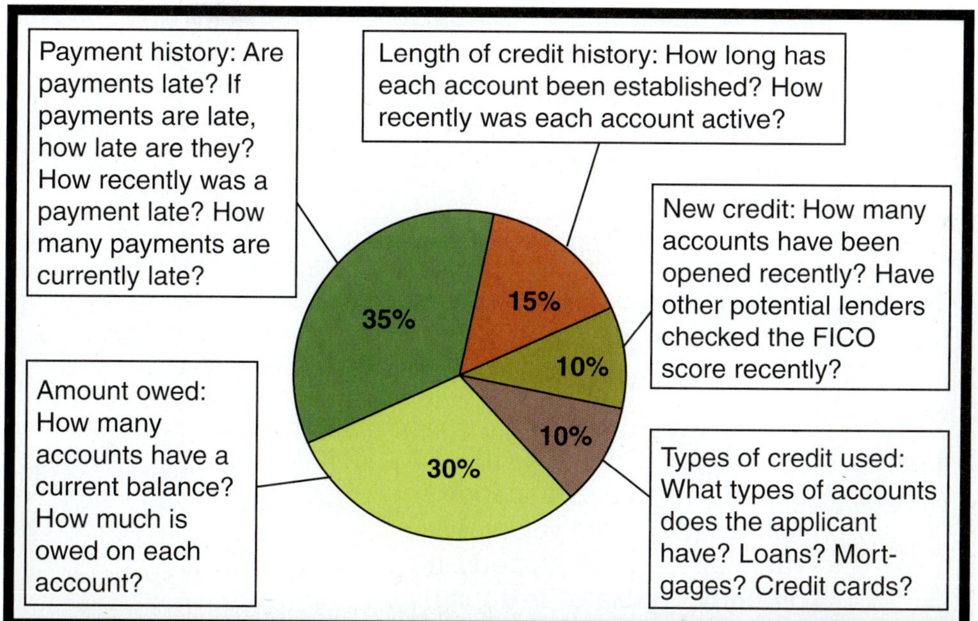

Figure 8-6.
FICO Score Elements

In the same way that lenders want to know about a consumer's job and other sources of income, they look at a company's cash flow. Cash flow represents what money is coming in to a business and what money is going out of a business. If the amount coming in is greater than the amount going out, the company has a positive cash flow. How much positive cash flow a company has is a factor in determining if a loan is approved and for how much.

Collateral is a factor in all secured loans. Lenders use specific formulas to determine the value of a company's collateral. Remember that collateral can be capital such as an office building, manufacturing equipment, accounts receivable, and even patents and other intellectual property. Patents and intellectual property have to do with ideas that belong solely to a company or organization. It is very important that the business disclose all liabilities and assets when applying for a loan. In addition to this being the ethical thing to do, keeping any information from the lender can lead to the loan being withdrawn.

Commercial debt ratios are another factor in determining whether a commercial loan will be approved. The most common **debt ratios,** which compare debt to income or assets, are the debt-to-income ratio, debt-service-coverage ratio, and loan-to-value ratio. Figure 8-7 provides an overview of these debt ratios. The greater the ratio, the greater the risk is to a lender.

Credit-Application Process

The credit application is an important step in the loan process for the customer and the bank. Sometimes, banks charge an application fee when a customer applies for a loan. The fee may be small or as much as a few hundred dollars. It pays for verifying employment, credit, and other

Ratio	Equation	Definition	Example
Debt	debt ÷ income or liability ÷ assets	Compares what is owed to what is owned	$\left[\frac{\$100{,}000}{\$500{,}000}\right] \times 100 =$ Ratio of 20%
Debt service coverage	debt payment ÷ income	Compares the amount needed to pay on a debt rather than the whole debt with income	$\left[\frac{\$2{,}500}{\$5{,}000}\right] \times 100 =$ Ratio of 50%
Loan-to-value	mortgage amount ÷ appraised value of property	Compares the amount financed to the value of a given property. It relates to equity	$\left[\frac{\$250{,}000}{\$750{,}000}\right] \times 100 =$ Ratio of 33%

Figure 8-7.
Commercial Debt Ratios

background information about the customer. If the loan is not approved, the applicant does not get the loan and the application fee is not returned.

In some cases, the borrower does not qualify for a loan, but someone with a better credit history is willing to cosign on the loan. A **cosigner** is an individual who signs the loan with the borrower, taking on equal liability for repayment. A loan application that has been rejected because the applicant is a high risk might be approved if a cosigner agrees to cosign on the loan.

Applying

The process of applying for a loan includes many steps, as shown in Figure 8-8. The customer completes the application provided by the lender. A bank representative is available to answer questions and give guidance on types of loans that may be most suited to the customer's needs.

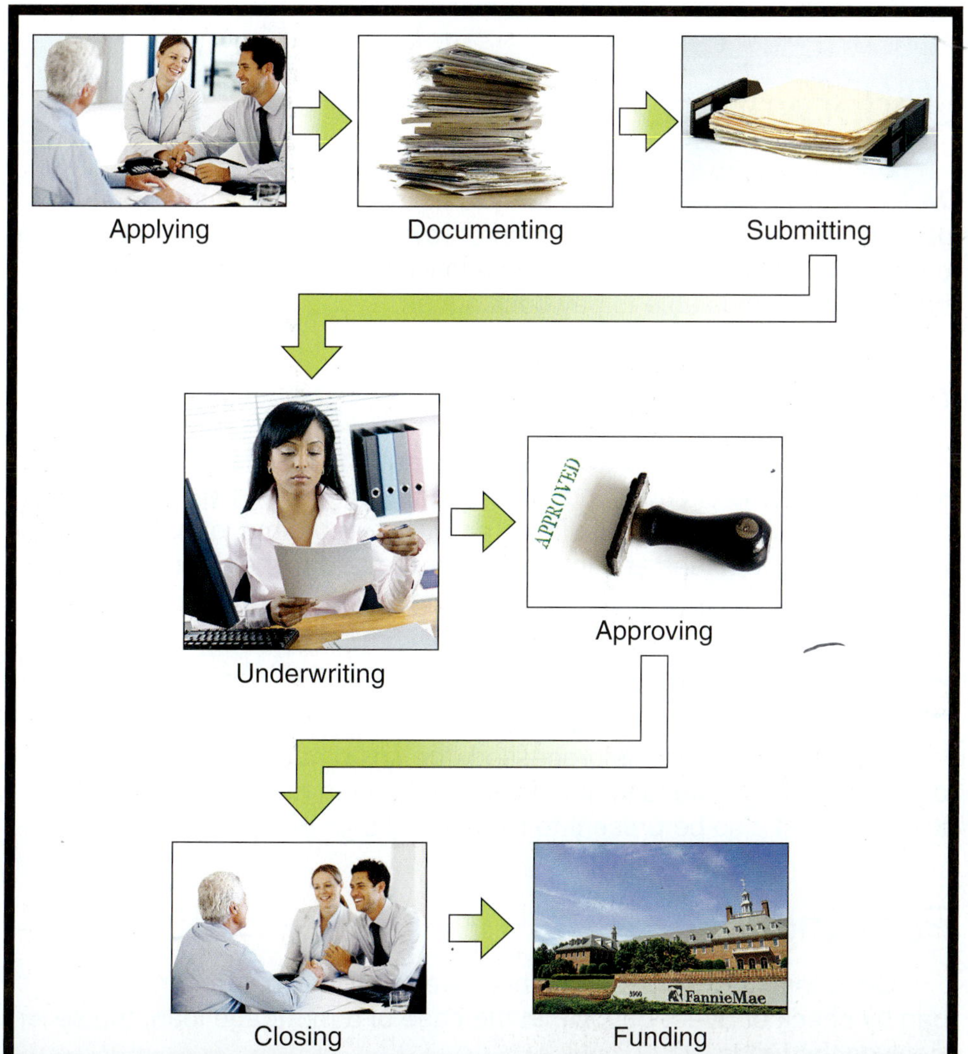

Source: Shutterstock (Yuri Arcurs, Stanislav Popov, KSR, jannoon028, Elena Elisseeva, Yuri Arcurs, Frontpage)

Figure 8-8.
Loan Application Process

Each lender may have its own processes, but will generally follow the same steps. This process can take days or weeks, depending on how complete the information is and how busy the lender is when the application is submitted.

Documenting

After filling out the application, customers are then asked to provide income tax forms, recent pay stubs, information about possessions and debts, and other documents that will demonstrate that the applicant can repay the loan. The bank also requests a credit report.

Submitting

The bank will verify all the information on the application and documentation that was provided. If there are any questions, the bank representative will contact the customer.

Underwriting

The final stage in the evaluation process for a loan is underwriting. **Underwriting** is when lenders analyze risks and set conditions on the loan. During this stage, the underwriter reviews the applicant's information to make certain that the applicant is a low risk. Banks want to make sure that the applicant is able to pay back a loan.

Approving

If the underwriter approves the applicant, the loan is approved. However, in some circumstances, even an applicant who did not meet all of the approval criteria might still be granted a subprime loan. A **subprime loan** is a loan with fees and interest rates that are higher than the rates given to a person who meets all of the underwriting criteria.

Closing

After the application is processed, the customer meets with the bank to review and sign the loan agreement. If the loan has a cosigner, the cosigner must also be present to review and sign the loan agreement.

Funding

Once the loan is closed, the borrower receives the amount of the loan by check or direct deposit. In the case of a mortgage loan, the seller receives the funds.

Checkpoint 8.3

1. List the five C's of credit.
2. What are three things that would show an applicant has good character?
3. How does a FICO score affect a loan application?
4. When considering the risk posed by a commercial loan, what three things do lenders look at?
5. Why would an applicant ask someone to cosign a loan application?

Build Your Vocabulary

As you progress through this course, develop a personal glossary of banking terms and add it to your portfolio. This will help you build your banking vocabulary. Write out a definition for each of the following terms, and add it to your personal glossary.

creditworthiness
character
capacity
capital
conditions
credit score
risk
credit bureau
FICO score
debt ratio
cosigner
underwriting
subprime loan

Section 8.4
Profits and Losses

Terms
nominal annual rate
annual percentage rate (APR)
periodic interest rate
finance charges
average daily balance method
previous balance method
adjusted balance method
default
bankruptcy
reorganization

Objectives
After completing this section, you will be able to:

- Distinguish between a loan's nominal annual rate, annual percentage rate, and periodic rate.
- Use three methods to calculate finance charges.
- Describe how bankruptcy affects lenders.

Source: Shutterstock (auremar)

Paying the monthly balance in full on your credit card will prevent finance charges.

Interest Rates

Loan applicants can be confused by a bewildering array of choices and terminology. First-time applicants are particularly vulnerable to this confusion. To protect consumers, lenders are required to disclose the nominal rate, the annual percentage rate (APR), and the periodic rate for every loan that is made.

The **nominal annual rate** identifies a loan's annual interest rate without the cost of fees or compound interest. When a consumer is faced with several loan options from different lenders that include different fees, it is difficult for the consumer to determine which loan is the best deal. Is it the loan with the 5% interest rate and several fees, or the loan with the 4.75% interest rate and several fees with different names and amounts?

The **annual percentage rate (APR)** is the annual cost of a loan, including all interest. The APR allows consumers to compare loans from different lenders at different interest rates with different fees. Lenders are legally required to provide the APR for every loan.

The **periodic interest rate** is the interest rate the lender applies to a loan's outstanding balance to calculate the finance charge each billing period. The periodic rate is the APR divided by the number of periods in the year. If the period is a month, the APR is divided by 12 because there are 12 months in one year.

If Jamal gets a new car loan with an APR of 6%, and he pays monthly, what is the periodic interest rate?

6% (annual percentage rate) ÷ 12 (number of periods) = .5% (periodic interest rate)

Calculating Finance Charges

Credit cards are open-ended loans. If the borrower does not pay the credit card debt in full every month, a balance is carried over to the next month. The item purchased ends up costing much more than the price indicated in the store. In fact, the buyer could still be paying for the item more than a year later.

Each month, most credit cardholders pay a **finance charge,** which is the cost of carrying the debt. The finance charge includes interest and fees, such as transaction fees, account-maintenance fees, and late fees for any overdue payments. A lender could charge a flat fee for finance charges, or calculate it as a percentage of the amount owed. Regardless of how it is calculated, the finance charge is *not* the same as the interest rate or the interest charged. The interest is part of the finance charge. Regardless of the method used to calculate finance charges, the charges are profit for the lender. The amount of profit is determined by the fees and interest rate.

Lenders may calculate finance charges on a credit card using various methods. However, three methods are used most often: the average daily balance, previous balance, and adjusted balance methods.

BIZ TIPS

A cardholder can avoid paying monthly finance charges if he or she meets the following criteria: pays the balance in full, makes no transactions that charge fees, and uses a credit card that does not charge an inactivity fee.

Average Daily Balance Method

The **average daily balance method** is a way to calculate finance charges by using the card's beginning daily balance. This is the most common calculation method used by lenders. The cardholder's account is credited the day a payment is received. Depending on the card's terms, new purchases may be added to the balance. Not every lender adds new purchases to the calculation.

To calculate the amount the cardholder owes:

Step 1. Subtract any payments made to the account that day from the beginning balance.

\$381.90 (balance) – \$20.00 (payment) = \$361.90

Step 2. Total the daily balances for the billing period.

\$361.90 (balance on day 1) + \$11,049.58 (sum of balances for each of the following 29 days) = \$11,411.48

Step 3. Divide the total by the number of days in the billing period to give the average daily balance.

\$11,411.48 (total of daily balances) ÷ 30 (days in the billing period) = \$380.38 (average daily balance)

Step 4. Multiply the average daily balance by the annual percentage rate multiplied by the number of days in the billing cycle and divide by the number of days in the year.

\$380.38 (average daily balance) × 12% (12% annual percentage rate) × 30 (number of days in the billing cycle) ÷ 365 = \$3.75 (finance charges)

Previous Balance Method

The **previous balance method** is a way to calculate finance charges by using the amount the customer owed at the end of the previous billing period to calculate the interest owed for the current month. Because this method is based on the balance from the previous billing period, payments, credits, and purchases made during the current billing period are not included.

To calculate the amount the cardholder owes:

Multiply the balance at the end of the previous billing period by the periodic interest rate to get the finance charges.

$381.90 (previous month's balance) × .01% (periodic interest rate: 12% APR ÷ 12 months) = $3.82

Adjusted Balance Method

The **adjusted balance method** is a way to calculate finance charges by using the balance from the previous month and subtracting payments made during the current period. New purchases are not included. This method is the most favorable for cardholders.

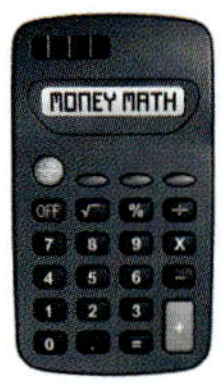

To calculate the amount the cardholder owes:

Step 1. Total the payments made in the current period.

$20 (payment made on day 5 of the billing cycle) + $50 (payment made on day 25 of the billing cycle) = $75

Step 2. Subtract the result from the previous month's balance.

$381.90 (previous month's balance) – $75 (total of payments made) = $306.90

Step 3. Multiply the result by the periodic interest rate to get the finance charges.

$306.90 × .01% (periodic interest rate: 12% APR ÷ 12 months) = $3.07

Loans in Default

Even though lenders carefully assess the borrower's ability to repay a loan, not every loan is repaid. **Default** is the borrower's failure to meet the terms of a loan agreement. Most often, a loan is in default because the borrower failed to make a payment when it was due.

The lender can sue the borrower for unsecured loans that go into default. For secured loans, the lender can take possession of the property used to secure the loan. The lender usually sells the property to reduce the amount of money lost by the default.

The process of collecting on defaults involves additional expenses for the lender. If a lawyer is required, the lawyer's fees must be paid. If a car has to be repossessed, someone has to be paid to retrieve the car. If real estate served as collateral for the loan, the borrower may need to be removed from the property. Then, the property must be sold to recover any profit or minimize the loss.

All of these activities require the lender to spend time and money. Also, the property might be worth less than it was at the time the loan was made. That means the lender cannot recover all of the money that would have been earned if the loan was repaid as stated in the loan agreement. You can see why lenders are so careful about the loans they grant.

Bankruptcy

Bankruptcy is a legal procedure that enables individuals or companies to eliminate or repay some or all debt under the guidance of federal bankruptcy courts. To declare bankruptcy, the borrower must be unable to repay debts from available assets. The purpose of bankruptcy is to provide individuals and businesses with a second financial chance. Bankruptcy generally remains in the borrower's credit record for 10 years. A borrower's bankruptcy also affects the lenders that have financial claims.

Bankruptcy is a second chance for borrowers. It allows them to start over financially. For lenders, it is a second chance to recover funds from a borrower who would not have otherwise been able to repay his or her debts.

Bankruptcies can be categorized as liquidation or reorganization. Laws govern both types of bankruptcies. They identify who can file bankruptcy, what kind of debt can be dismissed, and how debt and property are dealt with.

Liquidation

Borrowers who do not have the cash to repay a loan might still own property. Boats, jewelry, and vehicles are examples of property that can be sold for cash. The process of converting property into cash is *liquidation.* The bankrupt borrower may be required to liquidate property by selling it and giving the cash to the lender to repay the loan, as shown in Figure 8-9. The lender may also get a court order to have the assets seized and eventually sold.

Chapter 7 bankruptcy is a type of liquidation bankruptcy that can be filed to release an individual from personal responsibility for debt. Businesses can also file for Chapter 7 bankruptcy. However, Chapter 7 bankruptcy is more effective for individuals, because only individuals can be released from personal debt liability. The individual's property is sold and the funds are distributed to the lenders. Some property, such as clothing and furniture, is excluded.

Source: Shutterstock (OLJ Studio)

Creating and following a budget is a way to ensure bankruptcy can be avoided.

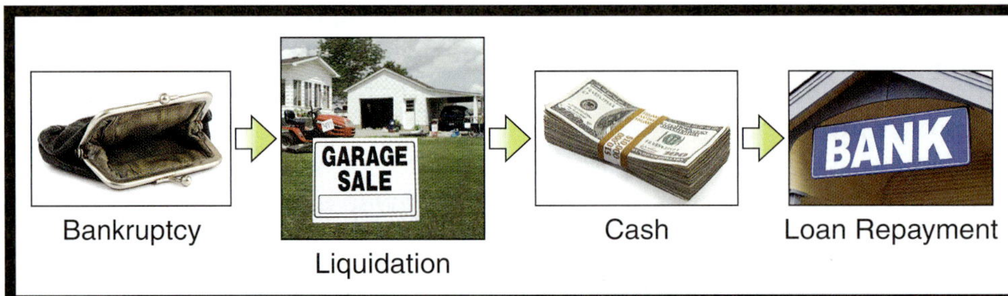

Source: Shutterstock (Andrey Eremin, Cathleen A Clapper, topseller, travis manley)

Figure 8-9.
Liquidation

Reorganization

In some cases, the borrower has a steady source of income, but still is not able to repay debt. For example, a married couple bought a house for $300,000. At the time, both were employed. Since then, the wife's company closed, leaving her unemployed. The economy is poor and unemployment is high. She cannot find another job. After nine months, they have used all of their savings and are not able to make loan payments. They still have his income and they do not want to liquidate their property. However, reorganizing their debt into smaller payments might enable them to meet their debt obligations.

Reorganization, in reference to bankruptcy, is the process of creating a repayment plan to repay debts without liquidating property. Essentially, the borrower reorganizes finances to repay debts. Individuals and businesses can use this type of bankruptcy.

Chapter 11 bankruptcy is a type of reorganization bankruptcy that can enable a company to make agreements with its lenders to repay loans while altering its own structure to prevent future problems. The company can change its structure by changing the way that it is organized or the type of business it operates. Closing or selling portions of its business that are not profitable can also be a change that will improve the company's financial standing.

Chapter 13 bankruptcy is a type of reorganization bankruptcy that enables an individual to make agreements with his or her lenders to repay loans without liquidating property. To file for Chapter 13 bankruptcy, the borrower must have a steady source of income. The borrower must also follow the payment plan established by the court.

BIZ TIPS

The Fair Debt Collection Practices Act (FDCPA), which was amended in 2006, protects consumers against creditors who try to use unfair techniques to force consumers to pay their past-due credit.

Checkpoint 8.4

1. What is the difference between the nominal annual rate and the APR?
2. What is the most common method used to calculate finance charges?
3. Which method used to calculate finance charges is the most favorable for borrowers?
4. What is the most common reason for loans to go into default?
5. Why is liquidation a possibility when dealing with bankruptcy?

Build Your Vocabulary

As you progress through this course, develop a personal glossary of banking terms and add it to your portfolio. This will help you build your banking vocabulary. Write out a definition for each of the following terms, and add it to your personal glossary.

nominal annual rate
annual percentage rate (APR)
periodic interest rate
finance charges
average daily balance method
previous balance method
adjusted balance method
default
bankruptcy
reorganization

Chapter Summary

Section 8.1 Loans

- Loans can be classified as consumer or commercial, open-ended or closed-end, and secured or unsecured.
- Many organizations and agencies exist to provide financial assistance and support to businesses, large and small.

Section 8.2 Real Estate Loans

- A loan made to purchase real estate is a mortgage loan. A mortgage loan is a closed-end secured loan.
- The characteristics of equity loans are similar to mortgage loans, and are often called second mortgages.

Section 8.3 Granting Loans

- Lenders use the five C's of credit to evaluate a loan applicant's creditworthiness—character, capacity, capital, collateral, and conditions.
- Lenders use a loan applicant's credit score to evaluate the risk in granting a loan. The FICO score is based on the individual's payment history, amount owed, or outstanding debt, length of credit history, new credit, and type of credit.
- The loan application process includes applying, documenting, submitting, underwriting, approving, closing, and funding.

Section 8.4 Profits and Losses

- Lenders must identify a loan's nominal annual rate, annual percentage rate, and periodic interest rate.
- The most common way to calculate finance charges is the average daily balance method. The previous balance method is the easiest way to calculate finance charges and the adjusted balance method is most favorable for borrowers.
- Most often, default loans are caused by borrowers who do not make payments on time. Collecting on loans in default require the lender's time and money.
- Liquidation and reorganization are two types of bankruptcies.

Check Your Banking IQ

Now that you have finished this chapter, see what you know about banking by taking the chapter post test.

www.m.g-wlearning.com
www.g-wlearning.com

Review Your Knowledge

On a separate sheet of paper or in a word processing document, match the following terms with the definition that fits best.

A. signature loan
B. credit bureau
C. subprime loan
D. default
E. underwriting
F. commercial loan
G. government-sponsored enterprise
H. closing costs
I. previous balance method
J. collateral

1. Gathers, analyzes, and summarizes credit-related information on consumers.
2. Chartered and supported by the government to promote a public interest.
3. Lenders analyze risks and set conditions on a loan.
4. When a company borrows money.
5. An unsecured loan.
6. Property pledged to secure a loan.
7. Failure to meet the terms of a loan agreement.
8. A loan with fees and interest rates that are higher than the rates given to a person who meets all of the underwriting criteria.
9. Uses the amount the customer owed at the end of the previous billing period to calculate the interest owed for the current month.
10. Fees applied when a mortgage is signed.

On a separate sheet of paper or in a word processing document, answer each of the following questions.

11. Why is the interest rate for an unsecured loan often higher than the interest rate for a secure loan?
12. What is the difference between a fixed-rate mortgage and an ARM?
13. If a home's value is $150,000 and the balance of the mortgage loan is $80,000, how much equity does the owner have?
14. What five elements are considered in the FICO score?
15. What is the purpose of bankruptcy?

Apply Your Knowledge

16. Using what you know about how a loan benefits a community, create a scenario in which an individual takes out a loan and describe how it affects his or her community.
17. Create a Venn diagram showing the similarities and differences between mortgages and home-equity loans.
18. Why do you think employers sometimes check the credit scores of their future employees? What might a person's credit score say about what kind of employee he or she might be? Write a paragraph in which you answer these questions.
19. Conduct research on the Internet regarding getting a small business loan. Create a flowchart that accurately depicts this process.
20. Create a print or video public service message that describes the dangers of misusing credit. Present your project to the class.

Working in Teams

Imagine a small business owner is attempting to open a new commercial account. On your own, think about the questions the lender would ask the small business owner. Also, think about the questions the small business owner should ask the lender. In groups of two or three, take turns role playing a banker and a small business owner in this scenario.

G-W Learning Mobile Site

Visit the G-W Learning mobile site to complete the chapter pretest and post test and to practice vocabulary using e-flash cards. If you do not have a smartphone, visit the G-W Learning companion website to access these features.

G-W Learning mobile site: www.m.g-wlearning.com
G-W Learning companion website: www.g-wlearning.com

Common Core

College and Career Readiness

Writing. Using what you have learned in this chapter about lending, edit a completed report you have already written about bank regulation and deregulation. Be sure to include any new knowledge you have gained since writing this report. Does this new information change your stance on a controversial issue? Does it change your understanding of the banking process? Convey any changes in your opinion or understanding in your new report.

Listening. Using the Internet, find at least three news broadcasts and three articles about the controversy surrounding Fannie Mae and Freddie Mac. Write a report in which you discuss the purposes and responsibilities of these entities, and how they were fundamentally changed during the Great Recession of the 21st century.

EVENT PREP Business Law

Business law is a competitive event you might enter with your career and technical student organization (CTSO). Business law is an individual event in which participants take an objective test that covers multiple legal topics. Participants are usually allowed one hour to complete the event. One of the topics that may be included on the test is *insurance as a means of risk management.*

To prepare for a business law event:

1. Well in advance of the date of the event, visit the organization's website.
2. Download any posted practice tests.
3. Time yourself taking the tests with the aid of a nongraphing calculator. Check the answers and correct any mistakes you may have made.
4. Conduct some research on the Internet regarding the legal topics that will be covered on the test. Print out the information you find to use as study material.
5. Visit the organization's website often to make sure information regarding the event has not changed.

9

Check Your Banking IQ

Before you begin this chapter, see what you already know about banking by taking the chapter pretest.

www.m.g-wlearning.com
www.g-wlearning.com

Payments

Section 9.1
Negotiable Instruments

Section 9.2
Using Checks

Section 9.3
Other Payment Systems

People and businesses are paid for products or services that they provide. Bank employees are paid to work in the bank. Professional athletes are paid to compete. Manufacturers are paid to make widgets. Radio deejays are paid to make your drive home more enjoyable. How is a bank involved in making these payments?

College and Career Readiness

Reading Prep. In preparation for reading this chapter, think about how payments have evolved with the increase of technology in banking. As you read, consider how the definition of *negotiable instrument* has changed in the light of technology.

Scan the code to view a Biz Kid$ video. If you do not have a smartphone, visit the G-W Learning companion website.

www.m.g-wlearning.com
www.g-wlearning.com

Section 9.1
Negotiable Instruments

Objectives

After completing this section, you will be able to:

- Define a negotiable instrument.
- Compare and contrast types of negotiable instruments.

Terms

negotiable instrument
on demand
payee
bearer instrument
maker
drawer
drawee
draft
note
check
bill of exchange
promissory note

What Is a Negotiable Instrument?

Unless you are doing volunteer work, you are generally paid for the work that you do. But your employer does not usually give you a thick wad of cash and a handful of change at the end of the day. Instead, you receive a paycheck, which is a negotiable instrument.

A **negotiable instrument** is a transferrable, signed document that represents the promise to pay a specific amount of money in the future or on demand. Although a stack of paper money and coins looks impressive, a single piece of paper worth the same amount is much easier to carry around! Put simply, negotiable instruments are easier to transport and more convenient than cash for large purchases. They also provide proof that a payment was made, which is not provided automatically when a cash payment is made.

Source: Shutterstock (jwblinn)

Using a negotiable instrument, such as a check, to pay for a car or house is much easier than bringing a bag of money.

Elements of a Negotiable Instrument

There are several types of negotiable instruments, but all of these types have certain elements in common:

- authorized signature
- specific amount
- unconditional promise to pay
- payment date
- payee

Figure 9-1 shows these elements on a check, which is a type of negotiable instrument.

Authorized Signature

Since a negotiable instrument is a legal document, it must be signed by an individual who has the authority to promise that the money will be paid. For example, your neighbor, Paul, cannot sign a negotiable instrument that promises money from *your* bank account to pay for *his* new car.

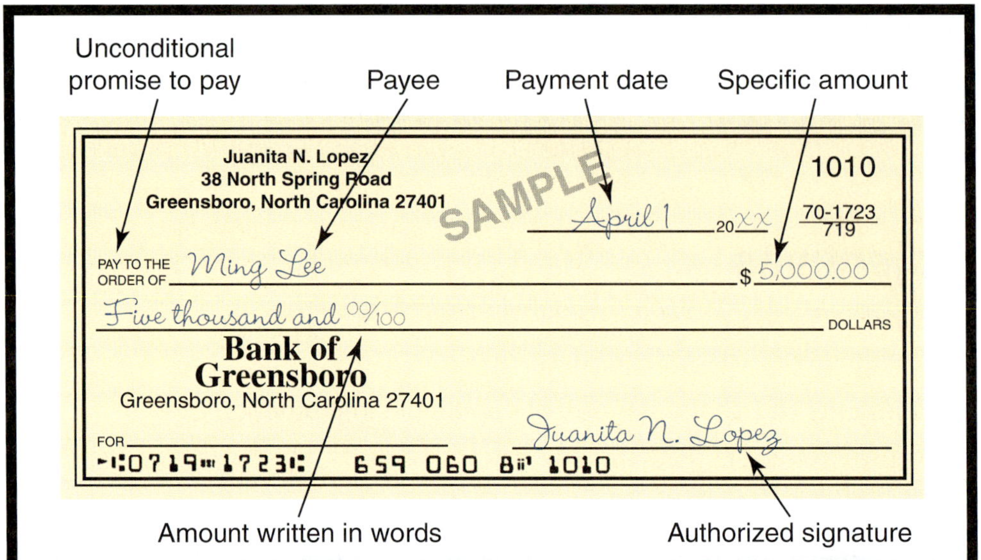

Figure 9-1.
Elements of a Check

Specific Amount

The value of the negotiable instrument must be stated. The value can include interest earned. If interest is included, the amount of interest or the interest rate must be defined in the negotiable instrument.

Unconditional Promise to Pay

A negotiable instrument is an unconditional promise to pay. A *condition* is a requirement that must be fulfilled before an event can occur. It limits or restricts an agreement. A conditional statement might be, “Maria will pay you $5,000 *if you grow the largest pumpkin in this state.”* The condition that must be met is growing the largest pumpkin in this state.

A negotiable instrument does not have conditions. The statement, “Maria will pay you $5,000,” is unconditional. Whether you grow the largest pumpkin or grow no pumpkin at all, Maria will pay you $5,000.

Payment Date

The negotiable instrument can specify a date for payment or the payment can be made on demand. The negotiable instrument can state that payment will be made on a specific day, such as January 5, 2025. It can also state a period of time, such as on the last day of each month. The date must be clear from the description.

A payment to be made **on demand** is made when the payment is requested, which could occur at any time after the negotiable instrument is created. If a date is not specified, the negotiable instrument is payable on demand. Presenting the check is demanding payment. The bank pays immediately.

Payee

The **payee** is the entity receiving the money. Negotiable instruments can be addressed to individuals, groups, companies, or organizations. On the check in Figure 9-1, the payee is Ming Lee. Other legitimate payees include Mr. and Mrs. Ming Lee, Nia and Derek Lee, Lee Industries, and Lee Charity Group. Any person, organization, or business that can be identified and receive payment can be a payee.

Sometimes, specifying a particular payee is not appropriate. Instead, the money should be paid to whoever is in possession of the negotiable instrument. In this case, the payee would be *bearer* or *cash.* When the bearer of a negotiable instrument is the payee, it is known as a bearer instrument. A **bearer instrument** is payable on demand to whoever has it.

Green Banking

Electronic check processing is a big step toward reducing paper usage in the banking industry. Checks are still paper. However, a lot of the other paper used for statements and other records has been reduced or eliminated. Reporting and communicating can be done electronically. The expense, paper documentation, fuel, and pollution caused by transporting paper checks among banks can be eliminated.

What Is the Bank's Role?

A negotiable instrument is created by a maker. The **maker** signs the negotiable instrument to validate it. The maker is also known as the **drawer** for some types of negotiable instruments. The maker authorizes the withdrawal of cash to pay the value of the negotiable instrument.

The **drawee** is the party who pays the value of the negotiable instrument to the payee. In many cases, this is the bank. Figure 9-2 shows the path followed by a negotiable instrument.

BIZ TIPS

The Bank of England was established in 1694. To encourage depositors, the bank issued notes in exchange for deposits. When a deposit was made, the cashier handwrote a note on the bank's paper and gave it to the depositor. Anyone presenting a bank note to the Bank of England was given the value of the note in gold or coins.

Types of Negotiable Instruments

There are two basic types of negotiable instruments: drafts and notes. The distinction between the two types is the way the unconditional promise to pay is handled. A **draft** is a negotiable instrument that orders the payment to be made. A check is a familiar example of a draft. A **note** is a negotiable instrument that promises payment, but does not order that the payment be made. A certificate of deposit (CD) is an example of a note.

Some examples of drafts and notes will be familiar to most bank customers. Others will be less familiar because they fill a specific need and are only used in a limited number of situations. All are negotiable instruments.

Drafts

Drafts clearly direct a payment to be made. On a check, for example, the line containing the payee's name usually says, "Pay to the order of," as shown in Figure 9-1.

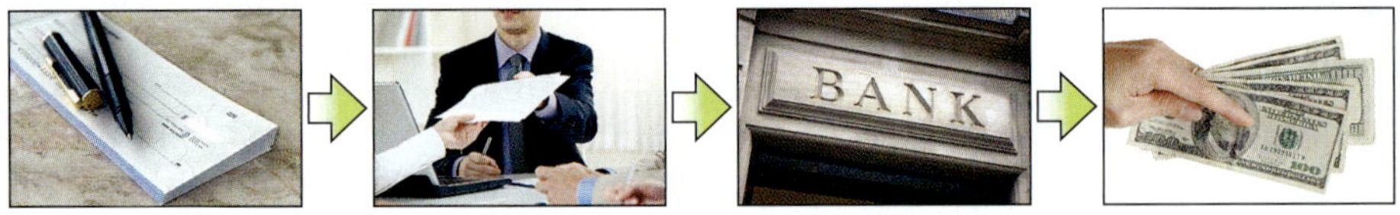

Source: Shutterstock (NAN728, Dmitriy Shironosov, brinkstock, Quang Ho)

Figure 9-2.
Path of Payment

Checks

Most bank customers are familiar with checks. They receive checks from employers or customers and they write checks to pay bills or make purchases. A **check** is a written order directing a bank to pay a specific amount from deposited funds. Because a check orders the payment to be made, checks are a type of draft. In addition to the basic check familiar to most customers, two other types of checks are used in limited situations: traveler's checks and money orders.

Traveler's checks are checks issued by a bank or other financial institution. The customer walks into the bank and buys traveler's checks at a teller window or orders them online from a bank or credit card company. A small fee is usually charged, which serves as income for the financial institution in exchange for the service.

Traveler's checks have several security features. Because they are purchased, they are not linked to a bank account or the customer's personal identity. The customer is protected from loss because traveler's checks can be refunded if lost or stolen. Each traveler's check has a serial number. Buyers should record the serial numbers and store them in a safe place separate from the traveler's checks. To claim a refund, the buyer reports the loss with the serial number.

Traveler's checks function as cash. To use a traveler's check, the owner simply signs it and hands it to a vendor like cash. They can be purchased in several denominations in a variety of currencies for different countries, making them popular for travelers.

A *money order* is another type of check. Although money orders can be issued by a bank or other financial institution, buyers can also purchase them at the post office or some grocery stores, for example. A small fee is charged for issuing the money order.

Money orders are used to pay a specific party. They are not used as cash, like traveler's checks, because they cannot be refunded if lost or stolen.

A *cashier's check* is similar to a money order. A cashier's check draws funds from an account at the same bank that issues a check. While money orders can be obtained from financial institutions and non-financial institutions, such as currency exchanges, cashier's checks can only be obtained from financial institutions.

Source: Shutterstock (Stephen Coburn)

A bill of exchange is often used in international transactions.

Bills of Exchange

Like any draft, a **bill of exchange** is a negotiable instrument that contains an unconditional order to pay a specific amount of money to the payee. The difference between a bill of exchange and a check is that a bill of exchange specifies a future date as the payment date.

A bill of exchange is used in commerce, particularly international trade. A buyer (the drawer) orders a bank (the drawee) to pay a specific amount to a seller (the payee) on a specific date that occurs after the merchandise has been delivered. For example, Latoya in Ohio is buying 5,000 crystal goblets from Joel in Rome. She sends a bill of exchange to Joel. On or after the specified date, Joel takes the bill of exchange to a bank to receive cash.

Notes

Notes promise that a payment will be made, but do not order a drawee to make the payment. A note acknowledges that the money is owed, but does not hand out the cash. Promissory notes and certificates of deposit are familiar forms of notes.

BIZ TIPS

In the 8th century, Arab merchants used a method similar to the bill of exchange to buy and sell products.

Promissory Note

A **promissory note** is the commercial version of an *I owe you (IOU).* It is an unconditional promise to repay a loan for a specific amount of money in the future or on demand. The repayment terms, such as the interest rate, must be detailed in the promissory note.

Certificate of Deposit

A *certificate of deposit (CD)* is a savings tool from the customer's viewpoint. From the bank's viewpoint, it is also a negotiable instrument. The bank is the maker, providing an unconditional promise to repay the customer's deposit, plus interest, on a specific date. Because the payment is promised, not ordered, a CD is a type of note.

Checkpoint 9.1

1. What elements must be in a negotiable instrument?
2. If a date is not specified in a negotiable instrument, when is it paid?
3. What are the two types of negotiable instruments?
4. How is a money order different from a traveler's check?
5. Why is a CD considered a negotiable instrument from the bank's perspective?

Build Your Vocabulary

As you progress through this course, develop a personal glossary of banking terms and add it to your portfolio. This will help you build your banking vocabulary. Write out a definition for each of the following terms, and add it to your personal glossary.

negotiable instrument
on demand
payee
bearer instrument
maker
drawer
drawee
draft
note
check
bill of exchange
promissory note

Section 9.2
Using Checks

Objectives

After completing this section, you will be able to:

- List the characteristics of a checking account.
- Describe the elements of a check.
- Distinguish between the common endorsement types.
- Explain how checks are processed.

Terms

ABA routing number
endorsement
blank endorsement
restricted endorsement
third-party endorsement
clearing
cancelled check
automated clearinghouse (ACH)
substitute check
image replacement document (IRD)

Checking Accounts

The main purpose of a checking account is the ability to withdraw funds from a bank account by writing checks. Checking accounts typically pay no or very low interest rates. This makes them a poor option for saving money. The liquidity of checking accounts is high, however. Customers can usually make an unlimited number of deposits and withdrawals without paying any fees for the account or the transaction.

Consumer checking accounts are opened and maintained by individuals. Commercial checking accounts are opened and maintained by businesses, groups, or organizations. Commercial accounts generally deal with large amounts of money, while consumer checking accounts contain less money. Other than this, most checking accounts are similar.

Most bank customers have a consumer or commercial checking account. Many banks consider checking account owners to be a pool of potential customers for other products and services the bank offers.

Checks

Checks have the same elements as other negotiable instruments, as well as additional elements that provide information related to the bank account. While there are variations in the layout, all checks contain the same basic information.

The elements on a check provide information about the checking account, the drawer, drawee, payee, and how the check is processed. Figure 9-3 provides an example of how these might appear on a check. The account owner is the party whose name is registered on the checking account from which the money will be withdrawn. Each owner of a consumer account or a representative for a commercial account has the authority to perform all transactions for the account.

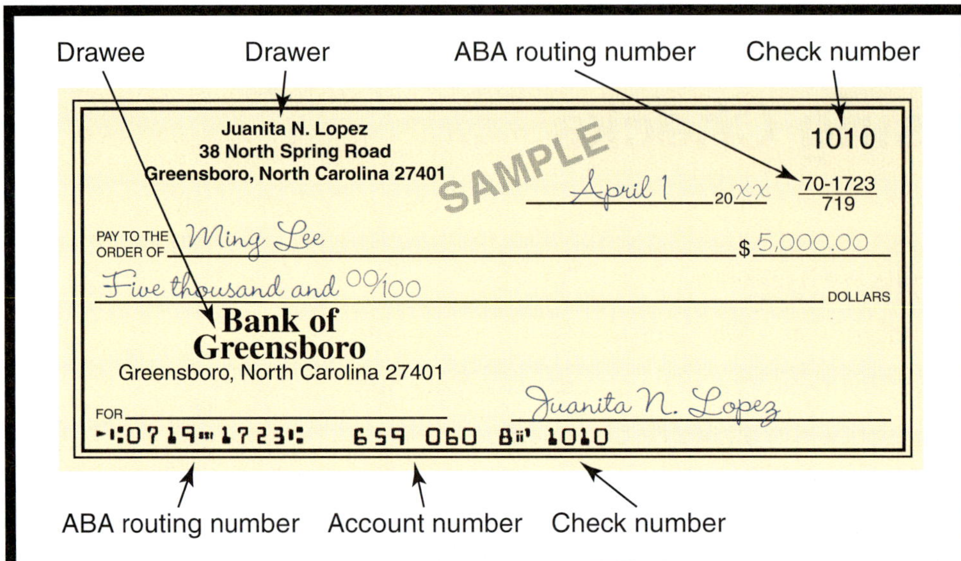

Figure 9-3.
Elements of a Check

The payee is the party to be paid. To cash a check, the payee has to sign the back of the check. The drawee is the financial institution that maintains the account. The name of the financial institution should correspond with the ABA routing number. The **ABA routing number** is a nine-digit number assigned by the American Bankers Association (ABA) to identify the financial institution responsible for paying the value of the check to the payee. It should correspond with the financial institution identified as the drawee.

The check number appears in the upper, right-hand corner. It is used to identify a specific check written from a specific account. Most checking accounts start with check number 101, but customers can usually specify the starting number.

An authorized signature is the account owner's signature or that of a legal representative. For consumer checking accounts, the account owner and the authorized signature should match.

The payment amount is the sum of cash to be paid to the payee. The amount is written in numerals as well as in words.

The day the check is written is the payment date. Checks are drafts that are payable on demand, so the check could be written and cashed on the same day.

Even though all checks contain the same elements, there is some variety in their appearance. Many people select personalized checks. A veterinary student's checks could have pictures of cats or dogs in the background. A business could include its logo, an image of its products, or a picture of its office.

BIZ TIPS

The American Bankers Association developed the ABA routing number in 1910. The number is issued only to federal- or state-chartered financial institutions that are eligible to have an account at a Federal Reserve Bank. Any new financial institution must submit an application to receive an ABA routing number.

Endorsements

The front of the check is not the only important information on a check. The back of the check is mostly blank when a check is written. By the time a check finishes its life cycle, any bank or individual that owned the check is identified on the back of the check. To cash or deposit a check, the payee must endorse it. An **endorsement** is the signature used to legally transfer the value of the check.

On the back of a check, an area is set aside for endorsements, as shown in Figure 9-4. In that area, the payees sign the check before presenting it to the bank.

Payees must follow several rules when endorsing a check. Bank tellers should be familiar with these rules so they only accept those checks that have been correctly endorsed. The payee's signature must match the payee's name as it appears on the front of the check. For example, if the payee is Aakash Patel, the signature must also be Aakash Patel.

If two payees are identified on the front of the check joined by the word *and,* both payees must endorse the check. For example, if the payees are Aakash Patel and Rosita Sanchez, both Aakash *and* Rosita must endorse the check. If two payees are identified on the front of the check joined by the word *or,* only one of the payees must endorse the check. For example, if the payees are Aakash Patel *or* Rosita Sanchez, Rosita can endorse the check alone.

If the payee's name is misspelled on the front of the check, the payee should endorse the check exactly as the name is shown—with the misspelling. Below the misspelled endorsement, the payee should sign the name correctly.

Three types of endorsements are commonly used. Figure 9-5 shows the most common types of endorsements. The differences between the endorsements are the restrictions placed on cashing or depositing a check. The blank endorsement, shown on the left side of the figure, is the least restrictive. The two restricted endorsements on the right side of the figure limit how the value of the check can be handled.

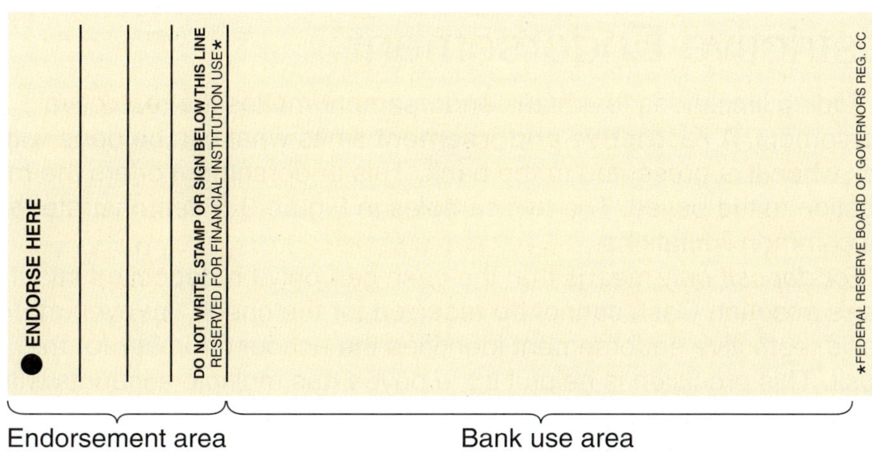

Figure 9-4.
Back of a Personal Check

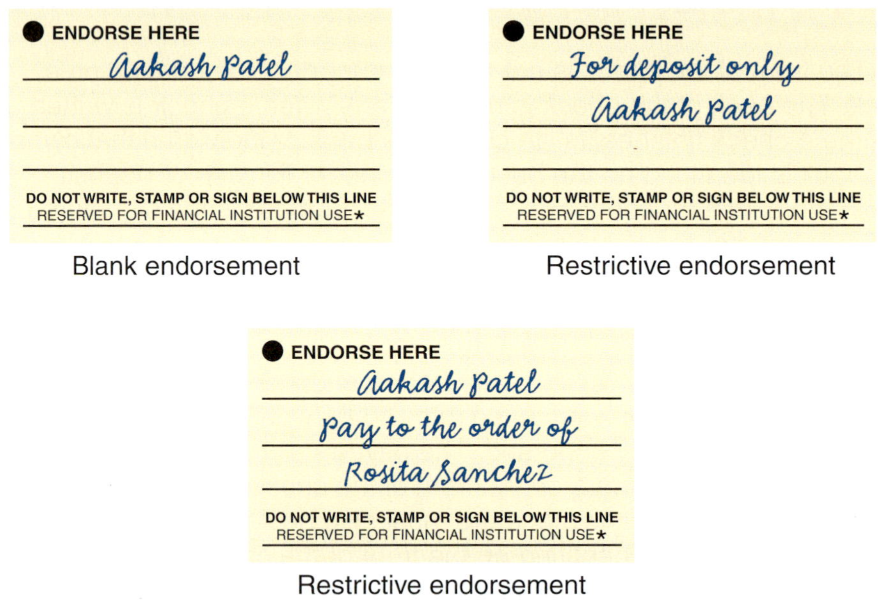

Figure 9-5.
Endorsements

Blank Endorsement

A **blank endorsement** is simply the payee's signature, without restrictions, in the endorsement area, as shown on the left in Figure 9-5. It is the most common, least-restrictive, and least-safe type of endorsement.

A check with a blank endorsement can be cashed by anyone who presents it to the bank. If the payee signs a blank endorsement and then loses the check, the finder becomes the owner of the check's value. The finder can take the check to a bank to receive cash. Account owners should be encouraged to use a blank endorsement only when standing in front of a teller to present a check for payment.

Restrictive Endorsement

Adding limitations to a blank endorsement makes it a restrictive endorsement. A **restrictive endorsement** limits what can be done with a check when it is presented to the bank. This endorsement offers the most protection to the payee. The two samples in Figure 9-5 demonstrate the most common limitations.

For deposit only means that the cash can only be deposited into the payee's account. Cash cannot be received for the check. An even more specific restrictive endorsement identifies the account number for the deposit. This precision is helpful if the payee has multiple accounts with the financial institution.

Third-Party Endorsement

A **third-party endorsement** transfers the payee's claim to the check's value to a third party. An example is shown in Figure 9-6. Banks will accept checks that have a blank or restrictive endorsement. However, most banks will *not* accept a third-party endorsement. These endorsements are considered to be risky because they are often forged.

For example, Aakash receives a check for $75 from Mateo. As it happens, he owes Meaghan Smith $75. To pay Meaghan, Aakash adds a third-party endorsement to the check he received from Mateo and gives the check to Meaghan. Meaghan may have trouble cashing or depositing the check because of the third-party endorsement.

Life Cycle of a Check

Checks are used every day to pay for anything from new shoes to farm equipment. How does a check transfer money from the drawer to the payee? This section discusses the process.

Honoring a Check

When a check comes into the bank, many elements are examined to determine if it is valid:

- date
- signature
- address
- identity of payee
- amount
- check number
- appearance

Date

What is the date on the check? If the date is more than six months old, most banks will not honor the check. Some checks, usually from nonprofit or commercial accounts, have shorter term limits, such as 30, 60, or 90 days.

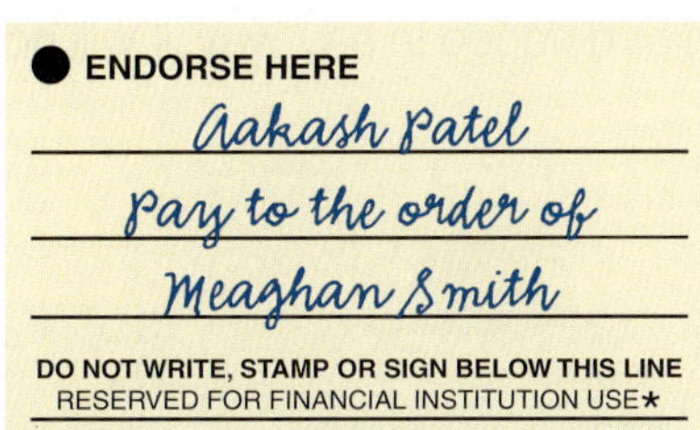

Figure 9-6.
Third-Party Endorsement

Signature

Is the signature legible? Tellers can compare the signatures on the check or endorsement to the signature on a driver's license or other identification. If the signatures do not match, the bank will reject the check.

Address

The address on the check should be a permanent street address, not a post office box. Post office boxes are not allowed because they are not permanent and can be easily used to commit fraud.

Identity of the Payee

The teller can request a legal identification source, such as a driver's license. Some banks require the teller to record the type of ID and the ID number that the payee presents.

Amount

The teller verifies that the amounts written in text and in numerals match. The amount in numerals must be the same as the amount written out in words. If they do not match, it could be an indication of fraud.

Check Number

Is the check number between 101 and 150? A large majority of bad checks have low check numbers. Customers using the same checking account long enough to reach a high number, say 1000, have usually not done anything to cause the bank to close their account, such as bouncing checks. Of course, not all low-number checks are trouble. In addition, many banks allow customers to choose the number at which their checks will begin.

ABA Routing Number

Is the ABA routing number correct for the drawer's financial institution? If it is the same bank, the teller should recognize the correct number.

Appearance

One edge of the check should be perforated. Only checks issued by the government or generated by a computer will not have a perforated edge. Checks today have many safety features. If a check seems to have been tampered with or is torn or defaced in any way, it will not be honored by the bank.

Source: Shutterstock (CREATISTA)

Banks look at all of the information on a check to determine its validity.

Acceptance

If a check meets the requirements outlined above, if it is drawn on the bank where it is presented for payment, and if it is presented by a customer of the bank, it should be honored. If a check meets these requirements, but the person presenting the check is not a customer, it should be honored if legitimate proof of identity is also presented. Banks are not legally required to honor checks that are presented by a noncustomer and are not drawn from one of the bank's accounts.

Processing a Check

After a check has been received by the bank, it is cleared for payment. **Clearing** a check is the process of approving a check and transferring funds from one account to another. In the past, the process of clearing a check took several days:

1. The drawer wrote the check and gave it to the payee.
2. The payee endorsed the check and presented it to the bank.
3. The payee's bank mailed the check to the drawer's bank.
4. The drawer's bank sent the payment to the payee's bank.
5. The **cancelled check,** which is a check that has been cleared, was returned to the drawer.

Because the process took several days, a drawer could write a check and then deposit money into the checking account to cover the check. Today, the process is much faster. Funds can be transferred the same day a check is written. Bank customers are cautioned not to write checks if they do not have enough cash in their account to cover the value of the check.

Of course, technology is at the heart of this increase in speed. Rather than mailing paper checks from bank to bank, electronic images are sent to an automated clearinghouse. An **automated clearinghouse (ACH)** is the system that processes these checks, transferring funds from the drawer's account to the payee's account. Everything happens on the same day or shortly after:

1. The drawer writes the check and gives it to the payee.
2. The payee endorses the check and presents it to the bank.
3. The bank sends an image of the check to the ACH.
4. The ACH transfers funds from the drawer's account to the payee's account.

Many banks no longer return cancelled checks to the drawer. A drawer occasionally requests a cancelled check to prove that payment was made. They can be given a **substitute check,** which is a paper copy of the front and back of the original check. Many banks also allow images of checks and deposits to be viewed online.

Since the 1990s, fewer and fewer paper checks have been written in the US. On the other hand, the number of electronic checks and transfers has also greatly increased. Electronic checks allow account holders to make payments on the Internet in the same way that they would pay for something

BIZ TIPS

The Office of Foreign Assets Control (OFAC) is part of the US Department of the Treasury. OFAC administers economic sanctions against countries, terrorists, and narcotics traffickers, and presents a list of those individuals that have been sanctioned to banks. Before cashing a check, tellers should reference this list to ensure that the parties identified in the check are not listed.

Source: Shutterstock (Tyler Olson)

Be sure there is enough money in your checking account to cover the checks you write.

Ethical Banking

If an account does not hold enough money to pay a check, the account has *insufficient funds (NSF).* Generally, the bank charges the customer a fee for any NSF checks. Intentionally writing a check that will bounce is not only unethical and expensive, it is illegal. If the drawer demonstrates the intent to defraud the payee, he or she can face criminal penalties.

with a check. These checks have more safety features than do paper checks. Both are governed by the same laws. Apps are another new development in banking. Apps allow customers at some banks to deposit checks by scanning them with their smartphones.

Legal Influences

Several legal developments made the modern check-processing system possible. These include the Federal Reserve Act of 1913, the Uniform Commercial Code of 1952, the Expedited Funds Availability Act of 1987, and the Check Clearing Act for the 21st Century of 2004.

Federal Reserve

The Federal Reserve plays the role of the *bankers' bank.* It provides two important services that formed the basis for today's check payment system:

- check processing
- electronic transfers

When two member banks use checks to transfer funds between them, Federal Reserve Banks can collect and pay the funds. Federal Reserve Banks can transfer funds between banks almost immediately. The Federal Reserve's capabilities made it possible to process checks and transfer funds. Electronic advances were needed to make it happen quickly and easily.

Uniform Commercial Code

The Uniform Commercial Code was established to bring uniformity to banking and lending transactions across the US. The code itself is not a law. However, most of its rules have been adopted as law by all 50 states. Without consistent practices for honoring and processing transactions, electronic banking would not be possible.

Expedited Funds Availability Act

In 1987, Congress passed the Expedited Funds Availability Act (EFAA). The EFAA led to rules that allowed quicker access to funds deposited as checks. The act remedied the practice of some banks extending the time between when funds were deposited and when they became available. During this time, called the *float,* banks showed deposits as their assets. This made the bank look like it had greater reserves and assets than was the case.

Check 21

Today's method of check processing would not be possible without the Check Clearing Act for the 21st Century, which is commonly known as Check 21. The purpose of Check 21, which went into effect in 2004, was faster check processing.

The major change was the **image replacement document (IRD),** which is another term for a substitute check. The ability to create a substitute check removed bank and customer concerns about the use of electronic records. Banks were no longer worried about the lack of a paper check that they could watch throughout the process. They could now watch an electronic copy of the check instead. Customers were no longer worried about the lack of a cancelled check at the end of the process. They could now view and print an electronic copy of the check as proof of payment. Because Check 21 enabled the creation of IRDs, banks and customers are not forced to be completely paperless.

Checkpoint 9.2

1. How is the drawee identified on a check?
2. Which type of endorsement is the least safe? Explain.
3. What is the purpose of a third-party endorsement?
4. What two steps did ACHs remove from the check-processing procedure?
5. How did IRDs remove bank and customer concerns about the use of electronic records?

Build Your Vocabulary

As you progress through this course, develop a personal glossary of banking terms and add it to your portfolio. This will help you build your banking vocabulary. Write out a definition for each of the following terms, and add it to your personal glossary.

ABA routing number
endorsement
blank endorsement
restricted endorsement
third-party endorsement
clearing
cancelled check
automated clearinghouse (ACH)
substitute check
image replacement document (IRD)

Careers in Finance Banking and Related Services

What Does a Computer Network Administrator Do?

Computer network administrators are members of the information technology (IT) career field, which focuses on the use of computers. Networks link computers to share and exchange information. **Computer network administrators** design and install new networks. They are also responsible for network security. Some of the activities performed by a **computer network administrator** include:

- creating new networks for business and financial institutions;
- supporting and maintaining a network after it is in place;
- updating software and troubleshooting and any problems that arise;
- adding and removing users to the network; and
- evaluating and correcting network security problems, which is especially important for financial institutions that handle financial and confidential information.

What Is It Like to Work as a Computer Network Administrator?

Computer network administrators usually work at a desk in an office environment. They may travel occasionally to branch offices when new computers are added to the network. As technology advances, the need for **computer network administrators** to travel to remote offices is less. More administration tasks can be performed through the administrator's own network connection rather than traveling to a remote location.

If you enjoy computer science and detailed, intricate work, a career as a **computer network administrator** might suit you.

What Education and Skills Are Needed to Be a Computer Network Administrator?

- college degree in business or information systems
- additional certifications may be required for certain employers
- problem-solving, analysis, and communication skills

Career Ladder

Chief Information Officer

Information Technology (IT) Manager

Computer Network Administrator

Section 9.3
Other Payment Systems

Objectives

After completing this section, you will be able to:

- Define a payment system.
- Describe the common types of electronic funds transfers.
- Explain how cards are used as payment systems.

Terms

payment system
electronic funds transfer (EFT)
automated teller machine (ATM)
cash card
direct deposit
wire transfer
automatic payment
bill-payment service
debit card

Payment Systems

Ways to pay for goods and services have evolved throughout the years. What is accepted as a form of payment has changed. A form of payment that is initially accepted reluctantly often ends up replacing the method people are currently most comfortable with. Figure 9-7 shows this development.

Today, money travels from pocket to pocket, wallet to wallet, and account to account. But, very little of it moves as cash. It moves as a check, a swipe on a debit card, or an electronic figure on a balance sheet. **Payment systems** are methods of transferring funds without using cash. Without them, money would not flow as smoothly as it does. Global trade would grind to a halt if buyers and sellers had to carry suitcases of cash to every transaction.

Checks are a common method of transferring funds. But, advances in technology have increased the number of payment systems available to consumers today. Electronic funds transfers are among the most common.

Electronic Funds Transfer

An **electronic funds transfer (EFT)** is any transfer of funds *started* by electronic means. EFTs generally include transactions on automated teller machines, direct deposits, wire transfers, automatic payments, and bill-payment services. Negotiable instruments, such as checks, are not EFTs, however, because the funds transfer is started by a document.

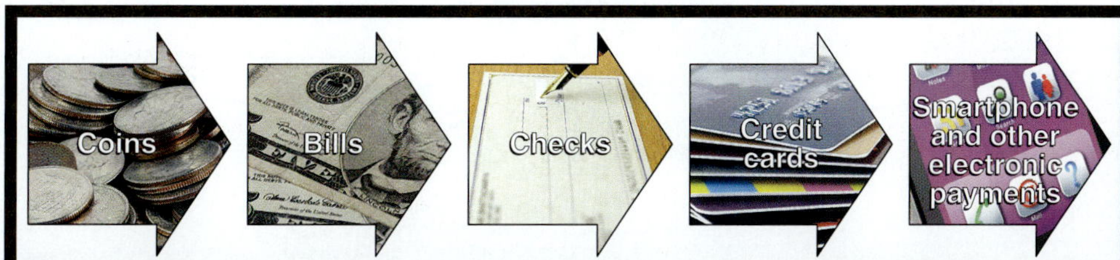

Source: Shutterstock (Brandon Alms, Seth E. Gallmeyer, neelsky, Solomin Andrey, mkabakov)

Figure 9-7.
Progression of Payment Systems

Automated Teller Machines

The automated teller machine (ATM) was a welcome technological advance for busy people everywhere. People no longer had to rush to a bank to make deposits or withdrawals during a busy lunch hour while the bank was open. Instead, they could go to a drive-through ATM after work, power walk to the ATM in a mall, or stroll over to an ATM near the beach while on vacation. Their banking activities were no longer tied to the bank's business hours.

An **automated teller machine (ATM)** is a computerized machine that allows a customer to perform basic banking activities, such as withdrawing cash or checking an account balance. If an ATM is not nearby, one might be there soon. A new ATM is installed approximately every five minutes.

Every customer with a bank account that can be accessed via an ATM receives a cash card. A **cash card** is a plastic card with a magnetic strip that can be read by an ATM. The customer simply inserts the cash card into the ATM, enters a PIN, and follows the on-screen messages to conduct transactions. Figure 9-8 shows the components of an ATM.

ATMs are a source of bank income. Customers can usually perform transactions at their bank's ATMs without paying a fee. However, a service fee is typically charged for using ATMs belonging to other banks.

Direct Deposits

Many employers pay their employees through direct deposit rather than cash or check. **Direct deposit** means that funds are added directly into a bank account by electronic means instead of a negotiable instrument being issued. This has two advantages. First, funds are immediately available since a check does not need to clear. Second, direct deposit is safe because it eliminates the need to transport a check.

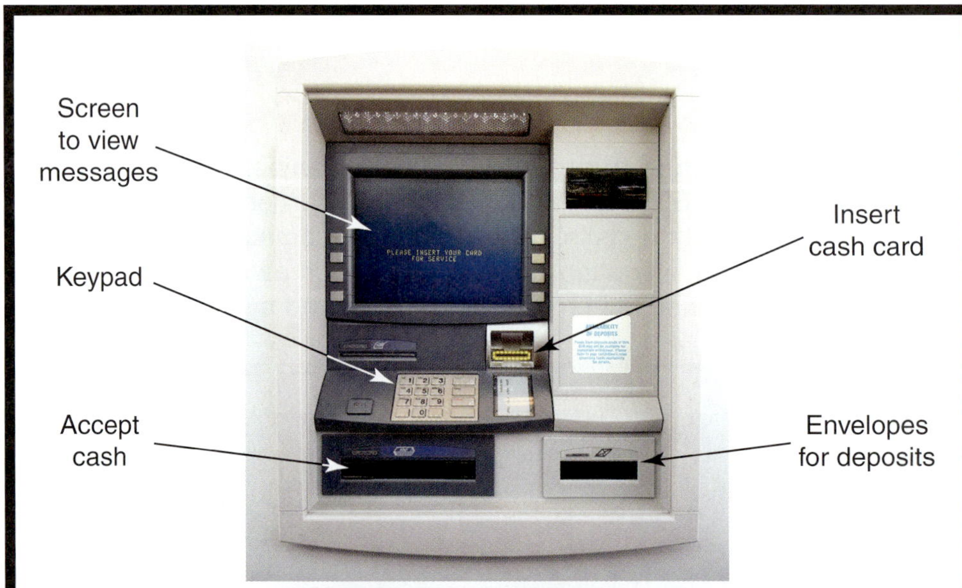

Source: Shutterstock (Amy Walters)

Figure 9-8.
Anatomy of an ATM

Wire Transfers

A **wire transfer** is an electronic transfer of funds from one location to another location. It is the fastest and safest way to transfer funds between locations. Typically, funds are transferred from one bank account to another bank account. This service is provided by several organizations and companies.

The Federal Reserve Wire Network (FedWire) is a system that connects the Federal Reserve Board of Governors, the Federal Reserve Banks and their branches, the US Department of the Treasury, and member depository institutions. This is one of the many services that the Fed provides to its member banks.

The Clearing House Interbank Payment System (CHIPS) is a privately held system that enables major banks around the world to electronically transfer funds with each other. Members are large banks that deal in US dollars. Small banks that want to participate, but cannot afford the service, may have accounts at larger banks that participate in CHIPS. This enables them to send and receive funds as well.

Automatic Payments

Most consumers have bills that must be paid on a regular basis. **Automatic payments** are preauthorized electronic funds sent from a customer's account to a vendor's account at regular intervals. The money is automatically transferred from the customer's account to the vendor without any request for that particular payment. Automatic payments are generally for a set amount each interval, such as a monthly mortgage payment.

For example, Bernard has a checking account and a mortgage loan. Bernard is afraid that he will forget to pay his mortgage, so he sets up an automatic payment for the length of the loan. Bernard makes this request only once. After the request is made, the recurring bill is automatically paid.

Bill-Payment Services

The difference between automatic payments and bill-paying services is the *automatic* feature. Automatic payments are set up by the customer once. All subsequent payments are made without additional action by the customer or the vendor. When using a **bill-payment service,** the electronic transfer of funds from a customer's account to a vendor's account must be requested by the customer or the vendor each time a payment is due.

This is more practical than automatic payments for bills that might vary in amount, such as electricity bills. This service can be provided by the bank or by the vendor. If it is provided by the bank, the customer usually requests the transfer. If it is provided by the vendor, the vendor makes the request to the customer's bank.

Source: Shutterstock (luchschen)

Debit cards can be used in ATMs or to make purchases.

Cards

The cash card used in an ATM is not the only type of card that can be used in a payment system. Credit cards, charge cards, and debit cards are payment systems as well. All three types of cards contain a magnetic strip that can be read by a machine.

Credit Cards and Charge Cards

Credit cards are used to buy products or services on credit. When making a purchase, the customer presents the credit card to the vendor. The vendor swipes the card through a device that reads the card's magnetic strip. The card's owner signs to authorize the transfer of funds. The vendor submits a request for payment and the customer's authorization to the credit card company. The credit card company pays the vendor and at the end of the month bills the customer for the expense. The customer goes home with his or her purchase without any cash exchanging hands.

Credit cards are open-ended loans that do not need to be paid in full every month. Charge cards work like credit cards, but the balance must be paid in full every month. Credit cards and charge cards usually limit the customer's spending to a specific amount. For example, Mateo's credit limit is $10,000. His older sister has the same type of credit card, but her credit limit is $25,000 because she has a longer credit history that is better than Mateo's.

Banks earn money for these cards by charging the vendors requesting payment, and banks also earn interest and fees on these cards from consumers. Depending on the characteristics of the specific card, the customer might pay a fee just to have the card, pay interest on the amount owed, and pay late fees if the customer's payment is made late.

Debit Cards

A **debit card** is a card that enables customers to electronically access the funds in their accounts. Debit cards are sometimes called *check cards.* Debit cards can be used in an ATM to get cash or can be presented to a vendor to pay for products or services.

Customers who use debit cards are not billed later like customers who use credit cards. Instead, money is immediately withdrawn from the customer's account and deposited in the vendor's account when the purchase is made.

To use a debit card, the customer must enter a password, usually called a *personal identification number (PIN).* This makes the debit card safer than cash or checks.

Whenever a debit card is used, either to make a payment or an ATM withdrawal, customers must be sure to record the amount in their account registers. The transaction must be included when balancing the account at the end of the month.

Checkpoint 9.3

1. How are ATMs a source of income for the bank?
2. What are two advantages of direct deposit from an employee's standpoint?
3. How does the Federal Reserve Wire Network participate in wire transfers?
4. What is the difference between automatic payments and a bill-payment service?
5. How is a debit card different from a credit card?

Build Your Vocabulary

As you progress through this course, develop a personal glossary of banking terms and add it to your portfolio. This will help you build your banking vocabulary. Write out a definition for each of the following terms, and add it to your personal glossary.

payment system
electronic funds transfer (EFT)
automated teller machine (ATM)
cash card
direct deposit
wire transfer
automatic payment
bill-payment service
debit card

Chapter Summary

Section 9.1 Negotiable Instruments

- A negotiable instrument is a transferrable, signed document that entitles an entity to receive a specific amount of money in the future or on demand.
- The two basic types of negotiable instruments are drafts and notes. Drafts order a payment, while notes promise a payment, but do not order that it be made.

Section 9.2 Using Checks

- The main purpose of a checking account is to receive funds from a bank account without having to get cash from the bank.
- Checks have the same elements as other negotiable instruments as well as additional elements that provide information related to the payment.
- To cash or deposit a check, the payee must endorse it. A signature used to legally transfer the value of the check is an endorsement.
- When checks are presented to the bank for payment, they are carefully examined to determine that they are legitimate. After checks are accepted, they are processed by an automated clearinghouse (ACH) and funds are transferred.

Section 9.3 Other Payment Systems

- A payment system is a method of transferring funds without using cash.
- Any funds transfer started by electronic means is considered to be an Electronic Funds Transfer (EFT).
- Credit cards, charge cards, and debit cards are also payment systems. Customers pay for credit card and charge card transactions when the card company bills them. Debit card transactions are immediately processed and paid.

Check Your Banking IQ

Now that you have finished this chapter, see what you know about banking by taking the chapter post test.

www.m.g-wlearning.com
www.g-wlearning.com

Review Your Knowledge

On a separate sheet of paper or in a word processing document, match the following terms with the definition that fits best.

A. drawee
B. blank endorsement
C. bill of exchange
D. cash card
E. substitute check
F. bearer instrument
G. direct deposit
H. electronic funds transfer (EFT)
I. cancelled check
J. restricted endorsement

1. Cleared check.
2. Plastic card that can be read by an ATM.
3. Pays the value of the negotiable instrument to the payee.
4. Funds added directly to a bank account by electronic means.
5. Limitations added to a blank endorsement.
6. Any transfer of funds started by electronic means.
7. Negotiable instrument that contains an unconditional order to pay a specific amount of money to the payee.
8. Payable on demand to whoever has it.
9. The payee's signature without restrictions.
10. Paper copy of the front and back of the original check.

On a separate sheet of paper or in a word processing document, answer each of the following questions.

11. Why does a negotiable instrument require an authorized signature?
12. When is a payment on demand made?
13. What is the difference between a consumer checking account and a commercial checking account?
14. List five types of EFTs.
15. How do banks earn money on credit cards and charge cards?

Apply Your Knowledge

16. Create a chart listing the types of negotiable instruments and the pros, cons, and major features of each.
17. Create an organizational chart showing the relationships between the entities in a negotiable instrument transaction. Make sure to include at least the payee, maker, drawer, and drawee, and provide an explanation of each entity's duties in the transaction.
18. Pick a bank to research. On the bank's website, look for a checking account disclosure or agreement. Specifically, look for the bank's policies on processing deposits. Write a summary of the bank's requirements for deposit processing and the responsibilities a consumer has in making a deposit. Why do you think these safeguards and penalties have been established?
19. Create a chart listing the types of EFTs and the major features of each. Include the pros and cons of each EFT from both the banker's and consumer's perspectives.
20. Research the electronic check conversion services provided by Federal Reserve Banks. Write a report in which you summarize the main advantages and disadvantages of this service.

Working in Teams

Working with a classmate, research the history of negotiable instruments. Write a report in which you consider the following questions: Where did the idea for negotiable instruments originate? How have they evolved over the years? How have they been adapted to fit the needs of 21st century bank customers?

G-W Learning Mobile Site

Visit the G-W Learning mobile site to complete the chapter pretest and post test and to practice vocabulary using e-flash cards. If you do not have a smartphone, visit the G-W Learning companion website to access these features.

G-W Learning mobile site: www.m.g-wlearning.com
G-W Learning companion website: www.g-wlearning.com

Common Core

College and Career Readiness

Reading. Locate a few summaries or opinions of Check 21 on the Internet. Determine the reasoning behind the provisions of this act. Write an evaluation of how the provisions of this act speak to the needs of bankers in the 21st century.

Listening. Find video footage of a speech describing the Uniform Commercial Code. Write a report in which you summarize the speaker's point of view, reasoning, use of evidence and rhetoric, word choice, points of emphasis, and tone. How do these contribute to the speaker's overall message?

EVENT PREP Extemporaneous Speaking

Extemporaneous speaking is a competitive event you might enter with your career and technical student organization (CTSO). This event allows you to showcase your communication skills of speaking, organizing, and making an oral presentation. You will be evaluated on your verbal and nonverbal skills as well as the tone and projection of your voice. This will be a timed event, and you will not be able to prepare for it before the competition. You will be given several topics from which to choose and a time limit to create a speech as well as a time limit to deliver the speech. Review the specific guidelines and rules for this event for direction as to topics and props you will be allowed to use. To prepare for an extemporaneous speaking event:

1. Read the guidelines provided by your organization. Make certain that you ask any questions about points you do not understand. It is important you follow each specific item that is outlined in the competition rules.
2. Ask your instructor for several practice topics on banking so you can practice making impromptu speeches.
3. Practice, practice, practice. Your speech will be judged by a panel of professionals.
4. Ask your instructor to bring together a panel that will listen to your practice speech and provide feedback.

Unit 3
Summative Assessment

On a separate sheet of paper or in a word processing document, use what you have learned in this unit to answer the questions that follow.

True/False Questions

1. *True or False?* Loans can benefit the entire community.
2. *True or False?* The five C's of credit are character, creditworthiness, capital, collateral, and capacity.
3. *True or False?* Electronic checks, transfers, and apps have replaced most paper checks today.
4. *True or False?* Compound interest pays interest on principal and accrued interest.
5. *True or False?* Automatic payments must be requested monthly.

Multiple Choice Questions

6. _____ are considered defined benefit plans.
   A. Roth IRAs
   B. SIMPLE IRA plans
   C. 401(k)s
   D. Pensions
7. The _____ method is the most favorable for cardholders.
   A. average daily balance
   B. adjusted balance
   C. monthly balance
   D. previous balance
8. Custodial accounts _____.
   A. are managed by an adult for a minor who is younger than 18 or 21
   B. pay higher interest rates than traditional savings accounts
   C. are opened and used without visiting a physical location
   D. have a higher minimum balance requirement and restrictions on the number of withdrawals
9. The _____ is the entity receiving the money.
   A. drawer
   B. drawee
   C. maker
   D. payee
10. Which of following is *not* true of an equity loan?
    A. Temporarily transfers cash to the borrower.
    B. Considered a first mortgage.
    C. Risks the borrower's real estate because it becomes collateral for the loan.
    D. A second way for lenders to earn money on the same real estate.

Visit the Biz Kid$ Website!

Unit 4

Bank Management

What You Will Learn

As you've already learned, banks are an integral part of our society. Banks work to grow the economy by lending out money and giving consumers a safe place to save. In this unit, you will learn how banks also function as businesses. Banks need to be managed, marketed, advertised, and evaluated just like any other business. You will also discover that banks offer a variety of important career opportunities. People working in these careers have a big impact on our economy.

Source: Shutterstock (Monkey Business Images)

Explore what skills and education are needed for a career in banking.

Chapter 10
Day-to-Day Activities

- Section 10.1 Organization and Management
- Section 10.2 Special Departments
- Section 10.3 Human Resources

Chapter 11
Selling the Bank

- Section 11.1 Marketing and Promotions
- Section 11.2 Building Relationships

Chapter 12
Banking Careers and Workplace Skills

- Section 12.1 Executive Careers
- Section 12.2 Banking Administration Careers
- Section 12.3 Managerial Careers
- Section 12.4 Operational-Support Careers
- Section 12.5 Employability Skills

Chapter 13
Bank Performance

- Section 13.1 Analyzing the Numbers
- Section 13.2 Assessing the Bank

Chapter 14
Ethics, Security, Fraud, and Workplace Safety

- Section 14.1 Ethics
- Section 14.2 Security
- Section 14.3 Fraud
- Section 14.4 Workplace Safety

Source: Shutterstock (.shock)

Learn why ethics and security are important to banks.

Biz Kid$ in Action

Manager Maria works at Sound Savings and Loans as a branch manager. Each day when she arrives to open the bank, she reviews the latest financial news to make sure her bank is in step with the economy. Then she reviews general e-mail inquiries and directs them to the correct employees. She needs to count out the tellers' cash drawers with each teller.

Manager Maria is proud about working at Sound Savings and Loans. The business has had excellent, stable performance, and Maria monitors it on a daily basis. Bank regulations have changed dramatically over the last few years. It's been a challenge to keep up with what these changes mean for customers and employees. Sound Savings and Loans has been a pillar of the community for years and has always funded the annual Holiday Walk and donated employee time to the local children's hospital. It is trusted in the community, and Manager Maria is proud to say, "When a customer leaves, they usually come back."

Banking Bits

Many banks have credit card security measures in place. If a purchase is made outside of a customer's normal purchase pattern, it will be flagged and the customer alerted to verify the transaction. Also, many credit cards have built-in protection from fraudulent transactions. But, it's much better not to get scammed in the first place.

Ensure a website is secure before providing your credit card number. A secure connection will often have *https* rather than *http* before the web address. Many browsers will show you a lock icon or other indication that the connection is secure.

Read your bank and credit card statements every month. Immediately call the issuer and credit bureaus if you see transactions you don't recognize.

Think you've found an online scam? Report it at the FBI's tips site: http://tips.fbi.gov.

Quick Tip! Building relationships also builds business opportunities. It's never too early to start building.

Let's get started! ⟶

Scan the code to view a Biz Kid$ video. If you do not have a smartphone, visit the G-W Learning companion website.

www.m.g-wlearning.com
www.g-wlearning.com

10

Check Your Banking IQ

Before you begin this chapter, see what you already know about banking by taking the chapter pretest.

www.m.g-wlearning.com
www.g-wlearning.com

Day-to-Day Activities

Think about what would happen if an official stopped calling a soccer game and began playing alongside one of the team members. Chaos would result. But why? Because the official was not doing the job the teams expected and needed him or her to do. It is important within any organization for people to play their parts and know how they impact the entire operation. This is true in sports as well as in any business, including banking. Jobs are assigned and an organizational structure is established based on each person's strengths and weaknesses. This ensures the bank runs as efficiently and profitably as possible.

College and Career Readiness

Reading Prep. Before reading, observe the objectives for each section in this chapter. As you read, focus on how the chapter is structured. Does this structure make points clear, convincing, and engaging?

Scan the code to view a Biz Kid$ video. If you do not have a smartphone, visit the G-W Learning companion website.

www.m.g-wlearning.com
www.g-wlearning.com

Section 10.1
Organization and Management

Objectives

After completing this section, you will be able to:

- Explain how organizational charts are used in the banking industry.
- Describe how banks are structured.
- Describe the role bank management plays in meeting bank goals.

Terms

organizational chart
department
branch office
manager
responsibility
authority
executive
board of directors

Organizational Charts

Organization and leadership are two important characteristics of successful banks. Organization provides a structure for action. Leadership structures an organization and directs its members. In a bank, employees perform certain roles and managers ensure that everyone stays on track.

A classroom is similar. In a classroom, it is easy to see who is in charge. The students report to the teacher, as shown by the organizational chart in Figure 10-1. An **organizational chart** is a diagram representing the structure of a company or organization. The position of each element shows its place within the group. The lines on the chart link workers to their supervisors.

A single classroom is not an accurate picture of your school. The teacher reports to the principal. The principal reports to the school district, and so on. Even a complex structure can be shown in an organizational chart. Figure 10-2 shows 27 students in nine classrooms at three schools in one school district. Your school district probably has many schools and principals, dozens of teachers, and thousands of students.

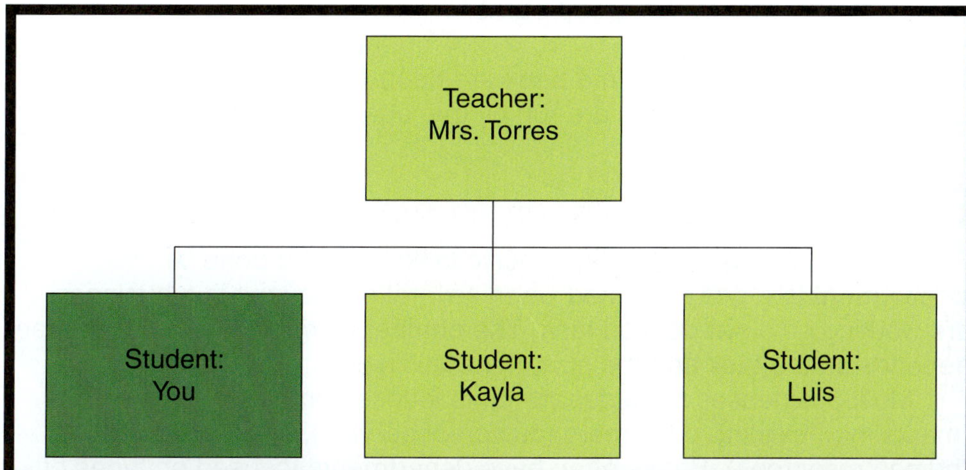

Figure 10-1.
Organizational Chart—Classroom

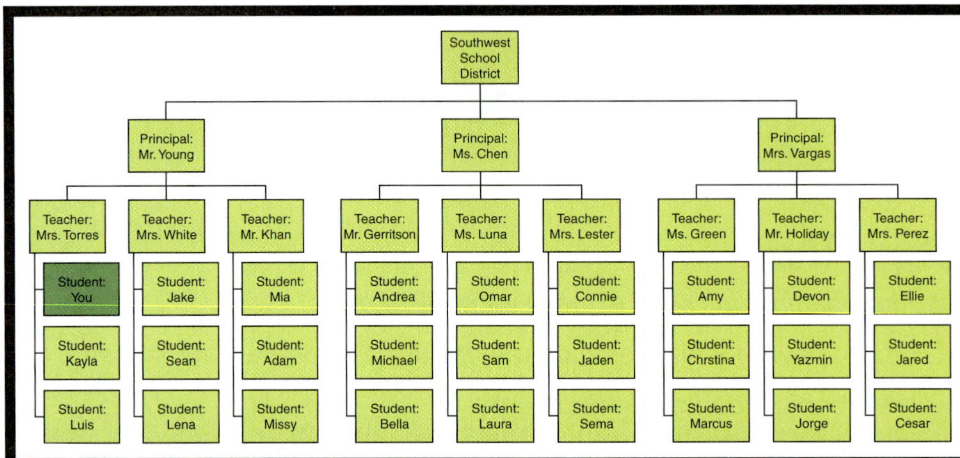

Figure 10-2.
Organizational Chart—School District

An organizational chart allows you to see the relationships among individuals and groups that might be difficult to explain in words. Looking at the chart, you can see how students are grouped into classes under one teacher, teachers in a school under one principal, and the schools under one district. These charts can be used just as effectively to demonstrate ranks within a business.

Bank Structure

The organizational structure of each bank is different. For example, depending on its size and business goals, it might have three or thirty employees focused on making home mortgage loans. If a bank does not make home mortgage loans, it will not have any employees focused on them.

Groups can be set up using several factors:

- function
- number of people performing the same function
- amount of money the group earns
- geographic location

The most common groups in a bank are departments and branches. Departments and branches are run by managers and executives.

Departments

For a business to operate, specific tasks must be done. A **department** is a group created when several employees in a business are working on a specialized task. The number of workers in a department depends on the task and the size of the business.

Most businesses have departments focused on new customers (marketing), existing customers (customer service), and employees (human resources). Banks often have departments focused on types of business as well. For example, a bank might have a department focused on loans or managing the bank's assets.

Branches

Banks have always been important in their local communities. To maintain a local presence and serve its customers, banks often have branch offices. A **branch office** is a banking facility that is not the bank's main location. These are commonly called *branches.* Large banks might have branches in several large cities. Headquarters may be out of state. Local banks might have several branches scattered around a single city.

A bank will open a branch office if doing so will increase profits. Branches are often located near other businesses. Each successful branch must be able to draw enough business from the local area to earn a profit.

Although banks differ, most branches have departments similar to the main location. Some functions, however, are specialized and stay in the main location. For example, all banks hire employees. However, a branch might have a dozen employees and hire only one or two new employees in a year. It is not necessary to keep a human resources department at the branch for so little work. Instead, the human resources department at the main location handles any tasks related to hiring employees for the bank *and* its branches.

Bank Management

Bank management relates to how a bank is run. Managers usually carry out the plans the executives develop. They also focus on the day-to-day operations of their departments. They supply the vision and structure of the bank. The executives are accountable to the shareholders who are represented on the board of directors. Each management level plays a role in making sure the organization's goals are met.

Managers

Each department reports to a manager. A **manager** is a bank employee who is in charge of a segment of a business. To effectively manage, the manager must have responsibility and authority. **Responsibility** is the duty to complete an assigned task well. Part of a manager's responsibility is to ensure that the group completes its tasks. If the group does not complete its tasks, its manager might be replaced.

In business, **authority** is the power to affect or direct a situation or a worker's behavior. For example, a loan department has a goal to make 20 new loans within a specific time period. If 20 loans are not made during that time, the manager might be disciplined or replaced. The manager has the authority to hire additional loan officers or make other changes to reach the goal.

The number of people who report directly to a manager differs. A department's goals and tasks and amount of functions it performs dictate the

Green Banking

Tellers record deposits and withdrawals on computer terminals. The terminals can display detailed information about customer accounts. The displayed information lets the tellers take advantage of cross-selling opportunities. This paperless form of marketing is good for the bank, the customer, and the environment.

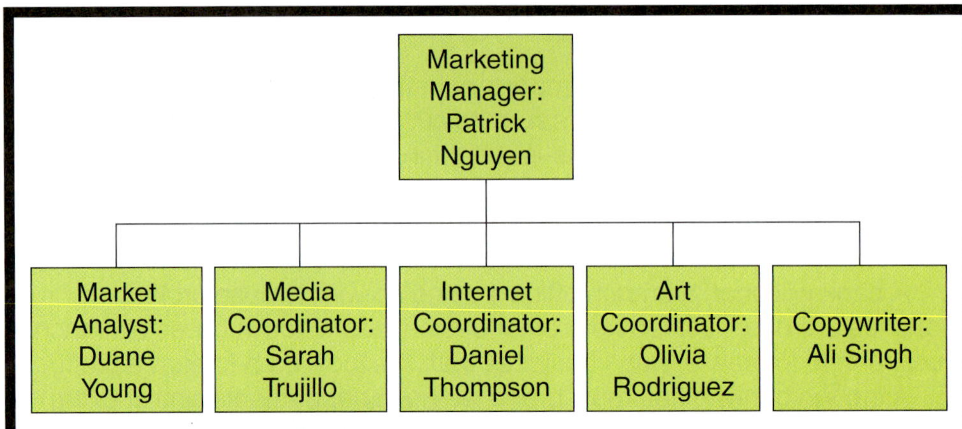

Figure 10-3.
Organizational Chart—Small Marketing Department

number of persons assigned there. In Figure 10-3, only five workers report to the manager of a small marketing department. Each worker's tasks differ from each other. The manager is responsible for verifying that all tasks are successfully complete. Together, they have the skills needed to accomplish most marketing skills. Each worker specializes in a particular task.

Executives

The top management layer consists of an executive team. **Executives** are managers who have the responsibility and authority to make decisions about the bank and how it conducts its business. Executives set the goals for the entire bank.

The structure of a bank's executive management depends on two main characteristics: size and ownership. Smaller banks have fewer executives than large banks. For example, a small, privately-owned bank might limit its executives to owners. Large banks that have shareholders often have a board of directors to manage the bank's growth.

Common executive positions include the chief executive officer, chief operating officer, chief financial officer, and president. Although the structure varies from bank to bank, Figure 10-4 shows a common structure. Other executives who report to the chief executive officer may focus on specific functions.

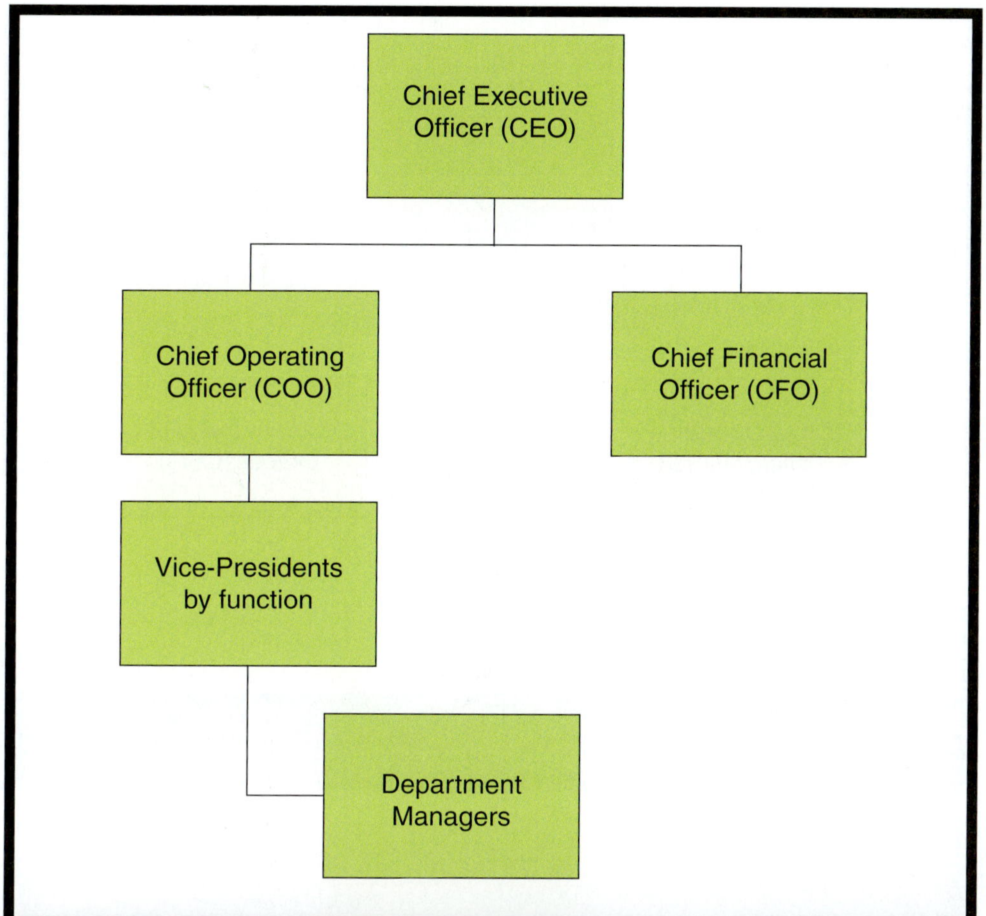

Figure 10-4.
Common Organizational Structure with Bank Executives

Board of Directors

The **board of directors** is a group of individuals elected by a bank's shareholders to represent the shareholders and guide the bank's policies and business decisions. The board of directors is the ultimate authority, making decisions that can affect the way the bank operates. The chief executive officer is often the top executive for the bank. However, in some organizations, the president is at the top. The board of directors has authority over the bank, as well as its highest executive.

The chief executive officer and other executives could be members of the board of directors. The chief executive officer or president must carry out the policies that the board establishes, regardless of whether he or she is a member of the board. A sample organizational chart reflecting this relationship is shown in Figure 10-5.

Typically, the board of directors selects one of its members to be the chairperson of the board. This individual leads the meetings, which occur several times a year. The bank's health is reported and policy decisions are made during these meetings.

Ethical Banking

Banks have access to customers' money and personal information. To reassure customers, some banks develop and publish a code of ethics that applies to all employees, regardless of rank. Each employee must take an annual refresher course.

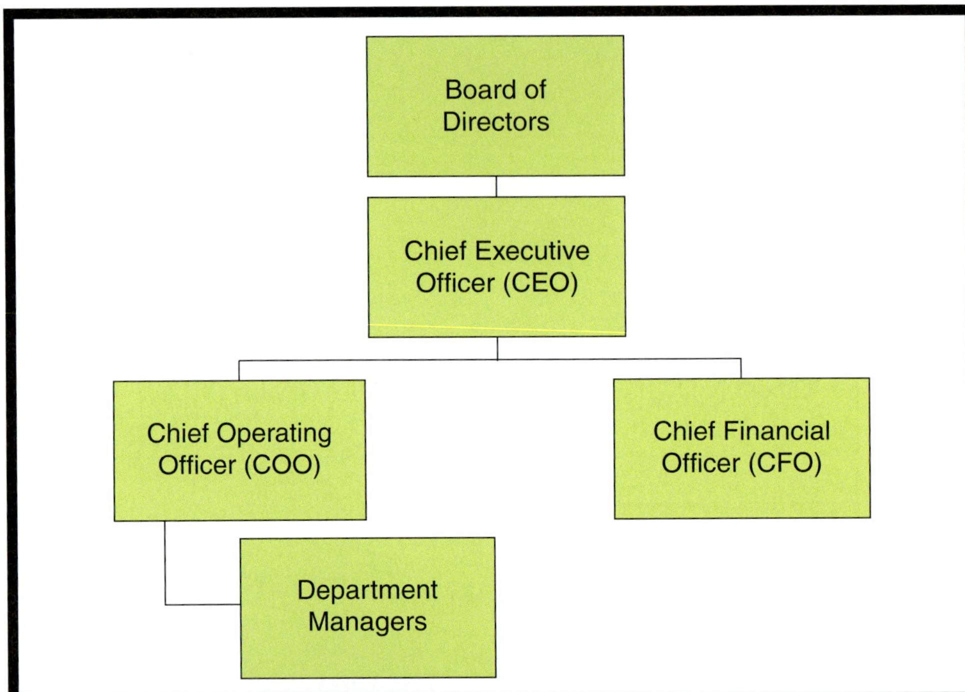

Figure 10-5.
Common Organizational Structure with Executives and Board of Directors

Checkpoint 10.1

1. Why are organizational charts used?
2. What are four factors that can be used to determine groups in a bank's organization?
3. Why would a bank open a branch office?
4. What are two qualities managers must possess to manage effectively?
5. Which executive is responsible for carrying out the policies that the board of directors establishes?

Build Your Vocabulary

As you progress through this course, develop a personal glossary of banking terms and add it to your portfolio. This will help you build your banking vocabulary. Write out a definition for each of the following terms, and add it to your personal glossary.

organizational chart
department
branch office
manager
responsibility
authority
executive
board of directors

Section 10.2
Special Departments

Objectives

After completing this section, you will be able to:

- Describe the special functions that banks perform.
- Explain the administrative tasks tellers perform.
- Explain how a bank collects funds from unpaid loans.
- Describe the role of compliance in bank operations.

Terms

safe deposit box
cash drawer
collection
foreclosure
repossession
garnishment
compliance

Operational Support

Although banks are like other businesses in many ways, they have some special functions that make them unique. Special functions include operational support, loan collection, and compliance.

Front-line operational support is performed by tellers. They are the most public faces in a bank. Tellers greet customers when they enter the bank or arrive at the drive-through window. They execute many of the basic functions that customers perform on a daily basis, such as cashing checks and making deposits. Without the operational support that tellers provide, most bank locations would have little customer interaction and less business.

Transactions

Tellers prepare, verify, and process deposit slips; cash checks after verifying the proper check endorsement; sell money orders and traveler's checks; inform customers of their account balance; and transfer funds from one account to another. All of these transactions are the services that customers perform on a regular basis.

New Account Functions

In many banks, the tellers help customers open new accounts. Tellers walk customers through the required account-disclosure packet and accept the initial deposit. They explain all of the account's characteristics and any unfamiliar terms to the customer and provide any additional information the customer requests. Larger banks may have a personal banker take care of this.

Source: Shutterstock (auremar)

Customer interaction is one of the primary ways banks retain their customers.

Safe Deposit Boxes

A **safe deposit box** is a strong storage container, usually metal, that is kept in the safest area of the bank. It is rented to customers, who use the boxes to store valuable items. Safe deposit boxes protect items from fire, flood, and theft. Each safe deposit box requires two keys to open it. One key is given to the customer and one is kept by the bank.

To access a safe deposit box, the customer brings the key and a valid ID. A bank representative checks the ID and the customer's authority to open the box. The representative and the customer will then use the two keys to open the box.

Customer Interaction

Tellers are often the first and most frequent contact customers have with their bank. The impression that tellers give to customers contributes to the bank's public image.

When customers come into the bank with problems, they often address the teller first. How the teller handles this initial contact affects customers' attitudes. Skilled customer interactions help banks to keep their customers happy.

Tellers also carry out the bank's marketing strategy. When tellers learn that a customer is interested in additional bank services, they can answer questions about the services and give the customer's information to an area specialist.

Balance the Cash Drawer

A **cash drawer** has separate compartments for different denominations of coins and bills. In stores, a cash drawer is part of a cash register. In banks, it is often a drawer that can be inserted and removed from the counter at the teller's workstation. At the end of each day, the tellers store their cash drawers in the vault.

Balancing a cash drawer is done by verifying that the drawer has the correct amount of cash after several transactions have occurred. Regulations do not govern when or how the cash drawers are balanced. Not all banks use the same procedures. Figure 10-6 shows an example of a teller balancing record. This form is used not only to keep track of the amount of money in a teller's drawer, but also what denominations the drawer contains. Cash in the drawer should reflect the system ending balance. Actual cash in the drawer should reflect the recorded amount. In practice, this record would be kept electronically.

Teller Balancing Record

Ending Balance	$2,429
Beginning Balance	$6,000

Drawer Count	
100s	5
50s	10
20s	50
10s	30
5s	25
2s	0
1s	4

Teller's Name Tom Peters

Employee Identification Number 3113

Figure 10-6.
Teller Balancing Record

Tom is a teller. At the end of the business day, he must count out his cash drawer. He must follow three steps to determine the ending balance:

Step 1. Count the number of bills he has for each denomination of currency and mark it on the teller balancing record.

100s	5
50s	10
20s	50
10s	30
5s	25
2s	0
1s	4

Step 2. Multiply the denomination of the bill by the number of bills in the drawer.

$100 denomination × 5 bills in the drawer = $500 in $100 bills

$50 denomination × 10 bills in the drawer = $500 in $50 bills

$20 denomination × 50 bills in the drawer = $1,000 in $20 bills

$10 denomination × 30 bills in the drawer = $300 in $10 bills

$5 denomination × 25 bills in the drawer = $125 in $5 bills

$2 denomination × 0 bills in the drawer = $0 in $2 bills

$1 denomination × 4 bills in the drawer = $4 in $1 bills

Step 3. Add the sums of each.

$500 + $500 + $1000 + $300 + $125 + $0 + $4 = $2,429 ending balance

In some banks, the head teller or manager counts the money in each teller's cash drawer at the beginning of the day. Only one teller is allowed to use each cash drawer on that day. Throughout the day, the teller records transactions on a computer terminal. At the end of the day, the amount of cash in the drawer is compared to the transactions the teller performed during the day. If the amount of cash in the drawer is correct, the cash drawer is *balanced.* The next day, the teller starts with a fresh cash drawer.

The cash drawer may be balanced more or less frequently than the above example. Some banks may require tellers to balance cash drawers at midday as well as the end of the day.

If a teller is unable to balance his or her cash drawer because it contains too much or too little cash, the cash is recounted. If the cash drawer differs from what it should be, a manager is alerted. Banks usually have an acceptable amount of error, and the manager is alerted only if the error is greater than this amount. If a teller's cash drawer has frequent errors, the teller's employment may be terminated.

BIZ TIPS

Cash needs fluctuate. Consumers withdraw cash from ATMs during the weekend, so more cash is in circulation on Monday than on Friday. Consumers also use more cash for shopping and vacations in December. After the holiday season, cash usage declines. Banks manage the cash they keep on hand to meet their customers' needs.

FedCash Services

FedCash Services are provided by the Federal Reserve Banks. Banks use these services to order additional currency and coins to meet the needs of their customers. Excess currency and coins are deposited with the Federal Reserve Bank. Damaged currency is deposited at the Federal Reserve Bank and removed from circulation.

Orders for currency and coins are prepared by the head teller or branch manager. When cash arrives from the Federal Reserve Bank, the head teller or manager counts the cash to verify the amount received. This must be done by two people, uninterrupted, performing the same tasks.

Loan Collection

No matter how careful banks are in making loans, some borrowers will not be able to repay the loan. When a loan is not repaid, it goes into collection. **Collection** is the transfer of past-due loans to a bank department or outside agency that attempts to gather full or partial repayment of the loan.

Source: Shutterstock (Andy Dean Photography)

The financial crisis of the 21st century saw many foreclosed homes.

Banks do not want to lose money, which can happen if a borrower is unable to repay a loan. To avoid losing money, banks have several options:

- take the property if the loan was secured
- negotiate with the borrower
- take court action to recover lost funds

When economic conditions are poor, the need for loan collection increases.

Secured Loan

A secured loan is backed by an asset. For example, a car loan is secured with the car and a mortgage is secured by the real estate. If the borrower is unable to repay the loan, the bank can take the property used to secure the loan. The bank can then sell the property to recover some of the funds lost by the borrower's inability to pay.

Foreclosure is the legal process of ending an owner's right to a property, usually caused by an unpaid mortgage loan. Foreclosure usually refers to real estate, including houses, commercial buildings, and land.

Repossession occurs when the bank takes property from a borrower who is not able to repay a loan. It generally refers to a car or other vehicle. However, it could be any property purchased with a loan or used as security for a loan. The bank then sells the real estate or other property and applies the proceeds of the sale to the loan. If any cash remains, the bank gives it to the borrower.

Negotiation

When a customer determines that he or she is unable to repay a loan, everyone loses. The customer loses any property that secured the loan. The bank loses the profit it planned to make on the loan. The community loses because foreclosed houses can remain empty. Businesses suffer because their customers have less money to spend. If a car is repossessed, the borrower loses transportation options, which could result in losing a job. Nobody wins.

Instead, the borrower and the bank could negotiate the terms of the loan. Reducing the interest rate and extending the length of the loan could reduce the monthly loan payment to an amount that the borrower could pay. Renegotiating the loan means that the borrower could keep the property while the bank would continue to earn a profit on the loan. The bank's profit might not be as high as it originally intended, but the bank avoids the expense of collecting an unpaid loan.

Court Action

A bank can take a borrower to court for an unpaid loan. The court may issue an order to garnish the borrower's income. **Garnishment** is withholding all or part of a borrower's salary to pay an outstanding unsecured debt or bounced checks. The garnished amount is automatically taken from the borrower's salary. Court action is often a last resort for an unpaid loan.

Compliance

Banks are heavily regulated to protect customers. Laws and regulations cover every aspect of banking from advertising to customer interactions. **Compliance** is the process of following these laws and regulations.

Banks hire compliance managers or compliance teams to ensure that the bank meets new and updated rules. Compliance personnel research and analyze the changes needed to follow the rules. If necessary, they explain the rules so all bank employees understand them. Departments take monthly department-compliance training.

Compliance staff develop new procedures, monitor the bank's actions, and prepare the bank's records for bank examiners. They often maintain a manual explaining bank policies and procedures. Their directions are carried out by employees throughout the bank.

Checkpoint 10.2

1. Which position in a bank is responsible for front-line operational support?
2. What are three hazards that safe deposit boxes protect their contents from?
3. How do banks use FedCash Services?
4. What are the three options a bank has if a borrower is unable to repay a loan?
5. What role does a compliance department play in a bank?

Build Your Vocabulary

As you progress through this course, develop a personal glossary of banking terms and add it to your portfolio. This will help you build your banking vocabulary. Write out a definition for each of the following terms, and add it to your personal glossary.

safe deposit box
cash drawer
collection
foreclosure
repossession
garnishment
compliance

Section 10.3
Human Resources

Objectives

After completing this section, you will be able to:

- Summarize the role of the human resources department.
- Explain the process involved in recruiting and hiring a new employee.
- Describe benefits that may be offered to employees.
- Explain the employee review process.
- Discuss the importance of maintaining employee records.

Terms

human resources (HR) department
career path
job fair
employment agency
interview
reference
benefits
performance evaluation
probation

Human Resources Department

To have the best employees, banks hire, train, and retain the best applicants. The **human resources (HR) department** finds and supports employees who contribute to the success of the bank. This department is often referred to as *HR.*

In a small bank, one person could be the entire HR department. Large banks could have a department manager, as well as managers and specialists in each function. The size of the department depends on the number of bank employees. Tasks can be separated into four categories:

- recruiting and hiring new employees
- managing employee benefits
- conducting or supervising employee reviews
- maintaining employee records

Recruiting and Hiring New Employees

To conduct its business, a bank needs the right people in the right jobs. One of the most important roles for the human resources department is recruiting and hiring new employees. In HR terms, recruiting is attracting the best people for positions in the bank. Recruiting and hiring employees is a multi-step process:

1. Recruit applicants.
2. Interview selected applicants.
3. Verify references.
4. Hire the best applicant.

Source: Shutterstock (Ali Mufti)

A job fair is an opportunity to learn about several hiring companies at once.

Recruiting Applicants

Finding good employees for a bank is not as simple as hanging up a help wanted sign in the window. Many jobs in a bank require a specific set of skills, experience, and education.

The recruiting method should match the role of the employee to be hired. For example, a college degree may not be required for tellers, but most bank managers have a college degree. Because of this, the methods used to recruit applicants for these two positions would vary. In general, several recruiting methods can be used:

- promotions
- media advertising
- job fairs
- college visits
- employment agencies

Promotions

Promoting from within is a recruitment method that encourages employees to excel at their jobs so they can progress on a career path within the bank. A **career path** is a series of jobs with increasing responsibility within a specific career. This is an excellent way to retain good employees.

To promote from within, current employees must be notified that a position is available. This could be done by:

- posting the job on a company bulletin board;
- including an announcement in a company newsletter;
- announcing the opening in a company meeting;
- posting a notice on the company website; or
- sending a company-wide e-mail.

Media Advertising

In the past, job seekers would search through the classified ads in the newspaper to find available jobs. Other than going to a company to ask if it had job openings, classified ads were often the only place job openings were found.

Today, the Internet is where companies often advertise open jobs. Businesses, including banks, advertise available jobs on their own websites, as well as general employment websites. Applicants are encouraged to submit applications through the website or e-mail. HR staff use keywords in the ads to get the attention of those with the skills and experience they are looking for. They may also use social media sites, such as LinkedIn®, to advertise the position.

Job Fairs

A **job fair** is a recruiting event attended by one or more companies that are seeking new employees. It gives job seekers the chance to learn about the companies and apply for available jobs. Most job fairs are held in a hotel or conference center. Often, colleges and universities sponsor job fairs on campus.

At a job fair, each company has a table or booth. Representatives speak to those who attend and may accept applications for specific job openings.

College Visits

Many positions in a bank require a college degree. Banks often work with colleges to set up interviews with graduating seniors. Banks invite students with specific majors to interview. This allows the bank to focus its search on those with the education they require.

Employment Agencies

Employment agencies match an employer's available jobs to workers who have the needed skills, education, and experience. They can be private companies or government agencies. The agency works with both employers and job seekers. When employers have a specific need, the agency finds qualified applicants for the position. This way, the employer does not have to waste time reviewing applicants who do not meet its needs.

Source: Shutterstock (Supri Suharjoto)

Many careers in the banking industry require a college degree.

Interviewing Applicants

A company usually interviews several applicants for an open position. An **interview** is a meeting between a company representative and the applicant. Discussion during the interview is meant to see if the applicant is a good match for the open position.

The number of times an applicant is interviewed varies. The applicant could be interviewed by representatives from HR, the manager of the specific department, and coworkers.

If necessary, the applicant's skills will be tested. For example, some banks may test an applicant's math skills.

An applicant's personal and professional ethics are particularly important in banking. Confidentiality, ethics, and honesty may be discussed during an interview.

Verifying References

After the applicant has passed the interview phase, the company will contact the applicant's references. A **reference** is a person who can provide information about the applicant's work history or character. The reference will be asked to verify information and recommend the applicant's work.

Hiring the Best Applicant

Criteria for how applicants will be judged will vary by the bank. However, education, work experience, technical skills, leadership, and interpersonal skills are signs of whether someone will make a good employee. Interpersonal skills include the ability to work with others. These skills will play a big part in whether the best applicant will become a valued employee. Hiring decisions cannot be based in any way on an applicant's age, gender, race, religion, or ethnicity. Some states exclude additional factors from consideration. When an applicant accepts the offer, the bank has a new employee.

Managing Employee Benefits

Employees receive salaries and benefits in exchange for their work. **Benefits** are services or privileges that an employer provides in addition to the employee's wages or salary. Benefits vary by company and position. Benefits can include:

- 401(k) and stock options;
- scholarships;
- free training;
- paid sick days; and
- wearing casual clothing on Friday.

Some benefits are standard for all employees. For example, all employees might receive free parking and direct deposit of their paychecks. Some benefits that vary by employee can be based on length of service or position. An employee who has been with the bank for ten years might get four weeks of vacation per year. A new employee may get only one week per year. A vice president might receive stock shares or a bonus if the bank performs well that year. A teller may not.

HR ensures that each employee receives the benefits he or she is entitled to. If a problem arises, such as a miscalculated bonus or incorrect fee paid for a class, HR deals with the problem.

BIZ TIPS

Health care is an important benefit for most workers. The Patient Protection and Affordable Care Act of 2010 requires companies with 50 or more employees to offer a health-insurance-benefit plan.

Reviewing Employees

At regular intervals, employees will have a performance review or performance evaluation. The objective of a **performance evaluation** is to look at how well an individual employee is doing his or her job. Employee evaluations are designed to fulfill many functions:

- clarify an employee's role in the organization
- determine whether strategic plans are being carried out
- open lines of communication
- assess the extent to which goals have been met
- gauge employee potential for advancement
- provide feedback to the employee and supervisor
- identify differences in expectations and outcomes
- discover areas for needed support or training
- conclude if performance level merits a pay increase

Source: Shutterstock (Apple's Eyes Studio)

Health insurance is a benefit that many companies offer their employees.

Typically, a performance evaluation occurs annually. When an employee is hired, an evaluation may occur after three or six months to check that the new employee is doing well. Reviews would occur annually after the first review. Many employers perform reviews on the employee's service anniversary, but some employers perform all employee reviews at the same time each year.

Figure 10-7 is an example of a performance evaluation form. In this example, the Function and Specific Observations column is tied to the job description.

North Creek Bank and Trust

EMPLOYEE PERFORMANCE EVALUATION

EMPLOYEE NAME: Felicia Smith

POSITION: Customer Service Representative

DATE EMPLOYEE BEGAN PRESENT POSITION: April 1, 20XX

DATE OF LAST APPRAISAL: April 1, 20XX

APPRAISER NAME: Tina Downey

APPRAISER TITLE: Customer Service Manager

Function and Specific Observations	Rating (1–5)
Work to service customer needs and requests. Felicia goes out of her way to make sure the customer is satisfied.	4
Provide product information and assist customers in product selection. Felicia's knowledge of financial products will increase with more exposure and training.	3
Assist customers with questions and resolve any issues that may occur. Felicia is a problem-solver who looks for the win-win resolution to all issues.	5
Consult, cross-sell and up-sell customers on additional bank products as licensure permits.	4
Provide back-up assistance with work overflow from other functional areas.	4
Provide initial technical support for products and services.	4
Receive all incoming inquiries (fax, paper, web, and phone) in assigned area and enter them into the system.	5
Make outbound calls to customers regarding questions and follow-up opportunities.	4
Maintain a pleasant demeanor.	5
Be punctual.	4
Dress appropriately and according to bank guidelines.	4
Work as part of a team.	4
Take personal responsibility for work product.	4
Total:	54
Average:	4.15

Figure 10-7.
Performance Evaluation Form

Careers in Finance
Banking and Related Services

What Does a Financial Manager Do?

Financial managers help direct the finances of a business or organization. **Financial managers** may have many different titles, including *controller, treasurer, finance officer,* and *branch manager.* **Financial managers** supervise workers who prepare financial reports. They develop strategies to meet the long-term goals of their employers. **Financial managers** who work in banks often manage departments, such as the accounting, budget, or credit departments. Some of the activities performed by a **financial manager** include:

- overseeing a business's investment and cash-management techniques;
- creating reports that summarize and forecast finances;
- developing long-term financial goals and strategies for a business; and
- creating and maintaining a budget to meet business financial goals.

What Is It Like to Work as a Financial Manager?

Financial managers typically work in an office environment. Because of their role in the financial planning of the business, **financial managers** often work very closely with management and executives. Depending on the nature of the bank for which they work, **financial managers** may be required to travel to customers or company branches.

Financial managers must be knowledgeable about current economic conditions and financial regulations. **Financial managers** in certain fields must acquire and maintain very specific knowledge about their field.

If you enjoy working on problems and creating long-term goals, a career as a **financial manager** might suit you.

What Education and Skills Are Needed to Be a Financial Manager?

- college degree in business administration, finance, or economics
- experience in banking or business
- strong problem-solving abilities
- excellent communication skills

Career Ladder

Chief Financial Officer

Financial Manager

Financial Analyst

Annual Reviews

The performance review is usually conducted by the employee's manager. Some companies also ask coworkers or workers who report to the employee to participate in the review.

The performance review can be tied to an annual increase in wages based on performance. An employee who performed well may receive a larger increase in salary than an employee who performed poorly.

Managers should keep an ongoing record of occasions when the employee's performance earned good or bad comments. This creates a balanced review that considers everything the employee did over the entire review period.

Unacceptable Performance

If an employee performs poorly, he or she may be placed on probation. **Probation** is a period of time in which the employee's performance is closely watched. If the employee continues to perform poorly, his or her employment may be terminated. If performance improves, he or she can be removed from probation.

If an employee's behavior is unethical, his or her employment could be immediately terminated. If the behavior is also illegal, the employee could be arrested. Because banking jobs often deal with confidential information and large sums of money, unethical and illegal behavior by an employee cannot be tolerated.

Maintaining Employee Records

Most businesses keep extensive records about every employee. The records cover every action and decision from first contact to last contact between the employee and employer. Employee records are intended to document events and actions taken. They meet government requirements for recordkeeping and protect the company if there is a dispute.

State laws about record access vary. Typically, employees are allowed to inspect most of their employee records on request. They are not allowed to see records about criminal investigations, reference letters, or documents obtained before they were hired.

As shown in Figure 10-8, employee records can be grouped by employment, financial information, performance, and exit from the company. State laws about how long records should be kept vary.

Some types of records should not be kept in personnel files. For example, results of drug-screening tests, injury reports, personal-credit history, background checks, and criminal-investigation results are not kept in personnel files. Generally, any information related to an employee's health history should not be part of a personnel file.

Employment	Financial	Performance	Exit
Application	Time sheets	Performance reviews	Final interview
Résumé	Tax forms	Training	Final performance review
Reference verification	Benefits	Skills	

Figure 10-8.
Employee Records

Checkpoint 10.3

1. What are the steps in recruiting and hiring a new employee?
2. List five recruiting methods.
3. Who conducts a performance review?
4. What are two possible consequences of poor work performance?
5. What personnel records are employees not allowed to access?

Build Your Vocabulary

As you progress through this course, develop a personal glossary of banking terms and add it to your portfolio. This will help you build your banking vocabulary. Write out a definition for each of the following terms, and add it to your personal glossary.

human resources (HR) department
career path
job fair
employment agency
interview
reference
benefits
performance evaluation
probation

Chapter Summary

Section 10.1 Organization and Management

- An organizational chart allows you to see the relationships among individuals and groups that might be difficult to explain in words.
- The most common groups in a bank are departments and branches.
- Departments and branches are run by managers and executives.

Section 10.2 Special Departments

- Tellers perform basic transactions, help customers open new accounts, assist with safe deposit boxes, interact with customers, balance cash drawers, and manage the currency and coins in their cash drawers and the bank.
- Banks have several options when collecting on unpaid loans: take the property if the loan was secured, negotiate with the borrower, or take court action to recover lost funds.
- Compliance managers or compliance teams ensure that the bank meets new and updated requirements.

Section 10.3 Human Resources

- The human resources department is responsible for four types of tasks: recruiting and hiring new employees; managing employee benefits; conducting or supervising employee reviews; and maintaining employee records.
- Recruiting and hiring employees is a multi-step process.
- The human resources department manages employee benefits, which can vary from bank to bank and employee to employee.
- Performance reviews are intended to verify that an employee is performing well. A performance review will also discover if additional assistance or training is needed.
- Employee records are intended to document events and actions taken. They meet government requirements for recordkeeping and protect the company if there is a dispute.

Check Your Banking IQ

Now that you have finished this chapter, see what you know about banking by taking the chapter post test.

www.m.g-wlearning.com
www.g-wlearning.com

Review Your Knowledge

On a separate sheet of paper or in a word processing document, match the following terms with the definition that fits best.

A. board of directors
B. cash drawer
C. foreclosure
D. executive
E. probation
F. garnishment
G. performance evaluation
H. organizational chart
I. career path
J. repossession

1. Legal process of ending an owner's right to a property.
2. Looks at how well an individual employee is doing his or her job.
3. Period of time in which the employee's performance is closely watched.
4. The bank takes property from a borrower who is not able to repay a loan.
5. Series of jobs with increasing responsibility within a specific career.
6. Has separate compartments for different denominations of coins and bills.
7. Manager who has the responsibility and authority to make decisions about the bank and how it conducts its business.
8. Diagram representing the structure of a company or organization.
9. Group of individuals elected by a bank's shareholders to represent the shareholders and guide the bank's policies and business decisions.
10. Withholding all or part of a borrower's salary to pay an outstanding debt.

On a separate sheet of paper or in a word processing document, answer each of the following questions.

11. Name three departments usually found in a business.
12. How are executives different from managers?
13. What is the last resort for collecting an unpaid loan?
14. What is one of the most important roles for the human resources department?
15. Name five of the functions of performance evaluations.

Apply Your Knowledge

16. Draw an organizational chart for your school or a familiar business or organization. Include at least three levels.
17. Select a local bank. Visit its website. Based on the information on the website, identify the managers and executives. Create an organizational chart to show their ranks.
18. Find an advertisement for a banking position. Based on the ad, describe the job responsibilities and the necessary skills and education.
19. Write ten questions that you would be asked if you interviewed for a teller position.
20. Research sample performance evaluations on the Internet. What employee qualities do managers and employers consider when creating performance evaluations?

Working in Teams

In a small group or with a partner, share a time when you were confronted with an ethical dilemma—a situation that had the voice in your head nagging you. Take turns discussing how you handled the situation and if you did so in an ethical manner. Have a representative of the group report to the class the key points of your group's discussion.

G-W Learning Mobile Site

Visit the G-W Learning mobile site to complete the chapter pretest and post test and to practice vocabulary using e-flash cards. If you do not have a smartphone, visit the G-W Learning companion website to access these features.
G-W Learning mobile site: www.m.g-wlearning.com
G-W Learning companion website: www.g-wlearning.com

Common Core

College and Career Readiness

Writing. Create a performance evaluation for a store or restaurant employee from a customer's point of view. What traits do you think are most important in this position? How can you tell if an employee is successful? Then, think about the last time you were in a store or restaurant and encountered an employee. How did the company's employee perform according to your requirements? Evaluate this employee based on your criteria. Afterward, reflect on the criteria you selected. Based on your evaluation of the employee, how would you adapt your performance criteria?

Speaking. In groups of three or four, imagine you are the human resources department of a bank and need to recruit applicants for three positions: teller, personal banker, and chief executive officer. Research the general qualifications and duties of these positions. Consider how you will evaluate and recruit applicants. As a group, develop a recruitment plan for these positions.

EVENT PREP

Personal Finance

Personal finance is a competitive event you might enter with your career and technical student organization (CTSO). The personal finance competitive event may include an objective test that includes banking topics. If you decide to participate in this event, you will need to review basic banking concepts to prepare for the test. To prepare for a personal finance event:

1. Read the guidelines provided by your organization. Make certain that you ask any questions about points you do not understand. It is important to follow each specific item that is outlined in the competition rules.
2. Review the checkpoint activities at the end of each section of the text.
3. Review the end-of-chapter activities for additional practice.
4. Ask your instructor to give you practice tests for each chapter of this text. It is important that you are familiar with answering multiple choice and true/false questions. Have someone time you as you take a practice test.

11

Check Your Banking IQ

Before you begin this chapter, see what you already know about banking by taking the chapter pretest.

www.m.g-wlearning.com
www.g-wlearning.com

Selling the Bank

Loyal customers are not born, they are created. For a bank to be successful, it must reach out to individuals and organizations that could benefit from the products and services it provides. Once a relationship with a customer is *born,* it must be nurtured. Banks nurture these relationships and create a positive public image by providing exceptional customer service.

College and Career Readiness

Reading Prep. In preparation for this chapter, use the Internet and printed materials to locate bank advertisements. Can you find any common themes in these advertisements? What does this tell you about the purposes behind bank advertisements?

Scan the code to view a Biz Kid$ video. If you do not have a smartphone, visit the G-W Learning companion website.

www.m.g-wlearning.com
www.g-wlearning.com

Section 11.1
Marketing and Promotions

Terms
need
want
market segment
target market
advertising
marketing
promotion
cross-selling
event-based selling

Objectives
After completing this section, you will be able to:

- Explain how customer needs and wants are used to identify a target market.
- Describe the components of a marketing strategy and how it is developed.

Meeting Customer Needs

Every consumer has needs and wants. A **need** is something a person must have to survive, such as food, clothing, and shelter. A **want** is something a person would like to have, but does not need to survive. The difference between a need and a want is easy to see when comparing the purchase of a house to the purchase of a ring. The house provides shelter, so it fills a need. The ring is a want, because you can survive without it.

How do a bank's products and services fit into a consumer's needs and wants? Every consumer needs money to purchase or acquire the items that are essential to life. A bank can help consumers save, earn, or borrow money. This helps them get what they need as well as some of what they want.

To create a *customer* from a *consumer,* a bank needs to be able to give the consumer what he or she needs. Banks do this by identifying their target market.

Identifying a Target Market

Banks, like every other kind of business, set up locations in areas where they can get customers. Banks design products and services to help meet the needs of the customers in the community they serve. No matter what product is being sold, not everybody will want to buy it. To reach the right consumers, banks first need to identify them.

What characteristics do these consumers have in common? Do they have similar incomes? Are they saving money to buy a house? Did they recently buy a car? Knowing the characteristics that possible customers have in common will help identify a market segment. A **market segment** is a group of consumers that share common wants and needs. The wants and needs of these consumers are different from consumers in other segments. Figure 11-1 shows examples of the four types of market segmentation: demographic, geographic, psychographic, and

Source: Shutterstock (Hannamariah)
A need is something required to survive.

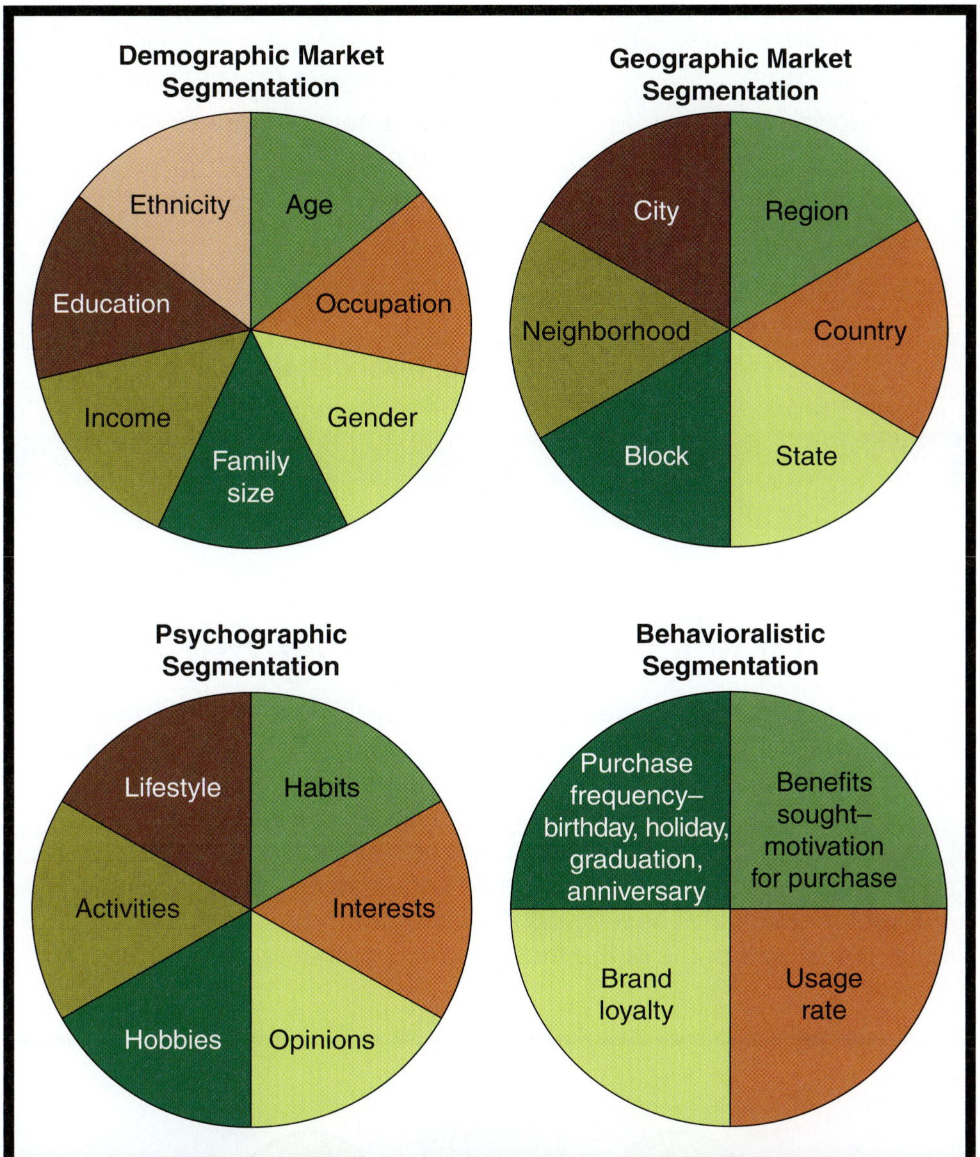

Figure 11-1.
Market Segmentation

behavioralistic. By breaking consumers into segments, banks can focus their marketing efforts on those who are most likely to become customers. This group is the target market. The **target market** is the market segment that will be the focus of the marketing strategy.

Matching Bank Products and Services to Needs and Wants

Once the bank identifies a target market, it can match the needs and wants of these consumers to its products and services. Products and services are designed or modified by analyzing the needs and wants of a certain market segment. In Figure 11-2, characteristics of mortgage loans (the product) are matched to first-time home buyers (the target market).

Characteristics of Mortgage Loan (Product)	Needs and Wants of First-Time Home Buyers (Target Market)
Small down payment	Small amount of money saved for down payment
Competitive interest rate	Low mortgage payments
Few closing fees	Low closing costs
Roll closing costs into the mortgage loan	Low closing costs
Flexible credit requirements	Approval with short credit history
No penalty for prepayment	Increased income over time

Figure 11-2.
Matching Product Characteristics with Target Market Needs and Wants

Developing a Marketing Strategy

When you think of marketing, you probably think of the advertisements you see on television. **Advertising** involves calling attention to a product or service, commonly through the use of paid announcements.

Advertising is only one part of marketing. **Marketing** is the process of introducing a product or service to the consumers who can purchase it. Marketing includes creating a salable item, setting a price, selecting a delivery method, and developing a strategy for promoting the item. Figure 11-3 shows some of the many aspects of marketing.

Figure 11-3.
Aspects of Marketing

Marketing professionals develop a plan that will help the bank meet customer needs while making a profit. Each marketing plan is developed around the *four P's of marketing:* product, place, price, and promotion. Figure 11-4 illustrates these.

The Four P's

Product

Source: Shutterstock (bannosuke)

What products or services meet the needs of consumers in the target segment?
Examples: certificate of deposit, savings account, mortgage, or mobile banking app.

Price

Source: Shutterstock (Lisa S.)

How much will the product cost the consumer?
Examples: fees and interest rates are paid as well as charged.

Place

Source: Shutterstock (June Marie Sobrito)

How will the product be available to customers?
Examples: online, at a bank branch, from an ATM or smartphone; regionally, nationally, or internationally.

Promotion

Source: Shutterstock (Jorge Salcedo)

How will the product be announced?
Examples: through television advertisements, billboards, the Internet, social media, or a combination of these.

Figure 11-4.
Four P's of Marketing

Creating Promotions

Promotion is an activity that increases consumer awareness of a product. Advertising is a type of promotion. Can you think of a television commercial that recently made you laugh? The funny commercial made you remember the product and is one way the company promotes it.

The methods and locations for promoting a product have changed. In the past, promotion relied heavily on advertising. Advertising meant promotions on television and radio or in newspapers and magazines.

Today, promotion is more dynamic. Advertising is only one option. Promotions can include almost any activity:

- distributing pens with the bank's logo
- sponsoring a city-wide event, such as a concert
- creating a website
- sending e-mail messages or social media updates to customers
- distributing calendars or some other daily-use product
- holding seminars to help customers that are considering financial milestones, such as buying a house, starting a business, or retiring

The banking industry has many regulations on promotions and advertisements. Interest rates, for example, must be stated in specific ways. Select terms must be avoided or included. If a certain balance must be maintained to take advantage of an account feature, that must be included as part of the advertisement. For example, if a customer must maintain a minimum balance of $2,000 to avoid a fee, that needs to be stated. In addition, the phrase *Member FDIC* must be included in anything that promotes a deposit account or the bank as a whole. This signifies that depositors are insured through the Federal Deposit Insurance Corporation. *Member FDIC* must also appear on the homepage of the bank's website. When mortgage products are advertised, the Department of Housing and Urban Development (HUD) requires that financial institutions state they are an equal-housing lender. Figure 11-5 provides an example of a compliant print advertisement.

Ethical Banking

It is unethical for a bank or any other business to take part in deceptive marketing. It is important for banks to not only comply with laws, but to ensure that any claims made are in no way misleading. This is not only an ethical and legal consideration, it is also good business.

Green Banking

Banks spend a lot of time and money on advertising costs. Although online marketing is becoming more common, some promotional materials are more effective in print form, such as brochures. Many banks are now using environmentally friendly supplies for their printed advertisements, such as paper made from sugar cane, rather than wood. Sugar cane actually biodegrades faster than wood and is cleaner to make. This can be a perfect alternative for paper stock used for marketing and promotional materials.

Making a Sale

Some type of contact is needed for a sale to happen. Selling occurs in many ways, but for banks, personal selling is the most common.

Each time a bank employee comes in contact with a customer, or potential customer, that employee is applying personal selling. Saying, "hello," "how can I help you?" and "is there anything else you need?" are examples of personal selling.

Cross-selling is a personal selling strategy that encourages existing customers to buy new products or services based on their previous purchases. Cross-selling is the result of

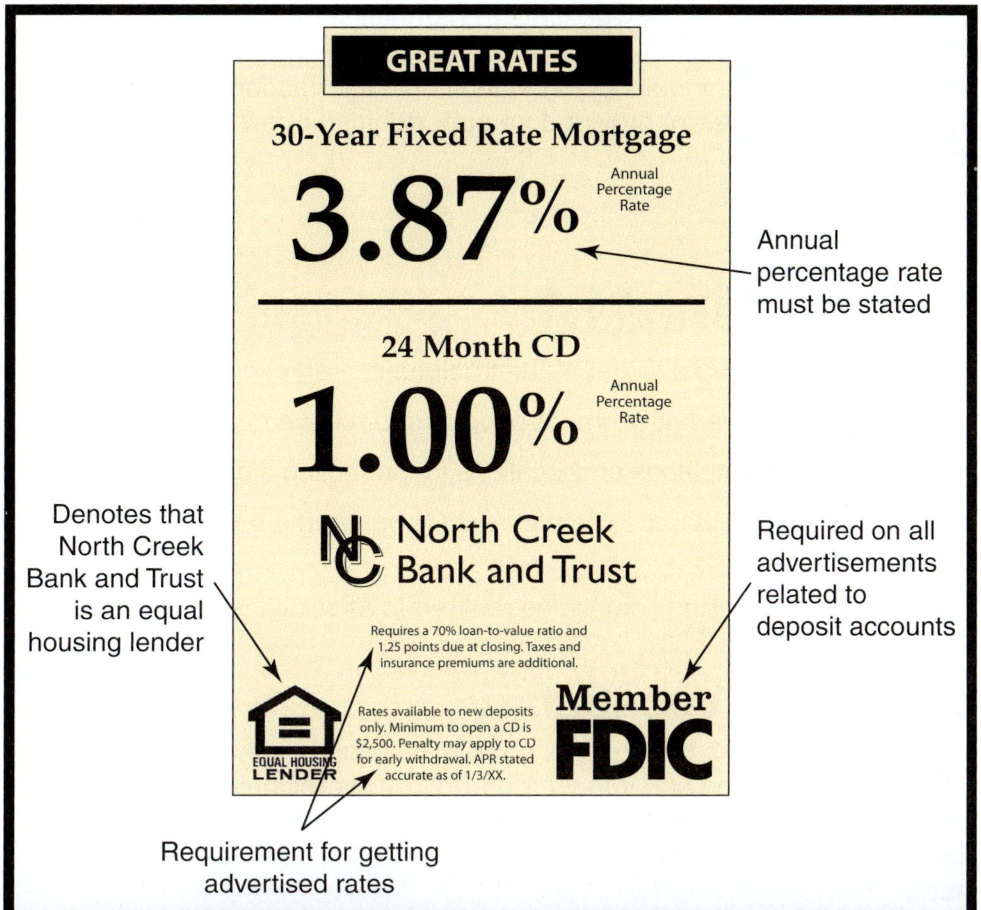

Figure 11-5.
Sample Advertisement

an existing relationship formed by selling a bank product or service to a customer. Therefore, it is sometimes known as relationship-based selling. For example, conversations between a teller and a customer might reveal that a customer with a savings account is saving for a down payment on a house. Tellers are trained to ask a checking customer if they would like to open a savings account. If they have a checking and savings account, the teller asks if they would like to have direct deposit or automatic bill pay. The more services a bank provides to a customer, the more likely the customer is to stay with that bank.

Cross-selling requires interaction between bank employees. Passing a customer's needs and wants along to a loan officer might result in making a mortgage loan to a savings account customer. Friendly interest from a bank teller reveals the customer's needs, and good communication among bank employees and bank departments could lead to a cross-selling opportunity. Customers who have several relationships with the same bank, such as a savings account and a mortgage loan, are more likely to be loyal to the bank.

Another form of personal selling is event-based selling. **Event-based selling** is when a bank employee contacts a customer because of an event that has recently happened with that customer. For example, a

BIZ TIPS

The Bank Holding Company Act, as amended in 1970, bans banks from making customers buy one product or service for them to be eligible for another product. For example, a bank cannot require that a customer buy homeowners insurance from a company owned by the bank to be eligible for a mortgage from the bank.

customer visits the bank's website and requests information about home mortgages. This information request event may trigger a personal email from the loan officer inquiring if any additional information is needed by the customer. The event provided an opportunity for personal selling from the bank.

Checkpoint 11.1

1. Why is setting up a target market helpful in marketing the bank?
2. What does a market segment of consumers have in common?
3. How have the methods and locations for promoting a product changed?
4. When must the phrase *Member FDIC* appear in a bank's communications?
5. Why is cross-selling sometimes referred to as relationship-based selling?

Build Your Vocabulary

As you progress through this course, develop a personal glossary of banking terms and add it to your portfolio. This will help you build your banking vocabulary. Write out a definition for each of the following terms, and add it to your personal glossary.

need
want
market segment
target market
advertising
marketing
promotion
cross-selling
event-based selling

Section 11.2
Building Relationships

Objectives

After completing this section, you will be able to:

- Describe the elements that create a positive image for a bank.
- Explain the importance of customer service in keeping customers.

Terms

public image
customer service
customer
rapport
word-of-mouth advertising

The Bank's Image

What qualities would you want a stranger to have when you consider giving him or her your life savings to hold for you? You would require the same qualities from your bank. When you think of a business, the ideas and opinions you have of it from your image of the business.

A business' **public image** is made up of the ideas and opinions that people have about the business. A positive public image makes it easier to hire and retain employees, acquire new customers, and keep current customers.

A bank must be seen as honest, stable, and an important part of the community. Even though all banks have to appear honest and stable, each bank also needs to appear unique in some way. Some banks appear different because they focus on a particular product or service that is not offered by other banks. Small, local banks often emphasize their customer service or community involvement. By examining a bank's promotions and, in particular, its advertisements, you can usually detect the public image the bank wants and how it is trying to achieve that.

The economic strength of a community often depends on its ability to get credit. Banks can contribute to the local economy by making loans to individuals and businesses. These loans help create jobs and bring revenue to its citizens. By working with the citizens, banks establish a positive public image. Banks provide the credit that helps the community run and grow.

In addition to the credit they provide, banks engage with the communities they serve in other ways. Banks often sponsor community events, such as marathons. Increasingly, they provide ongoing financial education to consumers. Bank executives often serve on civic boards and local chambers of commerce. Another way banks affect their communities is through the customer service they provide.

If the public image of the bank or the financial industry is damaged, the bank may need to repair its reputation with customers. For example, the financial crises of the early 21st century had a negative impact on the banking industry. In hopes of repairing some of the damage, many banks chose to replace managers, change how they qualified potential borrowers, and institute other policy changes. These were important steps to reestablishing the positive image of the banking business.

Source: Shutterstock (Yuri Arcurs)

Good customer service helps the bank's public image.

What Is Customer Service?

A customer enters the bank to buy traveler's checks for an upcoming vacation. The teller smiles, says hello, and issues the traveler's checks as quickly as possible. The teller then asks a few questions about how satisfied the customer is with checking and savings accounts service at the bank. The customer responds, "quite pleased" and leaves the bank. When did the customer service begin? When the customer entered the bank? When standing in line? When purchasing the traveler's checks?

Customer service includes all interactions between a customer and the bank. A **customer** is an individual, organization, or business that purchases a product or service. Customer service starts when the bank and the customer interact for the first time. This could be a click on a website, a comment about the bank that the customer overhears at work, or the use of an ATM at the mall. Every interaction is an opportunity to impress. Good customer service adds value to the bank and increases the customer's loyalty. It is the customer who judges the quality of the service. The difference between poor customer service and great customer service is the difference between losing and keeping a customer.

Source: Shutterstock (Alexander Raths)

Banks build rapport with customers through personal interaction and quality customer service.

Employee Behavior

Every bank employee is a customer service representative. Even though the bank may have dedicated customer service employees, each employee provides some type of customer service. Bank personnel must avoid any behavior that is unethical or inappropriate. Customers do not have to put up with rude or ignorant responses. It is easy for them to take their business to another bank that treats them well. Figure 11-6 shows examples of behaviors that reflect poor customer service and those that reflect good customer service. Remember that happy customers become loyal customers who will return to fill other banking needs. It costs much less to retain satisfied customers than it does to acquire new ones. To provide positive customer service, employees should always:

- address the customer by name;
- know the products and services that the bank offers;
- apply their expertise to the customers' needs to find the product that is right for him or her, not just what is profitable for the bank; and
- exceed in the customer's expectation for service.

	Poor Customer Service	Good Customer Service
The customer…	**The employee…**	**The employee…**
asks a question the employee does not know the answer to.	says, "I don't know."	says, "I will find out."
behaves rudely to the employee.	is rude in return, or refuses to deal with the customer.	remains courteous and businesslike.
disagrees with information provided.	argues with the customer.	tries to defuse the situation while remaining courteous.
asks that the employee take an additional step.	does not follow through because he or she will probably never see that person again.	follows through with the promise.
is waiting.	takes his or her time getting to the customer.	tries not to keep the customer waiting and acknowledges the wait when the customer is next.
is in front of the employee or on the telephone.	is distracted by another customer, coworker, or something else going on in the bank.	focuses on the current customer.
sees a bank employee doing something incorrectly.	corrects the coworker publicly.	waits until later to point out the problem or brings it to the attention of a supervisor.
does not complain about the service he or she has received.	assumes the customer must be satisfied.	asks if the customer's needs have been met and if there is anything further the employee can do.
is present when a problem arises.	blames the customer, a coworker, or the bank's processes for the problem.	takes responsibility and fixes the problem.
complains.	ignores it.	tells the customer that the employee will follow up on the complaint and fix the issue—and does just that.

Figure 11-6.
Focus on the Customer

Building rapport with a customer will increase his or her satisfaction with the bank. **Rapport** is a bond of mutual trust. It is central to a successful and ongoing business relationship. Never underestimate the power of a sincere smile. Other methods of achieving rapport are shown in Figure 11-7.

Financial products can be confusing for many people. Many of the financial decisions customers make will have a major impact on their lives. Bank employees should be able to explain the options the bank offers. If the employee does not know the answer, he or she should be able to readily find it. In some cases, the customer should be brought to an employee who is more familiar with the topic. For example, a loan officer could probably explain loan terms better than a teller, who does not deal with loans every day.

Although customers might be initially drawn to a bank by a product promotion, they are unlikely to continue as customers if their customer service needs are not met. When bank employees use what they know about the bank and its products to meet customer needs, they are contributing to the bank's success.

Customers expect good service. Whether a customer receives exceptionally good or poor service, he or she is likely to mention it to others. **Word-of-mouth advertising** is a type of promotion in which customers tell others about their experience with a specific business. The only control banks have over word-of-mouth advertising is the customer service they provide. It is up to the bank to foster positive relationships with customers by excelling in every interaction.

Rapport

Language
- Use speech and body language similar to that of the customer
- Be aware of your nonverbal communication as well as that from the customer

Cultural
- Find shared interests and experiences with the customer
- Be aware of cultural differences between you and the customer

Other
- Create a positive environment
- Be open to doing something for a customer for no immediate return
- Identify barriers between you and the customer and work to remove them

Source: Shutterstock (Pius Lee)

Figure 11-7.
Methods of Achieving Rapport.

Customer Services Offerings

Customer service representatives are an important part of customer services. However, quality products and services enhance the bank's image and generate customer loyalty:

- locations
- handicapped accessibility
- international services
- secure website

Locations that are convenient for customers are important with any business, including a bank. Persons with disabilities also need to have access that is appropriate to their needs. Ramps, teller windows, and lobby ATMs should be designed to accommodate a person using a wheelchair. The Americans with Disabilities Act (ADA) requires all buildings that welcome the public to meet accessibility standards. For example, as shown in Figure 11-8, a ramp can be provided as an alternative to using stairs.

International services are increasingly required by customers. Access to money and account information while traveling abroad is another factor. Credit and debit cards that work in foreign countries as well as other travel-rated services are ever more important to consumers.

Many people are now conducting most if not all of their banking online. The bank's website should be secure and easy to use. Information should be easy to find and services commonly offered by other banks should be available. For example, the ability to pay bills and check account balances should be provided.

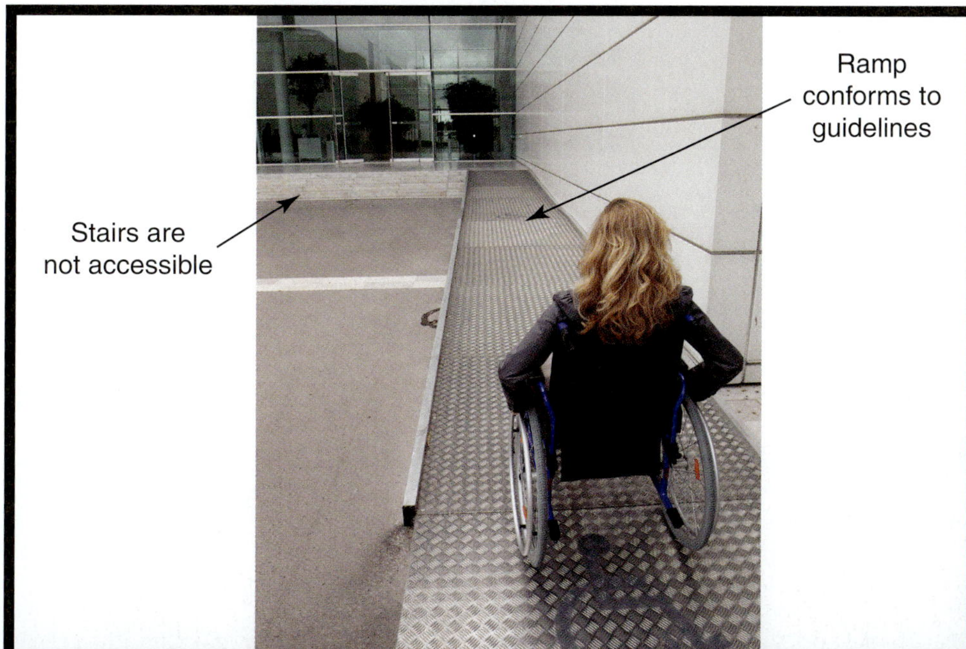

Source: Shutterstock (auremar)

Figure 11-7.
ADA Requires Public Buildings to be Accessible

Checkpoint 11.2

1. How does a positive public image help a bank?
2. List four ways that banks engage with the communities they serve.
3. How do banks control word-of-mouth advertising?
4. Why is it important for bank employees to be able to explain the options the bank offers?
5. What are four customer-service offerings that enhance a bank's image and generate customer loyalty?

Build Your Vocabulary

As you progress through this course, develop a personal glossary of banking terms and add it to your portfolio. This will help you build your banking vocabulary. Write out a definition for each of the following terms, and add it to your personal glossary.

public image
customer service
customer
rapport
word-of-mouth advertising

Careers in Finance
Banking and Related Services

What Does a Marketing Specialist Do?

Marketing specialists are responsible for the marketing, promotion, and sales of products and services. They are sometimes referred to as *product specialists,* because they often perform these duties for a specific banking product. **Marketing specialists** conduct surveys and make forecasts for the market for specific products. They develop advertisements, promotions, and pricing to accommodate the product's marketing plan. Some of the activities performed by a **marketing specialist** include:

- researching competing products and making recommendations on pricing and promotions;
- preparing sales brochures and other advertisements;
- gathering information from product users to determine customer satisfaction and ideas for improvements; and
- training sales and customer-service employees on product advancements.

What Is It Like to Work as a Marketing Specialist?

Marketing specialists spend time both traveling and working in an office environment. They are often attending conferences, meetings, and trade shows to gather information about market trends and competitors. **Marketing specialists** in the financial sector often specialize in one specific banking product and work under the direction of a marketing manager. Excellent communication and analytical skills are essential to a career as a **marketing specialist.**

If you possess an entrepreneurial spirit and enjoy conducting independent research, a career as a **marketing specialist** might suit you.

What Education and Skills Are Needed to Be a Marketing Specialist?

- college degree in business or marketing
- Master of Business Administration (MBA) is very helpful
- experience in marketing or bank management
- creativity

Career Ladder

Marketing Manager

Marketing Specialist

Marketing Analyst

Chapter Summary

Section 11.1 Marketing and Promotions

- To create customers, you must become familiar with consumers' needs and wants.
- Information about customers' needs and wants is used to identify a target market, match the characteristics of bank products and services to a target market, develop a marketing strategy, and create promotions.

Section 11.2 Building Relationships

- A positive public image makes it easier to hire and retain employees, acquire new customers, and keep current customers.
- Customer service starts when the bank and the customer interact for the first time.

Check Your Banking IQ

Now that you have finished this chapter, see what you know about banking by taking the chapter post test.

www.m.g-wlearning.com
www.g-wlearning.com

Review Your Knowledge

On a separate sheet of paper or in a word processing document, match the following terms with the definition that fits best.

A. marketing
B. rapport
C. event-based selling
D. public image
E. target market
F. word-of-mouth advertising
G. advertising
H. promotion
I. market segment
J. cross-selling

1. Customers tell others about their experience with a specific business.
2. Marketing strategy that encourages bank representatives to contact a customer when an event occurs.
3. Process of introducing a product or service to the consumers who can purchase it.
4. Activity that increases consumer awareness of a product.
5. Bond of mutual trust.
6. Encourages existing customers to buy new products or services based on their previous purchases.
7. Group of consumers that share common wants and needs.
8. Made up of the ideas and opinions that people have about a business.
9. Activity that calls attention to a product or service.
10. Market segment that will be the focus of the marketing strategy.

On a separate sheet of paper or in a word processing document, answer each of the following questions.

11. Describe the difference between a need and a want.
12. What distinguishes the members of a market segment from other consumers?
13. Name an event that could encourage a bank representative to contact a customer using event-based selling.
14. What are four aspects of a positive public image that banks strive for?
15. When does customer service begin?

Apply Your Knowledge

16. Create a chart listing some needs and wants of consumers. In the second column, list the products or services that banks provide to satisfy these needs and wants.
17. Create a chart of target markets that a bank might identify. Indicate on the chart which markets you are included in or excluded from.
18. Using Figure 11-6, add a fourth column titled Customer Service That Exceeds Expectations. For each situation, list customer service behaviors that would exceed customer expectations.
19. Think about an occasion when you witnessed inappropriate customer-service behavior at any business. Write a short summary discussing the encounter and what you think should have been done differently.
20. With a classmate, take turns role playing a customer-service situation at a bank. Imagine you are a bank representative answering a customer's questions about the savings accounts your bank offers. Ask your partner to rate your customer-service skills.

Working in Teams

Interview a classmate as if he or she were a client whose investment portfolio you manage. What information would you have to know about your client to understand what investments would be suitable? Create a pie chart that shows what percentage of your client's investable income you would place in stocks, bonds, treasury securities, and other assets, such as real estate. Present the chart to your client and your class, giving the rationale behind your choices.

G-W Learning Mobile Site

Visit the G-W Learning mobile site to complete the chapter pretest and post test and to practice vocabulary using e-flash cards. If you do not have a smartphone, visit the G-W Learning companion website to access these features.

G-W Learning mobile site: www.m.g-wlearning.com
G-W Learning companion website: www.g-wlearning.com

Common Core

College and Career Readiness

Speaking. Plan a marketing campaign based on increasing sales of an existing banking product or service. Using multiple types of visual and print displays, present your plan to the class. Ask your classmates to comment on the effectiveness of your marketing plan.

Writing. Keep an eye out for bank advertisements that you encounter. These can be found on television, in magazines, on social networking sites, on billboards, and multiple other places. Start a journal that documents where you found the advertisement, what was being advertised, who you think the target market for the advertisement is, and any aspects of the advertisement that contribute to the bank's public image. Update your journal throughout the semester, being sure to include advertisements from multiple types of media sources.

EVENT PREP

Financial Math

Financial math is a competitive event you might enter with your career and technical student organization (CTSO). The financial math event may include an objective test that includes banking topics. If you decide to participate in this event, you will need to review basic banking concepts to prepare for the test. To prepare for a financial math event:

1. Read the guidelines provided by your organization. Make certain that you ask any questions about points you do not understand. It is important you follow each specific item that is outlined in the competition rules.
2. Review the checkpoint activities at the end of each section of the text.
3. Review the end-of-chapter activities for additional practice.
4. Ask your instructor to give you a practice test for each chapter of this text. It is important that you are familiar with answering multiple choice and true/false questions. Have someone time you as you take the practice tests.

12

Check Your Banking IQ

Before you begin this chapter, see what you already know about banking by taking the chapter pretest.

www.m.g-wlearning.com
www.g-wlearning.com

Banking Careers and Workplace Skills

Have you ever heard of working *banker's hours?* Banker's hours used to mean a short workday that reflected the comparatively short number of hours a bank was open. Banker's hours today are often greater than nine to five to keep up with the demands of this complex and growing field. Banking is an exciting field that has an impact on just about every kind of business. A career in banking offers opportunities for employment and advancement to those who are willing to work hard and who have the skills and training the various positions demand.

College and Career Readiness

Reading Prep. Recall all the things you already know about banking careers. As you read, think of how the new information presented in the text matches or challenges your prior understanding of the topic. Think of direct connections you can make between the old material and the new material.

Scan the code to view a Biz Kid$ video. If you do not have a smartphone, visit the G-W Learning companion website.

www.m.g-wlearning.com
www.g-wlearning.com

Section 12.1
Executive Careers

Objectives

After completing this section, you will be able to:

- Describe the role and responsibilities of a chief executive officer.
- Explain the connection between the chief operating officer and the bank president.
- List the qualifications for a chief financial officer in the banking industry.
- Describe the difference between a chief technology officer and a chief information officer.

Terms

chief executive officer (CEO)
chief operating officer (COO)
president
chief financial officer (CFO)
chief technology officer (CTO)
chief information officer (CIO)

Chief Executive Officer

The **chief executive officer (CEO)** is appointed by a corporate board of directors and is accountable to the corporation's stockholders, the public it serves, and legal authorities for the actions of the bank. The CEO is responsible for setting the strategic vision of the bank and placing individuals into positions of authority to carry out that vision. If a bank has a board of directors, the CEO reports to the board and bases policies on the board's direction. Additionally, the CEO usually sits on the board of directors and may be the chairperson of the board. Recently, CEOs have taken on greater responsibility for *selling the bank,* a function described in depth in chapter 11.

An individual generally has at least ten years of high-level leadership experience as well as a bachelor degree in accounting or finance before being considered for a CEO position. Those serving in this role have a Master of Business Administration (MBA) and a strong background in technology.

BIZ TIPS

If you want to have a net worth of $1 million, determine at what point in your life you want to be worth that much; then save toward that goal!

Source: Shutterstock (AVAVA)

Executive positions require an advanced degree, such as an MBA.

Chief Operating Officer and President

The **chief operating officer (COO)** is the executive responsible for the bank's daily operations. In some circumstances, the **president** serves the function of a COO or even that of the CEO. The COO has the ultimate responsibility for the bank's operations and performance and is responsible for the bank's success or failure. The COO reports to the CEO, providing critical operations information that helps the CEO make policy decisions for the bank.

Department managers report to the COO. He or she uses information from the managers to track the departments' progress and verify that all departments successfully complete their tasks.

Skills and qualifications for a COO and a CEO are not altogether different. Both require a bachelor degree and an MBA. A COO or president focuses on how policies are reflected in day-to-day performance. Strong interpersonal skills are needed to be a successful COO.

Chief Financial Officer

The **chief financial officer (CFO)** is the executive responsible for financial planning, control, and record keeping for the bank. The CFO supervises all accounting tasks, including preparing and monitoring the bank's budget. The CFO reports to the CEO, providing critical financial information that helps the CEO make decisions involving the bank's finances.

Like other senior-level positions, academic preparation that includes a bachelor and master degree is required. A great deal of technical, legal, and technological knowledge as well as certification as a Certified Public Accountant (CPA) is required.

Chief Technology Officer and Chief Information Officer

The **chief technology officer (CTO)** is the executive responsible for developing new technology for use by the bank. This role has become increasingly central to banks as Internet and mobile banking have become growing parts of the banking industry. Information technology managers report to the CTO.

The role of the CTO varies from bank to bank. In some banks, the CTO sets the long-term direction of the technology the bank will use. In other banks, the CTO is also involved in the technology the bank currently uses and may be involved in resolving issues with implementing new technology. Sometimes a **chief information officer (CIO)** serves this function.

A great deal of technical knowledge is required to be a CTO. The ability to interact with different banking departments is also important. Many CTOs were information technology managers who have more than ten years of experience. An MBA is required in most instances, with a concentration in systems management being highly desirable.

Green Banking

Green banks, banks that are concerned with the environment, are gaining in popularity. Banks, like other corporations, are recognizing the importance of protecting the environment as they conduct business. Online and mobile banking are helping the environment. By doing business online, customers save gas by not making a trip to the bank. Many banks are offering special incentives to customers who choose to use these services rather than come into the bank for routine transactions.

Checkpoint 12.1

1. To whom is the CEO responsible?
2. What executive banking role is charged with setting the strategic vision of the bank and placing individuals into positions of authority to carry out that vision?
3. How do the duties of the CEO differ from that of a COO?
4. Why is it necessary for a CFO to be a CPA?
5. What previous career experience may help someone become a CTO?

Build Your Vocabulary

As you progress through this course, develop a personal glossary of banking terms and add it to your portfolio. This will help you build your banking vocabulary. Write out a definition for each of the following terms, and add it to your personal glossary.

chief executive officer (CEO)
chief operating officer (COO)
president
chief financial officer (CFO)
chief technology officer (CTO)
chief information officer (CIO)

Section 12.2
Banking Administration Careers

Terms

compliance officer
trust officer
trust
probate law
lending officer
loan officer
mortgage banker
underwriter

Objectives

After completing this section, you will be able to:

- Discuss the role of a bank's compliance officer in banking operations.
- Explain how financial advising is part of a trust officer's duties.
- Describe the role a lending officer plays in the loan process.
- Explain the relationship between a real estate professional and a mortgage broker.

Compliance Officer

The **compliance officer** is the person who must ensure the bank follows all state and federal laws and regulations. This person establishes how the bank will implement strategies for complying with laws and regulations and for completing the necessary reporting. Another important role for the compliance officer is to ensure all bank employees understand their roles in complying with laws and regulations.

A bank's compliance officer is often an attorney with a bachelor degree in finance or other business-related field. A person serving in this role must be highly ethical and honest. Recent legislation has lead to an increase in responsibilities associated with this position.

BIZ TIPS

Aim to save 10% of your income every week, and more if possible. The goal of saving on a regular basis is to make it a habit.

Trust Officer

A **trust officer** is responsible for providing customers with financial products and trust services. **Trusts** are established to help with the distribution of a person's assets after his or her death. A trust officer also provides financial advice to customers. Traditionally, trusts have generally been used by the wealthy, although this is changing as trusts are being used across all income brackets.

Source: Shutterstock (Andrey Burmakin)

A background in finance and law can lead to a career as a compliance officer.

A trust officer needs to have a general knowledge of business. In addition, a trust officer must know about investing, estate planning, and tax codes and laws, especially probate laws. **Probate laws** are those that pertain to settling the financial affairs of a person after he or she has died. Since a trust officer often provides financial advice, strong communication and interpersonal skills are required. A bachelor degree in a finance-related field is required.

Lending Officer

The **lending officer,** sometimes called the **loan officer,** is involved in evaluating applications for loans or lines of credit. The loans may be to individuals or businesses and can be offered for a variety of reasons.

A lending officer must have a general knowledge of business and the operation of the banking industry. Strong sales skills are also required. Because of the knowledge and skills required for this position, many upper-management positions are filled by people with experience as lending officers.

Some lending officers travel outside of the office. Commercial lending officers, for example, may travel to another city to complete a complex loan agreement. Most lending officers work a 40-hour workweek. However, additional hours may be required in some situations.

A minimum of a high school degree is required to be a lending officer. On-the-job training is then provided. However, it is common for a bank to require a bachelor degree in finance, economics, or a related field for a commercial lending officer.

Ethical Banking

Many banks mandate ethics training. Employees must participate in training sessions to maintain employment. The training itself usually centers on understanding the bank's code of conduct and all relevant laws.

Mortgage Banker

A **mortgage banker** is similar to a lending officer, except for he or she deals only with mortgage loans. The mortgages may be offered to individuals or businesses. A mortgage banker is also involved in servicing existing mortgages that have not been sold to another bank.

A mortgage banker spends a lot of time talking with real estate professionals and the person or business seeking the mortgage. Therefore, time is usually spent working outside of the office. Also, excellent communication skills are required. Additionally, a mortgage banker must know how to conduct a credit check. A 40-hour workweek is typical. However, more hours may be required in certain situations.

Mortgages are often sold by the initiating bank to another bank or other investors. The *mortgage-backed securities* market played a role in the events that lead to the financial crises in the early 21st century. With new and proposed regulations on mortgage-backed securities, a mortgage banker must keep up to date with all related rules and regulations.

A bachelor degree in finance, economics, or a related field is usually required to work as a mortgage banker. Beyond that, federal law requires mortgage bankers to be licensed. To maintain the license, certain continuing education credits must be earned.

Source: Shutterstock (Goodluz)

Mortgage bankers must have good communication and interpersonal skills.

Underwriter

An **underwriter** reviews the loan application and approves or denies the loan. This decision is based on the creditworthiness of the applicant, and software is usually used to help make the decision.

Underwriters work in an office. A 40-hour workweek is typical. However, in some cases additional work or travel may be required. Most banks require underwriters to have a bachelor degree in finance, economics, or a related field.

Checkpoint 12.2

1. What role does a compliance officer play in the banking industry?
2. In addition to a general knowledge of business, what else must a trust officer know to be a success?
3. Why is experience as a lending officer particularly helpful for someone who wants to move up in the banking industry?
4. Who do mortgage bankers most frequently deal with?
5. What criteria do underwriters use to determine if a loan is approved?

Build Your Vocabulary

As you progress through this course, develop a personal glossary of banking terms and add it to your portfolio. This will help you build your banking vocabulary. Write out a definition for each of the following terms, and add it to your personal glossary.

compliance officer
trust officer
trust
probate law
lending officer
loan officer
mortgage banker
underwriter

Section 12.3 Managerial Careers

Objectives

After completing this section, you will be able to:

- Explain the role of a bank manager.
- Describe the connection between workplace regulations and a human resources manager's duties.
- Identify the specific qualification of an information technology manager.
- Explain the relationship between a real estate professional and a mortgage broker.
- Describe what interpersonal skills are required of a public relations manager.
- Identify the education required for an accounting manager position.

Terms

branch manager
operations manager
human resources (HR) manager
information technology (IT) manager
public relations manager
accounting manager

Branch Manager

A **branch manager** oversees the day-to-day activities of one branch of the bank and is sometimes called an **operations manager.** Part of this is ensuring the activities of the bank are completed, but the branch manager must also develop a relationship with existing and potential customers. Many branch managers start working as a teller or customer service representative.

A branch manager must have good communication and interpersonal skills. In addition, attention to detail and the ability to organize and plan are needed.

Usually, a bachelor degree in finance or a related field is required to work as a branch manager. However, some banks will hire bank managers who have an unrelated bachelor degree if they have a master degree in finance or a finance-related field. Branch managers' workweek reflects the hours of operation of the bank, which will typically include hours on Saturdays.

BIZ TIPS

Be frugal! You aren't going to become a millionaire by spending all of your money.

Source: Shutterstock (Golden Pixels LLC)

Many branch managers work their way up from teller or CSR positions.

Human Resources Manager

The **human resources (HR) manager** is involved in employee relations for the bank. This includes recruiting new employees, ensuring employees receive proper training, and enforcing the bank's employment policies. The human resources manager represents the management to the employees and the employees to the management.

Part of the responsibilities of an HR manager is to implement regulations concerning employees. For example, hourly employees are guaranteed rest and lunch breaks. The HR manager must also ensure fair hiring and labor practices are followed.

An HR manager typically works in an office environment. Generally, HR managers work a 40-hour week. However, in some cases additional hours may be required. Depending on the bank, the HR manager may occasionally need to travel to employment fairs or for professional training.

A bachelor degree in human resources management or a similar field is usually required. A minor in finance or economics may be preferred by some banks. Additionally, a master degree is often preferred, and in some cases may be required.

Information Technology Manager

The **information technology (IT) manager** implements the policies and procedures set by the chief technology officer or chief information officer. If the bank does not have either of these positions, the IT manager sets the policies and procedures for the technology the bank uses. The IT manager directs the work of IT technicians.

An IT manager must have technical expertise in computer systems. In addition, an ability to set schedules and direct others is essential. Long hours may be required to meet deadlines or to correct problems with the computer systems.

A bachelor degree in a computer-related field is usually required to be an information technology manager. However, many banks may prefer a master degree. Beyond a degree, certification in specific computer technologies may be preferred or required.

Source: Shutterstock (AISPIX by Image Source)

The public relations manager is in charge of managing the bank's public image.

Public Relations Manager

The **public relations manager** is responsible for creating a positive image of the bank. This includes designing and implementing promotions, coordinating the bank's sponsorship of charitable activities, and providing information to journalists. Depending on the size of the bank, the public relations manager may have a staff or may work alone.

A public relations manager works closely with executives and top management. Often, the public relations manager is the face of the bank. As presenting the bank in a positive way is the primary responsibility of a public relations manager, he or she must be pleasant and accommodating. Excellent communication skills are required, as is an ability to remain positive even when discussing problems. Public relations managers often work long hours, sometimes on the weekends.

A bachelor degree in public relations or journalism is often preferred for public relations managers. However, a master degree may be required. Courses in advertising, public speaking, creative writing, technical writing, and business administration will be beneficial.

Accounting Manager

The **accounting manager** is responsible for the functions of the accountants and auditors in the bank. This includes making sure the bank's financial information is correctly recorded. The accounting manager may also work closely with the bank's executives to develop new financial products for the bank.

An accounting manager usually works in an office environment and generally works a 40-hour workweek. However, during certain periods, such as tax time or the end of the quarter, additional hours may be required.

Usually, a minimum of a bachelor degree in accounting is required, although many banks require a master degree in accounting or business administration with a concentration in accounting. Beyond a college degree, the accounting manager is usually a Certified Public Accountant (CPA). If the accounting manager is responsible for filing reports with the Securities and Exchange Commission, by law that person must be a CPA. In addition to CPA certification, other certifications may be required.

Checkpoint 12.3

1. What is another title for a branch manager?
2. In what banking career would you recruit new employees, ensure employees receive proper training, and enforce the bank's employment policies?
3. In addition to the ability to set schedules and others, what skill must an information technology manager have?
4. To create a positive image of the bank, what must a public relations manager do?
5. In what banking career would you supervise the accountants and auditors in the bank?

Build Your Vocabulary

As you progress through this course, develop a personal glossary of banking terms and add it to your portfolio. This will help you build your banking vocabulary. Write out a definition for each of the following terms, and add it to your personal glossary.

branch manager
operations manager
human resource (HR) manager
information technology (IT) manager
public relations manager
accounting manager

Section 12.4
Operational-Support Careers

Terms

- credit analyst
- loan processor
- bill and account collector
- repossession agent
- debt counselor
- credit counselor
- teller
- Certified Bank Teller (CBT)
- customer service representative (CSR)
- public relations specialist
- data processor
- accountant
- auditor
- title researcher
- examiner
- abstractor

Objectives

After completing this section, you will be able to:

- Describe the function of credit analysts and loan processors in making loans.
- Describe the connection between those in loan processing roles and a bank's profitability.
- Explain why tellers, customer service representatives, and public relations specialists are the key to how the bank is perceived by its customers and potential customers.
- Recognize how those in data processing careers manage increasing amounts of digital information.
- Describe the functions of accountants and auditors in the banking industry.
- Explain how the services provided by title researchers, examiners, and abstractors are important to banking operations.

Loan Origination

Lending is an essential service provided by a bank. When someone comes into the bank seeking a loan, many people work toward making sure the documents are correctly prepared and all the information is accurate. Without credit analysts and loan processors, no one could ever get a loan.

BIZ TIPS

Use your creativity. Everybody has a talent that is marketable. Use your creativity to make some extra money out of your personal experience.

Credit Analyst

A **credit analyst** looks at the credit worthiness of loan applicants. This includes projecting the future cash flow for the individual or business and determining how financially sound they are. A credit analyst typically works in an office, but may need to visit a business as part of determining its credit worthiness. Much time is spent on the phone investigating the loan applicant. As a result, a credit analyst may work more than the typical 40-hour workweek.

A bachelor degree in accounting is often required for a credit analyst. Additional on-the-job training is usually provided.

Loan Processor

A **loan processor** works with the lending officer to collect all of the required information from the individual or business applying for a loan. This includes verifying information on the application and performing a credit check. Once all of the information is collected and verified, the loan processor forwards the information to the underwriter, who approves or denies the loan. By separating the loan processor from the decision to approve or deny the loan, bias is removed.

Loan processors work closely with the lending officer. Much time is spent completing paperwork and communicating with loan applicants. A 40-hour workweek is typical.

A minimum of a high school degree is required to be a loan processor. However, completing a certificate program beyond high school is often recommended. Additionally, some banks prefer or require a bachelor degree in business, accounting, or a related field. Some states require loan processors to be licensed. In most cases, the bank also requires the loan processor to be bonded.

Source: Shutterstock (mangostock)

A loan processor collects and verifies a loan applicant's information.

Loan Servicing

The bank's job does not end after funds are dispersed. On the contrary, several processes that are part of the bank's routine operations center on loan servicing. When a borrower fails to repay a loan according to the terms of the loan agreement, bill and account collectors are called on to facilitate repayment. When a person's debt exceeds his or her ability to repay it, the services of a debt or credit counselor may come into play. Since the financial crises of the 21st century, an increasing number of borrowers have stopped paying on their loans. When a loan is not repaid, the bank loses money. Problem-loan management has become a big part of banks' loan-servicing operations.

Bill and Account Collector

A **bill and account collector** is responsible for getting customers to make overdue payments. Included in this career category are repossession agents. **Repossession agents** are people who take possession of property, such as a car, when payments have not been made for a period of time and turn the property over to the bank.

A bill and account collector spends a lot of time communicating with customers. Therefore, excellent communication and interpersonal skills are required. The work can be stressful because customers can be confrontational when pressed to make payments. Also, evening and weekend hours may be required in order to contact customers.

A minimum of a high school degree is required for a bill and account collector. However, most banks prefer completion of some college courses. Experience in a call center is helpful, since most of the time is spent on the phone with customers. On-the-job training will provide instruction in complying with the Fair Debt Collection Practices Act and appropriate state laws.

Debt Counselor

A **debt counselor,** or **credit counselor,** provides advice to a client on how to manage and reduce debt. Additionally, a debt counselor may help clients develop financial plans for remaining debt free in the future.

Debt counselors spend a lot of time communicating with the client. Most clients contacting a debt counselor are in stressful situations due to their debt. Therefore, a debt counselor must always be pleasant, positive, and sympathetic toward the client. In addition to spending time communicating with the client, a debt counselor spends time researching the client's financial information and resources that will assist the client.

A bachelor degree in finance, economics, or business is usually required to be a debt counselor. In addition, many states require debt counselors to be licensed or certified.

Customer and Community Relationships

The banking business has become more competitive since the Great Recession. Banks are under a lot of pressure to retain the customer base they have, even in the face of increasing fees and decreasing perks, while attracting new customers. Tellers, customer services representatives, and public relations specialists play a large role in how customers and the communities they serve perceive the bank. Banks, like other businesses, must maintain a positive image to maintain and grow their customer bases.

Tellers

Tellers are responsible for conducting transactions between the bank and the customer. This includes assisting customers in making deposits, cashing checks, paying property taxes, and making account withdrawals. Tellers are often thought of as the face of the bank because they are the point of contact between the bank and the customer.

Tellers stand for long periods of time. They must always be pleasant and courteous toward customers. Tellers usually have set hours of work. Depending on the bank, they may be required to work in the evenings or weekends.

A minimum of a high school diploma is required to be a teller. A background check is also conducted. On-the-job training is provided for the skills needed to be a teller. The Institute of Certified Bankers has established performance standards for bank tellers. Tellers can obtain **Certified Bank Teller (CBT)** certification by demonstrating expertise on a standardized examination.

Source: Shutterstock (OtnaYdur)

Accountants maintain the bank's financial records.

Customer Service Representative

A **customer service representative (CSR)** is a link between customers and the bank. Where the teller conducts the customer's business, the customer service representative assists the customer in resolving issues.

Customer service representatives spend a lot of time communicating with customers. A friendly and positive attitude is required. Often, when customers are contacting customer service, they are upset or confrontational. To deal with this, patience and the ability to remain calm to resolve the situation is essential.

A minimum of a high school degree is required to be a CSR. However, many banks require a bachelor degree in finance, economics, or a related field because the CSR position often provides entry into higher-level careers in the bank.

Public Relations Specialist

A **public relations specialist** carries out the policies and procedures outlined by the public relations manager. This includes initiating promotions, coordinating the bank's sponsorship of charitable activities, and providing information to journalists.

As presenting the bank in a positive way is a primary responsibility, a public relations specialist must be pleasant and cooperative at all times. Excellent communication skills are required, as is an ability to remain positive even when discussing problems. Public relations specialists often work long hours, sometimes on the weekends.

A bachelor degree in public relations or journalism is often preferred for public relations specialists. Courses in advertising, public speaking, creative writing, technical writing, and business administration will be beneficial.

Data Processing

A **data processor** deals with the management of digital information. This career category may include one of a variety of careers shown in Figure 12-1. The specific data-processing careers available depend on the bank. Most data processors work in an office setting. A 40-hour workweek is common, but this varies.

The educational requirements for a data processor depend on the specific career. Some data-processor careers require only a minimum of a high school diploma. However, some data-processor careers require a bachelor degree in accounting, computer science, or a related field. In some cases, a master degree or certificate program is preferred or even required.

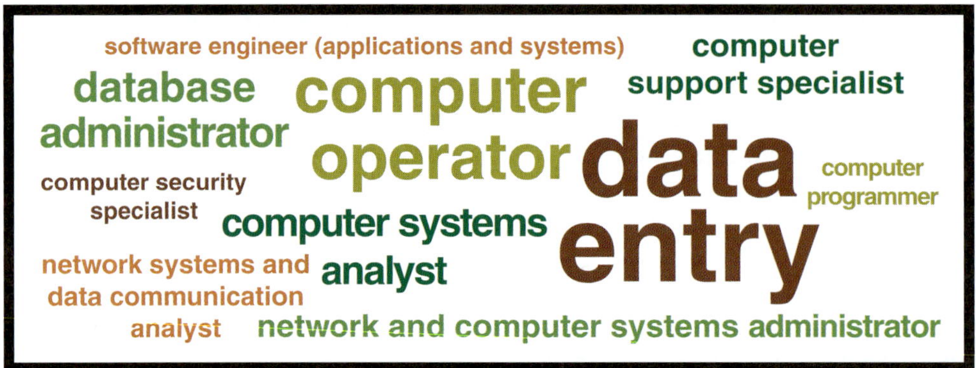

Figure 12-1.
Data-Processing Careers

Accountant and Auditor

An **accountant** is responsible for creating and maintaining accurate financial records for the bank. This includes transactions the bank completes, paying taxes and fees for the bank, and maintaining required public records. Accountants work with accounting clerks and report to the accounting manager.

An **auditor** verifies the bank's processes and procedures, checking for errors, mismanagement, and fraud. Auditors certify various reports the bank produces, including the quarterly and annual reports. Auditors typically report to the accounting manager.

Accountants and auditors work in an office. A 40-hour workweek is typical. However, additional hours may be required in some situations, such as during audits, ends of quarters, or tax season.

Usually, a minimum of a bachelor degree in accounting is required. Beyond a college degree, many accountants and auditors are Certified Public Accountants. Other certifications may be preferred or required by the bank.

Title Researcher, Examiner, and Abstractor

A **title researcher, examiner,** or **abstractor** searches real-estate records for details related to an assigned task. Titles, legal documents, and insurance documents may also be searched. For example, they may need to compile a list of contracts, legal documents, and mortgages attached to a particular title for real estate.

Work with computerized-database systems in an office is the standard working environment. A high school diploma is required, but coursework beyond high school will make a person looking for a job in this field more marketable. Knowledge of the court system is also a plus.

Checkpoint 12.4

1. What aspect of a bill and account collector's job can make it stressful?
2. What interpersonal skills must a credit counselor have?
3. What banking career is often thought of as the face of the bank?
4. In what banking career would you put your excellent communication skills to work to represent the bank in a positive way to the community?
5. What kind of work does a title researcher do?

Build Your Vocabulary

As you progress through this course, develop a personal glossary of banking terms and add it to your portfolio. This will help you build your banking vocabulary. Write out a definition for each of the following terms, and add it to your personal glossary.

credit analyst
loan processor
bill and account collector
repossession agent
debt counselor
credit counselor
teller
Certified Bank Teller (CBT)
customer service representative (CSR)
public relations specialist
data processor
accountant
auditor
title researcher
examiner
abstractor

Section 12.5
Employability Skills

Terms

interpersonal skills
communication
verbal communication
nonverbal communication
teamwork
team
leadership
problem solving
self-esteem
punctuality
ergonomics

Objectives

After completing this section, you will be able to:

- Explain the role interpersonal skills play in employee success.
- Identify the role sales skills play for banking employees at all levels.
- Explain how creative problem solving is an important skill in both daily life and the workplace.
- Describe how an employee or job seeker can conduct themselves in a professional manner.
- Explain how ergonomics can prevent workplace injury.

Interpersonal Skills

People skills, more commonly known as **interpersonal skills,** are how you handle interactions with other people. This includes not only your interactions with customers, but with your coworkers and management. To succeed in the workplace, you must have a positive attitude, be cooperative, and respect others.

Communication Skills

An important part of interpersonal skills is communication. Good communication is central to the smooth operation of any business. Through **communication,** you and your coworkers exchange ideas, thoughts, and information. The primary forms of communication are verbal and nonverbal:

- **Verbal communication** involves sending and receiving messages through speaking, listening, and writing.
- **Nonverbal communication** includes sending and receiving messages without using words. It involves body language, such as your facial expressions and your posture.

Listening and feedback are keys to effective workplace communication. If you do not understand what a coworker or supervisor has said, or if his or her nonverbal and verbal communication sends mixed signals, be sure to ask questions. Remember, maintaining eye contact tells the other person you are paying attention to what he or she is saying. Clear communication helps avoid costly mistakes and wasted time in the workplace.

Source: Shutterstock (Yuri Arcurs)

Teamwork and leadership skills are important for career success.

Skillful communication also applies to telephone conversations and written communication. Promptly answering the telephone with a positive tone of voice and pleasant attitude conveys a positive message about your employer. Likewise, written communication, such as letters and e-mails, requires special attention. Carefully craft the message to say precisely what you mean. Think about how others will interpret the message without hearing or seeing body language. Then, check your spelling, grammar, and punctuation. Unfortunately, many people do not give this attention to e-mails, which reflects negatively on not only you, but your employer. Never send a written communication, whether a printed letter or an e-mail, without checking spelling and grammar. Additionally, texting language is *not* acceptable in a business situation.

Periodically give yourself a communications checkup. Ask your supervisor to suggest areas in which you can improve.

BIZ TIPS

Back when coins were made of silver or gold, a person could have made an illegal living from shaving coins and selling the precious metal. That's why we now make ridges on the edges of coins.

Teamwork Skills

Another important part of interpersonal skills is **teamwork,** which is working with others to achieve a common goal. You are a member of a team, and it is important to be an integral part of that team. A **team** is a group of people with similar or complimenting skills who share a common purpose.

Employers seek employees who can serve efficiently on a team. Effective team members focus on the goals of the group. Creative ideas and solutions often develop from building on the shared ideas of others. With a team, all members help carry out tasks to meet team goals. Cooperation and effective communication among team members allows each person to express ideas fully and honestly. All team members use problem-solving skills to help build consensus on ways to meet group goals. Team membership involves striking a balance between group productivity and personal satisfaction.

Leadership Skills

The third important part of interpersonal skills is **leadership,** which is the ability to lead others to achieve goals or complete tasks. Employers want to know how you function as a team leader. If you have ever made a decision that helped others achieve a goal, you have used leadership skills. Leadership skills go hand in hand with problem-solving skills. Although a number of leadership styles exist, a democratic style of leadership is often favored. It encourages all group members to take initiative, help carry out goals, and assume responsibility for group accomplishments. Figure 12-2 lists the traits of effective leaders.

- Help individual team members resolve problems and differences of opinion
- Guide the team to overcome hurdles in reaching the team goals
- Work with the team to make changes happen
- Take responsibility for their actions and the actions of the team
- Be inspiring, flexible, and creative

Figure 12-2.
Traits of Effective Leaders

Sales Skills

Many of the careers in the banking industry require sales skills. In some careers, you will be directly selling banking products to a customer. In other careers, you may not be selling a product, but you must still sell the bank. As a representative of the bank, you must always present it in a positive way. This will help encourage customers to conduct business with the bank.

Analytical, Synthesis, and Creativity Skills

The ability to make responsible decisions and use problem-solving skills applies to the workplace and all other aspects of life. **Problem solving** includes the ability to analyze a situation or information, synthesize the material into a cohesive position, and creatively determine a solution or action. Using these skills well shows your employer that you can handle additional work responsibilities. Effective use of these skills can also strengthen team efforts and help all employees take pride in their work.

Your problem-solving skills can help you answer tough questions and resolve difficult situations. Often, problem solving involves adapting to a new way of doing things. Employers highly value employees who can solve problems effectively. Figure 12-3 shows the steps in the problem-solving process.

Positive Workplace Practices

Workplace success results from hard work, high motivation, and diverse skills. Whatever banking career path you choose, you will need to give it your best effort. Employees who are successful display energy, cooperation, and enthusiasm for their work. They follow instructions, take constructive criticism well, and finish tasks in a timely manner. Maintaining confidentiality is also an important workplace responsibility. Willingness to do more than what is expected and respecting the work of others are traits employers value.

The problem-solving steps include:

1. Clearly identify the real problem.
2. List alternative courses of action.
3. Evaluate the consequences of each course of action.
4. Choose an alternative and take action.
5. Assess the outcome for reference when facing future problems.

Figure 12-3.
Steps in the Problem-Solving Process

Employers want employees who are reliable, punctual, and responsible, and who present themselves in a professional manner. They want their employees to be capable of taking initiative, working both independently and with team members. Employees who have high **self-esteem** have a deep sense of worth and are able to work hard with a positive attitude.

Appropriate Dress Code

Banking as an industry tends to be conservative, and workplace attire usually reflects this. Women should wear a business suit, dress, or pantsuit with a blouse. Dress shoes should be worn. Some banks do not allow open-toed shoes, so check with your employer. Men should wear a business suit with a white or light-colored, long-sleeve shirt. A conservative tie and dress shoes should be worn.

Attire that is not acceptable includes shorts, denim, tee shirts, strapless or spaghetti-strap tops, low-cut blouses, and tight-fitting or baggy clothing of any kind. Also not acceptable is any manner of dress in which the undergarments are visible.

In addition, most employers look unfavorably on visible tattoos and body piercings. Men should not have any visible body piercings, including pierced ears. For women, the only visible piercings should be in the ears and they should be limited to one per ear. Women should wear only conservative earrings; bar earrings are not acceptable.

Personal Grooming

You should always be well groomed at work. You represent your employer, and by being well groomed, you project a positive image of your employer. Being unshaven is not acceptable, nor is wearing too much perfume or cologne.

Hair should be kept clean and neat. Generally, men should not wear their hair long. For those who choose to color their hair, the color should be conservative. Men should not have special hair treatments, such as frosted tips.

Punctuality

Punctuality is showing up on time. Even though many careers in the banking industry are paid a salary instead of hourly, punctuality is still very important. Failing to show up for work on time can lead to dismissal. You should also return promptly from breaks and lunches.

While punctuality is often thought of in terms of starting time for work, it also applies to meetings with coworkers and clients. Dependable employees keep their word and meet deadlines. Being punctual shows respect for those you work with and to clients. Remember, you are representing your bank, so showing up late to a meeting with a client reflects negatively not only on you, but the bank itself.

It is important to call your supervisor right away when illness or other emergencies prevent you from coming to work. Then, make alternative arrangements with your employer for making up work. Many people lose jobs because of failure to check in with a supervisor about time off.

Time Management and Organization

Successful employees prioritize their work assignments, complete them on time, and avoid wasting time. Time-wasting behaviors include talking with coworkers, making personal phone calls, texting, sending e-mail messages, or other nonwork activities during business hours.

Ability to determine which assignments are most important is a key organizational skill. When uncertain, ask your supervisor. It is important to avoid putting excessive effort into minor assignments, especially when a high-priority task demands attention.

Safe Workplace

Workplace safety in the US has continuously improved since the beginning of the 20th century. Gradually, workplace injury, death, and illness have declined due to a change in the type of work we do today and in the safety precautions that have been put in place. Many workers now spend extended periods of time in front of computers. This can result in injury that would cause a workers' compensation claim. **Ergonomics** is the science of adapting the workstation to fit the needs of the worker and lessen the chance of injury.

Checkpoint 12.5

1. What three interpersonal skills are necessary for success in the workplace?
2. What are the two basic forms of communication?
3. Making decisions that help an organization or others achieve a goal is an example of what important interpersonal skill?
4. Wearing jeans, a tee shirt, and unlaced athletic shoes to work at a bank is an example of violation of which positive workplace practice?
5. Being on time for work and returning promptly from lunch and breaks is an example of what essential skill?

Build Your Vocabulary

As you progress through this course, develop a personal glossary of banking terms and add it to your portfolio. This will help you build your banking vocabulary. Write out a definition for each of the following terms, and add it to your personal glossary.

interpersonal skills
communication
verbal communication
nonverbal communication
teamwork
team
leadership
problem solving
self esteem
punctuality
ergonomics

Chapter Summary

Section 12.1 Executive Careers

- The CEO provides strategic leadership and a vision for how the bank will grow.
- The COO or president has the ultimate responsibility for the bank's operations and performance and is responsible for the bank's success or failure.
- The CFO reports to the CEO, providing critical financial information that helps the CEO make decisions involving the bank's finances.
- The role of the CTO has become increasingly central to banks as Internet and mobile banking have become growing parts of the banking industry.

Section 12.2 Banking Administration Careers

- A bank's compliance officer is tasked with making certain the bank is abiding by state and federal regulations that govern banking operations.
- Trust officers must possess a general knowledge of business, as well as investing, estate planning, and tax codes and laws, especially probate laws.
- A lending officer evaluates applications for credit.
- Mortgage brokers handle new and existing mortgages for individuals and businesses.
- Loan applications are reviewed, and ultimately approved or denied, by an underwriter.

Section 12.3 Managerial Careers

- The branch manager, sometimes called the operations manager, typically supervises one of the bank's branches.
- Maintaining a safe and equitable workplace is among the duties of a human resources manager.
- In addition to great technological skills, an information technology manager must be able to set schedules, effectively train members of the IT team, and get along with the people working in all the departments of the bank.
- A public relations manager must always be pleasant even when confronted with negative situations.
- An accounting manager typically has a bachelor degree as well as a CPA designation.

Section 12.4 Operational-Support Careers

- Credit analysts and loan processors are essential to a bank's ability to make loans.
- Those working in loan processing roles, such as bill and account collectors and credit counselors, are important because a bank's profitability is linked to its ability to collect on the loans it makes.

- Tellers, customer service representatives, and public relations specialists are the link between the community and the bank, and should reflect the best qualities of the institution in their every interaction.
- Data processing roles in the banking industry have grown along with the increased need to manage huge amounts of digital information.
- Accountants and auditors help verify the accuracy and honesty of transactions for the bank.
- Because most of the lending done by banks centers on real estate, the services of title researchers, examiners, and abstractors are important.

Section 12.5 Employability Skills

- Well-developed interpersonal skills, such as communication, teamwork, and leadership, are the key to success in any workplace.
- An employee's sales skills have an effect on how the bank is perceived.
- Strong problem-solving abilities help employees advance in the workplace and build a productive team atmosphere.
- Appropriate dress, punctuality, and organization are important attributes of professionalism.
- Although the workplace is generally safer today than it has been in the past, workers can still help prevent on-the-job injury by taking simple precautions.

Check Your Banking IQ

Now that you have finished this chapter, see what you know about banking by taking the chapter post test.

www.m.g-wlearning.com
www.g-wlearning.com

Review Your Knowledge

On a separate sheet of paper or in a word processing document, match the following terms with the definition that fits best.

A. repossession agent
B. public relations manager
C. interpersonal skills
D. chief information officer (CIO)
E. auditor
F. probate law
G. ergonomics
H. chief operating officer (COO)
I. branch manager
J. mortgage banker

1. Science of adapting the workstation to fit the needs of the worker and lessen the chance of injury.
2. Similar to a lending officer, but deals only with mortgage loans.
3. Responsible for creating a positive image of the bank.
4. Verifies the bank's processes and procedures, checking for errors, mismanagement, and fraud.
5. Executive responsible for the bank's day-to-day operations.
6. Takes possession of property when payments have not been made for a period of time, and turns the property over to the bank.
7. How you handle interactions with other people.
8. Laws pertaining to settling the financial affairs of a person after he or she has died.
9. Sometimes serves the function of a CTO.
10. Sometimes called the operations manager.

On a separate sheet of paper or in a word processing document, answer each of the following questions.

11. How are the qualifications for a COO different from that of a CEO?
12. What is the role of a compliance officer?
13. What is the primary responsibility of a public relations manager?
14. How does a credit analyst determine the creditworthiness of an applicant?
15. What are the keys to effective workplace communication?

Apply Your Knowledge

16. The CEO provides vision for the future of the bank. Banks, other businesses, and some nonprofit institutions have vision statements. Research different vision statements on the Internet. Write a few paragraphs on how you think a bank's vision affects its operations.
17. Why do you think it is important for a chief information officer to be able to positively interact and communicate with individuals working in many different departments? Write a few paragraphs about the qualities that you perceive are most important to a CIO.
18. Log onto the Bureau of Labor Statistics website (www.bls.gov) and find information regarding the earnings and expected job prospects for one of the careers described in this chapter. After reviewing the information, write a report describing how this affected your interest in the career. Are you more or less interested in this career now? What qualities do you possess that would be helpful for a future in this career?
19. Can you think of a problem or issue in banking today? If you could create any innovation to improve banking, what would it be? Create a presentation about your new product or concept and present it to the class.
20. Create a fictional résumé for someone who wants to get a job in the banking industry. Develop the résumé to show how the applicant's prior experience, skills, and education match the qualifications for one of the careers discussed in this chapter. Be creative and be sure to use appropriate business communication conventions in your writing.

Working in Teams

In small groups, practice your verbal and nonverbal communication skills. Think of something that you know how to do that your classmates might be unfamiliar with. Think about the steps to complete this task, and teach your group how to do it. You can use any form of communication you think will work best. Afterward, ask your group to evaluate how well you communicated the procedure. Take turns evaluating your group members.

G-W Learning Mobile Site

Visit the G-W Learning mobile site to complete the chapter pretest and post test and to practice vocabulary using e-flash cards. If you do not have a smartphone, visit the G-W Learning companion website to access these features.

G-W Learning mobile site: www.m.g-wlearning.com
G-W Learning companion website: www.g-wlearning.com

Common Core

College and Career Readiness

Reading. Research vision statements of banks on the Internet. Write a report analyzing the purposes and central ideas, and how the style and content of the vision statement contribute to the text.

Writing. Choose the banking career discussed in this chapter that appeals to you the most. Using the Internet, research individuals who currently hold this position. Consider the education, experience, and skills that they had before they held this position. Then, write a plan to attain this career, starting with your graduation from high school. Use the information that you find as a guide for opportunities that might help you create this career path.

EVENT PREP

Finance Careers

Finance careers is a competitive event you might enter with your career and technical student organization (CTSO). This competitive event may include an objective test that covers multiple topics. Participants are usually allowed one hour to complete the event. One of the topics that may be included on the test is careers in banking. To prepare for a finance careers event:

1. Read the guidelines provided by your organization. Make certain that you ask any questions about points you do not understand. It is important you follow each specific item that is outlined in the competition rules.
2. Read the careers in finance feature in each chapter of the text. As you read each career, note an important fact or two that you would like to remember.
3. Do an Internet search for *banking careers.* Review any careers that you have not already read about. Make notes on important facts about each.

13

Check Your Banking IQ

Before you begin this chapter, see what you already know about banking by taking the chapter pretest.

www.m.g-wlearning.com
www.g-wlearning.com

Bank Performance

Performance in all industries is most often measured by profits. Managers are constantly striving for the same goal—to have a successful business. As with any business, banks cannot be successful if they do not stay profitable. However, most banks must not only earn profits, but also maintain the safety and soundness of the bank.

College and Career Readiness

Reading Prep. In preparation for reading the chapter, think about what makes a business successful. What is a successful business? How do business owners measure success? As you read, consider how the information in this chapter supports or contradicts your answers to these questions.

Scan the code to view a Biz Kid$ video. If you do not have a smartphone, visit the G-W Learning companion website.

www.m.g-wlearning.com
www.g-wlearning.com

Section 13.1
Analyzing the Numbers

Objectives

After completing this section, you will be able to:

- Explain the parts of a balance sheet.
- Describe the ratios used to measure bank performance.

Terms

balance sheet
asset
liability
stockholders' equity
ratio
net interest income
net interest margin (NIM)
return on assets (ROA)
net income
return on equity (ROE)
spread

Reading the Balance Sheet

Banks are usually for-profit businesses and are expected to generate revenue. Stockholders want a return on their investments in the bank. They want to know that their money is being carefully invested and that their returns are maximized.

For a bank or any other business to show it is successful, progress must be monitored. Measurements must be taken. Many of these measurements are based on the bank's income and expenses. Income includes both traditional and nontraditional services, including those shown in Figure 13-1.

Much of what is needed to understand how well a bank is doing can be found on the bank's balance sheet. A **balance sheet** is a document that reports a company's assets, liabilities, and stockholders' equity. Figure 13-2 is an example of what can be found on a bank's balance sheet.

The left side of the balance sheet shows the assets. **Assets** are what the bank owns. The right side shows the liabilities and the stockholders' equity. **Liabilities** are what the bank owes. Total **stockholders' equity** is the amount of capital owned by the stockholders.

Traditional Services	
Interest on loans	Gains on securities
Interest on securities	
Nontraditional Services	
Insurance products	Trust services
Life insurance	Individual clients
Health insurance	Corporate clients
Property and liability insurance	Asset management
Brokerage services	Investment services

Figure 13-1.
Sources of Bank Income and Expenses

West Creek Bank
Balance Sheet
August 31, 20XX

Assets			Liabilities		
Current Assets:			**Current Liabilities:**		
Cash	$50,000,000		Accounts Payable	$80,000,000	
Accounts Receivable	$140,000,000		Salaries	$90,000,000	
Total Current Assets		$190,000,000	**Total Current Liabilities**		$170,000,000
Plant Assets:			**Long-term Liabilities:**		
Equipment	$30,000,000		Notes Payable	$40,000,000	
Less Accumulated Depreciation	$2,000,000		**Total Long-term Liabilities**		$40,000,000
Total Plant Assets		$28,000,000	**Total Liabilities**		$210,000,000
			Stockholders' Equity		
			Capital Stock	$8,000,000	
Total Assets		$218,000,000	**Total Liabilities & Owner's Equity**		$218,000,000

Figure 13-2.
Bank Balance Sheet

BIZ TIPS

The Sarbanes-Oxley Act of 2002 mandates corporate disclosure of factors that can be used to evaluate the relative strength of a bank or other publically owned corporation.

Performance Ratios

One way of measuring how well the business is doing is to use ratios. A **ratio** shows the relationship between two numbers that have the same unit of measurement. By comparing various financial ratios to those from other businesses in the industry, comparisons can be made to see how the business is doing.

Suppose you want to compare a national chain store's profits to a local retail store's profits. It would be difficult to do so just by looking at the dollar amount of the profits each company made. The national chain store would have profits much larger than the local retail store. But, if you look at a profit ratio for each company, you could easily compare them.

Ratios are a more efficient way to make meaningful comparisons that are adjusted for the size of a business. Using banking ratios allows a comparison between small and large banks. There are three common ratios used by the banking industry: net interest margin, return on assets, and return on equity. Figure 13-3 shows the performance ratios for all FDIC-insured commercial banks for seven years.

Net Interest Margin

Interest received from customer loans or securities is the major source of income for banks. Interest paid on customer deposits is the major expense for banks. Loans and securities are called average earning assets when using this ratio. It makes sense that a bank would pay close attention to both of these types of interest. **Net interest income** is the difference between interest received and interest paid.

	2011	2010	2009	2008	2007	2006
Net interest margin (NIM) (%)	3.63	3.81	3.52	3.21	3.35	3.39
Return on assets (ROA) (%)	0.94	0.65	–0.10	0.13	0.93	1.33
Return on equity (ROE) (%)	8.42	5.88	–0.92	1.31	9.12	13.02

Source: FDIC Quarterly Banking Profile

Figure 13-3.
Selected Performance Indicators for FDIC-Insured Commercial Banks

$$\text{net interest income} = \text{total interest income} - \text{total interest expense}$$

Net interest margin is one of the most widely used ratios for measuring bank performance. **Net interest margin (NIM)** shows how much net income the bank is making on interest as a percentage of total assets. A high net interest margin is good. It shows the bank has kept interest income relatively high while keeping interest expense low. For example, a bank paid \$2 million interest on deposits and received \$6 million in interest income on loans. The bank's assets were \$125 million. The bank's net interest margin is 3.2%.

$$\text{net interest margin (NIM)} = \left[\frac{\text{interest income} - \text{interest expense}}{\text{total assets}}\right] \times 100$$

$$\text{net interest margin (NIM)} = \left[\frac{\$6{,}000{,}000 - \$2{,}000{,}000 \text{ (net interest income)}}{\$125{,}000{,}000 \text{ (total assets)}}\right] \times 100 = 3.2\%$$

In recent years, the NIM for banks has averaged 3.5%. A good NIM is above 5%, while a NIM below 2.5% is cause for concern.

Return on Assets

Return on assets is a widely used measure of performance for all businesses, not just banks. **Return on assets (ROA)** represents how much money a business makes for each dollar of assets the company owns. Bank assets are primarily loans and securities. A high ROA indicates the bank is performing well. It shows the bank has used its assets effectively to generate profits.

To calculate the ROA, the net income must first be calculated. **Net income** is the difference between the income and expenses of the business.

$$\text{return on assets} = \left[\frac{\text{net income (income} - \text{expenses)}}{\text{total assets}}\right] \times 100$$

For example, bank XYZ has total income of \$90 million, total expenses of \$60 million, and total assets of \$375 million. Return on assets is 8%.

$$\text{return on assets} = \left[\frac{\$30 \text{ million (net income)}}{\$375 \text{ million (total assets)}}\right] \times 100$$

$$\text{return on assets} = 8\%$$

For a bank, a good ROA is considered to be over 1%. The average ROA in recent years has been lower than that. During the financial crises of the early 21st century, many banks had a negative ROA because they had losses instead of profits.

Return on Equity

Investors buy stock in the bank hoping to make a return. Stockholders' equity is the difference between total assets and total liabilities of the bank.

$$\text{stockholders' equity} = \text{total assets} - \text{total liabilities}$$

Return on equity is another ratio that measures how well the bank is performing. This ratio applies to banks that have stockholders. **Return on equity (ROE)** tells the stockholder how much profit was made for each dollar invested by stockholders.

$$\text{return on equity} = \left[\frac{\text{net income}}{\text{stockholders' equity}}\right] \times 100$$

Source: Shutterstock (Stephen Coburn)

Bank performance is measured by return on assets and return on equity.

Banks, like other corporations, try to maximize the returns for those with an ownership stake. If the bank has a high return on equity, then the owners of the bank are receiving a good return on their investment. For example, a bank earns \$200,000 in income and pays \$50,000 in expenses. It has assets of \$2 million and liabilities of \$750,000. Its return on equity is 12%.

$$\text{return on equity} = \left[\frac{\$150{,}000 \text{ (net income)}}{\$1{,}250{,}000 \text{ (stockholder's equity)}}\right] \times 100 = 12\%$$

Historically, a good ROE for a bank has been above 10%. Currently, the average bank ROE is around 8%. During the financial crises of the early 21st century, many banks had a negative ROE.

Spread

An important measure of bank performance that is *not* a ratio is the spread. The **spread** is the difference between the average percentage rate the bank receives on loans made to customers and the average percentage rate that the bank pays on customer deposits.

spread = average interest rate on loans – average interest rate on deposits

If, on average, a bank charges a 10% interest rate on loans and pays out a 6% interest rate on deposits, then the spread is 4%. The bank is earning 4% above what it is paying depositors.

spread = 10% – 6% = 4%

The larger the spread, the more profit for the bank. A good spread is over 5%. However, during the financial crises of the early 21st century, banks saw average spreads of 3%.

The spread does not account for all sources of income or expenses. However, because interest from loans is the largest source of income and interest paid on deposits is the greatest expense, the spread gives a good overall picture of bank health.

Source: Shutterstock (Blend Images)

Spreads are an accurate indicator of a bank's success.

Checkpoint 13.1

1. What two factors are used to evaluate a bank's success?
2. Describe the difference between an asset and a liability.
3. What does a high net interest margin represent?
4. What is the historically average bank ROE?
5. Why is the spread useful if it does not consider all sources of income and expenses?

Build Your Vocabulary

As you progress through this course, develop a personal glossary of banking terms and add it to your portfolio. This will help you build your banking vocabulary. Write out a definition for each of the following terms, and add it to your personal glossary.

balance sheet
asset
liability
stockholders' equity
ratio
net interest income
net interest margin (NIM)
return on assets (ROA)
net income
return on equity (ROE)
spread

Section 13.2
Assessing the Bank

Objectives

After completing this section, you will be able to:

- Describe how the CAMELS model is used to evaluate the strength of a bank.
- Explain the risks to profitability that are unique to banks.

Terms

CAMELS
capital ratio
asset quality
liquidity
market risk
risk
interest rate risk
credit risk
liquidity risk

CAMELS

Measuring a bank's performance using ratios is a key indicator of success for our economy. Ratios help government agencies oversee banks to make sure they are successful and keep our nation running.

The **CAMELS** model is an international bank-rating system used by the US to evaluate the overall financial condition of banks and other financial institutions. There are six factors that make up the acronym CAMELS, as shown in Figure 13-4.

Each of the CAMELS characteristics is rated on a scale of one to five. One is outstanding, and five is poor. The ratings of the six factors are averaged for an overall score. A bank with a composite score of four or higher is considered a problem bank. Bank regulators monitor problem banks very closely, as the odds of the bank failing are high.

Capital Adequacy

If a bank has enough capital, it is less likely to fail than a bank with not enough capital. If a bank has a large amount of capital, it can more easily absorb losses and is more likely to survive. *Capital adequacy* is a term used to describe having enough capital.

The **capital ratio** shows how much capital the bank has relative to its assets. It is the most common way capital adequacy is measured. The capital ratio is calculated using a specific formula.

Capital adequacy
Asset quality
Management
Earnings
Liquidity
Sensitivity to market risk

Figure 13-4.
CAMELS

$$\text{capital ratio} = \left[\frac{\text{total capital}}{\text{total assets}}\right] \times 100$$

A good capital ratio is above 10%. If a bank has a capital ratio below 5%, it is considered seriously undercapitalized and will receive a low rating. An *undercapitalized bank* does not have enough capital to cover its expected risks.

Asset Quality

Banks are concerned about the quality of loans they make to customers. Interest on loans generates the largest revenue stream for the bank. If customers do not repay loans, the bank will be in financial trouble.

Banks are also concerned about the quality of securities they purchase. Treasury bills and government bonds are considered safe, but banks also invest in higher-risk deposits. **Asset quality** is the credit risk associated with the loans and investments held by a bank. A good asset quality rating shows that the bank is making wise decisions and should be able to continue generating revenue.

Green Banking

Sign up for electronic statements and plant a tree. This is just one approach used by more banks and credit unions to reduce paper consumption. Several financial institutions offer to plant a tree whenever a customer signs up for electronic statements. Usually, the bank sends a small amount, often $1, to the National Arbor Day Foundation, which plants trees throughout the country. Customers like the satisfaction of helping the environment, while banks save paper and cut expenses.

Management

Management is how the bank operates. Management quality is more difficult to measure than the other CAMELS factors. Past actions of the bank's management team are signs of how that group will handle future situations. In recent years, more focus has been placed on making the board of directors accountable for manager actions. Many point to the failure of executives and managers for the recent collapse of several high-profile banks and investment firms. In some cases, managers were not prepared for market changes and did not take corrective action when problems started to arise.

Earnings

Earnings are a key component of the CAMELS rating. Banks fail when earnings are consistently negative. Earnings may mean the difference between staying in business and closing the doors.

Successful banks find a way to generate positive earnings even in bad times. Regulators look for an upward trend in earnings. A bank can have one bad year, especially in a recession, and not go under. Earnings trends over several years are more accurate indicators of a bank's health.

The sources of a bank's earnings can also be critical. Regulators look for sources of income that can continue in the future. Banks are expected to earn most of their income from loans, securities, and fees. These ongoing sources of income can result in a higher earnings rating.

Liquidity

Liquidity is having enough cash available to meet normal withdrawals. The reserve requirement ensures banks will have a percentage of deposits in liquid assets. But, banks may need more than the required reserves to meet expected cash needs.

The first step to measuring liquidity is to examine bank deposits. The trend of deposits is important. If deposits increase, so should the bank's liquidity. However, banks must consider the stability of deposits. If many of the deposits are from new customers, the bank cannot project how long they are likely to keep their money in the bank because there is no deposit history. The bank must have sufficient liquidity to accommodate those customers who withdraw money. On the other hand, if deposits are from long-time customers, the bank will be better able to project how long those deposits are likely to remain in the bank.

After determining how much liquidity is needed based on deposits, sources of liquidity are examined. Does a bank keep sufficient cash on hand? Are there securities that can be quickly sold to obtain cash? Banks can also borrow from other banks or from the Federal Reserve Bank. These loans are usually very short term to meet immediate liquidity needs. Regulators will look at all the possible sources of liquidity when rating the bank.

Source: Shutterstock (Konstantin Chagin)

Banks must have enough cash available to meet the amount of customer withdrawals.

Sensitivity to Market Risk

Market risk is the chance that the value of an asset will change due to market conditions. Market conditions are those that affect how buyers and sellers are able to profitably interact. In recent years, bank profitability has been greatly affected by a huge number of mortgage defaults. The ability to manage risk is key to a bank's profitability.

Common Risks to Profitability

Being successful in any business is about balancing risk with reward. **Risk** is the chance of an event occurring and the likely outcome of that event. Will the business make money? Will the business be competitive? There are a lot of questions related to risk that businesses ask every day.

There are risks unique to banks, as shown in Figure 13-5: interest rate risk, credit risk, and liquidity risk. Successful banks keep risks at a tolerable level while maintaining positive earnings.

Ethical Banking

The quest for short-term gain without regard for long-term risk is unethical. Banks are continuously confronted with the need to maximize profits. Executives and other members of a bank's management team must balance profitability with ethical behavior.

Interest Rate Risk

Interest rate risk is the chance that a bank may lose revenue due to a change in interest rates. Interest rate risk is a great concern. Interest rates are constantly changing. This means a bank's revenue constantly changes. For example, if market interest rates on savings accounts increased from .1% to .5%, the bank would have to pay more interest to depositors. Profits would then decrease. Sometimes interest rate

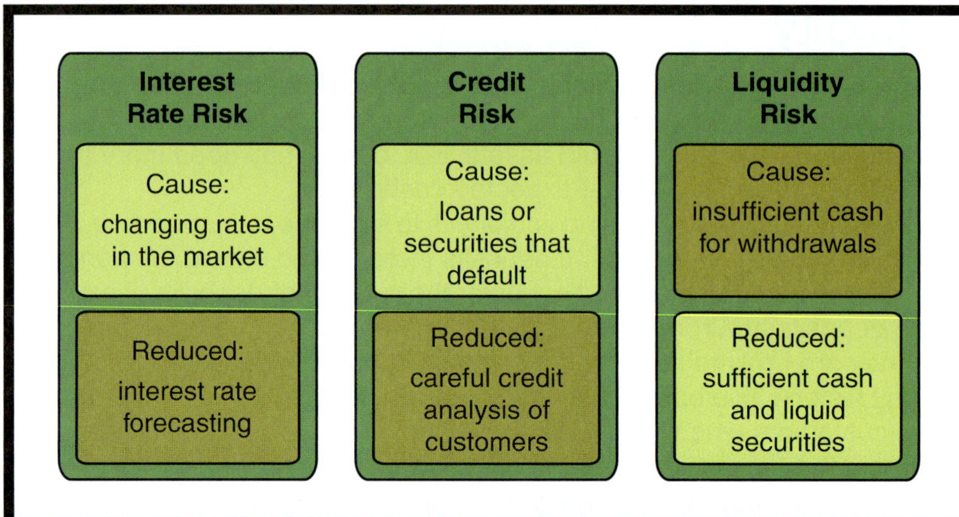

Figure 13-5.
Risks Faced by Banks

changes can be good for profitability. For instance, if market interest rates on savings accounts fell from .5% to .1%, the bank would pay less to depositors. Profits would then increase.

Interest rate risk also affects security prices. Securities include stocks and bonds. When interest rates rise, security prices generally fall, as shown in Figure 13-6. A bank that owns bonds would likely see the prices of those bonds fall if interest rates increased. If the bank had to sell the bonds during a period of rising rates, it could lose money on the bonds.

Banks try to forecast where interest rates are headed to reduce interest rate risk. Knowing the direction of interest rates helps banks determine the best mix of loans, securities, and deposits.

Credit Risk

Credit risk is the possibility that a borrower will not repay a loan. Since loans are the major asset of depository institutions, credit risk is always present. Credit risk is also known as *default risk.* A loan that is not repaid is said to be in *default.*

The first step toward reducing credit risk is to make good loans. Banks carefully analyze potential borrowers to determine if a loan should be granted. Credit analysis involves checking everything about borrowers that may affect their ability to repay a loan. These factors are often referred to as the *five C's of credit,* which are discussed in chapter 8.

Credit risk is often affected by the economy. When the economy is not performing well, many borrowers may have trouble repaying loans. Businesses make fewer sales and some workers become unemployed, increasing the chance of default.

A borrower's character also influences credit risk. Some borrowers choose not to repay loans even if they have the funds available. Others have financial situations that may prevent them from paying their loans, such as illnesses.

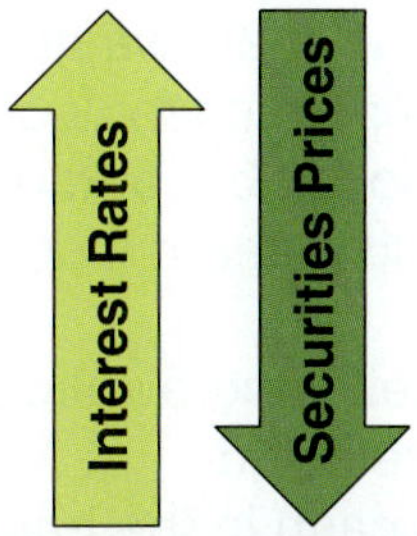

Figure 13-6.
Relationship Between Interest Rates and the Price of Securities

The *risk-return trade-off* is the idea that if banks or other investors want a higher return, they must accept a higher degree of risk. Short-term loans:

- turn over quickly;
- generally have low interest rates; and
- are liquid.

Generally, short-term loans are considered low risk.

Long-term loans tie up money for a longer period of time, so they are not liquid. They do, however, carry higher interest rates than short-term loans. During the time it takes to repay the loan, interest rates could rise. If this happened, the bank's money that could have been invested in a loan at a higher interest rate instead remains in a lower-interest loan. This would result in a lower return on assets. Long-term loans carry a higher risk-return trade-off.

Credit risk is closely watched by both banks and regulators since losses from bad loans are a primary reason for bank failure. Bank examiners spend more time examining a bank's loan portfolio than on any other area of the bank.

Liquidity Risk

Liquidity risk is the chance a bank cannot sell its assets quickly enough to make a profit and meet the demand for cash. A bank is said to be *illiquid* when cash going out exceeds cash coming in.

Banks expect a certain amount of money to be withdrawn each day. They know they must have sufficient liquidity to meet customer withdrawals. The reserve requirement, set by the Federal Reserve, makes all depository institutions set aside a percentage of deposits. The current reserve requirement is 10%. Two main events cause cash to leave the bank: customer withdrawals and new bank loans.

Source: Shutterstock (Blend Images)

Some financial institutions require advance notice before a large amount of money is withdrawn.

The major source of cash coming in, also known as *inflows,* is deposits made by customers into their bank accounts. Certain deposits are predictable, such as payroll checks. Other deposits may occur less predictably.

As with credit risk, liquidity risk has a trade-off. Banks can stay very liquid by keeping all deposits in cash. This means that any withdrawal could be met since the bank's money would be on hand. However, deposits that are not invested earn no income. In fact, because of inflation, money kept in cash declines in real value over time. A dollar bill is still worth one dollar, but one dollar buys less over time.

Banks must invest deposits to earn income. Banks generally handle liquidity risk in two ways:

- keep enough cash to meet withdrawal demands
- make investments that are liquid

Banks routinely keep enough cash in the bank to meet their average cash withdrawals. By checking the amount of cash actually withdrawn from the bank over a time period, banks can estimate how much cash they should carry. Some banks and credit unions require customers who want to withdraw large cash amounts to give the bank notice so they can arrange for a cash shipment. Often, a three-day waiting period may be imposed on large withdrawals so the bank has time to receive more cash.

Banks can further reduce their liquidity risk by having some very liquid investments that can quickly be turned into cash. Short-term securities such as treasury bills or certificates of deposit at other banks can give banks cash within a day or two. If a bank foresees more cash withdrawals than usual or vault cash is dwindling, it can sell the securities.

Checkpoint 13.2

1. What are the six factors that make up the CAMELS ratings?
2. Which of the CAMELS ratings is the hardest to measure?
3. How do banks reduce interest rate risk?
4. What is the risk-return trade-off?
5. Name the two events that cause cash to leave the bank.

Build Your Vocabulary

As you progress through this course, develop a personal glossary of banking terms and add it to your portfolio. This will help you build your banking vocabulary. Write out a definition for each of the following terms, and add it to your personal glossary.

CAMELS
capital ratio
asset quality
liquidity
market risk
risk
interest rate risk
credit risk
liquidity risk

Careers in Finance
Banking and Related Services

What Does an Internal Auditor Do?

Internal auditors verify the effectiveness of a bank's internal controls. They also check for mismanagement, waste, or fraud. Today, computer systems are also evaluated by **internal auditors,** since banks rely heavily on automated systems in so many areas. Compared to *outside auditors,* who are independent firms, **internal auditors** are employees of the bank. Some of the activities performed by an **internal auditor** include:

- examining the bank's financial and information systems, management procedures, and internal controls to ensure that records are accurate and controls are adequate;
- reviewing bank operations and compliance with bank policies and government regulations; and
- preparing reports for bank managers and directors that give a complete assessment of the bank.

What Is It Like to Work as an Internal Auditor?

Most **internal auditors** work in a typical office setting within the bank. Technology is rapidly changing the work of **internal auditors.** There are many specialized software programs that summarize financial information and records used by **internal auditors.** Computers allow auditors to extract information easier and reduce some of the tedious work associated with auditing. Increasing regulations and disclosure requirements have increased the demand for **internal auditors.**

If you enjoy analytical work and technology, a career as an **internal auditor** might suit you.

What Education and Skills Are Needed to Be an Internal Auditor?

- college degree in accounting or business administration
- master degree or CPA may be required by larger financial institutions
- efficient math skills
- high ethical standards

Chapter Summary

Section 13.1 Analyzing the Numbers

- Much of what is needed to discern how well a bank is doing can be found on the bank's balance sheet. A balance sheet is a document that reports a company's assets, liabilities, and stockholders' equity.
- Ratios are a more efficient way to make meaningful comparisons that are adjusted for the size of a business. Using banking ratios allows us to compare small and large banks.

Section 13.2 Assessing the Bank

- The CAMELS model is an international bank rating system used by the US to evaluate the overall financial condition of banks and other financial institutions.
- Interest rate risks, credit risks, and liquidity risks are unique to banks. Successful banks keep these risks at a tolerable level while maintaining positive earnings.

Check Your Banking IQ

Now that you have finished this chapter, see what you know about banking by taking the chapter post test.

www.m.g-wlearning.com
www.g-wlearning.com

Review Your Knowledge

On a separate sheet of paper or in a word processing document, match the following terms with the definition that fits best.

A. asset
B. stockholders' equity
C. net interest margin (NIM)
D. net profit
E. return on equity (ROE)
F. market risk
G. asset quality
H. capital ratio
I. credit risk
J. interest rate risk

1. Difference between income and expenses.
2. Chance that a bank may lose revenue due to a change in interest rates.
3. What the bank owns.
4. Shows how much net profit the bank is making on interest as a percentage of assets.
5. Credit risk associated with the loans and investments held by a bank.
6. Possibility that a borrower will not repay a loan.
7. Tells the stockholder how much return was made for each dollar of assets.
8. Shows how much capital the bank has relative to its assets.
9. Chance that the value of an asset will change due to changing market conditions.
10. Money a bank receives from investors in return for stock.

On a separate sheet of paper or in a word processing document, answer each of the following questions.

11. Why are performance ratios a more efficient way to make comparisons between bank profits?
12. What are the primary assets of a bank?
13. What is the most common way to measure capital adequacy?
14. How can a bank have a bad year and still receive a positive earnings rating?
15. How do banks manage liquidity risk?

Apply Your Knowledge

16. Research what interest rate local banks and credit unions are offering on car loans and savings accounts. Calculate the average interest rates on car loans and savings accounts. Assuming these institutions only make car loans and only offer savings accounts, calculate the spread.
17. Research how banks forecast interest rates. What factors do they consider? Which factors are of greatest importance? Write a summary of the information you found.
18. Using the Internet, research information about how other countries use the CAMELS rating system. Write a report on your findings.
19. Research different types of bank performance ratios. Create a chart of ratios not mentioned in the text and the values that they represent.
20. There are many factors that can cause a bank to fail. Using the Internet, research the different things that can cause a bank to fail. Write a report summarizing your findings.

Working in Teams

Working with a few classmates, imagine you are a group of bank examiners. The economy is in a recession and many banks are failing due to bad loans. Create a checklist of the things that you would like to know about the loans made by failing banks.

G-W Learning Mobile Site

Visit the G-W Learning mobile site to complete the chapter pretest and post test and to practice vocabulary using e-flash cards. If you do not have a smartphone, visit the G-W Learning companion website to access these features.

G-W Learning mobile site: www.m.g-wlearning.com
G-W Learning companion website: www.g-wlearning.com

Common Core

College and Career Readiness

Writing. Using the Internet, research the advice that experts have for banks, given what they think the market interest rates will be in one year. Make sure to look at, among other sources, newspaper and magazine articles, scholarly reports, and public addresses from prominent financial figures. Write a final research report in which you cite the sources that you used and the strengths and weaknesses of each. Be sure to consider the background and point of view of the sources that you find, as well as any bias that the author may bring to the issue.

Reading. Research information on the CAMELS rating system. What is the history of the rating system? Who monitors CAMELS? How are the ratings obtained? Are the results available to the public? Why or why not? Write a report in which you analyze the strengths and weakness of the CAMELS rating system, using information from your research and this text. Present your opinions to the class.

EVENT PREP

Public Speaking

Public speaking is a competitive event you might enter with your career and technical student organization (CTSO). This event allows you to showcase your communication skills of speaking, organizing, and making an oral presentation. Public speaking is usually a timed event you can prepare for before the competition. You will have time to research, prepare, and practice before going to the competition. To prepare for a public speaking event:

1. Read the guidelines provided by your organization. Make certain you ask any questions about points you do not understand. It is important you follow each specific item that is outlined in the competition rules.
2. Practice, practice, practice. Your speech will be judged by a panel of professionals. Practice your speech in front of your peers until you are comfortable.

14

Check Your Banking IQ

Before you begin this chapter, see what you already know about banking by taking the chapter pretest.

www.m.g-wlearning.com
www.g-wlearning.com

Ethics, Security, Fraud, and Workplace Safety

Banks hold more than cash; they hold secrets—personal information that customers want to keep private. What is Lin Zhang's salary at the ad agency? What does Omar Abaza keep in his safe deposit box? How much money does Sam Cutter owe on his house and car loans? Banks know all of that information and much more.

College and Career Readiness

Reading Prep. In preparation for reading the chapter, consider what the term *ethics* means to you. Have you ever been confronted with an ethical dilemma? As you read, focus on how ethics influence many of the safety features of banks.

Scan the code to view a Biz Kid$ video. If you do not have a smartphone, visit the G-W Learning companion website.

www.m.g-wlearning.com
www.g-wlearning.com

Section 14.1
Ethics

Objectives

After completing this section, you will be able to:

- Explain the importance of ethics in a bank.
- Describe how ethics affect day-to-day use of software and Internet access.

Terms

ethics
turnover
copyright
license
software piracy
freeware
shareware
netiquette
software virus

Importance of Ethics in Financial Institutions

In the past, banks protected one thing: money. Banks protected money by locking it in a vault. A *vault* is a secure area for storing valuable items, including cash and safe deposit boxes. Vaults are made from sturdy materials and designed to prevent unauthorized access. You may think that a vault can protect anything in a bank, but think again. Today, in addition to protecting valuable items in a vault, banks also protect information. Unfortunately, information protected by banks cannot be secured by locking it in a vault. The first line of defense to protect a bank's valuables, regardless of whether the valuables are items or information, is its personnel.

Bank personnel must have a strong sense of ethics. **Ethics** are the basic concepts and principles of moral behavior. An employee with strong ethics will always try to do the right thing. Employees demonstrate their ethics through honesty, integrity, and loyalty.

Honesty

What prevents an employee from engaging in illegal or unethical behavior? *Honesty* is the quality of being truthful and sincere. Honesty prevents an employee from behaving in ways that would hurt the bank, customers, or coworkers. How can honesty help the bank?

- Honest evaluations of procedures can lead to suggestions for improvement.
- Truthful explanations help everyone learn from an event.
- Honest exchanges with customers lead to long-term business relationships.

Source: Shutterstock (Peter Kim)

Bank vaults and safe deposit boxes are secure, but cannot protect digital information.

How does an employee's dishonesty hurt a bank? Banks, like other businesses, rely on their reputations. If a customer sees a single instance of a bank employee's dishonesty, the bond of trust is broken with that customer and the bank's reputation is harmed.

Integrity

Integrity is strong moral character. Employees with integrity will consistently refuse to compromise their ethical principles, regardless of any outside influence, punishment, or reward. They are viewed by others as always doing the right thing.

Employees with integrity are benefits to any business. How do bank employees with integrity benefit a bank? They:

- are dependable;
- do not make decisions based on personal rewards;
- demonstrate perseverance; and
- apply high ethical standards to decision making.

Clearly, employees with integrity provide another level of security for the bank. Additionally, they are good examples for other employees.

Loyalty

Loyalty is faithfulness to a commitment. In the business world, it is faithfulness to an employer or a supplier. It is easy to see when customers are loyal. They return to the bank for all of their banking needs. How can you tell that employees are loyal? They:

- say positive things about the bank;
- recommend the bank as an employer to others who are looking for work;
- work well with coworkers;
- produce a high quality of work and are highly productive;
- know the bank's products and take advantage of cross-selling opportunities;
- are friendly and respectful to customers and coworkers;
- have a positive attitude; and
- are not looking for another job.

Basically, loyal employees want the bank to succeed. They do their best to make it happen. Most of the benefits to the bank are obvious. One hidden benefit of loyal employees is low turnover.

Turnover is the number of employees hired to replace employees who left in a specified time period. Turnover is a business expense. In fact, it can be quite expensive. The obvious costs include the process of recruiting, interviewing, and training new employees. Turnover includes less obvious expenses as well. For example, cross-selling opportunities are lost because the new employee does

Green Banking

Banks, as well as other businesses, need to paint their walls from time-to-time. When given an opportunity, many banks look for green products that are safe for the environment. Banks minimize their carbon footprint by using wall paint that contains no volatile organic compounds (VOCs), which cause air pollution. This not only helps the environment, but can also reduce worker illnesses caused by sensitivity to fumes.

not recognize them. New employees tend to make more errors, which must be found and corrected.

High turnover has a negative effect on the remaining employees' and customers' attitudes. Employees are more likely to look for a new job or, at the least, to become more open to other job offers. Customers may quickly become impatient and dissatisfied when a new employee is not an expert at his or her job. If customers experience this too often, they are likely to leave.

Source: Shutterstock (Monkey Business Images)

Loyal employees have a positive attitude.

Day-to-Day Ethics in a Business

Bank employees protect the valuable items and information a bank holds. They also face the same ethical questions that are faced by employees in any business: use and misuse of business property and Internet access.

Business Property

Many employees seem to think, "If I use it at work, why is it wrong to use it at home, too?" The answer is easy: it is not yours. This simple rule applies to everything from paper clips to software.

Software

All software is protected by a copyright, although some software may be released by its owner for free use. A **copyright** is the exclusive right to copy, license, sell, or distribute material. In the US, an original work is copyrighted as soon as it is in tangible form. For example, if you write a story, as soon as the story is transferred from your mind to the paper or computer file, it is copyrighted. Almost everything found on the Internet is copyrighted, including images, music, videos, and textual information. A copyright statement is *not* required, and lack of a copyright statement does not mean the work has no copyright.

The *fair use doctrine* allows exceptions to copyright under certain limited situations. It allows for use of copyrighted material in teaching, news reporting, editorial commentary, and other similar situations. However, the copyrighted work cannot be claimed as your own. The situations in which the fair use doctrine can be applied are very specific and limited.

When you buy software, you are buying a license. A **license** is the legal permission to use a software program. All software has terms of use that outline what the license allows the software to be used for.

If you buy software, you have the license and you can use it on your computer. If a business buys software, the business has the license for the software. A software license allows you to use the software, just like a driver's license allows you to drive a car. **Software piracy** is the illegal copying or downloading of software. Never engage in software piracy.

Some software may only be lawfully used if it is purchased. This is known as *for-purchase software.* Demo software may be used without buying it, but demos are either limited in functionality or time. Other software, known as **freeware,** is fully functional and can be used forever without purchasing it. To be considered freeware, the software cannot be a demo or restricted version of software meant for purchase. **Shareware** is software that can be installed and used, then purchased if you decide to keep using it. Shareware usually has a notice screen, time-delayed startup, or reduced features. Purchasing the software removes these restrictions. Figure 14-1 identifies the differences between the software types.

The difference between a demo of for-purchase software and shareware is subtle. Typically, shareware software is not time limited. This means that the software remains functional forever with restrictions. Shareware is based on the honor system. Those who continue to use the software are expected to purchase it. A demo of for-purchase software, however, typically stops working after a period of time. In the case of a limited-feature demo, the best features are either not functional or are functional only for a limited time.

Public-domain software is similar to freeware in that it is free. However, freeware is copyrighted, while *public-domain software* either has no copyright, or the copyright has expired. Some photographs, music, videos, and textual information are in the public domain.

Business Devices

Office equipment includes everything from the computer on your desk to the photocopy machine and the company phone. All employees must be aware of appropriate use of office equipment.

Hardware, such as computers and photocopiers, are provided to employees to improve efficiency. In many cases, it would be impossible for an employee to even do the basics of his or her job without this equipment. Always be aware of what you are doing when using company hardware. For example, computers are company property and, as such, the company can look at information stored on them at any time it deems necessary. Do not store personal or inappropriate information on company computers.

Mobile devices, such as smartphones or tablets, provided by the company for employee use are company property. Always be aware that you represent the company when you use one of these devices. They should not be used for personal reasons without company approval. Additionally, be aware of any communication you send with these devices. Be sure it follows company policies for acceptable communication and behavior.

	Software Type		
Characteristics	**For-Purchase**	**Freeware**	**Shareware**
Cost	• Must be purchased to use • Demo may be available	Never have to pay for it	• Free to try • Pay to upgrade to full functionality
Features	Full functionality	Full functionality	Limited functionality without upgrade

Figure 14-1.
Characteristics of Software Types

Internet Access

Internet access provided by the company should be used only for business purposes. Checking personal e-mail or shopping online is not acceptable. When communicating using the Internet, you are a representative of the company. Proper netiquette should be followed.

Netiquette is the accepted social and professional guidelines for communicating using the Internet. Never use texting language in a business environment. It is unprofessional to do so. Also, always proofread and spell-check e-mails before clicking the send button. If you are sending e-mail to a customer in response to a question, texting a coworker, blogging about a bank product, or any other communication, it is important to follow the same common courtesy you would follow for a face-to-face discussion.

If you create publications or blogs for the bank, perhaps as a marketing function, you might think of using images, video, text, or sounds you find on the Internet. Remember, almost everything on the Internet is protected by copyright. This material is the result of someone's work and creativity. Without appropriate permission, you cannot use this material.

Software Viruses

Software viruses are computer programs that cause harm to computer systems. A virus may destroy customer data on the computer or collect information from the bank's network and transmit it to some other location. Viruses can be introduced by downloading infected programs from the Internet. They can also be contained in e-mail attachments or transmitted by visiting websites. In general, viruses can be file infections, boot-sector infections, worms, and Trojan horses. The characteristics of these types of software viruses can be found in Figure 14-2.

Virus Type	Characteristics	How It Spreads	Harm
File Infections	• Most common virus • Infects programs with .exe and .com extensions	Through downloaded or copied files	Carries out unwanted actions that can corrupt files or the hard drive beyond use
Boot-Sector Infection	Attaches to the part of the computer used to boot up	Floppy disks, other types of portable media storage devices, or downloads	Prevents the computer from booting up
Worms	Makes unwanted copies of itself on the computer it infects	Through e-mail	Damages the computer's hard drive or consumers' computer resources
Trojan Horse	Secretly performs unwanted functions	As part of a wanted program or app	• Bypasses security to retrieve information • Maliciously destroys files

Figure 14-2.
Common Software Viruses

Ethical Banking

In 2010, $58.8 billion (42%) of software in use in the world was pirated. Licensed software is considered to be better than pirated software because it is secure and dependable. Yet, software piracy has increased dramatically. It has doubled since 2003. Much of the piracy occurred in developing countries. Often, software pirates in these locations don't know that they are behaving illegally.

To deter a software virus infection, be sure to have high-quality antivirus software installed and kept up to date. Also, never open an e-mail attachment that you are not expecting. It is better to send an e-mail asking about the attachment before opening it than dealing with a virus infection. Avoid visiting questionable websites or downloading files from unknown sources to the computer.

Checkpoint 14.1

1. What are the two main things that banks protect?
2. How does an employee's dishonesty hurt a bank?
3. How does turnover cost money?
4. In what situations does the fair use doctrine allow exceptions to copyright?
5. How can you deter a software virus infection?

Build Your Vocabulary

As you progress through this course, develop a personal glossary of banking terms and add it to your portfolio. This will help you build your banking vocabulary. Write out a definition for each of the following terms, and add it to your personal glossary.

ethics
turnover
copyright
license
software piracy
freeware
shareware
netiquette
software virus

Section 14.2
Security

Objectives

After completing this section, you will be able to:

- Explain bank robbery deterrents.
- Describe what bank employees should do during a robbery.
- Describe what happens after a robbery.
- Explain how a bank creates a business-recovery plan.

Terms

deterrent
bandit barrier
bait money
dye pack
business-recovery plan (BRP)

Robbery Prevention

It is always better to prevent a crime than to react to one. Special deterrents are used to help prevent robberies. A **deterrent** is something that discourages an action. Just by their presence in the bank, some items and people can deter bank robberies. Sadly, they cannot prevent robberies entirely. Deterrents commonly used in banks include:

- closed-circuit digital video equipment;
- bandit barriers;
- greeter or security guard;
- an open floor plan; and
- signs.

Digital video equipment can be positioned to capture customers' faces at the teller windows, entrances, and ATMs. Seeing the cameras can often deter a robber who does not want to see his or her image on the evening news. A **bandit barrier** is a bullet-resistant, acrylic barrier at a teller window that protects a teller from a robber's physical contact or weapon. A bandit barrier is depicted in Figure 14-3. By removing the

Figure 14-3.
Bandit Barrier

threat of physical violence, a potential robber believes he or she is less likely to succeed.

A security guard or other bank employee can greet customers entering the bank. In addition, employees in other areas of the bank should have a clear view of the teller windows. That is why most banks have open floor plans with few, if any, blind spots. Something as simple as a sign stating that robberies will be investigated reminds potential robbers about alarms and cameras, and can be an effective deterrent.

Bank robberies most often occur on Fridays between 9 and 11 am. Increased awareness by bank employees during this time can help identify any suspicious individuals in the area. Suspicious activity may include a car idling in the parking lot or passing by the bank more than once. Reporting such activities to the police is a deterrent because the police will drive by the bank and be visible to potential robbers.

BIZ TIPS

The Bank Protection Act of 1968, which was revised in 1991, is intended to deter bank robberies. It requires financial institutions to install and maintain security devices, including a vault, nighttime lighting, an alarm system, and tamper-resistant locks.

During a Robbery

Despite the best deterrents, bank robberies occur. Bank employees undergo training to learn what they should do if a robbery does occur. During a robbery, bank employees focus on safety and protecting lives, not money. Bank robberies usually take only a few seconds or minutes, so the most important thing for everyone to remember is to stay calm. These guidelines tell bank employees how to act during a robbery:

- Follow the robber's instructions without making any suggestions.
- Give the robber the cash demanded.
- Notice everything the robber touches. Remember the robber's appearance, voice, speech patterns, and mannerisms.
- Keep any evidence, including the note, if the robber uses one.
- Do not draw attention to the robbery. If customers do not notice the robbery, they might not become involved in any way.
- Press the alarm button when it is safe.
- When the robber leaves, remember which way the robber went and a complete description of the robber's vehicle.

After training, bank employees often practice these techniques to ensure that they know what to do if a robbery actually occurs.

When cash is given to a robber, it should include bait money. **Bait money** carries serial numbers that have been recorded by the bank. When the robber is caught and the money is recovered, the serial numbers prove that the cash was stolen in a specific robbery. Some banks also train employees to include a pack of dye or a global positioning system (GPS) device in the cash they give to the robber. A **dye pack** is a radio-controlled device that, when set off, marks stolen cash with permanent dye.

Source: Shutterstock (auremar)

No amount of money is worth more than the lives of coworkers and customers.

Careers in Finance
Banking and Related Services

What Does an Insurance Fraud Investigator Do?

Insurance fraud investigators look into suspected fraud involving life, health, or homeowners insurance claims. **Insurance fraud investigators** work closely with investigation firms, insurance companies, and law enforcement agencies to recover losses caused by fraudulent insurance claims. Some of the activities performed by an **insurance fraud investigator** include:

- searching video footage, police reports, personal references, and financial records to investigate claims;
- reviewing information and suggesting additional investigation or surveillance activities;
- acting as a liaison between the insurance company and law enforcement authorities; and
- providing training on detection of insurance fraud for insurance company employees.

What Is It Like to Work as an Insurance Fraud Investigator?

Insurance fraud investigators often work long, irregular hours. They are often required to travel to meet with witnesses or claimants. Excellent interviewing and report-writing skills are essential to this position. **Insurance fraud investigators** must also be able to provide investigation suggestions and consider problems creatively.

If you enjoy detailed investigative work and posses strong negotiating skills, a career as an **insurance fraud investigator** might suit you.

What Education and Skills Are Needed to Be an Insurance Fraud Investigator?

- college degree, with courses in business, economics, and finance
- banking or law enforcement experience helpful
- analytical thinking skills
- creative problem-solving skills

Career Ladder

Chief Operating Officer

Insurance Fraud Investigator

Claims Adjuster

Always remember, it is just money. It is not as valuable as the lives and safety of the customers and bank employees.

After a Robbery

After a robbery, the focus is on identifying and capturing the robber. If the alarm was not triggered during the robbery, it should be triggered as soon as possible afterward. Notify the bank security officer. Stay in the bank until the police have approved your departure.

If a dye pack was included with the cash, a radio signal will trigger it as the robber passes through the doorway. When the dye pack explodes, anything exposed to the dye becomes stained—cash, clothing, and skin.

Footage from the closed-circuit video equipment can provide an accurate picture of the robber. Height markers are usually placed at the bank's entrance. An image of the robber entering or exiting the bank will provide an accurate height. Additionally, each employee should write down a description of the robber before speaking with anyone else.

BIZ TIPS

Bank robbery is a federal crime. In 2009, the Federal Bureau of Investigation (FBI) received reports of 6,000 bank robberies, which resulted in the theft of more than $45 million and 140 injured people.

Disaster Recovery

A robbery is not the only bad thing that can happen to a bank. Disasters such as hurricanes, tornadoes, and fires can also cause serious damage. In 1983, the Office of the Comptroller of the Currency ordered all banks to create a business-recovery plan. A **business-recovery plan (BRP)** is a written document that shows how a business will return to its pre-disaster condition. Recovery depends on having a plan, creating an alternative site for processing data, assigning tasks to individual employees, and testing the plan.

One of the most critical items in most disaster plans is restoring the bank's computer network and the ability to access and process customer data. Setting up a remote location from which data can be accessed is a large part of resuming business.

If only a single bank branch is touched by disaster, moving the bank's operations is relatively easy. However, if an entire area is destroyed or left without power because of a major disaster, recovery is much harder. A BRP should consider worst-case scenarios, such as a widespread disaster that destroys large areas and affects communication and power capabilities.

Banks test a BRP by conducting a mock disaster. The staged disaster allows banks to work out any kinks in the BRP so that things go smoothly if a real disaster occurs. This ensures that the plan works and also allows employees to practice their roles.

Checkpoint 14.2

1. How does a bandit barrier deter robberies?
2. When do most bank robberies occur?
3. Why is bait money often given to robbers?
4. What triggers a dye pack to explode?
5. What is one of the most critical items in a BRP?

Build Your Vocabulary

As you progress through this course, develop a personal glossary of banking terms and add it to your portfolio. This will help you build your banking vocabulary. Write out a definition for each of the following terms, and add it to your personal glossary.

deterrent
bandit barrier
bait money
dye pack
business-recovery plan (BRP)

Section 14.3
Fraud

Terms
bank fraud
identity theft
check fraud
embezzlement
phishing

Objectives
After completing this section, you will be able to:

- Explain the types of bank fraud.
- Define phishing and how bankers and customers can protect themselves from phishing schemes.

What Is Bank Fraud?

Bank fraud is a scheme intended to steal money or valuables under the control of a financial institution. Bank fraud is illegal. The penalty for bank fraud is a fine of up to $1 million, up to 30 years in prison, or both. Bank fraud can be broken into three categories:

- identity theft
- check fraud
- employee theft

Unlike robbery, which forces the bank to hand over cash, fraud is a web of lies and half-truths. Fraud is often not discovered until long after the crime occurred and the criminal has moved on to a new location and new victims.

Identity Theft

Every year, about nine million Americans have their identities stolen. **Identity theft** is stealing someone's personal information and using it to impersonate them. Personal information used in identity theft includes the victim's name, address, Social Security number, credit card and bank account numbers, and birth date. Information about the victim's family can be used to guess passwords or gain illegal access to the victim's money and credit. For example, banks used to ask for the maiden name of a customer's mother to confirm the customer's identity. Today, banks use a wider range of questions to confirm identity.

Source: Shutterstock (mikeledray)

Destroying personal and financial information can protect against identity theft.

To steal an identity, thieves need to obtain the information. They can obtain this information in hundreds of ways. Several are more common than others. The thief can take from the victim's mailbox any mail that was sent by credit card companies or other businesses. The thief can then use the account information to change the victim's contact information with the business. This enables the thief to make purchases that will be charged to the victim. Taking information from the victim's trash is another way to obtain personal information. Old receipts, check stubs, and other financial records are often thrown away when they are no longer needed, but can be recovered by thieves.

Thieves can take their scams to another level by stealing records or bribing employees of the victim's bank, employer, or vendors to steal records. Pretending to be a financial institution or a business and calling the victim to request the information is another ploy. A small device, known as a *skimmer,* can be attached to a legitimate card scanner or ATM to illegally record the card's magnetic strip and the victim's access code.

After stealing a person's identity, the thief can take control of the victim's bank account, make purchases, apply for loans, apply for jobs, and apply for additional credit cards. The thief could commit other crimes using the victim's identity. By the time the identity thief leaves, the victim could have a:

- mountain of debt that he or she is unable to repay;
- low credit rating;
- criminal record; and
- ruined reputation.

The victim could need legal counsel and a lot of time to repair the damage done by the identity thief.

The individual whose identity was stolen is not the only victim in identity theft. Financial institutions and businesses are also affected by the crimes committed. The bank loses funds, its reputation, and time. A business loses funds, merchandise, and time.

To prevent identity theft, personal information must be protected. The Gramm-Leach-Bliley Act requires all financial institutions to safeguard their customers' financial records and other personal information. Banks need to ensure that customers' personal information and passwords are protected. This information should not be exposed on paper, computer terminals, or computer networks. Customers should protect their own information by protecting their mail, shredding financial documents before throwing them away, frequently changing passwords, and carefully using their credit cards. If banks do not keep the information safe, they can be fined by the Securities and Exchange Commission.

Check Fraud

Check fraud is the illegal use of a check to take or use funds that do not belong to the person who signs the check. Check fraud accounts for much more theft of funds than bank robberies. Check fraud includes several possible activities:

- altering a legitimate check by changing the payee or the amount
- duplicating checks or making counterfeit checks
- forging the signature or the endorsement on a legitimate or stolen check
- sending an illegitimate bill for merchandise or service that was not purchased

Source: Shutterstock (Perig)

Monitoring employee behavior is a way to protect the bank from embezzlement.

Banks can prevent some check fraud by carefully examining checks, signatures, and identification when a check is presented for payment or deposit. Bank customers should keep their checkbooks in a secure location and verify that bills they pay are legitimate.

BIZ TIPS

All of the people who are involved in handling cash in the bank are trained in how to spot counterfeit bills. They carefully examine the bill's portrait, watermark, color-shifting inks, and serial number. If a counterfeit bill is suspected, the United States Secret Service is contacted immediately.

Employee Theft

Unfortunately, bank employees can also give in to temptation. With their knowledge of bank operations, they can take advantage of procedures in their banks. **Embezzlement** is the act of illegally taking funds or property entrusted to you. Embezzlers steal from their employers or organizations.

Bank employees may have access to the bank's funds. Bank employees may also have access to the funds deposited by customers. Depending on the embezzler's expertise and access, methods of embezzlement can differ. Embezzlement can include:

- transferring funds from customer accounts to an employee's personal account;
- accepting money for deposit that is never deposited into the customer's account;
- creating cashier's checks and depositing them into the employee's personal account; and
- manipulating the numbers on a deposit slip and keeping the difference between the reported deposit and the actual deposit.

The bank can protect itself from embezzlement by monitoring employee behavior. Cameras can capture employees' actions as well as customer transactions. A bank's best defense against employee theft is hiring employees with high ethical standards and a history of good behavior.

Phishing

Phishing, which is pronounced *fishing,* is a fun-sounding name for an activity that is not fun at all. **Phishing** is the use of fraudulent e-mails and copies of legitimate websites to trick people into providing personal, financial, and other data.

The most common form of phishing is done by sending an e-mail to the intended victim. The e-mail message pretends to be from a legitimate source, such as the victim's bank. The e-mail asks the victim to send certain information, such as an account number and password, or it provides a link to a web page. If the victim goes to the web page, the site looks legitimate, but it collects the information the victim enters. The information can then be used to commit fraud.

Banks can protect customers from phishing e-mails by keeping their customers' information secure. They can also warn customers if information has been stolen or if the bank knows that phishing e-mails pretending to be from the bank are circulating. Customers can protect themselves by using software that filters their e-mail. Legitimate businesses do not request confidential information via e-mail.

Checkpoint 14.3

1. Name the three categories of bank fraud.
2. What personal information can be used in identity theft?
3. How can banks prevent check fraud?
4. What is a bank's best defense for preventing employee theft?
5. How can customers protect themselves from phishing?

Build Your Vocabulary

As you progress through this course, develop a personal glossary of banking terms and add it to your portfolio. This will help you build your banking vocabulary. Write out a definition for each of the following terms, and add it to your personal glossary.

bank fraud
identity theft
check fraud
embezzlement
phishing

Section 14.4
Workplace Safety

Terms

falling hazard
lifting hazard
material-storage hazard
ergonomics
Occupational Safety and Health Administration (OSHA)

Objectives

After completing this section, you will be able to:

- Describe the most common types of work-related accidents in the office.
- Explain what role the science of ergonomics plays in workplace safety.
- Discuss the function of OSHA.

Workplace Accidents

Falling hazards, lifting hazards, and material-storage hazards account for most of the workplace accidents that occur in offices. **Falling hazards** are sources of potential injuries from slipping or falling. Falls are the most common workplace accident in an office setting. Falls can result in broken bones, head injuries, and muscle strains. Avoiding workplace falls is relatively simple:

- close drawers completely
- do not stand on a chair or box to reach
- secure electrical cords, rugs, and mats

Lifting hazards are sources of potential injury from improperly lifting or carrying items.

Most back injuries are caused by improper lifting. To avoid injuries resulting from lifting:

- make several small trips with items rather than one trip with an overly heavy load;
- use dollies or handcarts whenever possible;
- lift with the legs, not the back; and
- never carry an item that blocks vision.

Material-storage hazards are sources of potential injury that come from the improper storage of files, books, or office equipment. A cluttered workplace is an unsafe workplace. Material stacked too high can fall on employees. Paper and files that are stored on the floor or hall are a fire risk. To prevent injuries:

- do not stack boxes or papers on top of tall cabinets;
- store heavier objects on lower shelves; and
- keep aisles and hallways clear.

Source: Shutterstock (Martin Haas)

Always be cautious of potential hazards in the workplace.

Maintaining a safe workplace is the joint responsibility of the employer and employee. The employer makes sure the facility and working conditions are such that accidents are unlikely to occur. The employee uses common sense and care while at the office.

Worker Safety

Workplace safety in the US has continuously improved since the beginning of the 20th century. Gradually, workplace injury, death, and illness have declined. This is due to a change in the type of work done today and in the safety precautions that have been put in place. Many workers now spend extended periods of time in front of computers. This can also result in injury. **Ergonomics** is the science of adapting the workstation to fit the needs of the worker and lessen the chance of injury. Figure 14-4 depicts the best way for a worker to sit at a computer workstation.

OSHA

In 1970, the Occupational Safety and Health Act was passed. The Occupational Safety and Health Administration was established a year later. The **Occupational Safety and Health Administration (OSHA)** is a federal agency that enforces safety and health regulations in the workplace. OSHA's efforts have lead to a significant decline in workplace injuries and deaths since the 1970s.

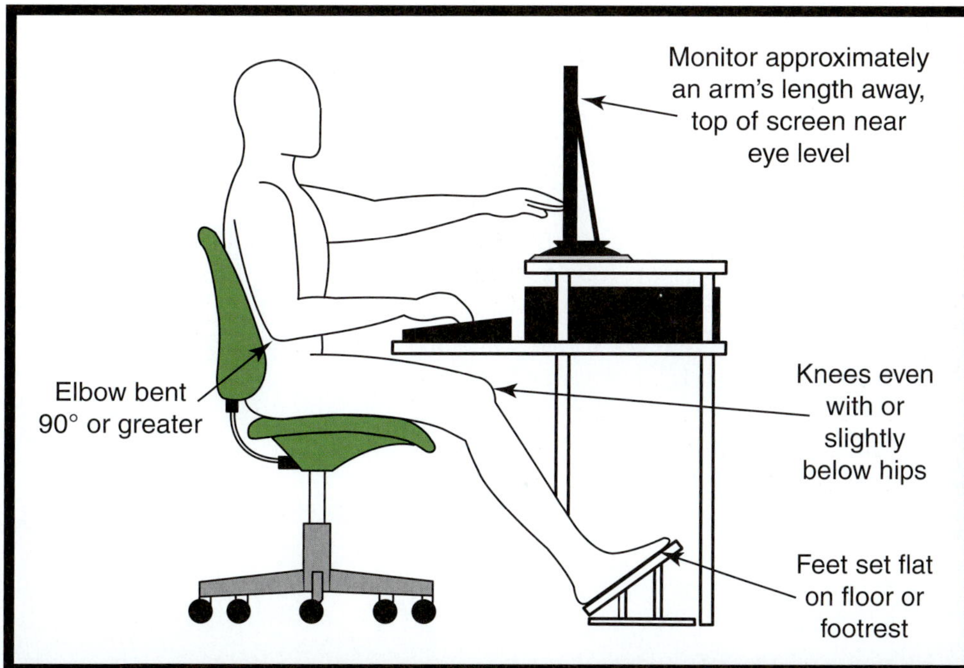

Figure 14-4.
Ergonomic Workstation

Checkpoint 14.4

1. What are the most common workplace hazards in an office setting?
2. Name two ways to prevent lifting injuries.
3. What is the employer's role in preventing material-storage hazards?
4. Why have workplace injuries, deaths, and illnesses declined since the beginning of the 20th century?
5. What is the role of OSHA?

Build Your Vocabulary

As you progress through this course, develop a personal glossary of banking terms and add it to your portfolio. This will help you build your banking vocabulary. Write out a definition for each of the following terms, and add it to your personal glossary.

falling hazard
lifting hazard
material-storage hazard
ergonomics
Occupational Safety and Health Administration (OSHA)

Chapter Summary

Section 14.1 Ethics

- An employee with strong ethics will always try to do the right thing, which is an advantage for the bank. Employees demonstrate their ethics through honesty, integrity, and loyalty.
- Employees must follow the copyright laws for software usage and the bank's rules for Internet usage.

Section 14.2 Security

- Banks can deter robberies by having closed-circuit video equipment, bandit barriers, greeters or security guards, open floor plans, and signs that remind customers of the surveillance equipment and FBI involvement in robbery investigations.
- During a robbery, bank employees focus on protecting lives and safety, not money.
- Dye packs and surveillance video are tools that can help to identify and capture a bank robber.
- A business-recovery plan describes how a business will recover from a disaster that affects the bank's computer network and the ability to access and process customers' data.

Section 14.3 Fraud

- Identity theft, check fraud, and employee theft are the three categories of bank fraud.
- Phishing uses e-mail and web pages to collect information that can be used to commit fraud.

Section 14.4 Workplace Safety

- Falling hazards, lifting hazards, and material-storage hazards account for most of the workplace accidents that occur in offices.
- Ergonomics is becoming increasingly important, as many workers now spend extended periods of time in front of computers.
- The efforts of the Occupational Safety and Health Administration have led to a significant decline in workplace injuries and illnesses since the 1970s.

Check Your Banking IQ

Now that you have finished this chapter, see what you know about banking by taking the chapter post test.

www.m.g-wlearning.com
www.g-wlearning.com

Review Your Knowledge

On a separate sheet of paper or in a word processing document, match the following terms with the definition that fits best.

A. bait money
B. license
C. freeware
D. embezzlement
E. bandit barrier
F. software piracy
G. ergonomics
H. copyright
I. turnover
J. identity theft

1. Fully functional software that can be used forever without purchasing it.
2. Science of adapting the workstation to fit the needs of the worker and lessen the chance of injury.
3. Carries serial numbers that have been recorded by the bank.
4. Stealing someone's personal information and using it to impersonate them.
5. Exclusive right to copy, license, sell, or distribute material.
6. Illegally taking funds or property entrusted to you.
7. Legal permission to use a software program.
8. Bullet-resistant, acrylic barrier at a teller window.
9. Employees who left in a specified time period.
10. Illegal copying or downloading of software.

On a separate sheet of paper or in a word processing document, answer each of the following questions.

11. What is the purpose of having a license for software?
12. How does an open floor plan deter bank robberies?
13. In the past, how did banks confirm a customer's identity?
14. What can bank customers do to protect themselves from identity theft?
15. Name three things you can do to remove falling hazards in the workplace.

Apply Your Knowledge

16. Imagine you are a bank COO concerned about the risk of bank robberies. Research deterrents used in banks other than those mentioned in the text. Then, write a report to your employees about robbery deterrents present in the bank, and how employees are to use them.
17. Banks used to commonly rely on the answer to only one security question to verify a customer's identity: what is your mother's maiden name? Today, many banks allow customers to choose up to three different security questions to verify their identity. Can you think of the reasons behind this change? Consider what security questions might provide greater security for bank customers. Write at least ten questions.
18. Research the consequences of identity theft. Write a report listing these consequences and the actions that consumers can take to prevent them.
19. Imagine you are a bank COO concerned about employee theft. Write a report to the board of directors detailing how you plan to prevent employee theft.
20. Using the Internet, research information on common phishing scams. What are some of the most common phishing scams? Write a guide of do's and don'ts for consumers trying to avoid getting caught in a phishing scam.

Working in Teams

Working with two or three classmates, imagine you are the HR department of a bank. You are trying to recruit for two teller positions. How will you test the ethics of potential job candidates? What questions will you ask? What body language will you pay attention to? Write an interview guide for managers to use when conducting an interview for these positions. Be sure to include information on the importance of hiring ethical employees.

G-W Learning Mobile Site

Visit the G-W Learning mobile site to complete the chapter pretest and post test and to practice vocabulary using e-flash cards. If you do not have a smartphone, visit the G-W Learning companion website to access these features.

G-W Learning mobile site: www.m.g-wlearning.com
G-W Learning companion website: www.g-wlearning.com

Common Core

College and Career Readiness

Speaking. Using the Internet, research information on ergonomic solutions. What are some products available to workers who need to create an ergonomic workstation? Imagine you are a salesperson for an ergonomics company. Prepare a professional presentation to the president of a bank on products that can help create an injury-free workplace. Be sure to include a description of ergonomics, a visual of each product, purpose of each product, and the injuries that each product helps to prevent. Present your sales pitch to the class.

Reading. Visit the OSHA website (www.osha.gov). Under the Publications tab, choose a report to read. Consider what the report tells you about OSHA's mission and responsibilities. Write a summary of your findings.

EVENT PREP

Banking Ethics

Banking ethics is a competitive event you might enter with your career and technical student organization (CTSO). The banking competitive event may include an objective test that covers multiple topics. Participants are usually allowed one hour to complete the event.

The event may be an objective test. However, it may also be a part of the competition in which teams participate to defend an ethical dilemma or topic. To prepare for a banking ethics event:

1. Read the guidelines provided by your organization. Make certain that you ask any questions about points you do not understand. It is important you follow each specific item that is outlined in the competition rules.
2. Review the ethics section in this chapter.
3. Read each of the ethical banking features that appear throughout the text.
4. Put a team together of others also interested in this event. Work collaboratively with your team to review and discuss each ethical banking feature in the text. How would you or your team respond to similar ethical situations?
5. Use the Internet to find more information about ethics and communication. Print this information for future study material.

Unit 4
Summative Assessment

On a separate sheet of paper or in a word processing document, use what you have learned in this unit to answer the questions that follow.

True/False Questions

1. *True or False?* A loyal employee wants the bank to succeed and does his or her part to make it happen.
2. *True or False?* A department is a banking facility that is not the bank's main location.
3. *True or False?* Credit risk is the chance that a bank may use revenue due to a change in interest rates.
4. *True or False?* The wants and needs of consumers in a market segment are different from those of consumers in other segments.
5. *True or False?* The CFO is responsible for the day-to-day operations of the bank.

Multiple Choice Questions

6. Which of the following is *not* an operational support career in a bank?
   A. Debt counselor
   B. Loan processor
   C. Public relations specialist
   D. Human resources manager
7. A balance sheet reports each of the following *except* _____.
   A. performance ratios
   B. stockholders' equity
   C. liabilities
   D. assets
8. Which of the following is *not* a function of employee evaluations?
   A. Gauge employee potential for advancement.
   B. Discover areas for needed support or training.
   C. Allow employees to review their personnel records.
   D. Conclude if performance level merits a pay increase.
9. Which of the following is *not* an aspect of a successful business-recovery plan?
   A. Assigning recovery tasks to individual employees.
   B. Creating an alternative site for processing data.
   C. Installing a bandit barrier.
   D. Testing the recovery plan.
10. Which of the following is *not* an example of customer service?
    A. A consumer visits a bank website.
    B. A consumer overhears a customer talking about his or her bank.
    C. A customer visits a bank branch to cash a check.
    D. None of the above.

Unit 5

History and Future of Banking

What You Will Learn

Have you ever heard the phrases *breadwinner* or *bring home the bacon*? While these phrases seem funny, both refer to earning money. That is because long ago, people used things like food, shells, and precious metals as money. In this unit, you will learn the history of banking from ancient Egypt to today. You will discover what led to the Great Recession of the early 21st century and the changes that it brought. Finally, you will explore what banking will look like in the future as technology brings new changes.

Source: Shutterstock (Theo Fitzhugh)

Discover the different forms money has taken throughout history.

Source: Shutterstock (Tyler Olson)

Learn how technology will continue to transform the banking industry.

Biz Kid$ in Action

The ATM machine has greatly changed how people do their banking. The first ATM appeared in the US in 1969, and at the time was considered revolutionary. Its impact on banking has been profound. Since then, there have been several amazing technological changes in banking, many geared toward making it more convenient for customers to access their funds.

Today if you live in Dallas, Texas, but need to access money while vacationing in Bangkok, Thailand, you only need to find an ATM that is part of a worldwide interbank network, such as Cirrus. The funds get pulled from your US account and get converted to Thai baht in the blink of an eye! But, all this convenience also means increased fraud, so security measures have evolved to keep up with the fast-paced growth of international banking and online transactions.

What will ATMs look like in the future? Maybe they will be voice activated, have thumbprint scans, or even have retina-scan security features. There's even speculation about robotic tellers and holographic bankers! The future of banking could be very exciting indeed.

Banking Bits

Currencies are bought and sold on a market called the *foreign exchange market* or *forex.* The forex is the largest market in the world. Four trillion dollars in currency changes hands every single day. It's such a big and complex market that it's very difficult to predict which way exchange rates will go. Big-time traders like governments and ultra-rich investors can try to move rates by buying or selling a lot of a currency at once.

Quick Tip! Be careful when accessing your bank accounts and personal information in public places, as this increases your chances of identity theft.

Let's get started! ⟶

Scan the code to view a Biz Kid$ video. If you do not have a smartphone, visit the G-W Learning companion website.

www.m.g-wlearning.com
www.g-wlearning.com

15

Check Your Banking IQ

Before you begin this chapter, see what you already know about banking by taking the chapter pretest.

www.m.g-wlearning.com
www.g-wlearning.com

Evolution of Banking

Banking and civilization go hand in hand. How a country's economy develops has a lot to do with the banking system it adopts. A country's economic strength is reflected in its banks, both private and central. The banking system in the US has evolved and adapted over time. To remain strong, it will have to continue to change in response to innovation.

College and Career Readiness

Reading Prep. In preparation for the chapter, research one of the laws discussed in this chapter. Keep in mind the main purpose and provisions of this law as you read.

Scan the code to view a Biz Kid$ video. If you do not have a smartphone, visit the G-W Learning companion website.

www.m.g-wlearning.com
www.g-wlearning.com

Section 15.1
Origins of the Banking System

Objectives

After completing this section, you will be able to:

- Explain how ancient civilizations set the stage for modern banking systems.
- Describe how banking evolved from the Middle Ages to the 18th century.

Terms

sovereign debt
money changer
bill of exchange
bank of deposit
goldsmith
fractional-reserve banking

Ancient Times

Even before there was money, there were banks. They were not in the form banks are today, however. These banks held livestock and crops for safekeeping. In addition, these banks made loans and paid interest on those loans. In ancient Egypt, stores of grain were held by individuals in a central location and debts were paid in quantities of grain. This continued long after coins came into wide use. Rules for how stored valuables should be handled were even part of the first written record of laws.

Banking in the form of taking in deposits and lending money took place in many ancient civilizations, as shown on the map in Figure 15-1.

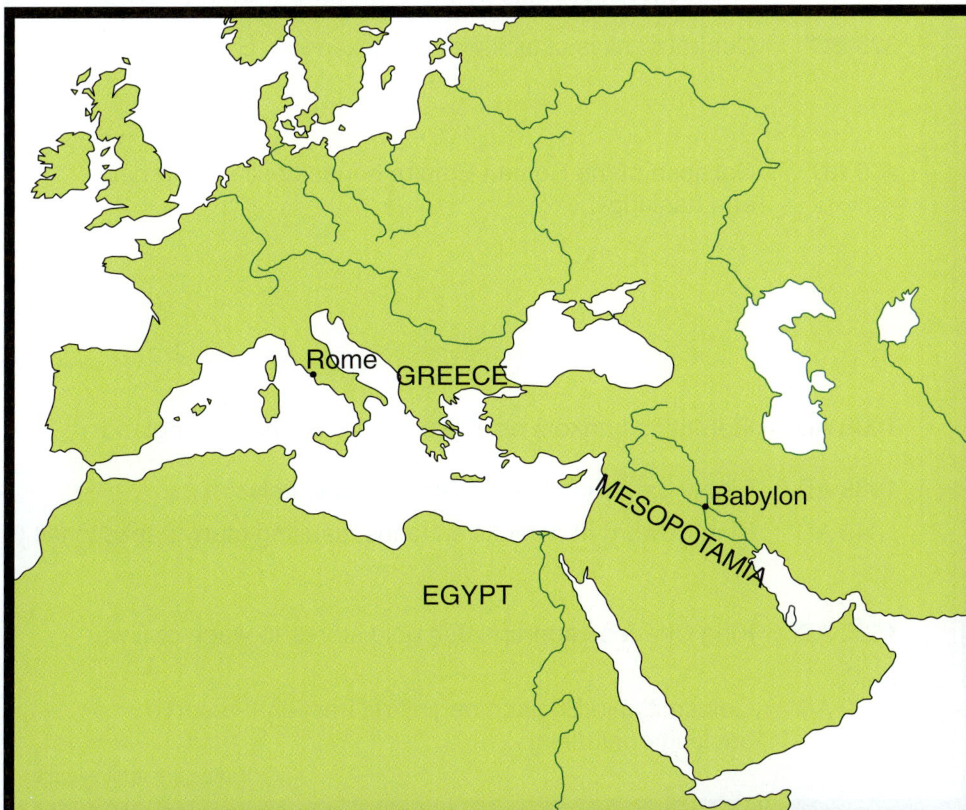

Figure 15-1.
Centers of Banking in the Ancient World

These civilizations included Babylon (present-day Iraq), Egypt, Greece, Mesopotamia (parts of present-day Iran, Iraq, Syria, and Turkey), and Rome.

Middle Ages to the 18th Century

A more recognizable banking system began to take shape during the Middle Ages (1066–1485). At the time, Italian bankers made loans to finance the wars, international trade, and exploration that characterized the era. These loans were made to countries, not individuals. **Sovereign debt** is a financial obligation incurred by a country. Like today, sovereign debt proved dangerous to lenders. Two of the most dominant banking families extended money to King Edward III to finance England's Hundred Years War against France. Edward defaulted on the loan, which led to the closure of the banks that had extended the credit. Figure 15-2 is a time line showing early developments in banking.

A more successful and well-known banking family, the Medicis, had better luck. For generations the Medicis provided an essential service to travelers and traders in an expanding world—money changing. **Money changers** exchanged

Date	Development
2500 BC*	Temples and palaces used to store valuables in Mesopotamia
1775 BC*	In Babylon, Code of Hammurabi sets forth rules regarding banking operations
350*	In Greece, customary interest rate for borrowing is 10%
325 BC*	Central bank is established in Alexandria, Eqypt
476 AD	Collapse of the Roman Empire brings decline in trading and banking
1290 AD	Florentine bankers establish bank branches in England
1338 AD	Eighty banks in operation in Florence, Italy
1345 AD*	King Edward III defaults on loans, causing many banks to fail
1630 AD*	King Charles I appropriates gold stores to wage civil war
1750 AD*	Goldsmiths in England begin first fractional-reserve banking operations

*Dates are approximate

Figure 15-2.
Early Developments in Banking

one country's currency for that of another for a fee. The word bank comes from the Italian word *banca,* meaning money changers' table.

To simplify doing business across borders, bills of exchange came into use. A **bill of exchange** is a type of negotiable instrument that is still used in international trade. During the Middle Ages, charging interest on loans was not allowed. Bankers got around this by using bills of exchange. A bill of exchange was issued in one country for a specific amount and used to pay for goods purchased in another country. A fee was charged to issue the bill as well as to redeem it.

Banks of deposit were the first depository institutions that arose during this time. Before banks of deposit existed, those with large sums of gold would store it in the king's mint. After England's Charles I took the gold to pay for a civil war, the practice stopped.

By the 18th century, **goldsmiths,** artisans who make items out of gold and other precious metals, began holding valuable objects for clients. In exchange, they would issue receipts stating the quality and quantity of the objects being held for the client. These receipts began to be traded and essentially used as currency in place of the precious metal held by the goldsmiths. Soon, the goldsmiths started lending out portions of the gold left with them. They took the chance that not *all* depositors would need *all* of their deposits back at the same time. This was the beginning of fractional-reserve banking. **Fractional-reserve banking** is the practice of keeping only a portion, or fraction, of deposits in the bank. The rest of the money is lent out or otherwise invested. Today, the portion kept is known as the *capital reserve.* The Federal Reserve Bank sets the capital reserve ratios for US banks.

BIZ TIPS

During the Middle Ages, double-entry bookkeeping was first used. In this system, ledgers have two columns: one for debits and the other for credits. Double-entry bookkeeping is the central principle in the accounting system used to this day.

Checkpoint 15.1

1. What was the role of banks in ancient times?
2. Which ancient civilizations had banks that took in deposits and loaned money?
3. Why did sovereign debt initially prove dangerous to lenders?
4. How did banks get around not being allowed to charge interest during the Middle Ages?
5. What modern banking practice was first started by goldsmiths?

Build Your Vocabulary

As you progress through this course, develop a personal glossary of banking terms and add it to your portfolio. This will help you build your banking vocabulary. Write out a definition for each of the following terms, and add it to your personal glossary.

sovereign debt
money changer
bill of exchange
bank of deposit
goldsmith
fractional-reserve banking

Section 15.2
Banking in America

Terms

- commodity money
- wampum
- land bank
- fiat currency
- Bank of North America
- continental
- National Banking Acts of 1863–1864
- Office of the Comptroller of the Currency (OCC)
- bank run

Objectives

After completing this section, you will be able to:

- Explain how currency issues affected the colonial economy.
- Describe how a common currency helped shape a new nation.

Colonial Times

Before the American Revolution, banks in the true sense of the word did not exist in the colonies. Without banks, there was no common item to use as currency. Instead, trade was conducted with foreign coins or through the use of commodity money. **Commodity money** is an item exchanged for something else of perceived value. Examples of commodity money include tobacco leaves, rice, and wampum. **Wampum** is a string of white beads made from shells by Native Americans and used for trade. Europeans used wampum in early trading encounters with the native peoples. Tobacco came to be used in the same way. Tobacco was not produced in England. It was, however, produced in great quantities in Virginia. People were issued receipts for stores of tobacco and used these as money. The value of the receipt, or note, was backed by the tobacco held in a warehouse. Tobacco leaves themselves were also used as a medium of exchange.

In the commercial port cities along the Atlantic coast, gold and silver coins were more routinely used. It is perhaps not surprising that in colonial America, a place populated by individuals from many other countries, the first currency to be used was foreign coins. Even after independence from England, the English pound, as well as French and Spanish currency, was used in the US for a time. Spanish silver coins were the most popular.

In 1716, the Massachusetts Bay Colony founded a government land bank. The **land bank** issued notes that represented credit secured by the value of land. These notes were used as a type of fiat currency. **Fiat currency** is a type of money backed only by the government that issues it. By 1750, every colony had issued its own fiat currency.

Source: Shutterstock (Caitlin Mirra)

Carpenters Hall in Philadelphia, PA is the original location of the First Bank of the United States.

Revolution and Independence

In 1781, the **Bank of North America** was founded to finance the Revolutionary War. It was the first commercial fractional-reserve bank to operate in what would become the United States of America. It was also a privately owned bank.

The Bank of North America was able to raise money to fund the war by issuing notes. These notes were called continentals. **Continentals** were a type of note intended to be exchanged later for coins. Eventually, the oversupply of continentals led them to become worthless.

The First Bank of the United States was created in 1791 as the new government's central bank. It oversaw the government's money and chartered banks throughout the country. In addition, it sold federal bonds. The money from the bonds was used to pay the debts the states had incurred during the Revolution.

In 1792, a national currency was set up by Congress. This gave the federal government permission to mint gold and silver coins. At that time, the dollar, modeled after the Spanish *real* (pronounced *ree-al*), was established as the nation's currency. All banks now had to hold gold and silver that could be exchanged for currency. This practice helped to control the economy.

The Second Bank of the United States was established in 1816. Opponents of the bank made sure its 20-year charter was not renewed. For the next 26 years, there were no federal laws governing banking operations. The chartering and regulating of banks was left to the states. It would be another 80 years before the US would again have a central bank. Chapter 5 of this text provides an in-depth discussion of the First and Second Banks of the US.

BIZ TIPS

When a country has two types of currency, the one that is perceived to have the lesser value will be circulated. The one that is thought to be of greater value will be saved, sometimes even hoarded. This is an expression of *Gresham's law,* a monetary principle dating back to 1558.

Free Banking Era (1837–1863)

The period between 1837 and 1863 is known as the *era of free banking.* During this time, paper money was issued by states, cities, banks, railroads, stores, and even some churches. By 1860, an estimated 8,000 different state banks were circulating their own paper money. When a bank or other issuer failed, the currency it issued became worthless. Currency was often only accepted within a small geographic area. A traveler going from New York to Boston might need a dozen different currencies to make the trip.

The Civil War saw a huge increase in federal spending. The war was financed by issuing paper money. The **National Banking Acts of 1863–1864** led to the creation of national banks that were chartered by the federal government. These acts also led to the creation of a uniform national currency.

Green Banking

The Emergency Economic Stabilization Act was passed in 2008 as a response to the financial crises of the early 21st century. The act's central focus is to provide stability and prevent economic disruption through the Troubled Asset Relief Program, better known as TARP. One of the act's lesser-known provisions relates to the use of renewable energy. It provides tax credits for the use of renewable energy sources, such as geothermal energy and wind energy from small wind farms.

During this time, the Office of the Comptroller of the Currency was established as a division of the Treasury Department. The **Office of the Comptroller of the Currency (OCC)** was the first federal agency charged with supervising banks. The federal government imposed a tax on bank notes, which brought the era of free banking to an end in 1865.

National Banking Era (1863–1913)

The nature of lending was much different in the national banking era than it is today. Lending was very short term. Banks only made loans that were to be repaid in 30 to 60 days. Lending guidelines were very strict. Loans were made to business owners and manufacturers to pay their employees and suppliers. Once the goods they produced could be sold, the loan would be repaid. The length of the loan was kept short to make sure the bank had enough money to cover customer withdrawal requests. Banking and, by extension, lending, was initially centered in urban areas on the East Coast.

As people began to settle in the West, there was an increasing need for loans. Banks began to appear in these areas. These banks also began to issue notes.

These banks mostly made loans to farmers and ranchers who needed money to:

- purchase land;
- buy equipment; and
- pay for shipping costs.

Farming and ranching were very dependent on weather and the prices people could pay for what was produced. Many banks made loans that were not repaid because the borrowers were unable to sell their crops or livestock at the price they thought they would. Sometimes, a whole season's worth of crops would be destroyed by weather. This made these banks and the notes they issued a risky investment.

From time to time, a rumor would spread that a bank was going to fail. Depositors would rush to the bank and withdraw all of the money from their accounts or redeem the notes the bank had issued. A **bank run** results when a large number of depositors lose confidence in the banking system and withdraw their money. When banks have less money to lend because they have fewer deposits, loans are not made. The loans merchants, manufacturers, farmers, and ranchers relied on were no longer available.

Significant bank panics occurred in 1873, 1893, and 1907. The panic of 1893 resulted in the worst economic depression the US had suffered up to that time. During these incidents, banks suspended payment on any deposit accounts. Many banks failed. People began to hoard money rather than deposit it.

By 1907, the nation seemed determined to find a solution to bank failures. A monetary commission was charged with investigating the problems in the banking industry. The commission's report became the model for the Federal Reserve Act of 1913. Figure 15-3 shows the growth and expansion of banking.

Source: Shutterstock (Jim Barber)

As Americans moved west, new banks opened to accommodate changing customer needs.

1716	Massachusetts Bay Colony charters government land bank
1775	Continentals are issued
1782	Bank of North America opens
1791	First Bank of the United States is chartered
1816	Second Bank of the United States is chartered
1837–1863	Era of Free Banking
1863	National Currency Act
1873	Bank panic
1893	Bank panic
1907	Bank panic

Figure 15-3.
Banking in America During the 18th and 19th Centuries

Checkpoint 15.2

1. Name three forms of commodity money used in colonial times.
2. Why was the Bank of North America founded?
3. What currency was the US's first national currency modeled after?
4. What was the downfall of the era of free banking?
5. Why were bank loans initially issued for only short periods of time?

Build Your Vocabulary

As you progress through this course, develop a personal glossary of banking terms and add it to your portfolio. This will help you build your banking vocabulary. Write out a definition for each of the following terms, and add it to your personal glossary.

commodity money
wampum
land bank
fiat currency
Bank of North America
continental
National Banking Acts of 1863–1864
Office of the Comptroller of the Currency (OCC)
bank run

Section 15.3
Banking Since the Federal Reserve

Terms

Federal Reserve Act
open market operations (OMO)
bank holiday
Emergency Banking Act of 1933
Federal Deposit Insurance Corporation (FDIC)
bank holding company
deregulation
savings and loan crisis (S & L crisis)
subprime lending
Emergency Economic Stabilization Act
Troubled Asset Relief Program (TARP)
Dodd-Frank Wall Street Reform and Consumer Protection Act

Objectives

After completing this section, you will be able to:

- Describe the influence of banking laws on the US economy from 1913 to 1970.
- Explain the subprime lending crisis and its impact on the larger economy.

1913–1970

In 1913, the **Federal Reserve Act** established the Federal Reserve Bank as the nation's central bank. The organization and operations of the Federal Reserve are fully discussed in chapter 5 of this text.

With the establishment of the Federal Reserve, the economy stabilized and grew. The monetary policy carried out by the central bank helped to finance US participation in World War I. After the war, the Federal Reserve used open market operations to control the amount of money available. **Open market operations (OMOs)** allow the Federal Reserve to buy or sell US treasury securities, which affects the money supply. One of the first uses of OMOs was to combat an economic depression in 1923.

Source: Library of Congress

The Great Depression brought economic hardship on many Americans.

Great Depression

Following World War I, the US became more urban, and industrial production greatly increased. The economy and the stock market prospered. The nation's standard of living greatly increased. American consumers bought more than ever before. However, this unprecedented prosperity would not last for long. A global economic collapse was on the horizon. This collapse, which would last until the beginning of World War II, became known as the *Great Depression.* Several factors lead to the Great Depression:

- the stock market crash of 1929
- widespread bank failures
- decreased demand for consumer goods
- harmful foreign trade policies that led to decreased demand for American goods in foreign markets

Many bank runs occurred during the Great Depression. Without sufficient deposits, banks were forced to close. Unfortunately, these bank runs caused a wave of bank failures that swept the country. Over 9,000 banks failed during the 1930s.

President Franklin Roosevelt took office on March 4, 1933. Two days later, he declared a bank holiday. The **bank holiday** closed all banks for four days to allow time for the creation of a plan to reopen them. Congress then passed the **Emergency Banking Act of 1933** on March 9 that helped to reform the banking system in the US. Under this act, also known as the *Glass-Steagall Act,* the Federal Deposit Insurance Corporation (FDIC) was established. **The Federal Deposit Insurance Corporation (FDIC)** insures depositors' funds to a certain limit. The FDIC reestablished faith in the US banking system.

BIZ TIPS

In addition to stabilizing and growing the economy, the central bank began to promote relationships with other central banks. The most notable of these was with the Bank of England.

Prosperous Times Bring Innovation

The period from 1940 through the late 1960s was a time of great bank stability. Even when the economy went into a recession or had a downturn, the banking industry remained relatively strong.

This period also saw much innovation. The first bank credit card was created by Franklin National Bank in New York in 1951. However, it was only accepted by a small number of merchants. Bank of America created the first general-purpose bank credit card in 1966. It soon became widely accepted. This card later became the Visa® credit card.

The first automatic teller machine (ATM) in the US was installed in 1969 by Chemical Bank in New York. This was the first time customers could deposit or withdraw money from their accounts without using a teller.

Starting in the late 1960s, banks began expanding, both in terms of geography and services. The bank holding company became popular. **Bank holding companies** own a number of banks and allow banks to set up branch locations. A bank holding company could buy a bank in a town, and it would become a member of the holding company. In effect, the bank operated as a branch of the holding company, but was technically not a branch. Today most banks are part of a bank holding company. The largest bank holding company is Bank of America with over 6,000 branches across the country and over 17,000 ATMs.

BIZ TIPS

The FDIC insurance limit was $2,500 in 1933. This may not seem like a lot of money. However, in 1933, it was more than most people had in the bank. Adjusted for inflation, $2,500 dollars in 1933 was equivalent to about $43,500 in 2011. The current amount insured by the FDIC is $250,000 per depositor per account type.

1970–Present

Regulations instituted after the stock market crash of 1929 did not permit a bank to provide investment services *and* banking services. However, due to deregulation acts passed in the late 20th century, banks are once again allowed to provide both kinds of services.

Due to deregulation, many non-banks, such as stock houses, began offering some banking services. New accounts with stockbrokers were very similar to checking accounts. Businesses could get financing by selling securities instead of applying for a bank loan. Money market accounts often paid better interest rates than savings accounts. Some customers decided they could survive without banks. They closed their bank accounts and put money in non-banks. Banks saw large declines in deposits in the late 1970s. Without deposits, banks were unable to make loans.

Source: Shutterstock (Shannon Heryet)

After World War II, there was a period of prosperity and financial stability in the US.

Deregulation

Many federal regulations controlled the nation's banks through the 1970s. However, banks did not like having their business controlled, and they lobbied to do away with regulations. **Deregulation** occurs when some or all regulations are abolished or overridden. In 1980 and 1982, Congress passed two major deregulation acts—the Depository Institution Deregulation and Monetary Control Act (DIDMCA) and the Garn-St. Germain Act.

Under these laws, banks could offer more services and types of accounts. Fewer restrictions were placed on banking operations. Banks could pay interest rates based on market rates. Deregulation was initially widely hailed by banks and customers alike. Banks could more effectively compete against other types of financial companies. Many customers returned to banks, as they now offered some of the same services as non-banks, and at competitive rates.

Savings and loan associations (S & L's) could then act like commercial banks. As a result of the deregulation, S & L's took many risks. Many S & L's failed, and depositors lost their money. The late 1980s saw many bank and savings association failures, known as the **savings and loan crisis (S & L crisis).** The Federal Savings and Loan Insurance Company could not cover all of the losses that resulted. Congress funded the S & L industry's reorganization in order to help protect consumers. This crisis cost taxpayers billions of dollars.

BIZ TIPS

The Depository Institution Deregulation and Monetary Control Act of 1980 removed the power previously given to the Federal Reserve's Board of Governors to set interest rates for savings accounts.

Deregulation was partly blamed for the S & L crisis, as it had allowed banks into riskier areas. More banks failed in the 1980s than at any time since the Great Depression. For the first time in its history, the FDIC ran out of money to pay the insured depositors of failed banks. Congress was forced to bail out the FDIC so it could pay off depositors.

Congress attempted to correct some of the problems of deregulation and essentially passed new banking regulations in the early 1990s. Some banking powers that had been extended with the deregulation laws were abolished with the new laws. Regulators became more diligent in examining banks. By the mid-1990s, the banking industry was once again doing well.

Source: Shutterstock (R. Gino Santa Maria)

During the subprime crisis, many home buyers were unable to make mortgage payments.

Congress decided to give deregulation another chance. Several bank laws were passed in the late 1990s that let banks establish a branch anywhere in the country and engage in insurance and securities activities.

Under the Glass-Steagall Act, banks were not allowed to engage in many financial activities, such as selling securities or insurance. Some of the bank failures during the Great Depression were caused by banks involved in riskier transactions in the securities markets. Regulators were trying to prevent banks from failing by restricting them to safer ventures.

However, the provision of this act that prevented a bank holding company from owning other financial companies was repealed in late 1999. This removed the barrier between investment banks and depository banks. As a result, investment banks could engage in providing credit to consumers, often in the form of backing home mortgages offered by depository banks. Because of this, investment banks became an important part of consumer credit. However, under the new regulations, they did not have to follow the same regulations as depository banks.

Subprime Crisis

As the new millennium began, credit was increasingly extended to consumers. Lenders began offering homebuyers low-interest mortgages that were larger than some buyers could afford. Those borrowers who represent the greatest risk of being unable to repay a loan are called *subprime borrowers.* **Subprime lending** is offering these high-risk borrowers loans.

Subprime borrowers are charged a higher interest rate than more creditworthy borrowers. If the loan is repaid, a bank could potentially make more money from a subprime loan than from a traditional loan. Many banks during the first decade of the 21st century were willing to take on more subprime loans. To transfer some of the risk the subprime mortgage borrower represented, banks sold these loans that they had bundled together. The bundled mortgage loans are called *mortgage-backed securities (MBSs).*

Most subprime borrowers were given adjustable-rate mortgages (ARMs). The initial interest rate on ARMs was low. The rate was usually reset to a higher rate after three years. Many buyers found themselves unable to make mortgage payments at the higher rate. In addition, homeowners often found that they owed more on their mortgage than their houses were worth. This is also known as an *upside down loan.* As a result, foreclosures increased. Banks were not being repaid for the subprime loans they were making. Banks and other institutions that had purchased mortgage-backed securities also suffered for these unpaid loans. As a result, many banks collapsed. The banks that were still solvent were reluctant to lend money in such a climate. Credit was not available to transact business.

In 2008, the federal government took action to help the economy. The **Emergency Economic Stabilization Act** gave the Secretary of the Treasury the power to buy up to $700 billion worth of troubled assets from banks. The *troubled assets* were in the form of mortgages, mortgage-backed securities, and other products that involved subprime lending. The **Troubled Asset Relief Program (TARP)** purchased the assets. The program was designed to be repaid once financial conditions improved. Despite this program, which is often called a *bailout,* many financial institutions still failed. In 2008, Washington Mutual (WaMu), a savings bank holding company, shut its doors. It was the largest bank failure in history.

Ethical Banking

Ethical conduct has been at the heart of banking relationships since banking began. The banking industry is only as strong as the ethical standards it holds itself to. Many have cited ethical lapses for triggering the Great Recession of the early 21st century. This led many banks to revisit their codes of ethics. Some codes were rewritten, made more specific, or monitored more vigorously.

As a result of the financial crisis, there have been many changes in the banking industry. The **Dodd-Frank Wall Street Reform and Consumer Protection Act** of 2010 increases regulation of the banking and financial services industry. However, calls for additional measures persist. Today, banks are investing a great deal of time and money in financial-literacy programs. Many of these programs instruct consumers about the appropriate use of credit. Globalization and technological advancements present challenges and opportunities for the banking industry. Figure 15-4 is a time line that shows banking developments during this time.

1913	Federal Reserve System is established
1917	US enters World War I
1929	Stock market crash is followed by Great Depression
1933	Emergency Banking Act is signed, establishing the FDIC
1941	US enters World War II
1966	First widely accepted credit card is introduced
1969	First ATM in the US is installed in New York
1980	Depository Institutions Deregulation and Monetary Control Act repeals some bank regulations in effect since 1933
1984	Failure of the Empire Savings & Loan Association sparks beginning of the S & L crisis
2001	Terrorists attack the US on September 11th
2008	Financial crises cause economic collapse Emergency Economic Stabilization Act is signed, creating TARP
2010	Dodd-Frank Wall Street Reform and Consumer Protection Act is signed

Figure 15-4.
Banking in the 20th and 21st Centuries

Checkpoint 15.3

1. How did the Federal Reserve control the amount of money available after World War I?
2. Name four causes of the Great Depression.
3. Why did Congress pass new banking regulations in the 1990s?
4. How might a subprime loan benefit a bank?
5. What was the Emergency Economic Stabilization Act?

Build Your Vocabulary

As you progress through this course, develop a personal glossary of banking terms and add it to your portfolio. This will help you build your banking vocabulary. Write out a definition for each of the following terms, and add it to your personal glossary.

Federal Reserve Act
open market operations (OMO)
bank holiday
Emergency Banking Act of 1933
Federal Deposit Insurance Corporation (FDIC)
bank holding company
deregulation
savings and loan crisis (S & L crisis)
subprime lending
Emergency Economic Stabilization Act
Troubled Asset Relief Program (TARP)
Dodd-Frank Wall Street Reform and Consumer Protection Act

Careers in Finance
Banking and Related Services

What Does a Stockbroker Do?

Stockbrokers sell financial products to individuals and businesses. They explain securities products and provide financial advice to their clients. **Stockbrokers** perform the functions of two different positions: financial advisor and securities salesperson. Therefore, they are responsible for both acting in their clients' best interests financially and generating securities sales. **Stockbrokers** are also responsible for developing and maintaining their own client base. Some of the activities performed by a **stockbroker** include:

- interviewing clients to determine their financial goals;
- monitoring US and international stock markets and reporting this information to clients;
- creating and monitoring clients' investment portfolios; and
- selling financial products, such as certificates of deposit, insurance, money market accounts, stock, and bonds.

What Is It Like to Work as a Stockbroker?

Stockbrokers generally work long hours under very stressful conditions. Beginning **stockbrokers** focus mainly on recruiting clients, which is necessary to remain successful in this position. **Stockbrokers** spend most of their time working with clients, and therefore must have excellent interpersonal skills. **Stockbrokers** must also constantly monitor the stock market, and advise clients based on changes in the economy. Therefore, an interest in both US and international markets is very helpful in this position.

If you have a strong desire to succeed and an interest in investing, a career as a **stockbroker** might suit you.

What Education and Skills Are Needed to Be a Stockbroker?

- college degree in business, finance, accounting, or economics
- federal and state licensing exams
- professional certifications helpful
- strong interpersonal skills

Career Ladder

Stockbroker

Floor Broker

Trading Clerk

Chapter Summary

Section 15.1 Origins of the Banking System

- In ancient times, "banks" held livestock and crops for safekeeping. They also made loans and paid interest on those loans.
- During the Middle Ages, Italian bankers made loans to finance the wars, international trade, and exploration. These loans were made to countries, not individuals.

Section 15.2 Banking in America

- Before the American Revolution, banks in the true sense of the word did not exist in the colonies. Instead, trade was conducted with foreign coins or through the use of commodity money.
- In 1781, the Bank of North America was founded to finance the Revolutionary War. It was a privately owned bank that was able to raise money by issuing continentals.

Section 15.3 Banking Since the Federal Reserve

- While the US economy was plagued by the Great Depression for the first half of the 20th century, the banking industry was relatively stable from 1940 to the late 1960s.
- As the new millennium began, credit was increasingly extended to consumers. However, homeowners often found that they owed more on their mortgage than their houses were worth. As a result, foreclosures increased and many banks collapsed.

Check Your Banking IQ

Now that you have finished this chapter, see what you know about banking by taking the chapter post test.

www.m.g-wlearning.com
www.g-wlearning.com

Review Your Knowledge

On a separate sheet of paper or in a word processing document, match the following terms with the definition that fits best.

A. Emergency Banking Act of 1933
B. fractional-reserve banking
C. Troubled Asset Relief Program (TARP)
D. open market operations (OMO)
E. money changer
F. Emergency Economic Stabilization Act
G. Bank of North America
H. sovereign debt
I. bank holding company
J. land bank

1. Established the FDIC.
2. Exchanges one country's currency for that of another for a fee.
3. Designed to be repaid after financial conditions improved.
4. Owns a number of banks and allows banks to set up branch locations.
5. Gave the Secretary of the Treasury the power to buy up to $700 billion worth of troubled assets from banks.
6. Keeping only a portion of deposits in the bank.
7. Financial obligation incurred by a country.
8. Issued notes that represented credit secured by the value of land.
9. Founded to finance the Revolutionary War.
10. Allows the Federal Reserve to buy or sell US treasury securities, which affects the money supply.

On a separate sheet of paper or in a word processing document, answer each of the following questions.

11. What were the first depository institutions to emerge during the Middle Ages?
12. Name the type of currency that was issued by land banks.
13. What were the duties of the First Bank of the US?
14. When President Roosevelt took office, what did he immediately do to help the US economy?
15. Why was deregulation initially hailed by businesses and consumers?

Apply Your Knowledge

16. Why do you think the banking industry in America originally centered around the East Coast? What geographic and economic features did these states have that helped the banking industry to develop? Write a paragraph describing your conclusions and the reasoning behind them.
17. Research the impact sovereign debt has had on the financial crises of the early 21st century. Write a summary of your findings.
18. How was the Bank of North America different from the First and Second Banks of the US? Using information provided in the text and independent research, write a short summary contrasting these banks.
19. Conduct research on the end of the Great Depression. When, how, and why did it end? Write a report on the factors that helped improve the economy.
20. While Bank of America created the first general-purpose bank credit card in 1966, credit cards existed years before then. Research the history of credit cards, including when and how they were first created. What was the original purpose and use of a credit card? Has this changed since the invention of the credit card? Prepare a presentation detailing your findings.

Working in Teams

In a small group, conduct research on the federal government bailout of 2008. Once you have a solid understanding of the provisions and purposes of this event, create a presentation to explain it to your classmates. Be sure to use graphics and other displays, as well as the information that your research revealed.

G-W Learning Mobile Site

Visit the G-W Learning mobile site to complete the chapter pretest and post test and to practice vocabulary using e-flash cards. If you do not have a smartphone, visit the G-W Learning companion website to access these features.

G-W Learning mobile site: www.m.g-wlearning.com
G-W Learning companion website: www.g-wlearning.com

Common Core

College and Career Readiness

Reading. Locate the full text of the Banking Act of 1933 using the Internet. Try to find terms and concepts within the text that you are familiar with. For a review of the major provisions of the Banking Act of 1933, see the information provided in chapter 6 of this text. What additional information can you learn about these things? Write a report of your findings, including any new or surprising information you learned.

Writing. Imagine you are living in the US during the Great Depression. Using what you know about this time period, write a narrative about living during this time. Your story should be based on the factual events of the Great Depression, but can be told from any perspective or include any details that help to tell the narrative.

EVENT PREP

Proper Attire

Some career and technical student organizations (CTSOs) require appropriate business attire from all entrants and those attending the competition. This requirement is in keeping with the mission of CTSOs: to prepare students for professional careers in business. To be sure that the attire you have chosen to wear at the competition is in accordance with event requirements:

1. Visit the organization's website and look for the most current dress code.
2. The dress code requirements are very detailed and gender specific. Some CTSOs may require a chapter blazer to be worn during the competition.
3. Do a dress rehearsal when practicing for your event. Are you comfortable in the clothes you have chosen? Do you present a professional appearance?
4. In addition to the kinds of clothes you can wear, be sure the clothes are clean and pressed. You do not want to undermine your appearance or event performance with wrinkled clothes that may distract judges.
5. Make sure your hair is neat and worn in a conservative style. If you are a male, you should be clean shaven. Again, you do not want anything about your appearance detracting from your performance.
6. As far in advance of the event as is possible, share your clothing choice with your organization's sponsor to make sure you are dressed appropriately.

Check Your Banking IQ

Before you begin this chapter, see what you already know about banking by taking the chapter pretest.

www.m.g-wlearning.com
www.g-wlearning.com

16

Financial Crises of the Early 21st Century

In good times and bad, banks play a major role in a country's economy. This is especially true of the financial crises that have occurred since the turn of the 21st century. Home prices fell, banks failed, and people lost their jobs as the economy shrank. The causes of these events are complex. But, it is important to understand two things: banks played a major role in creating the crises, and the crises significantly changed the business of banking.

College and Career Readiness

Reading Prep. In preparation for reading the chapter, read a newspaper or magazine article on the Great Recession. As you read, keep in mind the author's main points and conclusions.

Scan the code to view a Biz Kid$ video. If you do not have a smartphone, visit the G-W Learning companion website.

www.m.g-wlearning.com
www.g-wlearning.com

Section 16.1
Roots of the Crises

Terms

Financial Crisis Inquiry Commission
wage stagnation
consumer debt
default
excess capital
securitization
subprime lending
ratings agency
collateralized debt obligation (CDO)
housing bubble
derivative
toxic asset
Troubled Asset Relief Program (TARP)

Objectives

After completing this section, you will be able to:

- Explain what crises triggered the Great Recession.
- Describe what conditions led to the crises.
- Discuss how the crises caused an economic collapse.
- Explain how the crises were addressed.

What Were the Crises?

The economic crises affecting the country and the world today are some of the most significant economic events of the past 100 years. A series of economic crises were to blame:

- collapse of the market for products pinned to mortgage loans
- widespread failure of financial institutions
- inaccessibility of consumer and commercial credit
- high rate of job loss

The banking industry was affected, as were most other industries. In retrospect, consumers, lenders, investors, regulators, and policymakers all helped to create the economic collapse.

Source: Shutterstock (Norman Chan)

There were several causes to the financial crises of the early 21st century.

Causes of the Crises

The **Financial Crisis Inquiry Commission** was created in 2009 by the Fraud Enforcement and Recovery Act to determine what caused the widespread financial collapse. After reviewing millions of pages of documents, interviewing more than 700 witnesses, and holding 19 days of hearings, the commission concluded that the financial crises were avoidable and the result of *human action and inaction*. What were the human actions that caused the financial crises? While opinions vary somewhat, there are several causes that are generally agreed on:

- consumer debt
- excess capital
- securitization
- subprime lending
- unreliable ratings
- the housing bubble
- shortsighted banks

Consumer Debt

Until the 1970s, worker wages in the US were steadily rising. At a certain point, however, several factors combined to slow the growth of wages. **Wage stagnation** is the term for slow growth in wages. Factors leading to wage stagnation included the increasing power of computers, more people in the workforce from nontraditional sources, and competition from countries with lower wages. To continue increasing their material comfort, consumers turned to borrowing money.

In the years leading up to the financial crises, interest rates on loans were very low and there was a lot of money available to lend. This led to excessive borrowing across the financial system. **Consumer debt** is money owed by individuals for the purchase of personal goods and services. This includes car loans, but not mortgages. Consumer debt increased from 77% of annual disposable income in 1990 to 127% in 2007. Figure 16-1 shows the overall increase in consumer debt since 1944. When the amount needed to pay consumer debt began to exceed disposable income, people began defaulting on their loans. A **default** occurs when a borrower stops paying the money he or she owes on a loan. Loan defaults were one of the main drivers of the crises.

Excess Capital

While growth of worker wages slowed, worker productivity surged. Corporate profits also increased. At the same time, the US began importing more and more goods from other countries. Those countries,

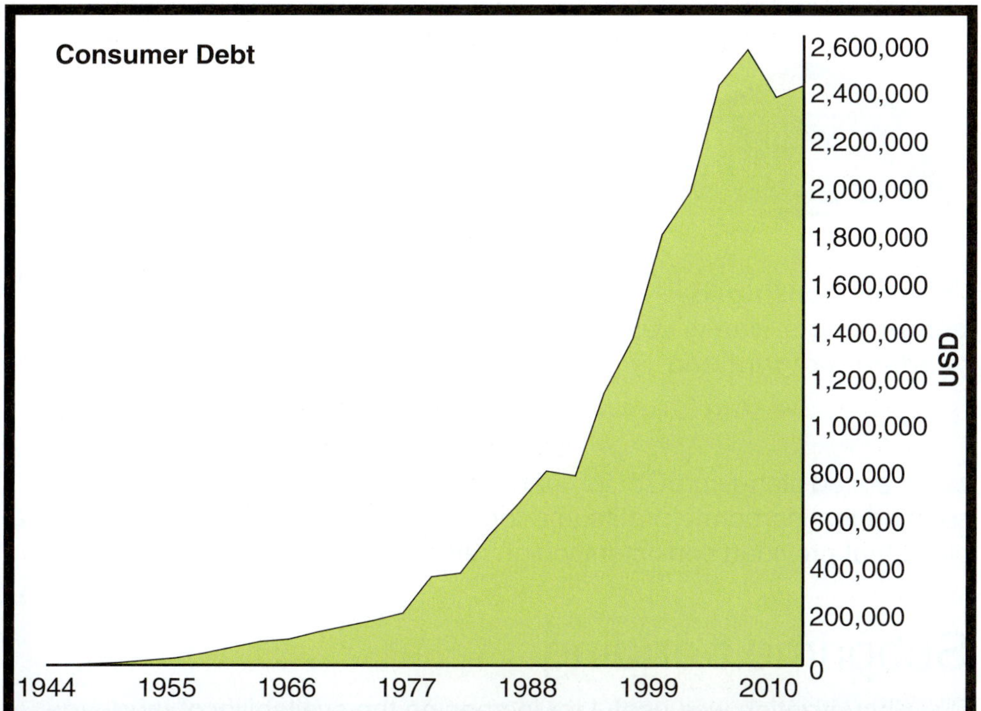

Source: Federal Reserve Board 2012

Figure 16-1.
Consumer Debt (1944–2010)

especially China, have very high savings rates compared to the US. High oil prices also sent a lot of US money to oil-producing countries. The money the US sent abroad came back in the form of investments in US treasury securities and other foreign investments. The owners of all this excess capital—corporations with high profits and exporters of oil and goods to the US—looked for places to invest it. **Excess capital** is the difference between what a company needs to run its operations and what it takes in. One place this capital ended up was in securitized mortgages.

BIZ TIPS

The two major institutions that bought mortgage loans and turned them into MBSs were Fannie Mae and Freddie Mac. Eventually, MBSs issued by investment banks became a major part of the market as well.

Securitization

Until the late 1960s, mortgage lenders made money on the difference between deposit rates and loan rates. That began to change with the start of securitization. **Securitization** is the pooling and packaging of loans to create securities. With the increasing use of securitization, the US housing market became a highly attractive place to invest.

Suppose a bank makes a $100,000 mortgage loan. Another financial institution buys the mortgage loan from the bank and combines it with other mortgage loans to create a security. This security is known as a mortgage-backed security (MBSs). MBSs can be traded like stocks and bonds.

MBSs investors get their returns from the money borrowers pay to service the loans each month. They also take on the risk that borrowers may not continue to pay. With securitization, a lender does not have to keep the mortgage until it is paid off. By selling the loan, the lender might make less money in the long run than if it had kept it in its portfolio. But, by selling the loan, it removes the risk associated with the loan. Securitization is used with all kinds of loans, including credit cards.

Green Banking

Some banks are encouraging consumers to be eco-friendly by offering special rates on loans for fuel-efficient cars or eco-friendly housing. By offering special loans for green products, banks can help customers reduce their carbon footprint and save on borrowing costs.

Securitization opened up an entirely new funding stream for the US housing market. The amount financial institutions could lend was no longer limited by the deposits they had on hand. Instead, investors could fund mortgage lending by investing capital in MBSs. The benefit of securitization to consumers was that it drove down interest rates on mortgage loans and made mortgage loans easier to get.

These securities were seen as a safe investment because they were backed by the US housing market, which had experienced steady growth for many years, as shown in Figure 16-2. It seemed that corporate profits and foreign capital had a safe place to go, a place that provided consistently high returns.

Subprime Lending

Securitization was useful for increasing the availability of mortgage loans. However, it also laid much of the groundwork for the financial crises. It allowed banks and mortgage brokers to transfer the risks associated with those loans to someone else. The lenders did not suffer

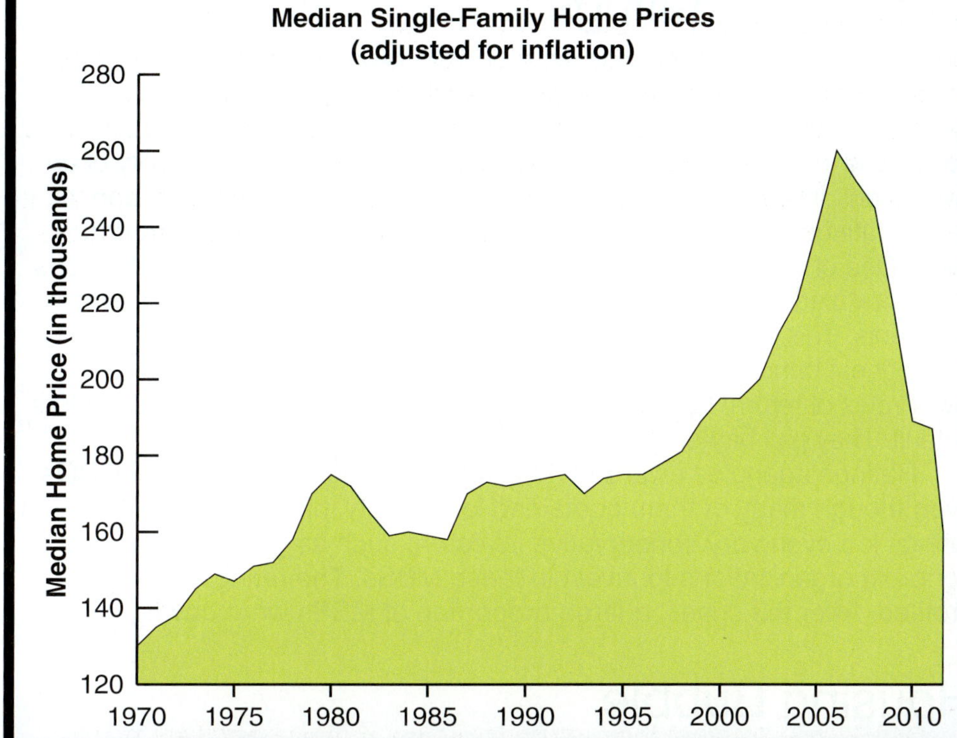

Figure 16-2.
Median Single-Family Home Prices (1971–2010)

the consequences in the same way that they would have if the loans were kept in their own portfolios.

At a certain point, there were not enough low-risk, high-quality mortgages being issued to meet the demand for MBSs. So, banks began to add higher-risk loans to their portfolios. One way to get more loans was to lower the down payment, income, and credit-score requirements. Another way was to reduce the degree to which banks verified a customer's borrowing ability. Loans made under these conditions are known as subprime. **Subprime lending** occurs when loans are made to borrowers that do not meet standard lending criteria.

Adjustable-rate mortgages (ARMs) also became popular. These loans allowed borrowers to get a low interest rate for a specified period, typically three years. After the initial period, the loan would reset to a higher interest rate and the monthly payment would go up, often drastically.

By the time the loans reset, the original loan had likely been sold and bundled into MBSs. The MBSs market meant the lender did not have to keep these risky loans. The risk could be passed on to other investors in the MBSs market. Because subprime loans command higher interest rates, they provided higher rates of return for MBSs investors, but at a higher risk.

Unreliable Ratings

Ratings agencies provide expert opinions on the financial strength of a given institution that issues securities, such as a corporation or country. Two of the best-known ratings agencies are Moody's and Standard & Poor's. Banks and investors relied on ratings agencies to evaluate the quality of an investment. Investment banks went to great lengths to make MBSs appear safe to ratings agencies by creating complex financial structures around them. One of their key strategies was to issue collateralized debt obligations. **Collateralized debt obligations (CDOs)** divide returns into *tranches,* or segments. This amounts to *re-securitization,* selling a segment of a security. The highest tranches get paid first, so they are the least risky, but offer lower rates of return. Lower tranches are more likely to be affected if debtors default. They pay higher rates in return for the additional risk.

Ratings agencies awarded AAA ratings to higher tranches of CDOs, even though many of them contained low-quality, high-risk debt. The high ratings led even very conservative investors such as governments and nonprofit organizations to invest in these MBSs. The ratings agencies profited. After the crises, a large proportion of MBSs were downgraded.

Housing Bubble

The **housing bubble** began with the increased access to credit by buyers who would not have been able to qualify for a larger mortgage or any mortgage. Home prices were already going up before the housing bubble began, as can be seen in Figure 16-2. Limited land, population growth, and the increasing cost of the commodities necessary to build homes drove price increases year after year. Rising home prices made it easy for consumers to refinance loans. By refinancing, they avoided ARM interest rate increases. In fact, the rising cost of housing is what led investors to see the US housing market as a "sure thing." This view also made home buyers believe that purchasing a house at the extent of their financial means, or in some cases above it, was a financially sound idea.

As more and more capital entered the US housing market, house prices began to dramatically increase. From 1998 to the bursting of the bubble in 2006, the average price of a house in the US increased 67%. The housing bubble was not limited to the US. Similar bubbles occurred in other countries as well.

With home prices going up 10% a year or more in some cities, the housing market seemed like a sure way to make money. People were buying houses, performing minor upgrades, and flipping them for big profits. *Flipping* is buying something, improving it, and then selling it for a profit very quickly afterward. Consumers took on more and more debt. This included second mortgages and cash-out refinancing, not to mention readily available credit cards and other lines of credit.

Shortsighted Banks

While the housing bubble inflated, the MBSs market continued to heat up. Investment banks created complex, yet lightly regulated financial instruments called derivatives. A **derivative** is a contract designed to manage risk and make money. As long as prices were going up and homeowners paid their mortgages, these instruments continued to make money for investors.

The banks invested very heavily in the MBSs they created. Because of loose liquidity requirements, banks used massive leverage to make those investments. In other words, they borrowed the money. Banks did this believing that even if some MBSs underperformed, US home prices would not collapse everywhere at once. They also overlooked the possibility that they would have problems continuing to borrow money. This proved to be a miscalculation when the crises hit and short-term lending dried up.

Crises Erupt

While the housing market looked healthy, the truth was that the quality of loans had been decreasing and rates of default had been climbing for years. Increasing home prices had hidden these facts because of the ease with which homebuyers could refinance. When homeowners got in trouble with one loan, they could refinance at a lower interest rate and keep their homes. By 2006, however, that was no longer possible. Heavily indebted consumers began to default on their mortgages in record numbers. This cut off the payments MBSs investors had come to rely on.

Securitization and derivatives were created to spread risk around. In fact, however, a small number of major financial institutions had huge, highly leveraged stakes in MBSs that turned out to be worthless. When those investments turned out to be much riskier than anyone had previously believed, they became very difficult to sell or even accurately price. In turn, the companies that held them were suddenly *insolvent,* or unable to pay their debts. The lending markets that had supported them dried up. They had no liquidity. The term **toxic asset** was coined to describe CDOs and MBSs that no one was willing to purchase. Some of the world's most respected financial institutions started to fail.

Bear Stearns, an 85-year-old global investment bank and brokerage firm, was purchased by Merrill Lynch for $2 a share in a government-sponsored takeover. Merrill Lynch, along with Countrywide, would later be purchased by Bank of America for pennies on the dollar. Lehman Brothers, a major investment banking firm, had over 26,000 employees when it declared bankruptcy.

Ethical Banking

The attraction of short-term financial rewards can be a real challenge. Some argue that the financial crises were caused by an unwillingness to see the potential danger in selling and trading products that were so lucrative. A strong personal code of ethics is the best defense against this type of temptation.

Source: Shutterstock (Losevsky Pavel)

Banks must ensure that borrowers are a good risk.

Careers in Finance
Banking and Related Services

What Does a Bill and Account Collector Do?

Bill and account collectors, often called *collection officers,* attempt to collect payment on overdue bills or loans. Banks and other lenders generally have their own collection departments. Some of the activities performed by a **bill and account collector** include:

- locating and notifying customers of delinquent accounts;
- soliciting payment on past due accounts;
- offering repayment plans or other help to customers;
- recording payments received on delinquent accounts;
- reporting missed payments to credit bureaus; and
- initiating repossession or other legal actions if an account remains unpaid.

What Is It Like to Work as a Bill and Account Collector?

Most of the work done by **bill and account collectors** is conducted in an office, often using computers and a variety of automated systems. Companies keep computerized records of accounts and previous collection attempts. **Bill and account collectors** spend most of their time on the phone tracking down and contacting people with unpaid debts. Sometimes **bill and account collectors** will make personal visits to customers. In order to reach customers when they are home, **bill and account collectors** are sometimes required to work evenings and weekends.

If you enjoy working with people and possess good negotiation skills, a career as a **bill and account collector** might suit you.

What Education and Skills Are Needed to Be a Bill and Account Collector?

- high school diploma; college degree preferred
- bilingual communication ability preferred
- computer skills and experience with telecommunication equipment
- excellent communication skills

Career Ladder

Loan Officer

Bill and Account Collector

Loan Service Clerk

Fannie Mae and Freddie Mac, formerly private, government-sponsored entities, were taken into conservatorship. The *Federal Housing Finance Association (FHFA)* was created for that purpose. *Conservatorship* gives legal control of an entity to another organization. The FHFA gave money to both entities to stabilize them and stopped many of their riskier practices.

AIG, one of the world's largest insurance companies, faced massive losses related to derivatives contracts. It was deemed *too big to fail,* but was bailed out with government loans. Morgan Stanley and Goldman Sachs changed from investment banks to bank holding companies. Washington Mutual was the largest bank failure in US history.

Addressing the Problem

The federal government decided to take bold action. The Emergency Economic Stabilization Act of 2008 was designed to save financial institutions and help the economy recover. It was passed by Congress and signed by President George W. Bush in early October 2008. One of the major provisions of the new law was the creation of a $700 billion fund known as the Troubled Asset Relief Program.

TARP

The **Troubled Asset Relief Program (TARP)** allowed the federal government to purchase assets (mostly loans) and equity from financial institutions in order to strengthen the institutions and prevent more failures. As the treasury bought up mortgage loans, MBSs, and other failing assets, losses were reduced. Many banks and other financial institutions with large losses were able to survive. Many economists saw TARP as the only way to prevent an economic catastrophe.

In terms of its cost to taxpayers, TARP was a success. It was originally estimated that the program would cost taxpayers close to $400 billion. However, banks and other institutions recovered and repaid the government much faster than expected. The total cost is projected to be less than $25 billion, perhaps even less than $10 billion. Money is still being repaid. As of 2011, TARP has recovered close to 99% of the funds provided by the US government.

TARP also gave banks and other lenders immediate cash that could be used to make loans. Since credit had been frozen, businesses and other borrowers were having a rough time getting necessary loans. The government wanted to ensure financing was available to help the economy recover from the financial crises. However, many banks chose to use TARP funds to strengthen their balance sheets rather than increase lending.

Although financial institutions were the intended target for TARP funds, some of the funds were used to help US auto manufacturers. Approximately $20 billion in loans to General Motors and Chrysler were made with TARP money. As with the financial institutions, the automakers were required to repay the government for any funds received.

TARP money was also used to encourage several bank mergers and acquisitions. More stable banks such as Bank of America, JPMorgan Chase, and Wells Fargo were encouraged to acquire smaller, weaker banks. Wells Fargo, for instance, was given TARP funds to help it acquire Wachovia Bank.

BIZ TIPS

TARP funds were not payments. They were loans. Companies that accepted TARP funds had to repay them with interest.

Help from the Federal Reserve, FDIC, and NCUA

Not all money that was used to help companies during the financial crises came from TARP. The Federal Reserve and the Federal Deposit Insurance Corporation (FDIC) also had programs that funded banks and other financial institutions. Deposit insurance from the FDIC and National Credit Union Association (NCUA) was raised to $250,000 per depositor. This action was taken to ensure depositors that the money in their bank accounts was safe even if the bank failed. This was intended to be a temporary move, but deposit insurance has been permanently raised to this level.

Bailout Versus Stimulus

Some confusion has arisen in recent years about what is referred to as the *bank bailout bill* and the *stimulus bill.* These are two very separate laws with different purposes. The Emergency Economic Stabilization Act, which created TARP, was aimed at helping saving banks and other financial institutions. The American Recovery and Reinvestment Act of 2009, often called *the stimulus,* was designed to help the economy get back on its feet and help average Americans. It was not a bailout bill. It included tax cuts for individuals, money to states for Medicare and unemployment benefits, and funds for transportation and other projects.

Source: Shutterstock (Denise Kappa)

TARP funds were used to assist the American automobile industry.

Checkpoint 16.1

1. What are the seven generally agreed on causes of the financial crises?
2. What factors led to wage stagnation in the late 20th century?
3. How did securitization fail to fulfill its purpose?
4. From a consumer's standpoint, why was TARP a success?
5. Describe the difference between the bank bailout and stimulus bills.

Build Your Vocabulary

As you progress through this course, develop a personal glossary of banking terms and add it to your portfolio. This will help you build your banking vocabulary. Write out a definition for each of the following terms, and add it to your personal glossary.

Financial Crisis Inquiry Commission
wage stagnation
consumer debt
default
excess capital
securitization
subprime lending
ratings agency
collateralized debt obligation (CDO)
housing bubble
derivative
toxic asset
Troubled Asset Relief Program (TARP)

Section 16.2
Effects of the Crises

Terms

Great Recession
recession
foreclosure
investment bank
Dodd-Frank Wall Street Reform and Consumer Protection Act
Consumer Financial Protection Bureau (CFPB)
debt ceiling
double-dip recession

Objectives

After completing this section, you will be able to:

- List the characteristics of the Great Recession.
- Explain the increased regulation of the finance and banking industry imposed after 2008.
- Describe the consequences of government spending during the crises.

Great Recession

The financial crises brought about the worst economic conditions in the US since the Great Depression. The **Great Recession** refers to the time during which the country most acutely felt the effects of the financial crises of the early 21st century. A **recession** occurs when the country has experienced negative economic growth for at least a six-month stretch. As measured against other recessions, the Great Recession lasted longer than others—20 months to an average of 16 months. It started in December of 2007 and lasted until June of 2009.

Source: Shutterstock (wavebreakmedia ltd)

Millions of Americans lost their jobs during the Great Recession.

At-risk banks stopped lending, causing business activity to slow to a halt. Stock values plunged. Investors in failed financial firms lost millions. Workers found their retirement accounts devastated by stock market losses. Consumers had large amounts of debt and were unable to spend at pre-recession levels. The US economy is largely driven by consumer spending, so the economy suffered. The Bureau of Labor Statistics reports that since the beginning of the recession, the US economy has lost 8.5 million jobs. It was, however, much less severe than the Great Depression, to which it is commonly compared.

When the housing bubble burst, home prices fell by 50% or more in some of the most highly inflated markets and an average of 30% around the country. Markets such as Las Vegas, Phoenix, and Miami had been highly inflated. Many homeowners had been counting on using the equity in their houses to finance education for their children or their own retirements. However, they lost much of this equity in the Great Recession, for example.

During the Great Recession, homeowners were no longer able to easily refinance. Those who could not afford monthly payments defaulted on their mortgages in record numbers. This led to high rates of foreclosure. **Foreclosure** is when the ownership interest in a piece of real estate is transferred to the lender. With demand for homes very low, banks were unable to sell foreclosed houses, leading to excess supply of and lower prices for houses.

As house values dropped, so did the real estate tax collections on those properties. This drop in tax revenue severely affected governments, forcing cuts in public services. Some local and state governments had to seek loans from the federal government to pay unemployment benefits.

Since 2008, corporate profits rose 27%. However, wage stagnation continued.

BIZ TIPS

The Great Depression lasted from the stock market crash of 1929 until the beginning of World War II, which the US entered in 1941.

Restructure and Regulation

The financial crises caused a number of financial institutions to fail. There were widespread failures in banks, securities firms, investment banks, and insurance companies. Banks and other lenders saw an increase in loan losses due to the recession. Heavily indebted consumers could not repay their loans due to job losses. Mergers also contributed to a decrease in the number of companies and banks. Some mergers were necessary to keep banks from failing. Others were undertaken as strategic business moves.

From 2008 to 2011, the number of banks in the US fell from 7,288 to 6,453. This was a drop of more than 11%. Most of the decline in the number of banks came from bank failures, with a smaller percentage coming from mergers and acquisitions.

BIZ TIPS

The recovery from the Great Recession is often referred to as a *jobless recovery*. The return to overall economic growth did not immediately reduce the unemployment rate.

Investment Banks

Regulations implemented after the stock market crash of 1929 led to the establishment of investment banks. **Investment banks** helped companies raise money through public offerings of stock or to otherwise make money from the stock market. Commercial banks were prohibited from providing these services. As part of the deregulation of the financial and banking industry that occurred during the 1990s, commercial banks were again allowed to perform investment banking functions. Commercial banks were now more exposed to the risks of the securities market. The banks that had most heavily invested in MBSs were subject to the greatest losses.

After 2008, the Federal Reserve saw the need to exercise more control over investment banks. These banks were given the opportunity to either merge with a commercial bank or apply for a bank-holding-company charter. Goldman Sachs and Morgan Stanley each chose to become bank holding companies.

Source: White House Official Photo (Lawrence Jackson)

Barack Obama signed the Dodd-Frank Wall Street Reform and Consumer Protection Act in 2010.

New Legislation

A major piece of legislation was passed in July of 2010. The **Dodd-Frank Wall Street Reform and Consumer Protection Act:**

- increased accountability of financial institutions;
- created a consumer financial protection organization; and
- established actions to prevent another financial crisis.

The act also provided for stricter regulation and examination of financial institutions to help prevent another large-scale crisis. More transparency is now required of banks and other financial firms. The act also mandates higher capital requirements to cover potential losses.

In addition, the act requires mortgage lenders to ensure a borrower's ability to repay the loan. In other words, the old standards of a 20% down payment, payments of no more than 28% of income, and credit verification, most of which were ignored or lowered prior to the Great Recession, have been restored. At the same time, the bill prohibits unfair lending practices, doing away with much of the subprime lending segment. Lenders and mortgage companies who do not comply with the new standards face penalties.

With respect to mortgage-backed securities, any company that sells MBSs must retain at least 5% of each one. In this way, if the security is a loss, the company that sold it would lose along with other investors. In addition, greater disclosure is required of MBSs so that investors can assess the risk.

The act also created an independent consumer-protection organization. The **Consumer Financial Protection Bureau (CFPB)** has the authority to ensure consumers get clear information about loans, mortgages, credit cards, and other financial products. It is also charged with ending hidden fees, abusive terms, and deceptive practices in lending.

BIZ TIPS

Since early 2008, the Federal Reserve has lowered the Federal Funds Rate to near 0% with a series of cuts, hoping to spur borrowing and investments.

Emerging Recovery

In general, banks are seeing more profits since the Great Recession. The FDIC reported that banks and savings associations saw total profits of $29 billion in the first quarter of 2011, up from $17 billion in the first quarter of 2010. In 2011, the number of troubled institutions was the lowest in more than three years.

The Great Recession is still having an impact on the economy and the banking industry. The pace of new loans is still lagging because some banks do not have sufficient liquidity to make loans. Others have been reluctant to lend. Banks and others are still working through loan and investment losses. A volatile and weak securities market and government-debt worries persist.

Debt-Ceiling Crisis of 2011

The Great Recession has caused significant problems with funding the federal government. The federal budget was already stretched due to reduced tax revenue as well as the expense of the wars in Iraq and Afghanistan. In addition, stimulus and bailout funds added more to the national debt.

Roots of the Crisis

The US government already used debt to finance much of its spending. The national debt doubled between 2004 and 2011, as shown in Figure 16-3. With growing spending and dropping revenue, the government needed to take on additional debt to meet its obligations. The **debt ceiling,** which is set by Congress, is the limit on the level of debt the government can take on. Congress must vote to raise the debt ceiling whenever the debt is projected to go above the established level, or the government must cease borrowing to pay its bills.

In 2011, the federal government needed to raise the debt ceiling to meet the requirements of the budget passed in April of that year. The House of Representatives insisted that the government cut spending before trying to borrow more money. The disagreement between the House of Representatives and the executive branch over the debt ceiling turned into a lengthy battle that lasted through the summer. If Congress failed to raise the debt ceiling, the government would be forced to begin paying down its debts instead of paying for services such as Social Security. Many economists agreed that failing to raise the debt limit could cause a double-dip recession. A **double-dip recession** occurs when a recovering economy goes into negative growth a second time.

BIZ TIPS

The Second Liberty Act of 1917 established the first debt-ceiling limit. Before then, when the government wanted to borrow money, it had to ask Congress for permission.

Year	Debt Limit
2004	$7,384,000,000
2005	$8,184,000,000
2006	$8,965,000,000
2007	$9,815,000,000
2008	$10,615,000,000
2009	$12,104,000,000
2010	$14,694,000,000
2011	$15,194,000,000

Source: US Treasury Department

Figure 16-3.
Debt Limits (2004–2011)

Compromise

The battle over the debt ceiling resulted in a compromise agreement in August of 2011. It consisted of trillions of dollars in spending cuts over ten years *and* an increase in the debt ceiling. The agreement was highly complex and controversial. Few of the required cuts were actually specified in the agreement.

Prior to the compromise agreement being reached, governments around the world criticized the US for being irresponsible. Most experts agreed that a US default on its debts would have been catastrophic for the world economy. A default could have triggered a global financial meltdown. Standard & Poor's credit-rating agency downgraded the US debt from AAA to AA+, the first such downgrade since the original rating was issued.

The compromise agreement prevented the US from defaulting on its debt. However, most experts agree that the US national debt is still growing at a dangerous rate.

Checkpoint 16.2

1. How did the Great Recession compare to other recessions historically?
2. How did the Federal Reserve exercise more control over investment banks after 2008?
3. What lending standards were restored with the Dodd-Frank Wall Street Reform and Consumer Protection Act?
4. Why was the US national debt already high in 2011?
5. What disagreement led to the debt-ceiling crisis of 2011?

Build Your Vocabulary

As you progress through this course, develop a personal glossary of banking terms and add it to your portfolio. This will help you build your banking vocabulary. Write out a definition for each of the following terms, and add it to your personal glossary.

Great Recession
recession
foreclosure
investment bank
Dodd-Frank Wall Street Reform and Consumer Protection Act
Consumer Financial Protection Bureau
debt ceiling
double-dip recession

Chapter Summary

Section 16.1 Roots of the Crises

- The economic crises affecting the country and the world today are some of the most significant economic events of the past 100 years.
- The Financial Crisis Inquiry Commission concluded that the financial crises were avoidable and the result of human action and inaction.
- While the housing market looked healthy, the truth was that the quality of loans had been decreasing and rates of default had been climbing for years. In 2006, heavily indebted consumers began to default on their mortgages in record numbers.
- The Emergency Economic Stabilization Act of 2008 was designed to save financial institutions and help the economy recover. One of the major provisions of the new law was the creation of a $700 billion fund known as the Troubled Asset Relief Program.

Section 16.2 Effects of the Crises

- The financial crises brought about the Great Recession. These were the worst economic conditions in the US since the Great Depression.
- From 2008 to 2011, the number of banks in the US fell from 7,288 to 6,453. Most of the decline in the number of banks came from bank failures, with a smaller percentage coming from mergers and acquisitions.
- The national debt doubled between 2004 and 2011. With growing spending and dropping revenue, the government needed to take on additional debt to meet its obligations.

Check Your Banking IQ

Now that you have finished this chapter, see what you know about banking by taking the chapter post test.

www.m.g-wlearning.com
www.g-wlearning.com

Review Your Knowledge

On a separate sheet of paper or in a word processing document, match the following terms with the definition that fits best.

A. collateralized debt obligation (CDO)
B. housing bubble
C. Great Recession
D. wage stagnation
E. excess capital
F. toxic asset
G. foreclosure
H. securitization
I. double-dip recession
J. debt ceiling

1. Pooling and packaging loans to create securities.
2. Slow growth in wages.
3. Limit on the level of debt the government can take on.
4. Began with the increased access to credit by buyers who would not have been able to qualify for a larger mortgage or any mortgage.
5. Difference between what a company needs to run its operations and what it takes in.
6. CDOs and MBSs that no one was willing to purchase.
7. When a recovering economy goes into negative growth a second time.
8. Divides returns into tranches.
9. Ownership interest in a piece of real estate is transferred to the lender.
10. Time during which the country most acutely felt the effects of the financial crises of the early 21st century.

On a separate sheet of paper or in a word processing document, answer each of the following questions.

11. What factors led to the high consumer debt that was present in the years leading up to the financial crises?
12. Why were MBSs seen as a safe investment?
13. Why do banks rely on ratings agencies like Moody's and Standard & Poor's?
14. List three effects of the Great Recession.
15. How did the Dodd-Frank Wall Street Reform and Consumer Protection Act reform MBSs?

Apply Your Knowledge

16. Study Figure 16-1. What are some consequences of excessive consumer debt other than those mentioned in the text? Write a few paragraphs about the effects that you can think of.
17. Research how the housing market affects the economy. Write a summary of the consequences of an increase or decrease in housing prices.
18. Visit the Moody's or Standard & Poor's website. Write a summary of your findings, including the purpose of the company, the ratings that they provide, and how their ratings are used by investors.
19. Find a website that compares the Great Depression and the Great Recession. Do you agree with the author that the recession was much less severe? What factors do you think contributed to these differences? Write a few paragraphs detailing your thoughts.
20. Research the history of the debt ceiling. Write a summary of your findings, including how it is determined and why it exists.

Working in Teams

With a partner, research recent opinions on the lasting effects of the Great Recession. What do modern scholars say about the solutions to the Great Recession? What do they think the forecast is for the US economy? Using the information that you find, create a presentation summarizing your personal predictions for the US economy and your reasoning behind these predictions. Present your findings to the class.

G-W Learning Mobile Site

Visit the G-W Learning mobile site to complete the chapter pretest and post test and to practice vocabulary using e-flash cards. If you do not have a smartphone, visit the G-W Learning companion website to access these features.

G-W Learning mobile site: www.m.g-wlearning.com
G-W Learning companion website: www.g-wlearning.com

Common Core

College and Career Readiness

Writing. Many argue that a lack of ethics is what spurred the financial crises of the early 21st century. What do you think? Research some of the major factors in the financial crises. Do you believe, along with the Financial Crisis Inquiry Commission, that the crises were a result of *human action and inaction?* What ethical issues in the US economic system have the financial crises brought to light? Write a paper on your stance on these issues. Be sure to include trustworthy sources in your explanations and reasoning.

Reading. Consider how the author uses the term *financial crises* throughout this chapter. How did your understanding of this term change as you were reading? Look up the word *crisis* in the dictionary. How did the author shape this definition to fit the subject matter in this chapter? Write a few paragraphs about what the term *financial crises* means to you after reading this chapter.

EVENT PREP

Leave Nothing to Chance

No matter what competitive events you will participate in for a career and technical student organization (CTSO), you will have to be well-organized and prepared. Of course, you will have studied the content exhaustively before the event, but you also have to prepare by making sure all the tools you need for the event, and for travel to the event, are taken care of. Confirming all of the details well in advance of an event will decrease stress and leave you free to concentrate on the event itself. To prepare for a competition, create a checklist of things you need to bring to the event:

- Appropriate clothing, which includes shoes and appropriate undergarments. See the event prep feature in chapter 15 for an in-depth discussion of appropriate attire.
- All technological resources, including anything that you might need to prepare or compete. Double-check to make sure that any presentation material that is saved electronically is done so on media that is compatible with the machines that will be available to you at the event.
- Identification and registration materials, including a valid form of identification.
- Study materials, including the flash cards and other materials you have used to study for the event.

Check Your Banking IQ

Before you begin this chapter, see what you already know about banking by taking the chapter pretest.

www.m.g-wlearning.com
www.g-wlearning.com

17

Bank of the Future

Financial institutions exist in the same economic environment as you. If economic conditions are good, a bank that makes good business decisions will flourish. When economic conditions are poor, financial institutions have to work harder to succeed. Anticipating challenges, taking advantage of new opportunities, monitoring local and global economic conditions, and following legal requirements form a recipe for a successful business.

College and Career Readiness

Reading Prep. Think about what you already know about how technology has changed banking. What do you think the future holds for the banking industry? As you read, evaluate how the ideas presented in the text compare to your own.

Scan the code to view a Biz Kid$ video. If you do not have a smartphone, visit the G-W Learning companion website.

www.m.g-wlearning.com
www.g-wlearning.com

Section 17.1
International Banking

Terms

- **Bretton Woods Conference**
- **International Bank for Reconstruction and Development (IBRD)**
- **International Monetary Fund (IMF)**
- **World Bank**
- **international financial institution (IFI)**
- **regional-development bank**
- **multilateral-development bank**
- **trade surplus**
- **trade deficit**
- **Export-Import Bank of the United States (Ex-Im Bank)**

Source: Shutterstock (Albert H. Teich)

Christine Lagarde was named Managing Director of the IMF in 2011.

Objectives

After completing this section, you will be able to:

- Identify types of financial institutions engaged in international banking and the types of international services they provide.
- List three types of financial institutions engaged in international banking.
- Describe the factors that affect currency values.
- Explain the banking services needed by international companies.

World Bank

The world used to be a much smaller place. Commerce among nations, particularly nations on different continents, was difficult, risky, and time-consuming. Most commerce was carried out within national borders. Nations that were poor had few resources and remained poor because they had no way to improve. Today, commerce can be conducted globally, which allows nations a greater market for goods and resources.

World War II, which lasted from 1939 to 1945, challenged many long-held ideas about the world. As part of the war effort, troops, machines, and products were shipped all over the world. There was a realization that nations could work together to improve conditions for everyone, including less-developed nations.

In July 1944, before the war ended, representatives from 43 nations met in Bretton Woods, New Hampshire. The **Bretton Woods Conference** established two important organizations: the International Bank for Reconstruction and Development (IBRD) and the International Monetary Fund (IMF), which together form the World Bank.

International Bank for Reconstruction and Development

The **International Bank for Reconstruction and Development (IBRD)** was created to speed up the process of reconstruction after World War II ended. It has 187 member nations that act as shareholders in the international organization. The members hope to increase the pace of economic progress, increase political stability, and encourage peace among nations. They agreed that international investments are a good source of income that could be used for reconstruction and development. Investments in foreign businesses are encouraged. The IBRD has two goals:

- provide loans at reasonable interest rates for long-term projects to improve productivity in the nation borrowing the money
- guarantee that loans made to a nation by others will be repaid

International Monetary Fund

The **International Monetary Fund (IMF)** is an international organization that was created to improve financial conditions in all nations. The IMF has 187 member nations. It has several goals:

- promote monetary cooperation among nations
- promote stability in the exchange rate among national currencies
- encourage the balanced growth of international trade
- help member nations that have difficulty making loan payments
- help nations reduce poverty

The IMF uses several methods to achieve its goals. It tracks economic developments in each nation and evaluates how those developments affect other nations. Each year, it creates a report for each nation that discusses that nation's economy. Nations can use the reports to review their country's progress and plan future actions. The IMF offers technical help and training in managing national finances. It lends money to low-income nations at low interest rates. In addition, it provides statistics and research information to all member nations.

World Bank's Goals

The **World Bank,** which consists of the IBDR and IMF, is an international organization that continues to work toward the goals established at the Bretton Woods Conference. To continue to improve conditions in all nations, the World Bank has focused on six main themes:

- help poor nations overcome poverty and encourage ongoing growth
- address the special needs of nations that have just ended a war
- help middle-income nations continue to develop
- actively address development issues that cross national borders, such as climate change and HIV/AIDS
- encourage growth and development in the Arab world
- collect information and make it easily available to everybody

Source: Shutterstock (Hector Conesa)

Increasing crop production in Ethiopia is one of the many projects of the WorldBank.

The World Bank is involved in a long list of projects in every corner of the world to support its goals. Sample projects include building irrigation systems in Ethiopia to increase the crops that can be harvested, improving energy efficiency in Ukraine, and improving health care in Nicaragua.

World Bank Group

While the World Bank consists of the International Bank for Reconstruction and Development and the International Monetary Fund, it also works with three other organizations. Together they form the World Bank Group.

International Finance Corporation

The *International Finance Corporation (IFC)* encourages the growth of private enterprise in member nations, particularly in the less-developed nations. It provides loans to private companies that support the activities of the IBRD. The IFC has 182 member nations.

Multilateral Investment Guarantee Agency

The *Multilateral Investment Guarantee Agency (MIGA)* is an organization that insures investments from citizens or corporations from any nation outside the developing nation in which the investment is applied. For example, an investment made by a US corporation in building a water treatment plant in Jamaica could be insured by MIGA. MIGA is made up of 175 member nations.

Green Banking

Advances in computer technology have improved hardware capabilities and performance. Often, terminals can be set up at several workstations and connected to a single server where the applications actually run. Sharing the computing power of a single server reduces the need for multiple computers, which reduces the amount of power used by the business.

International Centre for Settlement of Investment Disputes

The *International Centre for Settlement of Investment Disputes (ICSID)* is an institution that provides facilities and rules to settle disagreements between its members about international investments. ICSID is made up of 157 member nations.

Organization of International Financial Institutions

International financial institutions (IFIs) are financial institutions that have been established by more than one nation. They are owned by national governments.

Four IFIs are referred to as **regional-development banks,** because they focus on financing projects that improve their regions. The four regional-development banks are the African Development Bank, the Asian Development Bank, the European Bank for Reconstruction and Development, and the Inter-American Development Bank. Member nations of regional-development banks are not limited to the nations within the bank's region. The US is a member of all of the regional-development banks.

Multilateral-development banks are institutions that provide financing and advice to developing nations to encourage economic and financial growth. Multilateral-development banks include Bretton Woods institutions and regional-development institutions, as shown in Figure 17-1.

Currency

The value of a US dollar is 100 pennies, 20 nickels, 10 dimes, or 4 quarters, right? Yes, but if you are traveling in a foreign country that does not use US currency, it does not matter how many dollars, dimes, or quarters you have in your pocket. In order to buy something, you will need to use the currency of that country.

Changes in Currency Values

When you enter a foreign country, you can exchange your US currency into the type of currency used in that country. The value of each nation's currency changes constantly. The amount of the foreign currency that you receive for your US dollars changes as well. Multiple factors affect the value of a nation's currency.

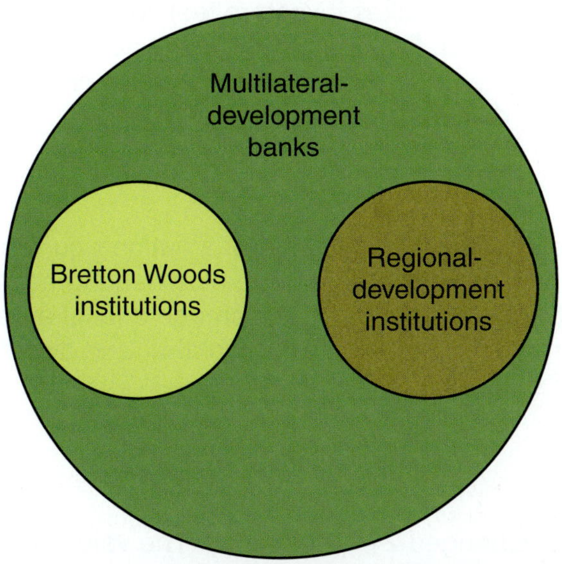

Figure 17-1.
Multilateral-Development Banks

Balance of Trade

Imports are products coming into a country. *Exports* are products going out of a country. A **trade surplus** occurs when a country exports more than it imports. A **trade deficit** occurs when a country imports more than it exports. The difference between the two values is the *balance of payments.* A US trade surplus could push up the value of the dollar. A US trade deficit could push down the value of the dollar. The US has seen a trade deficit every year since 1976.

National Debt

If a nation spends more money than it has, it must borrow money or take other actions to remain operational. This reduces the value of its currency.

In August 2011, the US government almost shut down because members of Congress could not agree on raising the debt-ceiling limit. Methods for reducing the national debt are hotly debated. In November 2011, the national debt was almost $15 trillion.

BIZ TIPS

In August of 2011, the credit ratings agency Standard & Poor's lowered the credit rating of the US one level from AAA to AA+. The agency cited political risks and the national debt as reasons for the downgrade.

Credit History

Nations have a credit history, just like individuals and organizations. If a nation fails to repay its debt, the value of its currency is reduced. The US has a good credit history, which helps the US dollar maintain its value.

Politics

Political uncertainty can be created by both national and international events. When investors do not know what to expect, they hold onto their money instead of spending or investing it. For example, war is expensive. It can increase national debt as well as political uncertainty. Uncertainty reduces the value of the nation's currency. All risk associated with doing business in a particular country is called *country risk.*

Political consistency makes investors feel confident. This increases the value of the US dollar. Politics in the US are consistent. Even when a new president is elected, the process is peaceful. Consistency increases the value of the US dollar.

Weather

Even the weather affects the value of a nation's currency. If the weather is not good for farmers, food may need to be imported. Tornadoes and other natural disasters damage a local area, but can affect a much larger area of the country. Poor weather and disasters reduce the value of a nation's currency.

Results

Currency is exchanged 24 hours a day. The values of all currencies constantly fluctuate. The factors that affect currency values and their effects are listed in Figure 17-2. However, these are just a few of the factors that change the value of a nation's currency. Every news story, serious storm, rise or fall of a leader's popularity, and many other events affect the value of each nation's currency. While one factor may increase the currency value, other factors decrease it. The constant push and pull among the factors cause the fluctuation in value.

Fluctuations in currency values can affect the finances of businesses that operate in more than one country. For example, a company may earn money in euros in France, but pay bills in dollars in the US. The company will find that it has less money to spend in the US if the value of the euro drops considerably. This is known as *currency risk.*

Current exchange rate: 1.3937 US dollars = 1 euro

1.3937 dollar-to-euro exchange rate × 250 euro = $348.425

250 euro is worth $348.43

Global Businesses

Many businesses operate on the world stage. A single business could have its headquarters in Boston, a manufacturing plant in Mexico, a data center in Sweden, and sales branches in London and Paris. Where should the company do its banking? Should it choose one bank in one location or one bank in each location? As companies grow and expand to other countries, they must choose the financial institutions that meet their banking needs.

Factor	Effect on Currency Value
Trade surplus	↑
Trade deficit	↓
Increased national debt	↓
Good credit history	↑
Political uncertainty	↓
Terrorism and war	↓
Political consistency	↑
Poor weather for agriculture	↓
Natural disasters	↓

Figure 17-2.
Factors Affecting Currency Values

Banking Needs of International Companies

As companies grow and become more sophisticated, they need banks that can keep up with them. As businesses become global, banks must become global as well. International companies may need multiple services from their bank:

- manage incoming payments for goods, including exported goods
- foreign currency exchange
- process *letters of credit,* which are binding documents a bank issues to guarantee payment when the goods are received
- Internet banking
- commercial lending
- asset management
- collection services
- expertise in local and global markets
- knowledge of local customs and businesses

Familiarity with the Export-Import Bank of the United States is also needed if the company exports goods. The **Export-Import Bank of the United States (Ex-Im Bank)** is an independent agency established by Congress to assist US businesses by financing the export of US products. The Ex-Im Bank supports US companies engaged in the overseas export of goods and services. It offers loans to US companies. It also provides guarantees that creditworthy foreign buyers will pay. In addition, it offers insurance to manage the risk that the goods will arrive at their intended destination. The Ex-Im Bank has partnered with the World Bank and various regional-development banks. It helped provide financing for projects with the potential to open markets to US exports.

The Overseas Private Investment Corporation (OPIC) was set up in 1971 as an independent agency of the US government. By facilitating private investment, OPIC seeks to increase US exports and advance foreign policy goals.

Banks That Provide Services to International Companies

Banks can be established in the US and expand to other countries. It can also happen the other way. A bank can be established in a foreign country and expand into the US. When a foreign bank opens a branch in the US, the branch must follow the banking regulations in both countries. This can become complicated. Banks must plan carefully before opening a branch in another country.

Source: Shutterstock (Rafael Ramirez Lee)

Many companies now do business all over the world.

Checkpoint 17.1

1. What is the name of the conference at which the World Bank components were created?
2. Why was IBRD created?
3. Name the five organizations that make up the World Bank Group.
4. How does war decrease the value of a nation's currency?
5. What is the purpose of the Export-Import Bank of the United States?

Build Your Vocabulary

As you progress through this course, develop a personal glossary of banking terms and add it to your portfolio. This will help you build your banking vocabulary. Write out a definition for each of the following terms, and add it to your personal glossary.

Bretton Woods Conference
International Bank for Reconstruction and Development (IBRD)
International Monetary Fund (IMF)
World Bank
international financial institution (IFI)
regional-development bank
multilateral-development bank
trade surplus
trade deficit
Export-Import Bank of the United States (Ex-Im Bank)

Section 17.2
E-Commerce

Terms

commerce
e-commerce
smart card
digital wallet
digital cash
mobile wallet
electronic check

Objectives

After completing this section, you will be able to:

- Define e-commerce.
- Identify the ways that customers can pay for products in an e-commerce transaction.

What Is E-Commerce?

Commerce is the exchange of products in a business transaction. **E-commerce** is the exchange of products in a business transaction using the Internet. For example, if you wander into a bookstore at the mall and buy a book, you are participating in commerce. If you buy the same book from the same bookstore through its website, you are participating in e-commerce.

Many transactions include elements of e-commerce. For example, if you used a credit card, charge card, or debit card to pay for the book in the bookstore, the cashier swiped your card through a card reader. The card reader uses an Internet connection to send your card's information to a company that processes the transaction. Even though you thought you were engaging in traditional commerce, it turned out that a bit of e-commerce was involved anyway.

Some retailers have only *brick-and-mortar stores,* which are physical locations that you can enter to see and touch the merchandise. Many businesses have both a physical store and an online store. An increasing number of businesses sell products only online. Operating a business that sells products without a brick-and-mortar store saves money for the retailer. The retailer does not have the expenses of a store location, such as building maintenance and rent.

Source: Shutterstock (AVAVA)

E-commerce is increasing as more retailers operate online-only stores.

Payment Options

In 2010, more than 80% of consumers shopped online at least once a week. In e-commerce, the seller and buyer usually do not meet in person. This means that the buyer cannot simply hand over the cash to pay for the purchase. Buyers pay for their purchases in a number of ways.

Credit Cards

Credit cards are open-ended loans issued by financial institutions. Credit card transactions are processed by the institution that issued the card. Merchants pay a fee for every credit card transaction.

BIZ TIPS

In Europe, the Single Euro Payments Area (SEPA) was set up by the European Payments Council. It established a uniform system of electronic payments throughout most of Europe.

Charge Cards

Charge cards are issued by financial institutions. The balance on charge cards must be paid in full every month. Charge card transactions are processed by the institution that issued the card. Merchants pay a fee for every charge card transaction.

Debit Cards

Debit cards are issued by financial institutions. Debit cards enable a customer to electronically access the funds in his or her account. Debit card transactions are processed by the institution that issued the card. Merchants pay a fee for every debit card transaction.

Smart Card

A **smart card** is a plastic card that has an embedded computer chip to store data. The card can carry a consumer's account and personal information. Interchange fees, which are discussed later in the chapter, are very low for smart cards.

Digital Wallet

A **digital wallet,** also known as an *electronic wallet,* is software on a buyer's computer that holds digital cash, files that confirm the digital wallet is valid, and information for billing and shipping. **Digital cash** is a form of currency that can be used online. The buyer transmits payment in the form of a digital certificate into the seller's account.

Source: Shutterstock (Supri Suharjoto)

Digital and mobile wallets store financial information for online payments.

Mobile Wallet

A **mobile wallet** is software on the buyer's mobile phone that holds digital cash, files that confirm the mobile wallet is valid, and information for billing and shipping. This is similar to a digital wallet, but the software is located in the mobile phone, rather than a computer.

Ethical Banking

Unethical individuals might set up a website, accept electronic payments, and then disappear without shipping products to the buyer. Before purchasing anything online, consumers should verify the seller. The Better Business Bureau evaluates sellers and informs consumers about sellers' trustworthiness.

Electronic Check

Electronic checks are the electronic version of paper checks. When a buyer presents a paper check to the seller, the seller runs the check through an electronic check scanner. The scanner captures the buyer's checking account information and the amount of the check. The information is electronically transferred to the Federal Reserve Bank. It takes the funds from the buyer's bank account and deposits them into the seller's bank account. Electronic-check-processing fees are lower than interchange fees and funds are transferred quickly, often on the same day.

Electronic payments are processed by the involved banks, credit card companies, and third-party payment-service providers. *Third-party payment-service providers* are independent companies that process payments for merchants. The fee charged to merchants varies.

Checkpoint 17.2

1. What is the difference between commerce and e-commerce?
2. What is a brick-and-mortar store?
3. What do credit, charge, and debit cards have in common?
4. How is information stored in a smart card?
5. What information does a mobile wallet contain?

Build Your Vocabulary

As you progress through this course, develop a personal glossary of banking terms and add it to your portfolio. This will help you build your banking vocabulary. Write out a definition for each of the following terms, and add it to your personal glossary.

commerce
e-commerce
smart card
digital wallet
digital cash
mobile wallet
electronic check

Section 17.3
Trends and Technology

Objectives

After completing this section, you will be able to:

- Describe the challenges faced by financial institutions.
- Identify trends in modern banking.
- Explain how technology has affected the banking industry.

Terms

hacker
firewall
smartphone
mobile banking
app
trend
social media
interchange fee

Challenges and Opportunities

Financial institutions face the same challenges of any business. In addition, financial institutions face challenges that are unique to the financial industry, including:

- keeping financial information secure;
- incorporating new technology for handling finances; and
- improving the public image of the financial industry.

Keeping Information Secure

Banks maintain a vast amount of information on computers. Much of this information is confidential. It includes customers' account details and the bank's internal business records. A thief can use or sell this confidential information, which can be used to steal a customer's funds or identity. The specific definition is debated, but one definition of a **hacker** is someone who has expertise in manipulating computer technologies. Not all hackers are malicious people out to cause harm or steal data or money. However, those who do are subject to criminal penalties. It has been estimated that hackers steal $1 billion dollars a year from banks. That is much more than the $43 million dollars stolen in 2010 by conventional robbers.

Hackers can also damage a bank's computer system by planting *computer viruses,* which are spread through file sharing and e-mail messages. These computer infections are known as computer viruses because they spread through computers like a cold or flu virus spreads through a group of people.

Banks can protect electronic information by maintaining a firewall. A **firewall** is computer hardware or software that provides security measures to prevent unauthorized access. A firewall is a basic way to protect a computer from unauthorized electronic access. Even your personal laptop has a firewall to protect it. Banks also hire experts in computers, networks, and software to protect the bank from hackers and develop software that helps the bank conduct its business.

Source: Shutterstock (Sergey Peterman)

Malicious computer hackers are subject to criminal penalties.

Careers in Finance
Banking and Related Services

What Does an Economist Do?

Economists study the economy and the factors that affect it. Among other things, these factors include interest rates, inflation, taxes, employment rates, and distribution of resources. **Economists** work in many different areas, including private businesses, financial institutions, and government organizations. Most **economists** also specialize in a particular area. Some of the activities performed by an **economist** include:

- gathering and analyzing data;
- monitoring legislation or competitors' markets and performing research on new issues;
- making recommendations to executives or policymakers based on research findings; and
- creating business forecasts or analyses based on data research.

What Is It Like to Work as an Economist?

Economists generally work a standard workweek in an office environment. They spend most of their time alone writing reports and charts. **Economists** also spend time in research teams, retrieving and analyzing data. Occasional travel to conferences or other events may be required. Patience and persistence are vital to this position, as **economists** spend a great deal of time studying data and problem solving.

If you enjoy detailed research and possess excellent writing skills, a career as an **economist** might suit you.

What Education and Skills Are Needed to Be an Economist?

- bachelor degree in economics; master degree preferred
- excellent analytical skills
- eye for detail

Career Ladder

Chief Financial Officer

Economist

Financial Analyst

Incorporating New Technology

In the past, customers physically went to the bank to do business. Automated teller machines (ATMs) were the first move toward computer-based interaction between banks and customers.

Today, anyone with Internet access can log on to a banking website. It is up to the bank to provide a secure platform for customers to perform financial transactions. This requires computer technology to conduct the transactions and protect those transactions from hackers. Users are responsible for security on their end of the transaction. For example, they should protect access to their passwords and computers.

Internet access is no longer limited to desktop or laptop computers. Smartphones can access the Internet, as well. A **smartphone** is a mobile device that not only acts as a cell phone, but also performs tasks such as:

- accessing the Internet;
- taking photos;
- sending e-mail messages; and
- running some software applications.

This technology has led to mobile banking. **Mobile banking** is the use of a smartphone or other mobile device to conduct financial transactions, including:

- checking an account's balance;
- making payments; and
- transferring funds.

Using a smartphone, customers can perform many banking transactions without going to the bank.

A bank can also create an app for customers to use. An **app** is a software application that runs on smartphones, tablets, and other mobile devices. The security and functionality of the app determines the security of the information and the transactions that can be performed using it.

BIZ TIPS

Chemical Bank opened the first ATM in the US at Rockville Center in New York on September 2, 1969. ATMs started becoming popular in the 1980s. By 2011, more than 1 million ATMs processed financial transactions all over the world.

Improving Public Image

A June 2011 report showed 36% of Americans had very little or no confidence in US banks. This distrust was caused by many factors. Many consumers experienced financial distress after the financial crises of the early 21st century. They had mortgage loans that they were not able to repay for houses that were not worth the money owed on the loan. Many blamed financial institutions for making loans that consumers were not able to repay. The bank bailout did not help the image problem banks faced. The bailout was not popular with many consumers.

Regaining consumers' trust and repairing the image of the banking system are big challenges. The impact is greater for large banks and major mortgage lenders than for smaller local banks. With less money to lend and close ties to their communities, local banks often made better lending choices. Still, the public image of the financial industry as a whole was affected by the recession, the burst of the housing bubble, and the bailout.

Source: Shutterstock (Sergey Skleznev)

Many banks have developed mobile banking apps.

Trends

A **trend** is a general movement or tendency. Trends are driven by consumer interests and business needs. The trend toward mobile banking was started by consumers' interest in using the new technology that became available with smartphones.

As banks create and expand their websites and move into mobile banking, the data transferred between banks and customers must be protected. Hackers and criminals who commit fraud are legitimate threats to banks and their customers. Protection from these threats is an important trend for bank departments focused on security and software development.

Use of social media for marketing is also a growing trend. **Social media** are forms of electronic communication used by groups of people to share information. Familiar types of social media include Twitter®, Facebook®, and YouTube™.

Changes in fee structures will also be a trend as banks try to maintain or improve their profits in the face of changing regulations. Banks charge merchants an **interchange fee,** also known as a *swipe fee,* every time a customer uses a debit card to pay for a purchase. The *Durbin Amendment* to the Dodd-Frank Wall Street Reform and Consumer Protection Act decreases by nearly half the interchange fee banks can charge merchants on debit card purchases.

The Durbin Amendment does not affect the interchange fee charged for credit card transactions. Interchange fees for credit card transactions are estimated to be $31 billion per year for the financial industry. The interchange fee for a credit card transaction is about 2% of the amount paid in the transaction. After the Durbin Amendment, banks will earn more in fees if the buyer uses a credit card rather than a debit card for any purchase that is more than $10.50.

Technology

Advances in technology have changed every aspect of modern business, including the financial industry. These advances have:

- increased the services a bank can offer;
- increased the number of customers that can be served;
- increased the amount of data that can be processed; and
- decreased the amount of time required to perform all of these tasks.

Increased Services

The ability of banks to provide a variety of services has received a boost from technology. Funds transfers, access to account information, and automated bill payments are among the services technology makes possible. Mobile banking has become increasingly popular and a service that customers expect banks to provide.

Increased Number of Customers Served

In the past, a bank could serve only the customers who waited in line for a teller's assistance. Today, a bank can serve customers who:

- wait in line at a bank;
- use ATMs;
- access the bank's website via a computer; and
- access the bank's website via a smartphone.

This has vastly increased the number of customers a bank can serve. Additional ways of interacting with a bank account allow banks to serve more customers.

Source: Shutterstock (Noam Armonn)

Technology has increased the services banks can provide.

Increased Amount of Data Processed

Banks maintain data about every customer and every transaction. Some data are simply stored, but much of it is processed in some way. Deposits are added to account totals and withdrawals are subtracted. Every transaction causes additional calculations. Thanks to computers, all of these data can be maintained and processed at a speed bankers could not have imagined before computers became business tools.

Decreased Amount of Time Required

All of these increases in technology have resulted in more and more work—for the computers. Even though banks process thousands of transactions every day, the number of employees needed to process the data has not increased at the same pace. However, the skills that banks look for in employees have changed to include computer literacy.

Checkpoint 17.3

1. How much money do hackers steal from banks in a year?
2. Name three financial transactions that can be completed on a smartphone.
3. What was the main provision of the Durbin Amendment?
4. How has technology increased the number of customers that can be served?
5. As the importance of technology has increased, how have the skills required of bank employees changed?

Build Your Vocabulary

As you progress through this course, develop a personal glossary of banking terms and add it to your portfolio. This will help you build your banking vocabulary. Write out a definition for each of the following terms, and add it to your personal glossary.

hacker
firewall
smartphone
mobile banking
app
trend
social media
interchange fee

Chapter Summary

Section 17.1 International Banking

- The World Bank and the World Bank Group work to improve conditions for all people by providing advice and information as well as financing projects that make real improvements.
- Multilateral-development banks, which include Bretton Woods institutions and regional-development banks, provide financing and advice to developing nations to help them grow and develop.
- The constant fluctuation of currency values is caused by the interaction of many factors.
- Global businesses require banks that offer international services.

Section 17.2 E-Commerce

- E-commerce is the exchange of products in a business transaction using the Internet.
- Electronic payment methods are used in e-commerce.

Section 17.3 Trends and Technology

- Financial institutions face the challenges of keeping information secure, incorporating new technology, and improving the public image of the financial industry.
- Banking trends include mobile banking, the use of social media, and changes in fee structures.
- Advances in technology have increased the services a bank can provide, the number of customers that can be served, and the amount of data that can be processed, while it has decreased the amount of time required to complete tasks.

Check Your Banking IQ

Now that you have finished this chapter, see what you know about banking by taking the chapter post test.

www.m.g-wlearning.com
www.g-wlearning.com

Review Your Knowledge

On a separate sheet of paper or in a word processing document, match the following terms with the definition that fits best.

A. mobile wallet
B. digital cash
C. commerce
D. Bretton Woods Conference
E. World Bank
F. multilateral-development bank
G. trade deficit
H. firewall
I. social media
J. interchange fee

1. Institutions that provide financing and advice to developing nations to encourage economic and financial growth.
2. Form of currency that can be used online.
3. Occurs when a country imports more than it exports.
4. Charged every time a customer uses a debit card to pay for a purchase.
5. Software on the buyer's mobile phone that holds digital cash, files that confirm its validity, and information for billing and shipping.
6. Established the International Bank for Reconstruction and Development and the International Monetary Fund.
7. International organization that continues to work toward the goals established at the Bretton Woods Conference.
8. Forms of electronic communication used by groups of people to share information.
9. Exchange of products in a business transaction.
10. Computer hardware or software that provides security measures to prevent unauthorized access.

On a separate sheet of paper or in a word processing document, answer each of the following questions.

11. How does the World Bank support its goals?
12. Why can it be complicated for a foreign bank to open a branch in the United States?
13. How are elements of e-commerce involved in most traditional transactions?
14. Who is responsible for security on a bank's website?
15. Why did many consumers lose confidence in US banks during the early 21st century?

Apply Your Knowledge

16. Visit the World Bank Group's website (www.worldbank.org). What are some of their current and past projects? How do these contribute to the overall mission of the World Bank Group? Write a report on your findings.
17. Research the international banking services provided by a national bank. Write a summary of your findings, including the services provided and the advantages and disadvantages of international banking.
18. Using the Internet, research the credit card reader app. What does this app do? What are some of the costs and benefits associated with using it? How does this product change your ideas about modern payment systems? Write a report detailing your stance on these issues.
19. Perform an Internet search for *bank hack.* What are some recent banking hacks? Write a short presentation on a recent bank hack and present it to your classmates.
20. Identify four products that can be sold, delivered, and used by electronic means alone. Compare your list to your classmates' lists.

Working in Teams

In small groups, research one of the four regional-development banks. What projects is this organization involved in? What kinds of services do they provide? Where do they operate? Create a presentation on this bank, and present it to the class.

G-W Learning Mobile Site

Visit the G-W Learning mobile site to complete the chapter pretest and post test and to practice vocabulary using e-flash cards. If you do not have a smartphone, visit the G-W Learning companion website to access these features.

G-W Learning mobile site: www.m.g-wlearning.com
G-W Learning companion website: www.g-wlearning.com

Common Core

College and Career Readiness

Writing. Create a classroom blog about the future of banking. Write a post about what you think will be most important to the financial industry in the future. Be sure to read and publish your comments to at least five of your classmates' posts.

Reading. Using the Internet, find an article about the future of banking. Write a summary evaluating the author's conclusions and supporting arguments. Be sure to consider his or her point of view, voice, and structure. Does the structure of the article make the argument clear, convincing, and engaging? How does this article compare to what you have already learned about the future of banking?

EVENT PREP

Day of the Event

You have practiced all year for this career and technical student organization (CTSO) competitive event, and now you are ready. Whether it is an objective test, written test, report, or presentation, you have done your homework and are ready to shine. To prepare for the day of the event:

1. At least two weeks before you go to the competition, create a checklist of what you need for the event. Include every detail down to a pencil or pen. Then, use this checklist before you go into the presentation so that you do not forget anything.
2. If you are making a presentation before a panel of judges, practice what you are going to say when you are called on. State your name, your school, and any other information that has been requested. Be confident, smile, and make eye contact with the judges.
3. When the event is finished, thank the judges for their time.
4. Be sure to get plenty of rest the night before the event so that you are rested and ready to go.

Unit 5 Summative Assessment

On a separate sheet of paper or in a word processing document, use what you have learned in this unit to answer the questions that follow.

True/False Questions

1. *True or False?* The Garn-St. Germain Act and DIDMCA were two deregulation laws passed in the 1980s.
2. *True or False?* Interchange fees for smart cards are very low.
3. *True or False?* Sovereign debt was safe for lenders in the Middle Ages.
4. *True or False?* The Emergency Economic Stabilization Act is also referred to as the *stimulus bill.*
5. *True or False?* TARP funds issued to banks and other institutions did not need to be repaid.

Multiple Choice Questions

6. _____ is the pooling and packaging of loans to create securities.
   A. Subprime lending
   B. A derivative
   C. Securitization
   D. A collateralized debt obligation
7. _____ is *not* an example of commodity money.
   A. A bank note
   B. Rice
   C. A tobacco leaf
   D. Wampum
8. The _____ decreased by nearly half the interchange fee banks can charge merchants on debit card purchases.
   A. Bretton Woods Conference
   B. Export-Import Bank of the United States
   C. World Bank
   D. Durbin Amendment
9. The Bretton Woods Conference established _____.
   A. the International Bank for Reconstruction and Development
   B. the International Monetary Fund
   C. the World Bank
   D. All of the above.
10. Which of the following was *not* a cause of the Great Depression?
    A. Harmful foreign trade policies.
    B. Increased demand for consumer goods.
    C. The stock market crash of 1929.
    D. Widespread bank failures.

Law Glossary

The number in parentheses indicates the chapter or chapters in which the law appears.

A

American Recovery and Reinvestment Act: Often called the *stimulus bill.* Designed to help the economy get back on its feet and help average Americans after the Great Recession; passed in 2009. (16)

Americans with Disabilities Act (ADA): Required all buildings that welcome the public to meet accessibility standards. (11)

B

bank bailout bill: See *Emergency Economic Stabilization Act* and *Troubled Asset Relief Program (TARP).* (15, 16, 17)

Bank Holding Company Acts of 1956 and 1970: Allowed banks to do business through holding companies that would have otherwise been banned. (6, 11)

Bank Protection Act of 1968: Required financial institutions to install and maintain security devices. (14)

Bank Secrecy Act: Required banks to report suspicious customer activities that might signify criminal activities. (6)

C

Check 21: Also known as the *Check Clearing Act for the 21st Century.* Enabled the creation of image replacement documents, which led to faster check processing; enacted in 2004. (9)

Check Clearing Act for the 21st Century: See *Check 21.* (9)

Community Reinvestment Act: Prevented redlining by requiring that banks and other depository institutions show that they are serving the credit needs of all people in their market area; passed in 1977. (6, 8)

Consumer Credit Protection Act: See *Truth in Lending Act (TILA).* (6)

Credit CARD Act: Protected consumers from unfair and deceptive credit card practices and gave cardholders additional rights; enacted in 2009. (3, 6)

D

Depository Institutions Deregulation and Monetary Control Act (DIDMCA): Removed many of the regulations passed during the Great Depression and allowed depository institutions to make more types of loans and investments; enacted in 1980. (6, 15)

Dodd-Frank Wall Street Reform and Consumer Protection Act: Increased regulation of the banking and financial services industry and created the Consumer Financial Protection Bureau; passed in 2010. (3, 6, 15, 16, 17)

Durbin Amendment: Amendment to the Dodd-Frank Wall Street Reform and Consumer Protection Act. Decreased by nearly half the interchange fee banks can charge merchants on debit card purchases. (17)

E

Electronic Funds Transfer Act: Established the rights and liabilities of consumers as well as the responsibilities of all participants in EFT activities in the US; passed in 1978. (1)

Emergency Banking Act of 1933: See *Glass-Steagall Act.* (6, 15)

Emergency Economic Stabilization Act: Often called the *bank bailout bill.* Helped the economy recover from the Great Recession by saving financial institutions and creating the Troubled Asset Relief Program; passed in 2008. (15, 16)

Equal Credit Opportunity Act (ECOA): Required all lenders to make credit decisions based solely on credit qualifications; passed in 1974. (6, 8)

Expedited Funds Availability Act (EFAA): Led to rules that allowed quicker access to funds deposited as checks; enacted in 1987. (9)

F

Fair Credit and Charge Card Disclosure Act: An amendment to the Truth in Lending Act that requires direct mail or telephone offers for credit cards to include specific information regarding fees. (6)

Fair Credit Billing Act (FCBA): Protected consumers from unfair billing practices and provided a way to correct billing errors; enacted in 1974. (6)

Fair Credit Reporting Act (FCRA): Required that credit bureaus collect and distribute information in a fair and legal manner and provided processes for correcting credit report errors; enacted in 1971. (6, 8)

Fair Debt Collection Practices Act (FDCPA): Protected consumers against creditors who tried to use unfair techniques to force consumers to pay their past-due credit; amended in 2006. (8, 12)

fair use doctrine: Allowed for the use of copyrighted material in teaching, news reporting, editorial commentary, and other similar situations, provided the copyrighted work is not claimed as your own. (14)

Federal Depository Insurance Corporation Improvement Act (FDICIA): Provided additional funding to the FDIC; passed in 1991. (6)

Federal Reserve Act: Established the Federal Reserve System; passed in 1913. (5, 9, 15)

Financial Institutions Reform, Recovery, and Enforcement Act (FIRREA): Commonly known as the *S & L bailout bill.* Strengthened banks and savings associations, and cleaned up the large number of failed institutions. (6)

Financial Services Modernization Act: See *Gramm-Leach-Bliley Act.* (6)

Fraud Enforcement and Recovery Act: Created the Financial Crisis Inquiry Commission to determine what caused the financial crises of the early 21st century; passed in 2009. (16)

G

Garn-St. Germain Act: Reduced bank regulations further and made it easier to save failing banks and savings associations; enacted in 1982. (6, 15)

Glass-Steagall Act: Also known as the *Emergency Banking Act of 1933.* Established the FDIC, introduced banking reforms, separated investment banking from commercial banking, and established an interest rate ceiling. (2, 3, 6, 15)

Gramm-Leach-Bliley Act: Also known as the *Financial Services Modernization Act.* Repealed several key provisions of the Glass-Steagall Act and allowed banks to engage in almost any financial activity; passed in 1999. (2, 3, 6)

H

Home Mortgage Disclosure Act (HMDA): Required most mortgage-lending institutions to report data related to mortgage loans to allow for greater transparency in lending. (6, 8)

Home Ownership and Equity Protection Act (HOEPA): For high-interest loans, it required that lenders verify borrowers' assets and determine if they are capable of repaying the loan; passed in 1994. (8)

Homeowner's Protection Act of 1998: Required lenders to tell borrowers when they no longer have to pay PMI on mortgages for homes the borrowers live in. (8)

I

Interstate Banking Act: Also known as the *Riegle-Neal Interstate Banking and Branching Efficiency Act.* Eliminated most restrictions on interstate bank branching, effectively overriding the McFadden Act; passed in 1997. (6)

M

McCulloch v. Maryland: Case in which the US Supreme Court ruled that the creation of a central bank was within the power of Congress; decided in 1819. (5)

McFadden Act: Gave individual states the right to set their own rules regarding out-of-state banks coming into the state; enacted in 1927. (6)

N

National Banking Acts of 1863 and 1864: Modified the National Currency Act, allowed the federal government to charter private banks, and created a uniform national currency. (5, 15)

National Currency Act: Created the Office of the Comptroller of the Currency; enacted in 1863. (5)

O

Occupational Safety and Health Act (OSHA): Established the Occupational Safety and Health Administration to enforce safety and health regulations in the workplace; passed in 1970. (14)

P

Patient Protection and Affordable Care Act: Required companies with 50 or more employees to offer a health-insurance-benefit plan; passed in 2010. (10)

R

Real Estate Settlement Procedures Act (RESPA): Required lenders to provide borrowers with a good faith estimate of all costs related to mortgage and closing costs; passed in 1974. (8)

Riegle-Neal Interstate Banking and Branching Efficiency Act: See *Interstate Banking Act.* (6)

S

Sarbanes-Oxley Act (SOX): Ensured accurate disclosure of a company's financial information by mandating greater transparency and accountability; enacted in 2002. (6, 13)

Second Liberty Act of 1917: Established the first debt-ceiling limit. (16)

S & L bailout bill: See *Financial Institutions Reform, Recovery, and Enforcement Act (FIRREA).* (6)

stimulus bill: See *American Recovery and Reinvestment Act.* (16)

T

Taxpayer Relief Act of 1997: Reduced tax rates, provided tax credits for all taxpayers, and established the Roth IRA. (7)

Troubled Asset Relief Program (TARP): Often called the *bank bailout bill.* Allowed the federal government to purchase assets and equity from financial institutions in order to strengthen them and prevent more failures; passed in 2008. (15, 16)

Truth in Lending Act (TILA): Also Title I of the *Consumer Credit Protection Act.* Required that all terms of and costs related to a loan must be provided to the consumer in writing; passed in 1968. (4, 6, 8)

U

Uniform Commercial Code: Established to bring uniformity to banking and lending transactions across the US; passed in 1952. (9)

USA Patriot Act of 2001: Required banks to report suspicious customer activities that might signify criminal activities. (6)

Glossary

The number in parentheses indicates the chapter or chapters in which the term appears.

401(k) plan: A retirement savings plan that enables employees to make tax-deferred or taxed contributions through payroll deductions. (7)

A

ABA routing number: A nine-digit number assigned by the American Bankers Association (ABA) to identify the financial institution responsible for paying the value of a check to the payee. (9)

abstractor: See *title researcher.* (12)

accountant: A bank employee who is responsible for creating and maintaining accurate financial records for the bank, including transactions, paying taxes and fees, and maintaining required public records. (12)

account holder: Anyone authorized to perform transactions in an account. (7)

accounting manager: A bank employee who is responsible for the functions of the accountants and auditors in the bank. (12)

account inquiry fee: A fee charged to check an account balance at an ATM. (3)

accrued interest: The amount added to the principal at regular time periods. (7)

acquisition: Occurs when one company buys another company and sets itself up as the new owner. (3)

adjustable-rate mortgage (ARM): A mortgage loan in which the interest rate may change over the life of the loan. (8)

adjusted balance method: A way to calculate finance charges by using the balance from the previous month and subtracting payments made during the current period. (8)

advertising: Calling attention to a product or service, commonly through the use of paid advertisements. (11)

aggregates: The different measures that are compiled from a collection of data sources by which the money supply is measured. (4)

annual percentage rate (APR): The actual annual interest rate paid over the life of a loan. (6, 8)

annual percentage yield (APY): The rate of return on an investment for a one-year period. (7)

app: Computer software program loaded onto a smartphone, tablet, or other mobile device that allows the user to perform specific tasks. (1, 17)

asset: Something owned by an individual or other entity. (3, 13)

asset quality: The credit risk associated with the loans and investments held by a bank. (13)

auditor: A bank employee who verifies the bank's processes and procedures, checking for errors, mismanagement, and fraud. (12)

authority: The power to affect or direct a situation or a worker's behavior. (10)

automated clearinghouse (ACH): Electronic network for financial transactions that processes credit and debit transactions, processes checks, and transfers funds between banks. (1, 9)

automated teller machine (ATM): A computerized machine that provides a means of self-service banking; allows a customer to perform basic banking activities, such as withdrawing cash, viewing account balances, initiating cash advances, and making deposits. (1, 9)

automatic payment: Preauthorized electronic funds sent from a customer's account to a vendor's account at regular intervals. (9)

average daily balance method: A way to calculate finance charges by using the card's beginning daily balance. (8)

B

bait money: Money that carries serial numbers that have been recorded by the bank. (14)

balance sheet: A document that reports a company's assets, liabilities, and stockholders' equity. (13)

bandit barrier: A bullet-resistant, acrylic barrier at a teller window that protects a teller from a robber's physical contact or weapon. (14)

bank: A type of financial institution. (1)

bank fraud: A scheme intended to steal money or valuables under the control of a financial institution. (14)

bank holding company: A company that owns a number of banks and allows them to set up branch locations. (15)

bank holiday: Four days in 1933 in which all banks were closed to allow time for creating a plan to reopen them. (15)

bank note: Intended to be used as currency, promised immediate payment by the bank that issued the note and backed by a government bond. (5)

bank of deposit: The first type of depository institution. (15)

Bank of North America: The first commercial fractional-reserve bank in the US, which was founded in 1781 to finance the Revolutionary War. (15)

bank panic: Widespread worry that banks do not have enough money to cover customer demands for withdrawals. (5)

bank run: Occurs when a large number of depositors withdraw all of their money from a bank at the same time due to fear that their money is unsafe. (5, 6)

banker's blanket bond: A type of insurance that covers a bank from losses due to robbery or theft. (1)

bankruptcy: A legal procedure that enables individuals or companies to eliminate or repay some or all debt under the guidance of federal bankruptcy courts. (8)

barter: The exchange of one good or service for another good or service. (4)

bearer instrument: A negotiable instrument that is payable on demand to whoever has it. (9)

beneficiary: The individual who receives financial protection from an insurance policy. (3)

benefits: Services, privileges, or rights that an employer provides in addition to the employee's wages or salary. (7, 10)

bill and account collector: A bank employee who is responsible for getting customers to make overdue payments. (12)

bill of exchange: A negotiable instrument that contains an unconditional order to pay a specific amount of money to the payee on a future date; often used in international trade. (9, 15)

bill-payment service: Electronic transfer of funds from a customer's account to a vendor's account that is requested by the customer or the vendor each time a payment is due. (9)

blank endorsement: The payee's signature. (9)

board of directors: A group of individuals elected by a bank's shareholders to represent the shareholders and guide the bank's policies and business decisions. (10)

Board of Governors (BOG): The governing body of the Federal Reserve System. (5)

bond: Represents money a government or company has borrowed from the bondholder. (2, 5)

branching: Opening banking facilities away from a bank's home office. (6)

branch manager: A bank employee who oversees the day-to-day activities of one branch of the bank; also called an *operations manager.* (12)

branch office: A banking facility that is not the bank's main location. (10)

Bretton Woods Conference: Held in 1944 to establish two organizations: the International Bank for Reconstruction and Development and the International Monetary Fund, which together form the World Bank. (17)

business finance company: Provides loans for businesses, such as retail stores. (2)

business-recovery plan (BRP): A written document that shows how a business will return to its pre-disaster condition. (14)

C

CAMELS: An international bank-rating system used by the US to evaluate the overall financial condition of banks and other financial institutions. (13)

cancelled check: A check that has been cleared. (9)

cap: The maximum increase that can be applied to a monthly loan payment, or the maximum interest rate increase when the rate is adjusted. (8)

capacity: A loan applicant's ability to pay debts as shown by cash flow. (8)

capital: A loan applicant's money, property, and other valuables. (8)

capital ratio: How much capital the bank has relative to its assets; the most common way capital adequacy is measured. (13)

captive finance company: Formed by a manufacturer to provide loans so the manufacturer can easily sell its goods. (2)

career path: A series of jobs with increased responsibility within a specific career. (10)

cash card: A plastic card with a magnetic strip that can be read by an ATM. (9)

cash drawer: A drawer with separate compartments for different denominations of coins and bills. (10)

central bank: A financial institution that oversees a nation's monetary system by regulating banks, lending money when commercial banks are not able to, and controlling the money supply. (1, 5)

certificate of deposit (CD): A savings account that requires a specific amount of money be held on deposit for a specific amount of time; also called a *time deposit* or *fixed deposit.* (7)

Certified Bank Teller (CBT): A certification available to tellers from the Institute of Certified Bank Tellers that is earned by demonstrating expertise on a standardized examination. (12)

character: A loan applicant's honesty and integrity as shown by how he or she handles debt. (8)

charter: A legal document issued by a federal and a state government that details how a bank is to be operated and how it will be regulated. (1)

check: A written order directing a bank to pay a specific amount from deposited funds. (9)

check fraud: The illegal use of a check to take or use funds that do not belong to the individual who signs the check. (14)

chief executive officer (CEO): A bank executive who is appointed by a corporate board of directors and is accountable to the corporation's stockholders, the public it serves, and legal authorities for the actions of the bank. (12)

chief financial officer (CFO): A bank executive responsible for financial planning, control, and record keeping for the bank. (12)

chief information officer (CIO): A bank executive involved in the technology the bank currently uses and responsible for solving issues with implementing new technology. (12)

chief operating officer (COO): A bank executive responsible for the bank's daily operations and performance. (12)

chief technology officer (CTO): A bank executive responsible for developing new technology for use by the bank. (12)

clearing: The process of approving a check and transferring funds from one account to another. (9)

closed-end loan: A loan that must be paid in full on a specific date. (8)

closing costs: Several fees that are applied when a mortgage is signed. (8)

coincidence of wants: Occurs when two people each want what the other has to offer. (4)

collateral: A borrower's property that is pledged to secure a loan. (8)

collateralized debt obligation (CDO): Divides returns into tranches, or segments. (16)

collection: The transfer of past-due loans to a bank department or outside agency that attempts to gather full or partial repayment of the loan. (10)

commerce: The exchange of products in a business transaction. (17)

commercial bank: A financial institution owned by investors that focuses on business customers, providing bank accounts along with specialized services such as foreign exchange, investment services, and capital loans; some also provide limited customer-oriented services, such as personal checking and savings accounts. (1, 2)

commercial loan: A loan made when a company borrows money. (8)

commission: A fee, such as the kind charged by a stockbroker for placing an order. (2)

commodity: Anything that is useful or has value. (4)

commodity money: Something of perceived value used as payment for something else of perceived value. (4, 15)

communication: The exchange of ideas, thoughts, and information. (12)

Community Reinvestment Act: Prevented redlining by requiring that banks and other depository institutions show that they are serving the credit needs of all people in their market area; passed in 1977. (6)

compensation: Wages and financial benefits earned by working. (7)

compliance: The process of following laws and regulations. (10)

compliance officer: A bank employee who ensures the bank follows all state and federal laws and regulation, and implements strategies for compliance and reporting. (12)

compound interest: Interest paid on interest. (7)

conditions: The overall environment in which a loan will be given. (8)

Consumer Credit Protection Act: See *Truth in Lending Act (TILA).* (6)

consumer debt: Money owed by individuals for the purchase of personal goods and services. (16)

consumer finance company: Provides high-interest personal loans to individuals who have poor credit. (2)

Consumer Financial Protection Bureau (CFPB): An independent consumer-protection organization that was created to protect the interests of consumers by making sure federal consumer-protection laws are enforced; it has the authority to ensure consumers get clear information about loans, mortgages, credit cards, and other financial products and is also charged with ending deceptive practices in lending. (6, 16)

consumer loan: A loan made when an individual borrows money for his or her use. (8)

continental: A type of note intended to be exchanged later for coins. (15)

contribution: An IRA deposit. (7)

cooperative: A business or organization that is owned by its members who cooperate to run the organization. (2)

copyright: The exclusive right to copy, license, sell, or distribute material. (14)

cosigner: An individual who signs a loan along with the borrower, taking on equal liability for repayment. (8)

counterfeit: A copy of something represented as the real thing. (4)

credit analyst: A bank employee who looks at the creditworthiness of loan applicants. (12)

credit bureau: A company that gathers, analyzes, and summarizes credit-related information on consumers. (8)

Credit CARD Act: Protected consumers from unfair and deceptive credit card practices and gave cardholders additional rights; enacted in 2009. (3, 6)

credit counselor: See *debt counselor.* (12)

credit risk: The possibility that a borrower will not repay a loan. (13)

credit score: A measure of risk based on a borrower's credit history. (8)

credit union: A financial institution that provides many of the same services as banks and S & Ls, but owned by its members and run on a nonprofit basis. (2)

creditworthiness: An assessment of a borrower's ability to repay a loan. (8)

cross-selling: A marketing strategy that encourages existing customers to buy new products or services based on their previous purchases. (11)

custodial account: A savings account managed by an adult for a minor. (7)

customer: An individual, organization, or business that purchases a product or service. (11)

customer service: The handling of all interactions between a customer and a bank. (11)

customer service representative (CSR): A bank employee who is a link between the customer and the bank and assists the customer in resolving issues. (12)

D

data processor: A bank employee who deals with the management of digital information. (12)

debit card: A card that enables customers to electronically access the funds in their accounts at an ATM or to pay for goods and services in stores or online. (1, 9)

debt ceiling: The limit on the level of debt the government can take on. (16)

debt counselor: A bank employee who provides advice to a client on how to manage and reduce debt; also called a *credit counselor*. (12)

debt ratio: A comparison of debt to income or assets, the most common of which are the debt-to-income ratio, the debt-service-coverage ratio, and the loan-to-value ratio. (8)

decentralization: Occurs when a central authority shares power with regional and local authorities. (5)

default: Occurs when a borrower fails to meet the terms of a loan agreement. (8, 16)

defined benefit plan: A retirement savings plan with a fixed amount of money that is provided to retired employees and is determined by qualifications, not company profit. (7)

defined contribution plan: A retirement savings plan with a fixed maximum amount that can be contributed each year. (7)

denomination: The unit in which money is available. (4)

department: A group created when several employees in a business are working on a specialized task. (10)

deposit: Money placed or transferred into a bank account. (2, 7)

deposit insurance: Insurance that covers the deposits of customers in the case of a bank failure. (2)

deposit insurance fund (DIF): Arranges for depositors to maintain their insured funds in the case of bank failure. Depository institutions pay premiums to this fund in order to pool their money and share risk. (2)

depositor: A customer who makes a deposit. (2)

depository institution: A type of financial institution at which customers deposit money in order to withdraw it later. (1)

Depository Institutions Deregulation and Monetary Control Act (DIDMCA): Removed many of the regulations passed during the Great Depression and allowed depository institutions to make more types of loans and investments; enacted in 1980. (6)

deposit slip: A form that an account holder fills out when making a deposit that is a record of deposit information. (7)

deregulation: Occurs when some or all regulations are abolished or overridden and governmental control is lessened. (6, 15)

derivative: A contract designed to manage risk and make money. (2, 16)

deterrent: Something that discourages an action. (14)

digital cash: A form of currency that can be used online. (17)

digital wallet: Software on a buyer's computer that holds digital cash, files that confirm the digital wallet is valid, and information for billing and shipping; also known as an electronic wallet. (17)

direct deposit: Funds that are added directly into a bank account by electronic means instead of with a negotiable instrument. (9)

discount broker: Stockbroker who places orders for customers at commissions lower than full-service brokers and may offer only limited services. (2)

discount rate: The interest banks pay to borrow money from the Federal Reserve Bank. (5)

distribution: An IRA withdrawal. (7)

dividend: A payment. (2)

divisibility: The ability to be broken into smaller units. (4)

Dodd-Frank Wall Street Reform and Consumer Protection Act: Increased regulation of the banking and financial services industry, established actions to prevent another financial crisis, and created the Consumer Financial Protection Bureau; more transparency is now required of banks and other financial firms; passed in 2010. (15, 16)

double-dip recession: Occurs when a recovering economy goes into negative growth a second time. (16)

draft: A negotiable instrument that orders a payment to be made. (9)

drawee: The party who pays the value of the negotiable instrument to the payee; often, this is the bank. (9)

drawer: The entity who signs the negotiable instrument to validate it; also known as the *maker*. (9)

dual banking system: Both state and federal governments pass and enforce bank laws. (6)

dye pack: A radio-controlled device that, when set off, marks stolen cash with permanent dye. (14)

E

e-commerce: The exchange of products in a business transaction using the Internet. (17)

e-compliance: Managing risks associated with electronic banking. (6)

electronic check: The electronic version of paper checks. (17)

electronic funds transfer (EFT): Any exchange of money from one account to another through computer-based systems that is started by electronic means. (1, 9)

embezzlement: The act of illegally taking funds or property entrusted to you. (14)

Emergency Banking Act of 1933: See *Glass-Steagall Act*. (15)

Emergency Economic Stabilization Act: Helped the economy recover from the Great Recession by saving financial institutions and creating the Troubled Asset Relief Program; passed in 2008. (15)

employment agency: A private or government agency that matches an employer's available jobs to workers who have the needed skills, education, and experience. (10)

endorsement: The signature used to legally transfer the value of a check. (9)

Equal Credit Opportunity Act (ECOA): Required all lenders to make credit decisions based solely on credit qualifications; use of gender, marital status, race, religion, age, national origin, or whether an individual receives public assistance benefits to determine whether that individual should get a loan is illegal; passed in 1974. (6)

equity: The difference between real estate's value and the amount owed for the real estate; equity belongs to the owner. (8)

equity loan: A loan that temporarily transfers cash to the borrower and is secured by the owner's equity; sometimes referred to as a second mortgage. (8)

era of free banking: The period from 1837 to 1863 during which all bank functions in the US were handled by state banks, and federal funds were held in the US Treasury. (5)

ergonomics: The science of adapting the workstation to fit the needs of the worker and lessen the chance of injury. (12, 14)

estate: The property and possessions of an individual, which may include property, cars, money, or other assets. (3)

estate planning: Preparing for the transfer of assets after a client's death. (3)

ethics: The basic concepts and principles of moral behavior. (14)

event-based selling: A marketing strategy that encourages bank representatives to contact a customer when an event occurs. (11)

examiner: See *title researcher*. (12)

excess capital: The difference between how much money a company needs to run its operations and how much it takes in. (16)

excess reserve: The funds available for a bank to loan out after its reserve is met. (4)

executive: A manager who has the responsibility and authority to make decisions about the bank and how it conducts its business. (10)

Export-Import Bank of the United States (Ex-Im Bank): An independent federal agency established in 1934 to assist US businesses by financing the export of US products, supporting US companies engaged in the overseas export of goods and services, offering loans to US companies, providing guarantees that creditworthy foreign buyers will pay, and offering insurance on exported goods. (8, 17)

F

Fair Credit Billing Act (FCBA): Protected consumers from unfair billing practices and provided a way to correct billing errors; enacted in 1974. (6)

Fair Credit Reporting Act (FCRA): Required that credit bureaus collect and distribute information in a fair and legal manner and provided processes for correcting credit report errors; enacted in 1971. (6)

falling hazard: A source of potential injury from slipping or falling. (14)

Farm Service Agency (FSA): Part of the US Department of Agriculture that provides financial and logistical support to commercial farms, often in the form of loans or guarantees. (8)

Fed: See *Federal Reserve System.* (5)

Federal Deposit Insurance Corporation (FDIC): An independent federal agency established in 1933 that provides deposit insurance up to $250,000 for depositors in insured banks and thrifts in the case of bank failure. (1, 2, 15)

Federal Depository Insurance Corporation Improvement Act (FDICIA): Provided additional funding to the FDIC; passed in 1991. (6)

Federal Home Loan Bank Board: A federal regulator agency that chartered and examined savings associations. (6)

Federal Open Market Committee (FOMC): The body of the Federal Reserve System responsible for making monetary policy. (5)

Federal Reserve Act: Established the Federal Reserve System; passed in 1913. (15)

Federal Reserve Bank: One of the twelve regional branches of the Federal Reserve System that were created to avoid establishing a central bank in a single location. (5)

Federal Reserve System: The central bank for the US that is responsible for the country's monetary system. Also known as the *Fed.* (5)

fiat money: Money that has value because the government says it has value. (4, 15)

FICO score: A credit rating used by lenders to predict an applicant's ability and willingness to repay loans. (8)

finance charge: The total dollar amount of interest and any other fees paid on the loan. (6, 8)

finance company: Issues loans to both individuals and businesses in order to make a profit, also known as a loan company. (2)

Financial Crisis Inquiry Commission: Created in 2009 by the Fraud Enforcement and Recovery Act to determine what caused the financial crises of the early 21st century. (16)

financial institution: Any organization or business that provides services related to money. (1, 2)

Financial Institutions Reform, Recovery, and Enforcement Act (FIRREA): Commonly known as the S & L bailout bill; strengthened banks and savings associations and cleaned up the large number of failed institutions. (6)

financial intermediary: An institution that acts as a go-between in financial transactions. (1)

firewall: Computer hardware or software that provides security measures to prevent unauthorized access. (17)

fixed deposit: See *certificate of deposit (CD).* (7)

fixed-rate mortgage: A mortgage loan in which the interest rate stays the same for the entirety of the loan's term. (8)

foreclosure: The legal process of ending an owner's right to a property and transferring it to the lender. (10, 16)

fractional-reserve banking: The practice of keeping only a portion, or fraction, of deposits in the bank. (15)

fractional reserve system: A system that requires banks and other depository institutions to keep a fraction of their deposits in reserves. (4)

freeware: Fully functional software that can be used forever without purchasing it. (14)

full-service brokerage firm: Advises customers on which securities to buy and helps manage investments. (2)

G

gain: An increase in income that occurs when a bank sells a security for more than its purchase price. (3)

garnishment: Withholding all or part of a borrower's salary to pay an outstanding debt. (10)

Garn-St. Germain Act: Reduced bank regulations further and made it easier to save failing banks and savings associations; enacted in 1982. (6)

Glass-Steagall Act: Also known as the *Emergency Banking Act of 1933.* Established the FDIC, introduced banking reforms, separated investment banking from commercial banking, and established an interest rate ceiling. (6)

gold-exchange standard: Allowed foreign governments, but not individuals, to redeem US dollars for gold. (4)

goldsmith: An artisan who makes items out of gold and other precious metals. (15)

gold standard: A system that determines how much gold each paper note represents. (4)

government-sponsored enterprise (GSE): An organization that is chartered and supported by the government to promote a public interest. (8)

Gramm-Leach-Bliley Act: Also known as the Financial Services Modernization Act; repealed several key provisions of the Glass-Steagall Act and allowed banks to engage in almost any financial activity; passed in 1999. (6)

Great Recession: The period of time during which the US most acutely felt the effects of the financial crises of the early 21st century. (16)

H

hacker: A person who has expertise in manipulating computer technologies. (17)

Home Mortgage Disclosure Act (HMDA): Passed in 1974 to require most mortgage-lending institutions to report data related to mortgage loans in order to allow for more transparency in lending. (6)

housing bubble: Increased access to credit by home buyers who would not have otherwise been able to qualify for a larger mortgage or any mortgage. (16)

human resources (HR) department: The bank department that finds and supports employees who contribute to the success of the bank. (10)

human resources (HR) manager: A bank employee who recruits new employees, ensures employees receive proper training, and enforces the bank's employment policies. (12)

I

identity theft: Stealing someone's personal information and using it to impersonate them. (14)

image replacement document (IRD): Another term for a substitute check, usually an electronic copy. (9)

inactivity fee: A fee charged if a customer does not make a transaction within a specified period. (3)

individual retirement account (IRA): An interest-earning savings account in which income taxes are deferred on some deposits and all interest until all or part of the balance is withdrawn at retirement age. (7)

inflation: When too much money in the economy results in rising prices. (4)

information technology (IT) manager: A bank employee who implements the policies and procedures set by the chief technology officer (CTO) or chief information officer (CIO) and directs the work of the IT technicians. (12)

installment loan: A type of closed-ended loan for a large amount of money that is repaid in smaller amounts over a specified period of time. (8)

insufficient funds fee: A fee charged by a bank when there is not enough money in an account to cover a transaction. (3)

insurance: Provides protection from certain risks that can cause financial loss. (3)

insurance company: A for-profit business that primarily sells insurance. (2)

insured: The person or thing covered by an insurance policy. (2)

interchange fee: A fee charged every time a customer uses a debit card to pay for a purchase; also known as a swipe fee. (17)

interest: A fee charged for borrowing money. (3, 7)

interest expense: Money that a bank pays to customers for the use of their money. (3)

interest rate: A stated cost for the use of borrowed money that is a percentage paid on top of the initial amount. (3, 4)

interest rate ceiling: The maximum rate that a bank can pay on certain deposits. (6)

interest rate risk: The chance that a bank may lose revenue due to a change in interest rates. (13)

International Bank for Reconstruction and Development (IBRD): An international organization with 187 member nations that was created to speed up the reconstruction after World War II; its goals are to increase the pace of economic progress, increase political stability, and encourage peace among nations. (17)

international financial institution (IFI): Financial institution that has been established by more than one nation and is owned by national governments. (17)

International Monetary Fund (IMF): An international organization with 187 member nations that was created to improve financial conditions in all nations; its goals are to promote monetary cooperation among nations, promote stability in the exchange rate among national currencies, encourage the balanced growth of international trade, help member nations that have difficulty making loan payments, and help nations reduce poverty. (17)

Internet bank: A financial institution with no physical location or building that customers access from anywhere with an Internet connection; also known as an online bank. (1)

interpersonal skills: How someone handles interactions with other people; also referred to as people skills. (12)

interstate bank: See *regional bank.* (1)

Interstate Banking Act: Also known as the Riegle-Neal Interstate Banking and Branching Efficiency Act; eliminated most restrictions on interstate bank branching, effectively overriding the McFadden Act; passed in 1997. (6)

interview: A meeting between a company representative and an applicant. (10)

investment bank: A financial institution that provides services for businesses, such as raising capital through the stock market. (1, 2, 16)

J

job fair: A recruiting event attended by one or more companies that are seeking new employees. (10)

jumbo CD: A CD for a large amount of money, usually $100,000 or more, with a high interest rate. (7)

L

land bank: A financial institution that issued notes, which represented credit secured by the value of land. (15)

leadership: The ability to lead others to achieve goals or complete tasks. (12)

legal tender: Money that must be accepted for payment of debts or to make purchases. (4)

lending officer: A bank employee who evaluates applications for loans or lines of credit; also called a *loan officer.* (12)

liability: What the bank owes. (13)

license: The legal permission to use a software program. (14)

lifting hazard: A source of potential injury from improperly lifting or carrying items. (14)

liquidity: The ability of a financial asset to be quickly converted into cash without any financial loss; having enough cash available to meet normal withdrawals. (3, 7, 13)

liquidity risk: The chance a bank cannot sell its assets quickly enough to make a profit and meet the demand for cash. (13)

loan: Money temporarily transferred to a borrower in exchange for repayment and interest. (8)

loan officer: See *lending officer.* (12)

loan policy: A guideline for balancing risk. (8)

loan processor: A bank employee who works with the lending officer to collect all of the required information from the individual or business applying for a loan. (12)

M

maker: See *drawer.* (9)

manager: A bank employee who is in charge of a segment of a business. (10)

market risk: The chance that the value of an asset will change due to market conditions. (13)

market segment: A group of consumers that share common wants and needs. (11)

material-storage hazard: A source of potential injury that comes from the improper storage of files, books, or office equipment. (14)

mature: When the fixed term of a CD expires and the account can be accessed without paying a penalty. (7)

maturity: The date on which a bond investor can receive the initial investment. (3)

McFadden Act: Gave individual states the right to set their own rules regarding out-of-state banks coming into the state; enacted in 1927. (6)

medium of exchange: Anything that is exchanged for goods and services, such as money. (4)

merger: When two companies agree to combine. (3)

mobile banking: The use of a smartphone or other mobile device to conduct financial transactions, including checking an account's balance, making payments, and, transferring funds. (17)

mobile wallet: Software on a buyer's mobile phone that holds digital cash, files that confirm the mobile wallet is valid, and information for billing and shipping. (17)

monetary policy: Regulation of a country's money supply to achieve economic goals and stability. (5)

monetary system: The mechanism a nation uses to provide and manage money for itself. (5)

money: Anything of value that is accepted in return for goods or services. (4)

money center bank: A very large, often international bank whose primary customers are businesses, other banks, and governments. (1)

money changer: Exchanged one country's currency for that of another for a fee. (15)

money market account: A savings account that pays a higher interest rate and requires a higher minimum balance than a traditional savings account. (2, 6, 7)

money market deposit account (MMDA): A deposit account similar to a money market mutual fund except that it is FDIC insured. (6)

money multiplier effect: The phenomenon that occurs when new deposits increase the money supply by more than the original deposit. (4)

money order: An amount of money that is purchased in an exact amount payable to a specific party. (3)

money supply: The total amount of money available in an economy at a given time in. (4)

mortgage-backed securities: Bonds that are guaranteed by the US government. (8)

mortgage banker: A bank employee similar to a lending officer who deals only with mortgage loans. (12)

mortgage loan: A secured loan made to purchase real estate; typically known as a mortgage. (8)

multilateral-development bank: Financial institution that provides financing and advice to developing nations to encourage economic and financial growth. (17)

N

national bank: A financial institution with offices all over the country. (1)

National Banking Acts of 1863 and 1864: Modified the National Currency Act, allowed the federal government to charter private banks, and created a uniform national currency. (5, 15)

National Credit Union Share Insurance Fund (NCUSIF): Established in 1970 to insure credit union deposits up to $250,000. (2)

National Currency Act: Created the Office of the Comptroller of the Currency; enacted in 1863. (5)

need: Something a person must have to survive. (11)

negotiable instrument: A transferrable, signed document that represents the promise to pay a specific amount of money in the future or on demand. (9)

negotiable order of withdrawal (NOW) account: Checking accounts that can pay interest. (6)

net interest income: The difference between interest received and interest paid. (13)

net interest margin (NIM): How much net profit the bank is making on interest as a percentage of assets. (13)

netiquette: The accepted social and professional guidelines for communicating using the Internet. (14)

net profit: The difference between the income and expenses of the business. (13)

nominal annual rate: A loan's annual interest rate without the cost of fees or compound interest. (8)

non-depository institution: A type of financial institution that does not accept deposits but accepts money from customers for the purpose of investing in business deals in order to spread risk and provide a means of investment. (2)

nonverbal communication: Sending and receiving messages without using words, such as through body language, facial expressions, and posture. (12)

note: A negotiable instrument that promises payment, but does not order that the payment be made. (9)

not-for-profit: Instead of paying profits to shareholders, money made by not-for-profit credit unions is returned to members in the form of higher interest rates on savings accounts and lower interest rates on loans. (2)

O

Occupational Safety and Health Administration (OSHA): A federal agency that enforces safety and health regulations in the workplace. (14)

Office of the Comptroller of the Currency (OCC): Established by the National Currency Act to create a uniform national currency and a system of national banks; was the first federal agency charged with bank supervision. (5, 15)

on demand: A payment made when requested. (9)

online banking: Allows customers to conduct financial transactions on a secure website operated by their bank; also known as home banking. (1)

open-ended loan: A loan that does not have to be paid in full by a specific date. (8)

open market operations (OMOs): Allow the Federal Reserve to buy or sell US treasury securities, which affects the money supply. (15)

operating expense: Costs incurred to keep a bank in business, such as utilities, rent, and wages. (3)

operations manager: See *branch manager.* (12)

organizational chart: A diagram representing the structure of a company or organization. (10)

overdraft: A negative balance. (3)

overdraft program: Provides funds to cover a check written on an account with insufficient funds. (3)

P

passbook: A small book kept by an account holder that is a record of savings account transactions. (7)

payday lender: Provides short-term high-interest loans designed to cover expenses until the borrower's next payday. (2)

payee: The entity receiving the money. (9)

payment system: Method of transferring funds without using cash. (9)

peer-to-peer payment (P2P): Allows for an immediate money transfer from one person to another. (1)

penalty: A fee for breaking the terms of an account. (7)

pension: A fixed sum of money a company provides for its retired employees. (7)

pension fund: Plan that provides retirement income for the employees of a business. (3)

performance evaluation: An assessment of how well an individual employee is doing his or her job. (10)

periodic interest rate: The interest rate the lender applies to a loan's outstanding balance to calculate the finance charge each billing period. (8)

phishing: The use of fraudulent e-mails and copies of legitimate websites to trick people into providing personal, financial, and other data. (14)

premium: Periodic payments made to purchase an insurance policy. (2)

president: A bank executive who often serves in the role of CEO or COO. (12)

previous balance method: A way to calculate finance charges by using the amount the customer owed at the end of the previous billing period to calculate the interest owed for the current month. (8)

prime rate: The interest rate that banks charge their best customers. (4, 5)

principal: An initial amount of money that is loaned or deposited. (7, 8)

probate law: Pertains to settling the financial affairs of a person after he or she has died. (3, 12)

probation: A period of time in which the employee's performance is closely watched, usually as the result of poor job performance. (10)

problem solving: The ability to analyze a situation or information, synthesize the material into a cohesive position, and creatively determine a solution or action. (12)

profit: When a bank's income exceeds its expenses. (3)

promissory note: An unconditional promise to repay a loan for a specific amount of money in the future or on demand. (9)

promotion: An activity that increases consumer awareness of a product. (11)

public image: The ideas and opinions that people have about a business. (11)

public relations manager: A bank employee who is responsible for creating a positive image of the bank, including the design and implementation of promotions, coordination of sponsorship, and providing information to journalists. (12)

public relations specialist: A bank employee who carries out the policies and procedures outlined by the public relations manager. (12)

punctuality: Showing up on time. (12)

R

rapport: A bond of mutual trust. (11)

ratings agency: An agency that provides expert opinions on the financial strength of a given institution that issues securities, such as a corporation or country. (16)

ratio: The relationship between two numbers that have the same unit of measurement. (13)

real estate: A section of land, the air above it, the ground itself, and any buildings on that land. (8)

recession: Occurs when the country has experienced negative economic growth for at least a six-month stretch. (16)

redlining: Occurs when a lender draws an imaginary red line on a map around one part of a community and does not make loans in that area. (6)

reference: A person who can provide information about the applicant's work history or character. (10)

regional bank: A type of financial institution that usually specializes in retail banking and does not operate internationally; also known as an *interstate bank*. (1)

regional-development bank: Financial institution that focuses on financing projects that improve their region. (17)

remote deposit capture: Records deposit information that the account holder would otherwise have to enter manually when making an electronic deposit. (7)

reorganization: The process of creating a repayment plan to repay debts without liquidating property. (8)

repossession: Occurs when a bank takes property from a borrower who is not able to repay a loan; generally refers to a car or other vehicle that was purchased with the loan or used as security for a loan. (10)

repossession agent: A person whose job is to take possession of property, such as a car, when payments have not been made for a period of time and turn the property over to the bank. (12)

representative money: A bill or coin that can be exchanged for an item of value. (4)

reserve requirement: The amount of money a bank must keep and not invest or loan out. (5)

reserves: A percentage of the bank's funds that is kept to ensure that money will be available for customers and is not available for loans; also known as required reserves. (1, 4)

responsibility: The duty to complete an assigned task well. (10)

restricted endorsement: An endorsement with added limitations on what can be done with the check when it is presented to a bank. (9)

retail bank: A type of financial institution that provides services for customers, such as deposit accounts, mortgages, auto and personal loans, and credit cards. (1)

retirement: A person's withdrawal from active participation in a job or business. (7)

return on assets (ROA): The amount of money a business makes for each dollar of assets it owns. (13)

return on equity (ROE): A ratio that tells the stockholder how much return was made for each dollar of profit. (13)

risk: The chance that an unfavorable event will happen to a person or property. (3, 8, 13)

S

safe deposit box: An individually secured container usually kept within a bank vault to store valuables. (3, 10)

Sarbanes-Oxley Act (SOX): Ensured accurate disclosure of a company's financial information by mandating greater transparency and accountability; enacted in 2002. (6)

savings: The portion of income that is not spent. (7)

savings account: A deposit account at a depository institution that earns interest and provides a safe place to store money. (2, 7)

savings and loan association (S & L): A type of financial institution that helped customers save money by allowing small deposits and home loans; also known as a savings association or thrift institution. (2)

savings and loan crisis (S & L crisis): The failure of many savings and loan associations in the late 1980s. (15)

savings association: See *savings and loan association*. (2)

secured loan: A loan backed by the borrower's property. (8)

securities: Financial instruments that pay interest or give the investor part ownership of the company; issued by investment banks. (2)

securities firm: A type of financial institution involved in the trading of securities in financial markets; also called a brokerage firm, stockbroker, or bondbroker. (2)

securitization: The pooling and packaging of loans to create securities. (16)

self-esteem: A sense of worth. (12)

share account: A savings account at a credit union. (2)

share draft account: A checking account at a credit union. (2)

shareware: Software that can be installed, used, and then purchased if you decide to keep using it. (14)

signature loan: See *unsecured loan*. (8)

SIMPLE IRA plan: An IRA-based retirement savings plan that gives small employers a simplified method to make contributions toward their employees' retirement. (7)

Simplified Employee Pension (SEP): A retirement savings plan established by a business for its employees or owners to which the business directly contributes. (7)

Small Business Administration (SBA): An independent agency of the federal government that was created in 1953 to help Americans start and grow businesses, often in the form of loans. (8)

smart card: A plastic card that has an embedded computer chip to store data. (17)

smartphone: A mobile device that not only acts as a cell phone, but also performs tasks such as accessing the Internet, taking photos, sending e-mail, and running some software applications. (17)

social media: Forms of electronic communication used by groups of people to share information. (17)

social security: A federal program that includes financial benefits intended to supplement retirement savings for Americans. (7)

software piracy: The illegal copying or downloading of software. (14)

software virus: Computer programs that cause harm to computer systems. (14)

sovereign debt: A financial obligation incurred by a country. (15)

spread: The difference between the average percentage rate the bank receives on loans made to customers and the average percentage rate that the bank pays on customer deposits. (13)

statement: A record that shows all of the activity that has occurred in an account during a covered time period. (7)

stock: A security that gives the purchaser part ownership in the company, known as equity. (2, 3)

stockholder: An investor who expects to make a return from his or her investment in stock. (2)

stockholders' equity: The money a bank receives from investors in return for stock. (13)

store of value: Something that can be saved, or stored, to use at a future date. (4)

subprime lending: The offering of loans to high-risk borrowers that do not meet standard lending criteria. (15, 16)

subprime loan: A loan with fees and interest rates that are higher than the rates given to a person who meets all of the underwriting criteria. (8)

substitute check: A paper copy of the front and back of the original check. (9)

surcharge: A fee charged by an ATM when cash is withdrawn, also known as a convenience fee. (3)

T

target market: The market segment that will be the focus of a marketing strategy. (11)

team: A group of people with similar or complimenting skills who share a common purpose. (12)

teamwork: Working with others to achieve a common goal. (12)

teller: A bank employee who is responsible for conducting transactions between the bank and the customer. (12)

term: The number of years a loan will exist. (8)

third-party endorsement: An endorsement that transfers the payee's claim to the check's value to a third party. (9)

time deposit: See *certificate of deposit (CD).* (7)

title researcher: A bank employee who searches real-estate records for details related to an assigned task. (12)

toxic asset: An asset with no liquidity. (16)

trade deficit: Occurs when a country imports more than it exports. (17)

trade surplus: Occurs when a country exports more than it imports. (17)

trading: The buying and selling of securities by a broker. (3)

transaction account: A bank account that allows the owner to use it to pay a third party, such as a checking account. (2)

treasury and cash management services: Services offered by banks related to cash management, such as accounting services, capital services, collections services, credit card services, and information services. (3)

trend: A general movement or tendency. (17)

Troubled Asset Relief Program (TARP): Often called the bank bailout bill; allowed the federal government to purchase assets and equity from financial institutions in order to strengthen them and prevent more failures; passed in 2008. (15, 16)

trust: A legal document that defines a customer's assets and how those assets should be handled. (3, 12)

trustee: The person or institution that controls financial assets for the customer. (3)

trust officer: A bank employee responsible for providing customers with financial products and trust services. (12)

Truth in Lending Act (TILA): Also Title I of the *Consumer Credit Protection Act.* Required that all terms of and costs related to a loan must be provided to the consumer in writing; passed in 1968. (6)

turnover: The number of employees hired to replace employees who left in a specified time period. (14)

U

underwriter: A bank employee who reviews loan applications and approves or denies a loan. (12)

underwriting: When lenders analyze risks and set conditions on the loan. (3, 8)

underwriting spread: The difference between the price paid by the investment bank and the price sold to the public. (3)

unit bank: A bank with one location, usually in a small town or rural area, that serves local customers, tends to invest locally, and knows the challenges of the local community. (1)

unit of account: A common measure of what something is worth. (4)

unsecured loan: A loan that is not backed by collateral, only the borrower's signature; also called a *signature loan.* (8)

V

verbal communication: Sending and receiving messages through speaking, listening, and writing. (12)

W

wage stagnation: Slow growth in wages. (16)

wampum: A string of white beads made from shells by Native Americans and used for trade. (15)

want: Something a person would like to have, but does not need to survive. (11)

wire transfer: An electronic transfer of funds from one location to another location. (9)

word-of-mouth advertising: A type of promotion in which customers tell others about their experience with a specific business. (11)

World Bank: An international organization that works toward the goals established at the Bretton Woods Conference to improve the conditions in all nations. (17)

World Bank Group (WBG): A group of international organizations whose mission is to ease poverty around the world by giving loans and grants to developing countries. (8)

Index

C

D

E

F

G

H

I

J

L

M

N

O

P

R

S

W